Deric Longden was born in Chesterfield in 1936 and married Diana Hill in 1957. After various jobs he took over a small factory making women's lingerie, but began writing and broadcasting in the 1970s. The demands made on him by Diana's illness, subsequently believed to be a form of ME, forced him to sell the factory, and since then he has devoted himself to full-time writing, broadcasting, lecturing and after-dinner speaking. *Diana's Story*, published in 1989, some years after Diana's death, was a bestseller. It was followed by *Lost for Words*, *The Cat Who Came In From the Cold*, *I'm A Stranger Here Myself* and *Enough to Make a Cat Laugh*. Deric Longden's first two books were adapted for television under the title *Wide-Eyed and Legless*, and an adaptation of *Lost for Words* was first screened in January 1999, attracting an audience of more than 12 million viewers. Starring Dame Thora Hird and Pete Postlethwaite, *Lost for Words* won the Emmy for best foreign drama in 1999. Deric Longden married the writer Aileen Armitage in 1990 and now lives in Huddersfield.

D0609839

A Play On Words

Deric Longden

CORGI BOOKS

A PLAY ON WORDS
A CORGI BOOK : 0 552 14660 9

Originally published in Great Britain by Bantam Press,
a division of Transworld Publishers

PRINTING HISTORY
Bantam Press edition published 1999
Corgi edition published 2000

1 3 5 7 9 10 8 6 4 2

Set in 11/13pt Palatino by
Kestrel Data, Exeter, Devon.

Corgi Books are published by Transworld Publishers,
61–63 Uxbridge Road, London W5 5SA,
a division of The Random House Group Ltd,
in Australia by Random House Australia (Pty) Ltd,
20 Alfred Street, Milsons Point, Sydney, NSW 2061, Australia,
in New Zealand by Random House New Zealand Ltd,
18 Poland Road, Glenfield, Auckland 10, New Zealand
and in South Africa by Random House (Pty) Ltd,
Endulini, 5a Jubilee Road, Parktown 2193, South Africa.

Printed and bound in Great Britain by
Cox & Wyman Ltd, Reading, Berkshire.

A Play On Words

Chapter 1

My eyes snapped shut as I pulled open the thick study curtains, the bright morning light etching its way in through my lids. Hardly had any sleep again last night. I could kill those damn birds.

There are two of them, a tall one and a short one, and they sit on the chimney stack, by the skylight, and wake me with a start at twenty-two minutes past four every blessed morning. The tall one is into light opera and performs highlights from *The Desert Song* and *Madam Butterfly*, while the short one is a throwback to the old music-hall days. He's brought his act up to date and now specializes in impressions of mobile phones, selections from Nokia and Ericsson, and one day I'm going to wring his bloody neck.

They also have a friend who visits every now and then. His conversation is somewhat limited. He bellows '*Hello, Kevin*' at six-minute intervals, but it must have been his morning off.

The park across the narrow lane from our house was almost empty except for a gardener, armed with a black plastic bin-liner, rounding up the wrappings from last night's fish and chips.

The Coke tins had already been spirited away by a freelancer. You can get forty pence a kilo for them down at Alcan, but you have to be up early or they're gone.

From time to time the council have a crackdown on the offending muck-spreaders. They call them litter louts. My neighbour Patrick calls them arseholes and I think Patrick has it by a short head.

An old man eased himself down on the bench two storeys below me. I could see the checkered top of his cloth cap and the narrow spread of his hunched shoulders. He held a cardboard pizza box out at arm's length, distastefully, between finger and thumb, and dropped it in the bin-liner as it floated by.

The door swung open and Aileen staggered into my study. She placed two full bottles of milk on my desk and then, shivering dramatically, pulled her robe tight around her.

'Why is fresh air always so draughty?'

Fresh air changes its mind far too often for her liking. She's basically your centrally heated sort of woman. If she wore a more sensible robe she wouldn't feel the cold half as much. It's nothing more than a wrap of thin cotton with lacy bits you can see right through, totally unsuited to the English climate. I bought it for her.

I peeped in through one of the lacy bits and congratulated myself on my good taste.

'Why do I have two bottles of milk on my desk?'

She was most surprised to see them there and

said that she didn't really know. Then she thought about it. As she did so she slumped down in the recliner chair and searched her pockets for a pack of cigarettes.

'I think you'll find there's a small brown-paper parcel for you in the fridge.'

I got up to go and get it. She's always like this in the morning. Her body goes walkabout while her mind is still having a lie-in.

'It'll be on that shelf in the door. The one where we keep the milk. Take those with you if you're going.'

She pointed to the two bottles of milk and leaned over to steal a cigarette from my packet on the side table. I keep them over there so that they are well out of my way while I'm working. If they were on my desk I would be forever reaching out and taking one. As it is I am forever walking over to the side table.

Those thieves who go around stealing small brown-paper parcels from unattended fridges would have no trouble whatsoever in locating ours, even though we keep the fridge hidden, tucked away behind one of twenty-three identical wooden doors.

There will invariably be a cat sitting staring at the fridge, willing the door to swing wide open. This morning there were three of them, all lined up, doing their level best to remember the PIN number.

'Excuse me.'

They didn't. They never do. They sat with

their bums glued to the lino and simply swayed backwards so that the door brushed up against their whiskers as I tugged it open. They made copious notes for future reference.

'Take this down. Ham on bottom shelf. Garlic sausage on second shelf. Can't see on top shelf, but it smells like chicken. Small, unidentified, brown-paper parcel being spirited away. Follow and report.'

They followed me upstairs. It's amazing how cats who set off hard on your heels can be sitting there waiting for you when you arrive.

Thermal jumped up on my desk. He spends most of his working day up there, stretched out under the anglepoise lamp, performing the various duties that come thick and fast when you are acting-unpaid-officer in charge of paper clips.

He keeps them on their toes. If it wasn't for him, he says, the paper clips would just lie there in that little plastic thing doing absolutely nothing all day long. So he keeps them on the move and sees to it that they hardly have a minute to themselves. By five o'clock they are absolutely knackered. I don't know what I would do without him.

Tigger gave the parcel a tentative sniff and then gestured to William who immediately strolled over to offer a second opinion. William sniffed at it. In William's opinion this was a parcel not to be sniffed at and so after nothing more than a perfunctory snuffle he walked away in disgust. I passed it over to Aileen.

'It's addressed to you.'

'I know. I sent for it. But it's for you really.'

The bright blue QVC logo told me that she had ordered it from the shopping channel on television. QVC has changed Aileen's life. With her limited sight she can't make out the jewellery that adorns her own fingers, or even see that which hangs around her neck. Earrings are one of life's great mysteries for her and so she has always relied upon my expert description as we gaze in through the jeweller's window.

'It's a sort of bluey-green stone, with a sort of gold thingy all around it.'

But on the shopping channel they have huge close-ups, and if she puts her nose right up to the screen the pendants and rings are twenty-seven inches across. It's wonderful. She can almost see the lobster-claw fastening on today's special offer and a sharp click on the mute button does away with all that waffle and blather that unfortunately comes along with the pictures. A quick telephone call and she has added yet another item to her collection.

But this one was for me, she said. I tore open the parcel and then eased back the lid of a small brown box. It felt expensive. I looked at the invoice – it was expensive. Aileen inched closer.

'Well?'

'It's a ring.'

'It was on special offer. Let me see.'

She slipped the eternity ring on her finger and

it fitted perfectly. I passed her the magnifying glass from my desk.

'It's beautiful, isn't it?'

'Very.'

'I like that.'

She gave me a big kiss and went off to get dressed. At the door she paused and looked back.

'Thank you, love. You must think a lot of me.'

I do, of course, and it would appear that I am also very generous.

I always make myself a large cup of coffee at ten o'clock in the morning. Ten o'clock on the dot. It sets me up for the day. By this time I have already made myself a large cup of coffee at nine twenty-three and another at a quarter to ten, but I wouldn't miss my ten o'clock cup of coffee for anything. It sets me up for the day.

I took it over to the window and looked out at the park. The old man was still there, sitting on the bench. He didn't seem to have moved a muscle since I saw him last. Then his cap swivelled slightly to the left as a young Alsatian came over to have a word with him.

They seemed to be getting on rather well until a shiny black Labrador, chasing a bright red frisbee and not looking where he was going, crashed without ceremony into the Alsatian's rear end.

There was no animosity. The two dogs examined each other closely in order to assess the damage. They made a thorough job of it. They seemed to be enjoying themselves and it was some time before they decided that the matter was probably best left in the hands of their respective insurance companies.

An old man in a cloth cap is no match for a bright red frisbee and so the two dogs lolloped off together across the park, leaving him alone on his bench except for a couple of sparrows who were conducting a mopping-up operation on the grass verge.

He looked rather lost. There's something about a pair of shoulders as seen from a second-storey window that is a dead give-away. Off duty, with nothing to occupy them, they seemed tired and weary. A pair of shoulders who had seen it all and done it all over a period of some eighty-odd years and who now realized that this was as good as it was going to get.

I wished the dogs had hung around and kept him company. I like sparrows, they are gutsy little devils, but if it's conversation you're after, forget it.

I wrote for an hour or more, the time seemed to fly by, and then a very damp cat jumped up on my knee and broke my concentration. I think he might have broken my left testicle as well – I must have it checked.

William doesn't enter a room – he takes it by surprise. He bursts in, having started his run somewhere along the M62. The door flies open and suddenly there's a huge black and white blur scattering papers and sleeping cats and turning hearthrugs into instant hump-backed bridges.

I took him to see the vet not long ago. We were shown into an antiseptic consulting room, white as snow with just a single well-scrubbed table and a freshly sluiced tile floor.

But from the moment I carried William in through the door the room became incredibly untidy. As Mrs Roger turned him upside down to examine his undercarriage I could see her glancing around, thinking, I must have this place done out – it's a disgrace.

It's not that William is a scruffy cat. His white bits are as white as you can get and his black bits glisten like newly polished ebony, but his hair is as fine as silk and the slightest breeze keeps it constantly on the move so that even when he's fast asleep he appears to be either on his way back from somewhere or just about to leave.

I dried him off and then did the same for Thermal. He hadn't been anywhere and was as dry as a bone but he has an equal-time clause built into his contract and he expects me to honour it.

I wondered if I ought to go out and dry off the old man. He had been sheltering under a tree and, now the rain had stopped, was making his way back to the bench. He plucked a tabloid newspaper from inside his jacket, spread it on the wet seat and sat down once more.

Something wasn't right. He'd been there for just over three hours now and I was beginning to worry about him. Perhaps if I went out and took a stroll in the park I might come across him unexpectedly, have a word or two and put my mind at rest.

Seen from my high study window the people in the park look as though they have just stepped out of a painting by Lowry, executed during his little known thick-brush period. They have put on a bit of weight perhaps, but still not enough to spoil the illusion. This, however, was the first time I had met a Lowry figure in the flesh. What there was of it.

His thin fingers shuffled the *Daily Mail* along the bench as I sat down beside him, then he muttered out of the corner of his mouth.

'Bit damp. Here, have shome of thish.'

He offered me the centre spread and I caught a glimpse of a woman who claimed that a famous cosmetic surgeon had gone and given her the wrong nose, and now one of her boobs had collapsed. I plonked my bottom down on top of her. It just wasn't her day.

'Thank you very much.'

We sat in silence for a moment or two. The sparrows were still at it. They were now working on a filled pizza crust and were about to experience a cheese surprise. Then the old man turned and gurned, I suppose you might call it – his mouth moving on rubbery gums, in all directions at once.

'Have you any idea what time it ish?'

I glanced at my watch.

'Just gone half-past twelve. You've been here for three and a half hours.'

He flashed me a questioning look, gums cocked and at the ready but saying nothing.

'I work up there,' I explained, pointing over my shoulder towards my study window. 'I was rather worried. I wondered if you were all right.'

He looked searchingly at me then moved a little closer, whispering so the sparrows wouldn't hear.

'I've been to the dentisht. I had an acshident with my teeth. Dropped my top shet in the shink and they've shent 'em off to Batley to be repaired. They won't have 'em back until five o'clock.'

His gums took some time to settle down after that little outburst. It must have been the longest sentence they'd ever attempted on their own and they were beginning to feel the strain.

'You can't sit here until five o'clock. It's going to rain again.'

'Have to.'

The sky was black as thunder over Almondbury and it was on its way here any minute now.

'Have you come far?'

I knew I couldn't leave him out here in the park – not for another four hours or so.

'No. I jusht live up Marsh.'

Marsh came out as clear as a bell, the perfect address for a man who has just dropped his top shet in the shink. But it was no more than half a mile away and he saw the look on my face.

'I can't go home. Me and my wife have been

married for shixty-three yearsh thish year and in all that time I've never let her shee me without my teeth. And I'm not shtarting now.'

I took him into the lounge and settled him down in front of the television. He was confused by the profusion of remote controls.

'Forget that one – it's for the video. That's the one you want, for channels one through to five and then if you press number six you can use this other one for the satellite channels. All you have to do then is . . .'

But I'd lost him. Thermal had jumped up on his knee and was pounding out a greeting.

'Good afternoon. My name is Thermal. Welcome to our home.'

The old man stroked his head and Thermal walked up his chest to have a closer look at his cap.

'You're a grand lad, aren't you?'

'Thank you. You're very kind.'

I left them to it and went to make a cup of tea. I had been very touched by the old man's reason for not wanting to go home. Romance comes in surprising packages.

'Would you like a sandwich?'

His gums panicked at the thought and were mightily relieved when he declined the offer.

'Right, I'll be just upstairs if you want anything.'

By the time I came down again he'd mastered the remote controls and was changing channels at a rate of knots. Thermal must have talked him through it. He was still tucked up on the old man's knee and William had perched himself on the arm of the chair. They settled down to watch a rerun of *The Likely Lads* on UK Gold. The old man turned to me.

'Can I ashk you shomething?'

'Of course.'

'I heard a woman'sh voice.'

'My wife.'

He still had his cap on and he adjusted it slightly to give himself a little extra thinking time.

'She won't be coming in here, will she?'

His gums shuddered in embarrassment at the thought and tucked themselves in behind his lips.

'No, don't worry. And if you do happen to bump into her she won't be able to see you. She's registered blind.'

'Oh thank God for that,' he said, easing himself back in his chair. 'That'sh grand ish that.'

When the time came for him to make his way down to the dentist the rain was still battering against the window panes, and so I gave him a lift in the car.

'It'sh very good of you.'

'It's no trouble.'

The garage doors had forgotten they were supposed to go up and over and by the time I had shown them what to do I was soaked to the skin. I should have asked him if I could borrow his cap.

Perhaps not. I doubt if the two of them had been separated since birth. He gave it a short sharp tug as he settled himself in the car and the brim twanged happily and bounced back down again.

'Wouldn't you think,' he said, 'that they'd lend you a shpare shet of teeth, jusht to be going on with? Whenever I had a shervice the garage alwaysh made sure I had a courteshy car.'

The perfect day comes in all shapes and sizes. Seeing the kids, the grandchildren, an unexpected cheque in the post. Aileen's lovely face as her fingers stroked the eternity ring.

Today it had arrived courtesy of a set of false teeth. Courtesy teeth. I could just see the dentist's receptionist looking through her records.

'I'm very sorry but Mrs Raynor hasn't brought them back yet. She should have had them here by four o'clock – it's very naughty of her.'

Perhaps they would carry discreet advertising, like the courtesy car I borrowed from the Body Shop while they were busy putting mine back together again. They had their name written all over the door and it was very effective. A woman came up to me in the multi-storey car park and asked my advice on essential oils.

A letter printed on each tooth. That was it. *False Teeth, courtesy of . . .* – I pulled the car to a halt and glanced at the dentist's nameplate – *Townend, Denham, Millington-Smith and Luty.* No, perhaps not. Bit of a mouthful, that.

They would need something a little more racy. *Supertooth* or *Gnashers Galore*? No, still not quite right.

The old man had one leg out of the door and was about to step out onto the pavement. He half turned and gave me a great big smile.

'Thank you very much,' he said. 'You're very kind.'

It came to me in a flash. *Gums R Us.* That was it. I shall patent the idea and make a fortune.

'No, really,' I replied as he waved goodbye. 'Thank *you*.'

Chapter 2

I gave the cat flap a quick squirt of WD40. That's about as technical as I get. The cat flap is on its last legs and no wonder. It handles more traffic than the turnstiles at Wembley stadium.

There was a time when it stood proudly at the cutting edge of technology, an electronic wonder that opened and shut whenever the cats' collars gave it the password.

Nowadays it just hangs on in there, wincing every time a furry little head bops it in the stomach. Denton started the rot. He's a ginger tom from down the road, built like a brick outhouse and as thick as two short planks. He has spent his entire life at the cutting edge of total ignorance.

And yet it didn't take him long to come up with a solution. He would sit outside, waiting for one of our cats to come bounding out, and then he would catch the cat flap with one paw before it could swing to.

Once in he would mop up enough food for a whole army. His only problem was that he couldn't get out, not until one of the residents came bounding back in again. That's how I caught him. He was waiting by the cellar door with his paw cocked ready, and his overloaded stomach slung close to the ground.

If a thicko like Denton could crack our security system then it wasn't worth a light. Our new-found technology had been downgraded from white hot to stone-cold sober in no time at all. Collars mysteriously went missing and the cat flap swung open to all comers.

We began to welcome a string of no-hopers, an endless procession of beaten-down losers in search of a square meal and a bed for the night.

I had fixed the cat flap in the cellar because I wasn't about to cut holes in solid oak doors that are over a hundred years old. The cellar would serve as a halfway house, I thought, and it couldn't have worked out better.

It's very cosy. The central heating boiler stokes the place up to gas mark 37 and there's a perfectly good carpet that didn't quite match the new three-piece suite. Light pours in through a window set halfway up the cellar steps, illuminating a vast array of extras designed to maximize feline potential. For the musically inclined a piano stands in one corner, and my sturdy old Amstrad sits on the workbench, should they wish to hone their literary skills.

They have an elderly microwave oven which still works in ten-second bursts, long enough for a medium-rare mouse, and there's a television set that is quite capable of receiving BBC2 if the wind is in the right direction and nobody moves.

Best of all there's a vast collection of cat baskets, gathered from some of the finest second-hand shops in West Yorkshire, each of them fitted with a plumped-up cushion to ensure maximum creature comfort.

And yet every morning, when I go down to feed this shifting population, I find them fast asleep on the piano, under the piano, in the sink, up on the top shelf, literally on a bed of nails. Anywhere but in the custom-built accommodation.

Arthur was the first stray to arrive. Tigger found him in the park and brought him home. Both his back legs had been broken and so had his tail, but his dignity was still intact. I always imagined he might have been a town councillor in a previous existence. One of those decent, working-class chaps. Miner's helmet during the day and a bowler hat by night, circa 1928. I remember him from a photograph I once saw hanging on the Town Hall staircase. Never made Mayor, but he could have if he hadn't always put others first.

Two hundred and seventy-one pounds' worth of vet's fees later Arthur decided to repay me by moving in permanently, and he was worth every penny. It broke my heart when he died a couple of years later.

Others come and go. Little Chap appears once a fortnight and I can't make him out. He's the mildest, gentlest, most civilized of cats and yet he chooses to live a life full of drugs, booze and women.

So every two weeks or so we dry him out, feed him up and let him sleep for twenty-four hours. Then he's off out with the lads again. I keep telling him he needs a hobby – he says he's got one.

My WD40 had worked wonders on the cat flap and I was out weeding the garden when Little Chap staggered up the side path and collapsed in a heap in the courtyard.

'Just give me a minute, old son, and I'll be with you.'

He half sat up, wondering how he could stop this paving stone from going round and round. He slid his bum over on to the adjoining slab, but that one was just as bad, and so he decided to lie down, close his eyes and let his mind and body go with it.

'Why on earth do you do it?'

I'm sure he would have answered me if he'd had any idea where the voice was coming from. He half opened one eye, grinned at the stone mushroom and fell fast asleep. I would take him down to the cellar as soon as I had sorted out this weed.

I have never been able to understand why people who come over as all weak and watery are said to be weeds. Those posh plants with their double-barrelled names and a family tree as long as your arm, with roots that go way back, they don't know they're born.

'My dear, I simply can't cope with this soil – far too acid for my liking. And look, there's a horrid *little stone in the way. It's just too much.'*

Reared under glass and spoilt to death, they are a load of old pansies. Not at all like the weeds who embarrass them by moving in next door. The weeds are tough and wiry. The sort of plant you need on your side when war is declared and the going gets tough.

Especially this little devil. If I had to guess I would say he was one of a large family brought up in Tesco's car park just outside Leeds, where his mother had had to force her way up through two feet of concrete for her first glimpse of daylight. He was determined that his own kids were going to have a better start in life and so when the time came to move on he drifted for miles until he floated over Greenhead Park. Then a crosswind caught him and he missed it by fifty yards or so. Never mind, perhaps it was for the best. The gardeners over there were professionals and would have had him on his bike in no time at all. Whereas over here his opponent was a bit of a prat who couldn't tell one end of a trowel from the other. He had never had it so good and he wasn't giving in easily.

I had been digging him out for months now and he always came back for more. Cut his arms and his legs off and he'd head-butt you.

'Come on – make my day.'

I filled in the hole, raked over the soil and covered it with three inches of forest bark. Down below I could hear the stretcher-bearers going about their duty.

'We can rebuild him.'
Make no mistake – he'd be back.

Little Chap has his favourite spot in the cellar, an old deckchair with a bellying canvas that almost touches the floor. The other cats prefer to be high up on the top shelf, tucked just underneath the ceiling out of harm's way. When I push open the door in the morning they look like a row of targets on a fairground shooting gallery.

But when Little Chap staggers in through the cat flap he needs to collapse somewhere handy. More often than not this will be on the concrete floor, just short of the carpet, and he will lie there, a couple of feet inside the cat flap, until his kindly landlord comes and picks him up and arranges his limbs neatly on the deckchair.

This time he hadn't even made it as far as the door, and so I scooped him up off the paving stone and carried him, limp and bedraggled, down the cellar steps.

I used to worry about him. The first time he arrived I thought he was dying, so I had him up at the vet's before you could say worming powder. They gave him an injection but couldn't find anything wrong with him.

'He's just knackered.'

They told me to feed him up and let him rest, which I did – only the other way around. He slept for the best part of a weekend and then on Monday morning he marched right into the kitchen and played hell with me.

'Food.'

He has a way with words. He stretches them. If I don't attend to him immediately he goes straight into overdrive.

'*Foo-oo-oo-ood.*'

It's very effective. But right now all he wanted to do was sleep. The eye that had quivered slightly as I elbowed open the cellar door closed again as I laid him gently in the deckchair. His left ear had turned itself inside out and tucked itself under his cheek. I flicked it and it twanged to attention. That was better. He'd be all right now.

My life is full of contradictions. Most of it is spent at home, with bursts of creativity constantly interrupted by the need to feed and nurture an army of short-haired cats and a long-haired woman.

Aileen plays her part. She deals with the day-to-day accounts and specializes in arranging amazingly good deals and terrifying tradesmen. They can't pull the wool over her eyes. Nature did that years ago and so she never sees the pain on their faces as she asks them if they wouldn't mind doing that again please, and properly this time.

Since she bought me a wok my cooking has come on in leaps and bounds. I can now stir-fry with the best of them, but there are times when it's nice to opt out of the domestic grind and hop onto the celebrity circuit for a change, where someone else does the cooking and I get spoilt to death.

Today I was off to talk at a literary lunch down in the Midlands. I was about to drive out of the car wash when the lady came over to have a word with me. I don't know her name. I know her only as the Lady with the Limp.

She does go on a bit, so I wound down the window and asked if she would mind meeting me over by the pumps so that I could get the car fed and watered while we talked.

I had already taken fifty pounds' worth of unleaded petrol on board by the time she arrived and my mind had slipped inexorably into that boring mode where it insists on reminding me that my mortgage was only eleven pounds, twelve shillings and threepence a month when I first married.

Her limp seems to be getting worse. Since Christmas it appears to have developed a secondary limp all of its own, a somewhat theatrical version of the original, and I felt rather guilty at having dragged her over here.

'Sorry, but I'm in a bit of a hurry.'

She never listens to what you say. I have learned over the years that every Monday morning she comes out of the house with a fresh topic of conversation, honed to perfection over the weekend, and then she tries it out on everyone she meets. Sometimes she has the sense to realize that it's running out of steam by Wednesday and so she'll switch to something else, but more often than not she can keep it going for the full seven days.

It's all rather sad and I'm usually more than

happy to give her as much time as she needs, but I was cutting things rather fine today.

'It's my brother.'

Her brother crops up rather a lot. He was once bitten by a dog and she thought he might have rabies. Did I think it was serious? A partridge he shot fell out of the sky and landed on his head and she thought he might have concussion. Did I think it was serious?

'What's happened to him now?'

'He's dead.'

Now that did sound serious. Just about as serious as you can get.

'Oh. I'm very sorry.'

I lifted the bonnet and inserted the dipstick while she told me all about it. Given his past record I did think he might have tried a little harder, put some effort into making his final exit that bit more entertaining. Apparently he died in bed, as a result of being very old.

But just as I thought he'd let me down, his sister came at me with a second wave.

'You know he was a gillie up in Scotland, a sort of gamekeeper?'

I didn't, but it was easier to say yes. It also went some way towards explaining the partridge.

'Well, he says in his will that he wants to be buried on the estate, out on the moors where he worked.'

I thought that was very romantic and I told her so, but she wasn't listening.

'What I want to know is – can they do that?

I thought you had to be buried in creosoted ground.'

The thought sustained me all the way through a four-mile tail-back on the M42 and just about made up for me missing the soup, the main course and the summer pudding.

I did manage to grab a cup of coffee, only to find that it had been brewed from a wartime recipe when you couldn't get coffee, which made me feel that perhaps missing the meal hadn't been such a bad thing after all.

A lady leaned over from next door but one on the top table and told me that she was supposed to introduce me.

'Do you write your books under your own name?'

It's surprising how often that one crops up. It meant that she'd never read a single word of mine and hadn't even heard of me before today. I have been tempted more than once to say that no, I write all my books under the pseudonym of Dick Francis.

'No. I call myself Dick Francis.'

Her eyes widened.

'Oh. I've heard of you.'

Before I could stop her she was on her feet, but then so was Madam Chairman who had been sitting between us and heard every word. She took over, with all the authority of a woman who owns a large chain of dress shops and knows exactly what she's doing.

'I'll see to this, Rita.'

She gave me a wonderful and very knowl-edgeable introduction and then a sharp kick on the ankle as she sat down.

'Forty minutes,' she said. 'No more.'

Thermal was waiting for me on the gatepost when I arrived home. It was way past his tea-time. He was weak with hunger and not best pleased.

'That woman trod on me.'

'Well, you know Aileen can't see you. You have to keep out of her way.'

I opened the door and let him in. The others were nowhere to be seen but they wouldn't be long. They can hear a tin being opened at three hundred paces. I filled four saucers with Whiskas duck and turkey in gravy and took one down to the cellar for Little Chap.

They must be using a new recipe these days, I thought. At one time the gravy looked good enough to eat, but now the glaze seemed to disappear very quickly. One minute the bowl of Whiskas looked as though somebody had recently been at it with a varnish brush and the next it was just a pile of uninteresting lumps leaning against each other, bored out of their skulls.

This one seemed right enough, but Little Chap was in no condition to take advantage of it. Curled up on his deckchair like a Danish pastry, he was still out like a light.

I was on my way back up the stairs when the truth dawned on me. I nipped out through the back door and peered in through the kitchen window. Thermal was moving along the line of saucers, his tongue flashing in and out like a little pink spatula on speed. I had caught him red-handed, but he denied it of course.

'*I never.*'

'Oh yes you did. I saw you.'

'*You mean you were spying on me?*'

'I was keeping an eye open.'

He thought that was despicable. If we couldn't trust each other, he said, what future did we have as a family unit?

But I was ready for him.

'And what future do we have if you go licking the gravy off everyone else's Whiskas?'

'*I was testing it.*'

'It doesn't need testing.'

'*Oh, so we're an expert on cat food now, are we?*'

He stormed off in a huff and Thermal in a huff is something to behold. He beat the living daylights out of Aileen's fireside rug and then belted several small ornaments off the mantelpiece, before setting about a poor innocent little toilet roll who had never hurt anyone in his life.

Eventually his huff sent him off across the lane where Bridie would take him in and spoil him and tell him what a clever boy he was. It must have been getting on for midnight before he came back and told me all about it.

Apparently he's worried about all this BSE. His theory is that the answer lies in the gravy. BSE has a bitter taste to it, he says, and he can tell it straight off. His dad once worked with the caretaker at the Technical College, so he knows all about it.

As senior cat he decided it was his task to sample each meal and maybe even lay down his life for the others. Isn't that wonderful? I had tears in my eyes before he had finished. He's an example to us all.

Chapter 3

Before the interview began, she smiled and told me she had read all my books, which is always comforting and not usually the case with radio presenters.

'You seem to like women.'

'I do.'

She glared at the two men who were drinking tea from cardboard cups on the other side of a glass partition. I may have imagined it, but the two of them seemed to be melting slightly at the edges.

'Not like this bloody lot here.'

She pushed her chair away from the console, leaned back and stretched her arms high above her head. Her legs went on for miles and miles before disappearing under a shiny leather pelmet she had slung around her waist. I tried hard not to look at them and failed miserably.

'They think we're only good for one thing,' she growled, nodding her head towards the two men, who had now decided to drink their tea standing up.

'Whereas you look at a woman from the inside, don't you?'

Yes. Any minute now, I thought. If she leans back an inch further. But then thankfully the red light changed to green and we were on the air.

She was very good at her job and even managed a few questions I had never been asked before, but there is the one that crops up time and time again.

'Do all these things really happen to you?'

'Of course they do.'

'You don't make them up?'

'Of course I don't.'

But I don't think she believed me and I just can't understand why. My adventures are very small adventures that could happen to anyone. Like most people I bumble through as best I can, through a life filled to the brim with the mundane and the microscopic. And yet rarely a day passes without it suddenly deciding to take off at right angles.

As it did on the way home. I got lost. From an island on the ring road I suddenly found myself in the middle of an industrial estate and then in a car park surrounding an out-of-town Asda, before magically entering a motorway service station from the wrong side, down a one-way country lane and in past a sign that read *Lorries Only*.

There were trucks of all shapes and sizes. Some parked up for the night, others manoeuvring and unloading. They towered above me, making me feel like a little lad on a bicycle. I decided to get the hell out of there, the way I came in.

I reversed back up the one-way lane, keeping a mere half an eye on the rear-view mirror as I stared straight ahead through the windscreen, hoping that any casual passer-by would think I was going forward and not backwards.

'Hey, look. His wheels seem to be going the wrong way round, just like they do in the movies. Isn't that amazing?'

The narrow lane was no more than half a mile long and I had almost made it when a fleet of enormous lorries appeared, shipping in emergency supplies of frozen chips and fun-sized Mars bars. The drivers pipped encouragingly and waved at me with clenched fists as they hauled their pantechnicons out of my way and up onto the grass verge.

I smiled and waved back. We are all part of the same brotherhood, I suppose.

Half an hour later I was hopefully heading north on one of those dual carriageways that have been handcrafted out of solid concrete in order to make you think your tyres have gone flat.

I realized I was going in the wrong direction entirely when I saw the radio station looming up on my left once more, so I pulled off the road and into its car park to try to work out just where I had been going wrong, and to have a quick look at my tyres.

The station had been buttoned up for the night. Just a single light showed in an upstairs window from where an agony aunt was doling out advice to the sad and the lonely. I switched on the car radio.

'. . . and don't forget. If you have a problem just ring me on . . .'

'How the hell do I get out of this place?' I shouted up at the lighted window but she took no notice of me and in no time at all she was up and running once more, dishing out advice to a young man who suffered from terminal acne.

Over on the corner of the road opposite, jutting out into the pavement like a double-breasted battleship, there was either a very popular pub or a penal institution for young offenders – it was hard to tell which. Most of the ground floor windows had been boarded up like a kennel in a Tom and Jerry cartoon, with great rough wooden crosspieces and six-inch nails.

A couple of seriously bald bouncers stood guard at the main entrance, enforcing a strict dress code. If you were a man you had to wear a vest and have had your ears pierced, while the women were required to leave their navels uncovered for inspection at all times.

An unmarked police car with its windows all steamed up was parked right across from the pub, so I decided to go and ask if they could point me towards the A38. It was one of those anonymous white panda cars that creep up behind you when you are doing fifty in a built-up area and there were two men sitting in the front seats. One wore a purple padded anorak with orange sleeves and the other one had more sense.

I tapped on the glass and waited as the electrics buzzed and the window slowly wound its way down. They had a huge thermos flask stuck between them and enough sandwiches to last a lifetime.

'Yes?'

'I'm sorry to bother you, but could you direct me towards the A38?'

They glanced quickly at each other and then the officer in the passenger seat leaned across his colleague's knee to face me.

'How would we know?'

'Well, you're policemen. Aren't you?'

They exchanged glances once more and then the driver casually leaned back in his seat, the tip of his cigarette dancing in time with his lips.

'And what makes you think that?'

'Well, you've got one of those blue lamp things stuck on the roof of the car.'

His eyes snapped shut and the cigarette froze in his mouth.

'Oh shit.'

His hand crept up out of the open window, his fingers exploring the roof until they came across the lamp. He plucked it off its suckers and pulled it inside the car without even looking at it, as though it had never existed, and shoved it down in the well by his feet. Then the window buzzed once more and slowly wound its way up, shutting me out.

I didn't even smile until I was back in my

car, conscious that they would be watching me through the rear-view mirror. I wondered how long they had been parked there on plain clothes surveillance – a couple of weeks judging by the quality of the cigarette smoke in the car. I wanted to run into the radio station and tell them.

'You see it does happen, and right outside your own windows.'

It was ages before I came across the A38 and even then I found I was heading down south instead of up north. But what the hell – it had been worth it.

My friend Trevor Evans told me that he was once on plain clothes duty in a shopping mall, as part of a highly trained surveillance team. They were in constant radio contact with one another. He was wearing his Sunday best suit, a crisp white shirt and an Abercrombie overcoat, when a woman rushed up to him.

'Excuse me, officer. I've lost my little girl.'

They searched around and found the child, who had come to no harm, and then Trevor asked the mother how she had managed to crack his disguise.

'Tell me, how did you know I was a policeman?'

The woman, who was in the midst of a joyous reunion, alternately hugging and then belting the living daylights out of her small daughter, paused for a moment and looked up.

'You kept mumbling into your jacket.'

Little Chap was fast asleep when I arrived home, just the other side of the wrought-iron gate so that I couldn't push it open without disturbing him. I bent down and whispered through the bars.

'Come on, now. Let's be having you.'

As usual he seemed to have fashioned himself a cosy little hollow in the middle of a paving stone and was flat on his back with all four legs stuck up in the air. Charming is a word that springs to mind. Gormless is another.

I pushed the gate open very gently at first. I didn't want to alarm him and in that respect I succeeded beyond my wildest dreams. He had no idea he was being swept slowly across the path by a wrought-iron gate until he found himself nestling on a pile of dead leaves that had settled down in the far corner for the duration.

Then a pungent mixture of indignation and rotting foliage brought him bouncing back into the land of the living. He scrambled to his feet and threw back his head.

'*Foo-oo-oo-ood.*'

William watched in deepest admiration from his grandstand seat on top of the gatepost. He would never dare do that. For all his energy and enthusiasm he still can't quite believe his luck.

After what must have been several months of self-catering out there in the wild, he still can't believe that he has at last hit upon a place where they serve a full English breakfast every morning, a little light lunch around noon and a nourishing evening meal with all the trimmings. Give or take the gravy.

No, it was too good to last and he wouldn't dream of rocking the boat. Most of the time he takes his new life in his stride, picking up tips here and there from the other two residents on what is to be expected of a young cat around the house.

But he still has days when his old insecurities come rushing back to wrap themselves around him like a shroud. Sometimes, if I make a sudden move towards him, he will race from the room and hide until he feels it's safe to come out, or at least until he has forgotten exactly why he happens to be cowering under the single bed in the spare room.

He peered down at the indignant little furball who was still standing four-square by my feet, his head thrown back, demanding to be fed immediately. You never know. It might be worth a try.

'*Foo-oo-oo-ood.*'

'Oh shut up, William.'

'*Sorry. My mistake. Oh my God, I've gone and done it now.*'

I could hear Aileen up in her office tapping away at her computer. She could be working on her new book or taking a little time out to surf the Internet.

I don't delve into the deeper possibilities of

the computer. The journey from Amstrad to Compaq laptop in just under twenty years has been quite heady enough for me. There are some things I can't take in. I have to reread the manual every time I use the fax machine. It's nothing to be proud of – quite the opposite – but I have learned over the years that when it comes to modern technology, if I am going to take in something new, then something that I have already stored in my head has to be sacrificed to make room for it. Since I mastered the Compaq I can no longer remember what all the lights and switches are for on the car dashboard and I confuse the stalks on either side of the steering wheel, the one for the windscreen wiper and the other for the horn. It makes for some interesting journeys.

But when it comes to rustling up six individual meals in a matter of a few minutes then I'm your man.

I fed Little Chap first, otherwise he would have started on the hearthrug.

'Foo-oo-oo-ood.'

He hadn't eaten for a day and a half to my knowledge and it could have been much longer. I had checked on him before I left home. He was fast asleep. His food had been left untouched and he would have needed a hammer and chisel to fight his way through the thick black crust, so now he nearly tore the saucer out of my hand as I plonked it down in front of him.

The other three cats sat and watched, dumb-struck and awestruck, as he plunged his head deep into the pile of Whiskas tuna and chicken, seeming to take in as much through his ears and nose as he did through his mouth.

As he came up for air Tigger turned away in disgust and then strolled over to the low shelf by the wine rack, where she keeps an open packet of Walkers barbecued beef and onion crisps, jammed in among a set of Japanese tea cups that look very pretty but are far too small to be of any use.

Thermal tagged along behind. He has never been able to manage a whole barbecued beef and onion crisp on his own, they make his eyes water, but he quite likes to mop up the crumbs afterwards.

Tigger reached a paw through the gallery rail and expertly plucked from the packet a large fat crisp, a healthy young male by the look of him, and then she hurled it over her shoulder onto the carpet by the dining table.

She's learned over the years that a cat hasn't been engineered for eating crisps on a smooth kitchen floor. They tend to lie flat, hugging the lino, and her nose gets in the way as she chases them round as she would an ice hockey puck, whereas on the carpet they lodge in the pile, standing tall and proud, just asking for it.

She steadied the crisp between her two front paws and then delicately nibbled all round the outside edge until she had reduced it from a reasonable facsimile of Greenland to an absolutely perfect scale model of the Isle of Man.

Then she turned it upside down and finished it off, starting at the Point of Ayre and working her way up towards Castletown, leaving Thermal to mop up the port of Douglas as far inland as Union Mills and as far north as Onchan while she ambled over to the shelf for seconds.

Little Chap was halfway through his pudding by the time I managed to feed the other three. He'd had Whiskas tuna and chicken for starters followed by a main course of Whiskas tuna and chicken, with a sizeable portion of Whiskas tuna and chicken on the side. For pudding he chose a small tin of Sainsbury's tuna in brine. Apparently it made a nice change.

'Coffee?'

'No. I couldn't, really.'

'Chocolate mint?'

'Perhaps later.'

Three small heads turned away in unison from their individual saucers as they watched him waddle off down to the cellar, as fine an example of synchronized gawping as I have seen in a long time. Then two of the heads swivelled back to the business in hand while Thermal turned and glared long and hard in my direction.

'I had to feed him first. It was an emergency.'

Thermal considered this for a moment. And when Thermal considers something he considers it with his whole being. His forehead furrows until you could almost screw his ears off and then the shock wave travels the length of his body, before finally being released into the community with a petulant flick of the tail.

'As long as it doesn't become a habit.'

Aileen and I discussed the welfare of our itinerant lodger over dinner. I had prepared a herb salad with feta cheese and roasted peppers, followed by fiorelli pasta in mushroom and garlic sauce, garnished with squares of bacon, asparagus tips and sweetcorn. I mention this only to point out exactly what can be achieved in ten minutes flat, to prove that my cooking has come on in leaps and bounds over the past few years, and to show off unashamedly.

Aileen is very encouraging. More often than not, when she first comes to the table she hasn't the slightest idea what is on the menu, and she still can't see what I have set down before her once she has taken her seat, with her head hovering just inches above her plate. But she is always ready with an enthusiastic word or two.

'Oh, lovely. I smell tuna.'

For some time now I had been worrying about Little Chap and wondering whether or not to have him neutered. But he never seemed to stay conscious long enough for me to take him to the vet. When he wasn't sleeping he was eating and when he wasn't either eating or sleeping, he wasn't here.

Apart from that he wasn't really my cat. He didn't seem to have a home of his own, but he was most certainly house-trained. He never sprayed, always popped out to use the toilet and then made sure to leave it as he would have expected to find it.

Most of the time he stayed down in the cellar, where Tigger had taken him the first time she brought him home, half starved and as weak as a kitten. He was much smaller than Thermal then and scared to death of him until he realized that Thermal was nothing more than a big soft kid at heart, and now he occasionally came up into the house and mingled with the others for a moment or two.

This would usually be on the day before he left for yet another walk on the wild side. He would stick close to Tigger as she took him on a tour of the establishment and he would make a half-hearted attempt to show interest in her new padded scratching post, complimenting her on her good taste.

But you could see he was becoming rather edgy and it wouldn't be long before he made his excuses and took to the courtyard, where he would pace the perimeter wall for a good hour or so before suddenly leaping down the other side and racing off towards the park and another two or three weeks of dissipation.

He would make a break for it tomorrow by my reckoning, after a good night's sleep and a nourishing breakfast of Whiskas tuna and chicken on toast.

Aileen chased a rogue asparagus tip round and round her plate. It wasn't the sort to give up easily, so eventually she abandoned her fork and went after it with forefinger and thumb. With nowhere to hide it cowered as far away as possible, holding its breath until the inevitable happened. I felt sorry for it.

'That was very nice.'

'Thank you.'

I poured freshly ground coffee from the cafetière and then spent some time with a teaspoon, removing a flotilla of little bits and pieces from each cup. I've become used to the little devils now. I take my time about it and wait for the stragglers to come up for air.

'Do you think I should take Little Chap to be seen to?'

'He's heading for an early grave otherwise.'

It did seem to be the obvious thing to do and yet I had my doubts. He was a free spirit. He could have settled down with us, but instead he had chosen a life of wine, women and song. We don't do a lot of singing in our house.

'It's like taking Oliver Reed to be neutered.'

'In that case I'm all for it.'

The next morning, armed with a rather swish cat transporter and accompanied by Thermal as my personal cat translator, I went down to the cellar to get him.

'Be sure to tell him it doesn't hurt.'

'You tell him. I was sore for a week.'

Little Chap was fast asleep on the boiler as I pushed open the door, but after a healthy yawn and a really good stretch he made us most welcome. In fact he made it all too easy for me.

He jumped down and strolled over to the pet carrier, sniffed appreciatively at the plastic door hinges and then walked inside.

'Rather well made, isn't it?'

I closed the door behind him and carried him out of the cellar. Thermal followed us upstairs.

'You wouldn't have got me as easily as that.'

Cats have a way of making you feel guilty. If Little Chap had lost his temper I could have coped with that, but he just sat imprisoned on the passenger seat of the car, staring at me through the bars with his big blue eyes.

'I never thought you would stoop to such a trick.'

I felt even worse on the way back. Little Chap had decided he wanted no part of this, so the vet had had to coax him out by standing the carrier on its end and tipping him onto the table. It must be hell being smaller than everyone else. The vet had given him a cursory examination and then handed him over to me.

'He's already been done.'

Thermal was taunting a small Yorkshire terrier when we arrived home, but as soon as he saw the car pull into the side road he jumped down from the wall and led us into the courtyard.

'It was a much longer job in my day.'

As soon as I pulled back the bolts of his cage Little Chap was off and I can't say I blame him. He made straight for the wrought-iron gate and squeezed between the bars. He didn't even look back and by the time Thermal and I reached the end of the path he had already negotiated the narrow road and was streaking off across the park.

A large Alsatian gave chase but was soon pulled up short by his extending lead, and an old mongrel who wouldn't have been seen dead on a lead – not in a million years – thought about it for a moment or so and then decided to carry on watering his tree.

Thermal and I walked back up the path together. The carrier sat all forlorn in the court-yard with the door standing wide open. I picked it up and took it down the cellar steps. Thermal raced on ahead of me.

'Got any more bright ideas?'

Chapter 4

There is something wonderful about being married to a woman who will wait for me on the wrong street corner, casually chatting up an alarming young man who is being given a wide berth by everyone else in the vicinity. She couldn't see him of course, but she thought he was charming.

'He had a lovely big dog with him. It licked my hand.'

It was a Rottweiler.

'He said he was from Manchester.'

I guessed as much. He had *Man Utd* tattooed lengthways up both arms, along with *Mum* and *Dad* on either side of his neck, and the individual letters of *Love* and *Hate* were stamped upon each of his fingers. A red and blue snake reached up from underneath his T-shirt and was about to make a meal of his Adam's apple before going on to have a swing on the ring through his left nostril.

He hung on for a while after I arrived but then, tossing the remains of his burger and French fries down on the pavement, he turned and lurched off in the general direction of Market Square.

'He wanted to know where the church was.'

I watched him cross the road and carry on down towards the parish church. He had a small haversack slung over one shoulder. He wouldn't get much lead in that. Perhaps the Rottweiler had a van parked nearby, ready for a quick getaway.

'Come on. I'll buy you lunch at the Theatre Bar.'

We always seem to have so much to talk about. I find that amazing. Two people who spend each and every day together, working, eating and sleeping, ought to have nothing left to say and yet we never shut up. Except when we take time out and indulge in a little eavesdripping, as Aileen puts it.

Our conversation gradually ground to a halt as we tuned in to the two women nattering away at the next table. One of them had moved with the times – almost, and was power-dressed from top to toe in chain-store Versace, with huge pads that sat to attention on each of her shoulders, like two stone lions either side of the steps of a municipal building.

Her companion had decided to stay put in the 1950s and it suited her. She wore a shapeless cloth coat, belted around her considerable middle, and had topped off the ensemble with a matching felt hat. The fact that it matched the curtains behind her rather than the coat she wore only added to the charm of the outfit.

They were deep in conversation, verbally disembowelling a mutual acquaintance.

'He's a bad 'un, is that one, Jessie,' muttered Shoulder Pads, her earrings swinging indignantly as she tossed her head. 'I wouldn't give him the time of day.'

'Oh come on now, Beryl. There's some good in everyone.'

'Not in him there isn't.'

'Yes, there is, love. As long as you're prepared to look for it.'

There was a pause as Beryl, as we had now come to know her, racked her brains for the killer punch.

'Oh aye. What about Adolf Hitler then?'

There was an even longer pause as Jessie considered this and then, folding her arms across her chest, she finally admitted defeat.

'Well yes, I must admit I could never quite *warm* to him.'

All the way home Aileen carried on the conversation, leaning back in her seat with her bare feet stuck up on the dashboard – an exercise which completely defeats the object of her wearing a seat belt in the first place and means that in the event of an accident her knees will be driven straight through her ribcage. I've told her a thousand times, but still she takes no notice.

'Anthony Hopkins in *Silence of the Lambs*. Now I could never quite warm to him.'

'Put your feet down.'

'Joseph Stalin – I could never quite warm to him either.'

'If we have an accident you'll finish up about three foot tall.'

'Mickey Mouse. Now he's another one I never could quite warm to.'

'If I have to brake sharply you'll – Mickey Mouse?'

'Little tosspot, with that high squeaky voice of his. Absolutely no talent whatsoever. Never could stand him. Not a patch on Tom and Jerry.'

I drove home in silence, listening to her as she vented her wrath on Colonel Gaddafi, Idi Amin and Francis the talking mule. So much to learn about her – so little time.

She wasn't warming to Gerry Adams as we walked up the garden path. A young woman had seen us coming and was waiting patiently on the front step. She had with her a little girl, the type of kid you don't often see around these days – washed, ironed and pre-shrunk and wearing a dress straight out of *Little House on the Prairie*.

They smiled identical smiles – the sort of smile that forgives you, for you know not what you do. These smiles have a mission to explain. To them, every day is a Sunday and they are determined that you should listen to their half-baked ideas. This was the sort of smile that should have been strangled at birth.

'Do you love animals?'

I mean, what sort of a question is that? She had a regular army of cats milling around her feet, waiting for me to stick the key in the front door, and young William had gone and perched himself on her left foot, looking for all the world like a very small vicar with his shiny black coat and gleaming white ruff. He smiled at me. The sort of smile that says it is suffering from acid indigestion and is about to break wind at any moment.

Aileen had stopped short at the sound of the voice.

'Who is it?'

'It's a young lady – two young ladies. I think they have come to tell us about God.'

'*He* loves animals,' declared the young woman as I pushed open the door.

'I should hope he does,' muttered Aileen. 'What sort of God would he be if he didn't love animals?'

The two of them smiled at her, oozing tolerance from every pore. Good job she couldn't see them.

I rather enjoy a good religious debate. I always lose in the end. Should I find myself ahead at any particular stage then I get terribly embarrassed about it and concede the point immediately. Besides, letting the other person win always makes them feel better and isn't that what Christianity is all about? Of course, it is also what cowardice is all about.

Aileen on the other hand, with her clear, crisp mind, employs a lethal brand of cold, hard logic to destroy the opposition and where's the fun in that?

The older of the two girls had just launched herself into a well-rehearsed sales pitch when I glanced down the path and noticed something missing.

'Oh, my God!'

I don't think she had ever made such an instant conversion in her short life and it took her completely by surprise. She paused and took a deep breath, ready to press home her advantage.

'My balls have gone.'

The girl reached out an arm and drew her young companion close to her side. The Lord might have rendered me harmless but she was taking no chances. I turned to Aileen, who was busy apologizing to Thermal for having cracked him around the back of the neck with her handbag. I pointed down the path.

'They were there when we went out. I'm sure they were.'

In fact I knew they were. Thermal had waved us off, his four paws tucked up tightly together as he balanced precariously, like a performing seal, on one of the two stone balls that sat on a solid plinth and topped off the huge stone gateposts.

And now they had gone. The two gateposts stood bareheaded either side of the wrought-iron gate and I felt the anger rise in me. They had been up there for over a hundred years, cemented in and skewered by an iron rod. It would have taken at least two men to prise them off. Maybe the same two men who turned up with a flat-bed lorry a year ago and carted off my pavement.

I despise thieves. When they are caught I think their favourite possessions should be taken from them and destroyed as a matter of course. An eye for an eye – a ghetto blaster and a twenty-nine-inch television set for two stone balls. Makes sense to me.

Then I remembered the stone mushroom. My grandmother's, my mother's and now mine, it stood alone in the front garden – serving as a lookout post for all four cats and as a stage for a tap-dancing squirrel who visited every now and then and put on shows for the troops.

I inherited the mushroom along with two stone pig troughs which were now overflowing with soil and flowers and would have needed a JCB to shift them. But the mushroom would be easier meat and it was a great relief to see it was still there.

An unpleasant coating of gunge-covered shell showed that our resident thrush had once again been using it as a chopping board in order to disembowel some poor unfortunate snail, but at least it was untouched by human hand and I could live with the beak. I would have a word with him later and ask if he wouldn't mind tidying up after himself.

Patrick, my neighbour, peered over the hedge. You have to be as tall as Patrick to peer over the hedge. I peered through the branches, at a spot just to the right of his left nipple, as his rich Irish voice brushed against the topmost leaves.

'Have you seen what they've done?'

'Yes.'

'Gone and pinched your balls.'

'I know. I've just found out.'

'Bastards. They want castrating.'

Now there was a thought. An eye for an eye and a ball for a ball. Even more appropriate than the ghetto blaster.

Patrick worries about me. He thinks I am too trusting. He has to restrain himself from frisking the guide-dogs-for-the-blind lady as she's pushing an envelope through his letter box.

'You need to keep a better eye on things.'

'I know.'

'You can't afford to relax for a moment.'

Patrick wandered off to tell his wife Sarah all about it and I thought I had better go in and ring the police. The two girls had made their escape and were now across the road, leaning heavily on Gwen's doorbell. I wished them luck. The doorbell works well enough, but Gwen's hearing doesn't. I always take my mobile phone with me and ring her from her own doorstep. Even so it can take a good half hour – you have to catch her as she's dusting the phone.

The police were much quicker and very sympathetic. There was a lot of it about apparently and did I need counselling? I said I didn't. They had offered us counselling once before, after one of our hanging baskets went missing, but we'd managed to struggle on without it and three years later we had almost come to terms with our loss. Curiously enough, I don't remember anyone asking me if I needed counselling after I found my first wife drowned in the bath.

That afternoon I worked on the screenplay of *Lost for Words*. Yorkshire Television had decided to take a chance on me. They had sunk a lot of money into the project and sets were being built and a cast was being assembled. I was now working on the third draft and hoping that there would be no need for a fourth.

Thermal worked with me. He had already sorted out his paper clips for the day and was now busily chewing the rubber bit off the end of a pencil, quietly, so that he wouldn't interrupt my train of thought. He's very good that way.

Even so my mind kept skipping back to the two stone balls. The thought that somebody must have been casing the joint for some time and then maybe even watched us as we left the house, was unsettling. A phone call to Architectural Antiques of Elland had told us that they would be worth around four hundred and fifty pounds and almost impossible to replace. But it wasn't the money. We had been invaded. Our privacy had been violated and it puts you on edge.

Every now and then I felt the need to leave my desk and go over to the window to see if the garage was still where I had left it. It was, but I had an uneasy feeling that somebody might be round the back, out of sight, slipping castors underneath, ready to roll it away as soon as dusk fell.

Viewed from up above, the gateposts looked like a couple of lonely skinheads waiting at a bus stop, until William decided to do something about it.

He clambered up to the top and then spread himself out in the sunshine, his thick little body immediately upholstering the jarring white of the naked cement, his luxuriant black tail hanging down the side so that his gatepost was turned into a dead ringer for Davy Crockett. Now if I could find myself another cat just like William I might be able to save myself a bob or two . . .

A movement in the front garden caught my eye. Just a flutter under the flowering privet. The thrush perhaps, back with a slug to stir-fry or yet another snail to fricassee. Then I saw the squirrel. A born athlete, he was limbering up with a series of stretching exercises. He is a very professional little squirrel and takes his business most seriously – he believes a pulled muscle to be the mark of an amateur and something to be avoided at all costs.

Thermal had to see this. I plucked him from the desk, hoisted him up on my shoulder and pointed him in the general direction of the front garden. The squirrel had just done a handstand on the garden wall and was about to attempt a triple somersault with half twist and rupture.

'Can you see him? Over on the wall, by the gate.'

Thermal shifted himself slightly and then peered deep into my left ear.

'*I think you've got a bit of wax.*'

'Never mind that.'

I plucked him off my shoulder and held him out to dry in front of me.

'There. Straight ahead of you.'

The squirrel was now performing excerpts from *Riverdance* on a low-lying branch, just to the left of the ornamental chimney pot. He was a natural, but Thermal missed him. He was busily examining a small imperfection in the window sill.

'*You want to touch that up. It'll spread like wildfire.*'

'Never mind that.'

I pressed his body up against the window pane and his nose went a funny shape and spread all over the glass.

'*I can't breathe.*'

'Sorry. I just wanted you to see this. There, look. He's on the stone mushroom.'

The squirrel had chosen the mushroom as the perfect place to take a standing ovation. He bowed to all four corners of the garden and then, somewhat disappointed that no-one had thought to throw flowers, he turned and made his way back to the park.

Thermal in the meantime had screwed his head upside down and was having a good look at the underside of the pelmet.

'You missed it.'

'*Missed what?*'

You can't point a cat at anything. They just don't want to know. They think you are trying it on. Thermal's neck takes on all the qualities of a bendy toy if I so much as attempt to draw his attention to anything interesting and his eyes cross over each other until they almost meet up round the back of his neck.

It's so disappointing. I can't really enjoy anything thoroughly unless I share the moment with someone else. If there's a good film on the television and I am on my own, I want to run out and drag people in off the street.

'Here, come and look at this. You'll love it.'

The other cats are just as bad. Tigger comes running to fetch me the instant she spots anything that takes her fancy, such as a spider on the hearthrug.

'*Come and watch this. I'm going to duff him up and I want a witness in case he sues.*'

But if I try to share one of my quality moments with any of them – forget it. The trouble is I can't forget it. I'm a born sharer, and so when the thrush appeared as the next turn on the bill I grabbed hold of Thermal once more.

'Look at that. No, not there – over there by the roses. Can you see him? He's got a huge worm. Yes, I know they're very pretty curtains, but that's not what I'm on about. Look at the thrush, for God's sake.'

I'd have been better off with a glove puppet. I planted Thermal down on the table and watched on my own as the thrush completed his act by tossing the poor worm high in the air before catching it on the way down and swallowing a good two thirds of it. The remaining third wriggled desperately in the vice-like beak for a moment or two, trying to make a break for it. But it wasn't best equipped for such an intricate manoeuvre and finally went the way of all flesh.

Patrick reappeared in his front garden, a spade in one hand and a can of lager in the other. He snapped open the can, rammed the spade deep into the soft earth and sat on the handle. He's my kind of gardener, is Patrick.

Over his head I could see his stone gateposts, exact replicas of mine. Both his balls were missing. Better go and tell him. He'd want to know. A trouble shared is a trouble halved.

Chapter 5

I sat waiting my turn. Four of us were due to speak and I was to be on last. A quarter of an hour each, we had been told, and the young man who was to start the ball rolling was now into his twenty-fifth minute and had just begun to read a great slab from his newly published novel.

At first they were known as the Angry Young Men, and then came the Brat Pack. Nowadays the breed has been watered down by the Martin Amises and Will Selfs of this world and comes under the general heading of the Aren't I a Little Rascal school of literature. This one had spent the first twenty minutes venting his wrath upon London's publishing establishment and it hadn't gone down too well up here in North Yorkshire.

The chairman was the editor of the local newspaper and he'd just about had enough. He rose to his feet. A small man, he had somehow seemed much taller sitting down, but his voice had been honed on junior reporters for more years than it cared to remember and it could take the skin off at forty yards.

'Going to have to stop you there, young man. Sorry to tear you away from yourself, but it's nearly twenty-five to three now and if we go on at this rate we'll none of us be home for *Coronation Street* – and we can't have that, can we?'

The young man sat down, blithely unaware of what a prat he had made of himself, and the chairman introduced the next speaker. She was young and pretty and nervous as hell. The audience took to her immediately and decided to help her along by listening intently and laughing out loud at her occasional jokes.

The young man turned and whispered to the chairman.

'I think I was aiming a bit above their heads.'

'No, not at all, young man. They knew exactly what you were on about – it's just that they didn't give a bugger.'

As I drove home I thought about my very first literary luncheon. There were three of us writers on the bill. The other two had been at the same university, and together they combined to shut me out and make me feel as though I had been brought along to serve the drinks.

One had recently edited a book of historical quotations and the other, a knight of the realm, had spent the latter part of his life as a political commentator for the BBC. He had written about his life and so had I. He recounted personal conversations with Winston Churchill and

Clement Attlee and I told the audience about my mother and Nellie Elliot.

I learned something that day. If he's not presented with a certain energy and warmth, Winston Churchill doesn't sell anywhere near as many books as Nellie Elliot, and I was still signing hardback copies long after the other two had given up and gone off to drown their sorrows at the bar.

Since that day I have strutted my stuff at hundreds of these lunches and Aileen says it's because I like to show off. For herself she picks and chooses, because for days before the event her nerves gnaw away at her stomach lining until she's pretty much of a wreck. It's just not worth it. She shakes all the way there. She can't use notes and she can't see the audience, but once she stands up to talk she is quite brilliant and enjoys herself immensely. She can't think why she doesn't do this more often – until the next time.

I enjoy meeting other writers. Some can be a pain in the neck, but on the whole they are a very democratic bunch of people who spend most of their days working in isolation and relish being let out to play. Most of them don't give a toss whether you sailed through university or were thrown out of school at the age of fourteen, whether you write romantic fiction or are rumoured to be heading straight for the Booker Prize. As long as you have started a book and stuck with it for some three hundred pages, then they know the agonies you must have been through and are more than happy to welcome you to the fold.

I also enjoy meeting the readers. It is very rare to come across someone actually reading one of your books. Writing is a solitary business and so, to a certain extent, is reading.

And perhaps it's for the best. Leslie Thomas, of *Virgin Soldiers* fame, once walked into the foyer of a hotel and saw a woman curled up on a settee, engrossed in one of his paperbacks.

'She's reading my book. I'm going to tell her.'

He walked over and sat down beside her.

'Sorry to bother you, but that's my book.'

The woman stood up, closed the paperback and handed it over to him.

'Here, you can have it. It was lying on the settee when I came in.'

It's a humbling experience. I was shopping in Marks and Spencer's food hall not so long ago, taking a few minutes out to help one of the staff. She wanted to know where the hell the bags of ready-sliced runner beans had gone and hidden themselves, and since I spend more time in the shop than most of the staff, she naturally asked for my assistance.

I took her over and pointed them out. Marks and Spencer's like to keep their shelves in a continual state of evolution – they don't want us resting on our laurels. No sooner have the unsliced loaves and currant teacakes made a comfortable home for themselves on the second shelf down and congratulated one another on finding such a pleasant place to bring up their little baps . . .

'*Our family has lived on this very spot for generations, your father and his father before him.*'

'*How long is that, mam?*'

'*The Wednesday before last.*'

'*Wow!*'

. . . No sooner have they settled down to a nice quiet life, with an unrestricted view of the wines, spirits and sparkling elderflower cordial, than it's time for the Easter eggs to take centre stage and the poor old loaves find themselves turfed out without so much as a by-your-leave and shoved in a corner next to the tinned cat food and sundry items.

Even I get confused at times, and I was in the process of tracking down a jar of beetroot slices – I prefer the crinkle-cut variety – when I became aware of a navel winking at me from across the aisle.

It was situated halfway between a pair of faded denim jeans and a cotton T-shirt. The T-shirt had been knotted a couple of times in order to allow the navel plenty of room to breathe and it was taking full advantage of its freedom.

'Excuse me.'

I couldn't remember ever having heard a navel talk before, but then I realized that the voice was coming from higher up, from the owner of the navel, a vivacious young woman with a sing-song voice that sparkled just as brightly as her long blond hair and soft golden tan.

'I hope you don't mind . . .'

To hell with the crinkle-cut beetroot. There were more important things in life.

'. . . but my mother would like a word with you, if it's no trouble.'

I hadn't noticed her mother. She was the sort of mother you don't notice. Dressed from head to toe in navy blue – shoes, tights and pleated skirt, with a snow-white Peter Pan collar peeping out from under a navy crew-neck sweater. She moved in on me.

'Sorry to be a nuisance, but are you him?'

I wasn't too sure whether I was him or not.

'Which him would that be exactly?'

'The writer.'

I preened a little, but not so you would notice.

'Yes – that's right.'

She moved in even closer, surrounding me in a sea of navy blue.

'Tell me. What's your name?'

'Deric Longden.'

She thought about it for a moment and then shook her head.

'No,' she said. 'That's not it.' She patted my arm gently. 'Never mind, love – it'll come to me.'

And with that the two of them wandered away, pausing only to pluck a jar of crinkle-cut beetroot from a nearby shelf. I wandered over and picked up a jar myself, but all the fun had gone out of it by then.

Aileen was weeding under the bedroom window as I pushed open the gate and walked up the path. At least *she* knows who I am. She shielded her eyes with a delicate hand and peered in my general direction.

'Who is it?'

'It's me, love.'

She smiled and reached that delicate hand of hers out towards a towering lily with a posh name. It's been in our family for over eighteen months now and is settling in very well. Aileen gave it a tentative yank.

'No. It's me.'

'Sorry.'

She felt her way along until she came across a small buttercup who was fooling around with a friend and not paying enough attention. Before he knew what had hit him, he found himself stuffed upside down in a black plastic bucket.

'*Oh sod it.*'

Aileen rose to her feet and gave me a kiss.

'How did the luncheon go?'

I find it very comforting to be married to someone who understands, from personal experience, that some you win and some you lose. One day you might just scrape through by the skin of your teeth and the next day you are quite brilliant. It's the way it is and I can always tell her the honest truth without loss of face.

'I was brilliant.'

'Told you not to worry.'

I was about to tell her just how brilliant I had been when William came racing in through the gate like an electrified spaniel. He was soaked to the skin and we hadn't had a drop of rain for a week.

William is very good at getting soaked. It's what he does best. Three or four times a week he streaks in through the kitchen door, dripping all over the place. At first I wondered if perhaps he was a special breed of cat who just happened to sweat a lot, but now I think that somewhere close by there lives someone who harbours a grudge against him and who keeps a hosepipe cocked and at the ready for whenever William decides to put in an appearance.

I took him into the kitchen and gave him a quick rub-down with a warm towel. He loves that, especially the bit where he lies on his back and I give his tummy a good seeing to, finishing him off by firmly ringing out his tail through both of my hands.

'Any messages?'

'You were a bit rough with my tail that time. In future, if you could just—'

'I was talking to Aileen.'

'Oh. Sorry.'

Aileen fished her tape recorder from out of her jeans pocket and plonked it down on the kitchen table. It saves her the laborious business of having to make notes, half on little bits of paper and half on the tablecloth. She pressed the play button and we both sat and stared at the little black box as it relayed an edited version of the day's events.

'Margaret rang. She won't be coming up this week, but she says she'll see you in Leeds next Thursday.'

Margaret Mathieson is a mover and a shaker. A wonderful lady, she gets things done. She was the executive producer of *Wide-Eyed and Legless* and after coming to see us had taken away the half-finished screenplay of *Lost for Words*. She rang me from London the very next day.

'Finish it.'

Then when the BBC eventually turned it down she told me not to worry. 'I'll get it made if it takes me fifteen years.'

I suggested that perhaps she might put that a little differently when next she spoke to Dame Thora Hird. It's hardly the sort of thing an actress wants to hear when she's fast approaching her eighty-eighth year.

Now Margaret had found a loving home for the play with Yorkshire Television and things were buzzing. Aileen pressed the button once more.

'Andrew Sanderson would like the large photo of you in your white angora bonnet and your white bootees. Also the one of your mother in Blackpool.'

Andrew was designing the sets for the play and I was to take pride of place on the mantelpiece in my mother's lounge. Ah, the glory of it all.

The machine cleared its throat once more.

'And the cats need a bag of fresh litter for their trays and don't forget the bottle bank.'

Aileen knows how to bring me down to earth, and William illustrated her point by practising one of his famous handbrake turns in his litter tray. Little lumps of damp gravel flew halfway across the kitchen floor and I went off to get the vacuum cleaner before fetching young William a smart clip across the backside.

It's a ten-minute journey up to the bottle bank and back and it usually takes me an hour or so. Something always happens and if it doesn't I hang around until it does.

Those of us who love the village of Marsh know that it lives and breathes and hums with activity, but to the casual motorist, driving up from the centre of Huddersfield towards the M62, it's just another dreary stretch of main road, to be negotiated at sixty miles an hour if at all possible.

They wouldn't notice that Lloyds Bank is about to have a new sign fitted and that while the workmen have nipped off to enjoy a tea break someone has gone and sorted out the pile of old letters and rearranged them under the window so that they now read DONKY BALLS.

At sixty miles an hour they wouldn't see that the old man waiting on the pavement edge has a racing pigeon peeping out of his raincoat pocket. As I pull up to let the two of them cross the road the pigeon looks right and left and then right again before giving me a grateful nod as the old man sets off slowly for the other side.

The casual passer-by wouldn't know how pleased we were when we heard the news that the old carpet shop, which had been boarded up for years, was about to be given a facelift. The Co-op have sold it. It's now a liquor store, all dressed up in black and red and called Booze Busters and at night we sit and think fondly of the good old days when it was tastefully boarded up.

The Co-op have also changed the name of their supermarket further up the road. At first it was Leo's, but now they have stuck in a row of new tills and renamed it the Pioneer. Down in town their large department store has changed its name to Living. I don't know why they bother. People still say, 'If you're going anywhere near the Co-op, get me a bag of sugar and a pound of leeks.'

Still, bless them, they do have a bottle bank round the back of the store. It must be a nightmare for those living in glass-smashing proximity to the bins, but is a boon for us red wine drinkers who live well out of the way and come up with the empties only once a month.

As I nosed my car into the park I happily gave way to a man with a pushcart. He smiled and eased his contraption into a vacant parking space. I hadn't seen anything like it for years. Right out of *Steptoe and Son*, it had been built around four huge pram wheels, dating from the days when prams were a status symbol and roughly the size of the Royal Coach. The wheels had been grafted on to what looked like a wardrobe that had died on its back after a long illness, and two wooden shafts provided the power steering.

I pulled into the space next to him and

watched him out of the corner of my eye. He was a short man but he was wearing a pair of very tall trousers that had been especially designed to keep his nipples warm in winter. He wore a coat of many colours – a splash of emulsion here, a dab of gloss there – and a blue and white bobble hat that would have gone well with a fishing rod by the side of a garden pond.

I pushed open the car door and he peered down the length of his cart to make sure I didn't scratch it.

'Nice car.'

'Thank you.'

'What sort is it?'

'It's a Jaguar. A Sovereign.'

'Very nice.'

It is at this point that I always start apologizing for my good fortune.

'It's getting on a bit now. Had it since it was a pup.'

I wanted to tell him how much I admired his pushcart but worried that it might sound patronizing.

He put his nose to the car window and stared in at the seats.

'Leather?'

'Yes.'

'Very nice.'

I desperately wanted to reciprocate.

Lovely shafts. I bet it can't half shift.

I moved round to the rear end and flicked open the boot. He followed me and stood by my side. He shook his head sadly.

'Wouldn't do for me. Hardly get owt in there.'

Then his mobile phone went off. He had to dig deep to find it. It was buried in his left-hand trouser pocket, just under his armpit, and he almost dislocated his shoulder in his attempt to locate it. In the end he fished it out through a hole in the lining.

'Hate these things. It'll be my partner.'

It was his partner and he told him that he would meet him in Rochdale later on that evening. I glanced at his pushcart and imagined it belting down the fast lane of the M62.

'Just a minute – got a call waiting.'

He pressed whatever it was he had to press as he wandered away towards the store. It was his wife who was interrupting, apparently, and he was not amused. He didn't like being disturbed during business hours.

I can remember when rag-and-bone men carried balloons about their person. Now it's a mobile phone with Call Waiting and they have fellow directors in Rochdale and they wouldn't even give my Jaguar house room. Once again I had managed to come third in a two-horse race.

Then another contender came up fast on the outside. This time it was a proper tramp – not one of your upwardly-mobile rag-and-bone men. He had all his worldly possessions stuffed in an old supermarket trolley that seemed intent on going sideways, and he stopped by the turbo-charged pushcart and sighed deeply. One day, if he ploughed all his profits back . . . He shook his head sadly. No, it was too late for that now.

He came over to see what I was doing. His trolley had a mind of its own. It had seen all the other trolleys lined up behind the Co-op and the herding instinct was still strong. The tramp wrestled with it until it gave in quietly and then they both came and stood by my side and stared at the array of empty bottles in my boot.

'You've been busy.'

'How do you mean?'

'That stuff. You don't half knock it back, don't you?'

'No, I wouldn't say that.'

'I would.'

He shuffled forward a couple of paces and stuck his head deep in the boot, his lips moving in time with his brain as he deliberately counted the bottles. It seemed to take for ever.

'Forty-seven. Forty-seven bottles.'

He straightened and caught sight of the two whisky bottles I was trying to hide behind my back.

'Forty-nine.'

'Yes. Well, I don't come up here all that often. I stack them in the cellar until it's worth the trip.'

'Oh aye?'

'Yes. And there are two of us and we have lots of friends round.'

I couldn't believe I was defending myself like this, especially to a man who had half a bottle of gin and a cheese sandwich nestling on that wire tray where harassed mothers normally plant their toddlers.

'Anyway. Red wine is good for you. Prevents you having heart attacks.'

He sniffed.

'So that's what they're saying now, is it?'

I reached in and picked up a crate of empties.

'Here, let me give you a hand.'

He took it from me and balanced it on the top of his trolley. The trolley groaned, it was getting too old for this sort of thing, but the tramp somehow found space for the other two as well and the three of us trooped over towards the bins.

I began hurling my collection through the hole in the green bin and my new-found friend grabbed hold of another crate and began to toss the contents into the mouth of the white one.

'They don't go in there.'

'How do you mean?'

'They're green bottles.'

'I know they are.'

'So they go in the green bin.'

He took a pace backwards so that he could get a wider view of the situation.

'You mean they've got a different bin for each colour?'

'Yes.'

'Brown, white and green.'

'Yes.'

'So the brown bottles go in the brown bin and the green bottles go in the . . .'

'That's right.'

He selected four brown bottles and walked over to the brown bin, lobbing them one by one through the hole. Then he turned back the blanket covering his trolley and took out two empty gin bottles that were tucked up among his winter clothing. He dropped them in the white bin with a certain tinge of regret.

'Somebody thought this system up, you know. Sat in an office and thought it up.'

'I suppose they must have done.'

He sighed as we turned back towards the car.

'There's some clever minds about, you know.'

I offered him a couple of pounds for his trouble and he said, no, really I shouldn't, there was no need to, that wasn't why he had given me a hand, if we couldn't help one another without money coming into it then what was the world coming to, and then he took it.

His trolley was still champing at the bit, dying to go and have a word with the free-range trolleys who were hanging out round the back of the Co-op. Some of them were grazing idly in and around the parked cars while a more motivated bunch were all lined up by the ramp, eager to be back on the shop floor. A rather furtive-looking couple of wire baskets seemed to be having sex in the disabled parking bay.

I headed my car out towards the exit and then sat there, waiting for a break in the traffic. Meanwhile the tramp had staggered up the slope with his belongings and begun to road test some of the newer-looking trolleys.

The first one had a fit of the staggers, I could see that from down the other end of the car park. It wobbled from side to side as he tried to keep it in a straight line. The next one seemed a much better bet as he gave it a whirl up and down the ramp before sticking it alongside a Volvo, where he could keep an eye on it while he made his mind up.

All this time the old trolley, jam packed with all his bits and pieces, watched his performance with a nervous eye. Was this the parting of the ways? Was he about to be thrown on the scrapheap? Had it really come to this?

His owner disappeared between two parked cars and came out pushing a bright young thing, all shiny metal and bouncing wheels, that pranced ahead of him like a young colt.

Without a second thought the tramp began to decant his belongings from his faithful old friend, piling them high in the young pretender. And then they were off across the car park without a backward glance. The worn old trolley stood there desolate and abandoned.

I found a gap in the traffic and pulled out into the road. As I curved round the car park I saw the trolley beginning to move. Now the weight had been taken from its shoulders it very slowly began to run backwards down the slope, then, gaining speed, it swung round, dancing across the tarmac like a pit pony released into the sunlight after years of darkness below ground.

Through my rear-view mirror I watched it sailing downhill until it smacked into a pleasant-looking bunch of trolleys who were having a quiet smoke and a natter down by the neatly kept bushes.

They made a space for him and he settled in among them, rubbing shoulders with them, one of the gang again. I smiled and pulled out into the main road. I love a happy ending.

Chapter 6

I had spent the whole morning at my desk, trying to lose an extra six minutes out of my screenplay in order to accommodate the commercial breaks.

When I recorded *Lost for Words* for the audio version it weighed in at just over seven hours' reading time. I had already pared that down to one hour and twenty minutes by being brutal and cutting both of my kids out of the story.

'*Sorry, kids, you're out.*'

'*Well, stuff you then.*'

Actually they took it very well and I did manage to work in a reference to them so that the television audience would at least know they existed.

Now I cut that out as well, but I had to extend the part of my mother's cat Whisky, and so I was back to square one.

'*I've left my mother's cat in.*'

'*Well, we know where we stand now, don't we?*'

At least I had managed to sit at my desk for almost three hours without interruption and that for me was fast approaching a personal best, even if I still wasn't getting anywhere.

I always manage a wry smile when I hear authors saying that they cut themselves off from the real world by taking an office away from home, or that they work to a strict timetable. They should try fitting in their literary endeavours with cooking three and a half meals a day, doing all the shopping and picking their wife up whenever she falls over one of the cats.

I sometimes think the cats do it on purpose.

'Let's get him out of that office – go and trip Aileen up.'

'Why does it always have to be me? I did it yesterday.'

I must admit though that I rather welcome the interruptions. Those golden moments when the intercom buzzes and Aileen is on the other end.

'Can you help me? I've lost a stamp.'

When I pushed open her office door she was on her hands and knees under her desk, sweeping the floor with her fingers.

'I'm sorry to bother you but I've just licked a stamp and it's disappeared.'

She sat back on her heels so that I could investigate.

'Can you see it?'

'Yes, love.'

'Where is it?'

'It's stuck on the end of your nose.'

*   *   *

82

But so far this morning not a single interruption, and I was just beginning to feel like a proper writer when this rather small and, it must be said, incredibly stupid vole marched into my study, sat down on the hearthrug and began to polish his whiskers.

I don't know how he got in, but he certainly hadn't thought it through. This vole was not the sort of vole destined to explore the dizzy realms of higher education. He certainly hadn't taken an 'O' level in survival techniques.

There were three cats in my office at the time of his arrival. Thermal was fast asleep on my desk, serving as combination paperweight and book-rest. Tigger was fast asleep on the fax machine, her tail tucked inside the paper guide, so that if I had needed to send a fax she would probably have gone along with it. William, for reasons known only to himself, was sitting in the fireplace, staring up the chimney. He has done that a lot recently. It's his new hobby. We have chimneys in practically every room and William has stared up them all – for hours on end. One day he will appear on *University Challenge*.

'*William Cat – reading chimneys.*'

I sat as still as I could, which is very still. I am extremely good at sitting still. I have been practising ever since I was a child. So had the vole apparently. Or maybe he was on some illegal substance. Whatever it was it certainly wasn't speed.

He sat on the hearthrug, inches away from William's tail, and inspected the quality of the weave. Not of William's tail – of the rug. It's Chinese and I am very fond of it. It's the only hearthrug that never leaves its post. All the others creep surreptitiously around the house during the night and have to be rounded up and sorted out next morning.

I thought about what to do next. If I made a move I would wake Thermal and Tigger. William would turn around and the vole would be history. What would David Attenborough do in a situation like this?

Well, if his past record is anything to go by he would nip behind the nearest bush and whisper sweet nothings into a microphone while the three cats tore the poor little devil to pieces, and I wasn't having that.

Tigger's glass water bowl was on the floor by my foot. The other two share a bowl in the kitchen, but Tigger refuses to share with anyone. She says it's unhygienic. She read it in a book somewhere.

Very slowly I bent down and picked up the bowl. I had filled it first thing this morning and now I needed to empty it. As quietly as I could I trickled the water into the waste-paper bin. It seemed to take for ever and sounded so loud that I was sure it would wake them up.

Thermal opened just the one eye and glared at me in disgust.

'For goodness' sake, man – use the litter tray.'

But Tigger woke up with a start and as she did a fax came through. This is always the highlight of her day. She jumped down and began to attack the paper for having the temerity to squeeze its way out of our machine.

William strolled over to let her know that he was there if she needed him and at that point the vole suddenly realized what a mess he'd got himself into.

He almost had kittens. Fortunately he ran over towards me to have them and as he hesitated for a moment, wondering how best to negotiate the north face of my desk, I dropped the glass bowl over the top of him.

The fax was forgotten. Tigger and William raced over to see what was going on and Thermal leaped off the desk to join them.

I must say I was rather impressed with myself and I was even more impressed with the vole when I joined the cats and studied him at close hand.

Distorted by the thick glass, his head seemed to fill the entire bowl – it looked enormous. He snarled and the cats backed away. It was the first time they had seen a sabre-toothed vole.

'What the hell is it?'

'I've no idea, but don't get too close.'

I slipped a clipboard under the bowl and carried him down the stairs to the courtyard, where I let him go. But he just sat on the step and stared at the empty milk bottles for a moment or so and then began to smarten up his whiskers once again.

'Go on. Get out of here.'

He was making a really good job of his whiskers and I wondered how he managed to keep them looking so bright and shiny without the aid of an expensive conditioner.

'Push off.'

But he wasn't your 'wash and go' type of vole. He took his time and he took a lot of trouble. He didn't know the meaning of split ends and dandruff. In fact he didn't seem to know the meaning of anything very much and he was just about to start plucking his eyebrows when Patrick yelled at me through the hedge.

The vole was off like a shot. One minute he was quietly considering the possibility of adding the odd highlight here and there and the next he was well on his way to breaking the land speed record for voles with learning difficulties.

I know how he felt. He's a good man is Patrick, but the power of his voice always startles me. I think it's to do with his being Irish and their long history of large families. As a kid you have to shout to be heard and it never leaves you. Bridie, from across the back lane, doesn't need to ring the doorbell. We can hear her muttering to herself as she walks across the courtyard, and when Kealen, who is one of eleven, has a coffee with us in the kitchen, the pan lids quiver with every word she utters.

Even so, Patrick takes some beating and the privet hedge winced as his voice whistled through the leaves.

'Are you there, Deric?'

'Yes.'

'I can't hear you.'

That's the trouble with us one-off kids. We don't speak up. I shouted that yes, I was there and then retreated into the small hallway off the kitchen where his dulcet tones wouldn't ricochet off the four garden walls. He told me that the police had just rung to say they had recovered the stone balls from the gateposts. They were bringing them up for us to identify that afternoon.

All through this conversation I ran in and out of the hallway, shouting out my replies and then diving for cover before Patrick could resume his assault. It was good news and I passed it on to Aileen before going to tell the cats.

Thermal was asleep on my desk, Tigger flat out on the fax machine and William staring up the chimney. I think I might get a pet vole. They are much more fun.

That afternoon I was due in Leeds, at the Yorkshire Television studios, for a session with the producer of the play, Sita Williams, together with Alan J. W. Bell, who was to be the director.

I wondered what to wear. Writers are supposed to look wild and dangerous, so I spent some time staring into the depths of my wardrobe. You may have seen those literary pundits on late night television, looking for all the world as though they have come to the studio straight out of bed, hair in a frenzy and wearing clothes that would have looked more at home selling copies of the *Big Issue*.

Well this artistic image doesn't just happen. It

takes time to look as scruffy as that, you have to work at it, and it takes even longer to look wild and dangerous. It took me ages and I failed miserably. I looked more like the vole I had rescued earlier on. We both had that vulnerable air about us, as if we cared too much what other people thought. So I decided to go for the lovable look instead.

The blue jacket with the brown shoes suggested that perhaps there was just the merest hint of the rebel hidden in there somewhere and I contented myself with the thought that I could always look wild and dangerous next time, when I wasn't in so much of a rush.

In fact the only rebel on duty at that moment was my right sock. I suppose on any other day it might just as easily have been my left sock, but today it had been randomly chosen as my right sock and there was something not quite right about it.

It seemed to be all ruckled up under the sole of my foot and try as I might I couldn't sort it out. So I changed my socks and still the right foot was just as uncomfortable, wrinkled up as though it was frowning. Perhaps it was the shoe that was causing the trouble.

So I changed my shoes and still the right foot was acting up, just as grumpy as ever. It was like walking across a freshly ploughed field. So I took off both my shoes and my socks and embarked on a barefoot hike across the bedroom carpet.

Perhaps it was the carpet? I had a go in the bathroom where the floor covering is as smooth as a bowling green and still my right foot felt as though it had recently been corrugated.

It must be the foot itself. I ran my hand over the length of my bare sole and I couldn't feel anything wrong with it, so I lay flat on the floor and, with the help of the magnifying mirror balanced on the edge of the bath, tried to make out what the trouble was.

Then Aileen came in and fell right over the top of me and while we were lying there, side by side, on the bathroom floor, we discussed feet.

'Do you ever feel as though one of your feet has been corrugated while the other one is perfectly all right?'

'No.'

It wasn't a long discussion and it solved absolutely nothing at all, but I felt a lot better when she said that I looked very smart indeed and sounded as though she really meant it.

Some people wouldn't take too much notice of a blind woman's opinion but I do, mainly because I love her and trust her and also because I become very desperate at times.

I also left her to identify the stone balls when the police arrived that afternoon, so I had no idea what might be waiting for me when I arrived home.

The Yorkshire Television studios in Leeds look as television studios ought to look and that isn't always the case. There are those that could easily be mistaken for a potted meat factory, but here in Leeds a vast reception area leaves you in no doubt whatsoever.

Waves of contestants for *The Price is Right* or *Countdown* gather on settees under enormous photographs of Bruce Forsyth and Richard Whiteley. David Jason, thinly disguised as Frost, stares across the room at a vast trophy cabinet, while over at the yuppie-free reception desk they somehow manage not to sound patronizing as they deal with people like me.

I had hung around outside, waiting for the automatic doors to spring open, and it wasn't until someone came barging through from the other side that I realized they weren't automatic at all. You had to push them. I could only imagine what I must have looked like from the reception desk.

Man in blue jacket and brown shoes stands outside building and waits patiently for a moment or two, giving the double doors plenty of time to acknowledge his presence. When they don't he waves his hand uncertainly from side to side in a vain attempt to attract their attention before taking a couple of paces backwards, and then he approaches once more, this time in what he imagines to be a more confident manner. The doors continue to ignore him, and so he tries a little jump in the air to see if that will do the trick. It doesn't, and he stands there looking puzzled and forlorn until a man he believes he once saw doing strange things to a sheep in *Emmerdale* barges through from the other side.

It's all very sad. Some deep-rooted politeness

gene always insists that I say thank you to automatic doors as they let me in or out, just as I never fail to thank that rather pleasant woman who operates the speaking clock, together with her colleague who so efficiently manages the 1471 service all on her own.

'You were called today at 14.30 – the caller withheld their number.'

'Thank you.'

I thanked the doors anyway, just to be on the safe side, and passed embarrassedly through reception on my way to the meeting.

Sita and Alan were waiting for me and after a quick cup of coffee we settled down to work. Over the past few weeks Sita and I had met several times in her office at the Granada studios in Manchester and I found her to be warm and witty and hugely experienced, with a long list of credits to her name. We had already gone through the play scene by scene and I admired her and liked her a lot.

Now we were about to go through it line by line and this can be a soul destroying business for the writer. Up until now the plaudits had come thick and fast. All those concerned at Yorkshire Television had told me that I had something very special and for weeks now I had gone around with a great big smile on my face.

They loved it, they said, but the fact that they had budgeted the best part of a million pounds on a single drama was the greatest compliment of all.

Selling a single play to television these days is no task for the faint-hearted, especially if that play is singularly lacking in cops and robbers. We didn't have a handsome young vet and nobody took their clothes off. There were no car chases, no lesbian love scenes and nobody got shot. We did have a doctor, several nurses and a couple of hospitals, but then you can't change the world overnight.

Alan Bell started the ball rolling on page two.

'Do we need that line?'

'Yes.'

'Why?'

'Er . . .'

I couldn't for the life of me think why we needed that line. I couldn't even remember having written it. As a writer I am a marathon runner rather than a sprinter and I needed to lie on the floor in a darkened room for a while, think about it, have a bath, turn it over in my mind and then sleep on it.

They wanted answers right now and they were spinning off each other.

'What about scene nine?'

'*What* about scene nine?'

'Do we need it?'

I slipped slowly from the settee and sat on the floor. I tried to look intelligent, making notes in my unreadable handwriting as the two of them unravelled my play like some lousy piece of knitting. They must know what they were talking about, they'd done it all before.

Then as the afternoon wore on we started

putting bits back in. We did need that line and scene nine proved to be absolutely essential and I began to realize that I had written a pretty tight script after all.

Sita and Alan were throwing ideas about and some of them were very good indeed, but they were freshly plucked ideas and needed work and I had laboured on this play for six solid months.

By the time Keith Richardson, the head of drama at Yorkshire Television, joined us, my fragile self-confidence had perked up a little and I was making notes I could almost read, which was a great improvement.

Then Sue Jackson, the casting director, popped her head round the door and spoke to Keith.

'Pete Postlethwaite says yes, he'll do it.'

A broad smile crept across Keith's face and the two of them discussed money for a while, then they upped it and Sue went off to clinch the deal. Sita was very excited and so was I, even though I had never heard of him.

'He's wonderful. Haven't you seen *Brassed Off*?'

'No.'

'*Sharpe*?'

'No.'

I think I was a bit of a disappointment to them. Later on I learned that Alan Bell didn't know much about him either but he had been bright enough to keep his mouth shut.

Alan Bell is probably best known as the

director of the BBC comedy *Last of the Summer Wine* and we'd had lunch together with Keith a week or so before at Alan's club in London.

As we stepped into the club foyer an attendant had barred my way.

'Sorry, sir.'

I wasn't wearing a tie and they wouldn't let me in until I had sorted one out from a selection they kept in a shoebox under the counter at reception.

I picked the sort of tie that instantly marks the wearer out as having either been educated at Eton or spent several years as an officer in the Guards, and yet as I knotted it round my neck it was patently obvious to anyone with half an eye open that I was more likely to have attended the Manor secondary modern school in Chesterfield and gone on to serve as a senior aircraftsman in the RAF at Hereford.

'Looks very smart, sir.'

I couldn't understand why they'd let Keith in. He was certainly wearing a tie, but then he wears them so loosely slung that it's hard to tell whether they are supposed to be round his neck or helping to keep his trousers up.

Alan looked the part until he took his overcoat off and it was discovered that he wasn't wearing a jacket underneath.

'Sorry, sir.'

The powers that be wouldn't let him into the dining room of his own club until he found one and they didn't keep a selection of jackets in their shoebox.

So Keith and I took our seats at a table in the dining room and talked about him as we worked our way through the best part of a bottle of wine until, some twenty minutes later, he arrived, wearing an ill-fitting jacket he had torn off the back of one of the lavatory attendants.

'Looks very smart, sir.'

It was fashioned out of royal blue nylon, with the bright yellow logo of the cleaning company stamped large across the left breast pocket. It fitted where it touched and was humming with static electricity, but all was well with the world. He was wearing a jacket and that was what mattered. Strange places, these London clubs.

It was well into the evening before Sita, Alan, Keith and I hammered out the closing sequence. The leading character, my mother – played by Thora Hird – had already died in hospital before the end of the play but I wanted her to have the final word in voice-over.

'I'm going nowhere without my teeth.'

I had fought hard for the line and I seemed to have won. Sita went off to find someone who could give her a docket for the taxi back to Manchester and Alan headed off towards his hotel. Keith, who doesn't seem to have a home to go to, sat back in his chair and smoked his umpteenth cigarette of the day.

I was very lucky that the play had finished up in his hands. He had fought like mad to get it networked, he believed in it completely, and now he had Pete Postlethwaite. Keith was the sort of man you needed on your side in this business and he smoked even more than I did. What more could anyone want?

On the way home I called in at the video shop and the woman disappeared among the display racks to find me a copy of *Brassed Off*. It didn't take her long.

'Have you seen it before?'

She was staring down at me from behind the counter as I sat on the floor and tried to sort out my corrugated sock.

'No, I haven't.'

'Oh, you'll love it. Pete Postlethwaite is absolutely brilliant.'

And he was. I didn't even wait to put the car away. I parked up by the side gate and rushed in to watch the film with Aileen. We laughed and cried and then watched the film all over again as we ate our dinner. While Pete was on the screen you couldn't take your eyes off him, and he had some stiff opposition.

We shed real tears as he lay in a hospital bed and the brass band played 'Danny Boy' from down on the lawn beneath his window and we cheered his rousing speech in the Albert Hall. We even gave him a round of applause as the credits rolled and I can't remember ever clapping the television before.

Then we replayed the bits and pieces we had especially loved before sitting back with what was now an early morning cup of coffee.

'Just think. He's going to be playing me.'

Aileen smiled and stroked my hand.

'Yes. And you've got your balls back as well.'

I had forgotten my balls.

'Are they all right?'

'Yes. The police put them in the garage, down the right-hand wall so you can still get the car in.'

I had forgotten about the car as well and it was pitch black outside. I switched on the headlights and a stray cat stood mesmerized for a moment as I pulled into the garage. I wanted to tell him about the cellar where he could get a warm bed for the night and a hot breakfast first thing in the morning, but he quickly pulled himself together and was gone.

And so were the balls. Not a sign of them. Someone had nipped into the garage and pinched them while we were watching the film.

Chapter 7

I could have taken the ring road and given Chesterfield a miss but I don't get too many opportunities to drive around my childhood haunts. Even though the town is changing at a rate of knots, it still holds many memories for me.

I checked my watch. Half an hour and I must be off. Just time to have a look at the old house in Heaton Street where I was born and from there it's only a hop, step and a jump along Old Road and then a sharp left into Storrs Road.

My mother didn't travel very far. Four houses from birth to death and all of them within the same square mile. It makes life very convenient when you are taking a trip down memory lane.

I pulled up across the road from number forty-three and switched off the engine. It was here in 1936 that my mother had been dragged away from a card game at midnight and rushed off to hospital in Bob Pearson's van. She hadn't wanted to go, she was winning and she had a good hand, but I had insisted on being born.

They say I hung on until she had made it to

the foot of the hospital staircase before making my first appearance. I wasn't a difficult birth. I couldn't wait to get out into the big wide world and apparently my dad was very proud of me that day, probably for the first and last time in his life.

My mother and I went to hospital together not so very long ago, a year or so before she died, and she asked if we might drive down Heaton Street so that she could have a look at the old house. I had pulled up on this very spot and for the umpteenth time she told me that the little garden wall had once sprouted iron railings.

I remembered them well. My father painted them a couple of times a week. He would always have a drop of paint left over from his latest job and it seemed a pity to waste it.

For three days they would be jet black with silver knobs and then I would come home from school to find they had magically turned olive green with brown and gold knobs. They were his pride and joy, until one day the powers that be came to cut them down.

'It's because of the war. They are going to make guns out of them.'

My father was heartbroken. I remember my mother trying to make him feel better, while I sat in the corner and tried to imagine the British Army going over the top, firing cardinal-red guns with big gold knobs on the end.

As my mother and I sat there a lady with lilac hair came hobbling round the corner of

Rhodesia Road. I can't remember her name, but I do remember that over the years her hair had changed colour about as often as our railings.

She recognized my mother and came over to have a word with her. In fact she managed to have several thousand words before my mother was able to grab an opening and butt in. In the meantime I almost hypnotized myself by staring at her pale pink scalp as it shimmered in the sunlight through the thin lilac covering.

At last the woman made the mistake of asking a question, which was where my mother entered into the conversation.

'What are you doing down here, then?'

'I just thought I'd stop and have a look. I'm going in hospital to have an operation.'

We then had ten solid minutes of my mother's medical history, ranging from that dreadful time in her schooldays when they thought she would never pull through, to the moment a fortnight ago when she came over all peculiar and had to lie down.

'Are you going private?'

'No, of course not.'

My mother seemed surprised at being asked such a stupid question.

'Deric's coming with me.'

I cruised slowly along Old Road, past the little shop at the top of St Thomas's Street. My mother was still calling it Hooley's, I think it was, long after Mr Drury had taken the business over. Then when Mr Drury retired after ten years or so and sold it on, she immediately decided to start calling it Drury's. She was always one owner behind and it didn't really matter until she came over all sophisticated and acquired one of those newfangled chequebooks. The new owner took it in his stride, waiting until she'd left the shop before crossing out the name Drury, inserting his own, and then forging her initials in order to make it all legal and above board.

The half-hour was ticking by, so I wasn't able to spend much time on the other two houses. The fourth, where my mother first saw the light of day, had been pulled down long ago and the site was now part of the grammar school playing fields.

A week ago a team from Yorkshire Television had covered this same route, taking notes and photographs of her last two homes so that they could recreate the interiors in the studio back in Leeds.

I waved to an old neighbour of my mother's who stopped weeding long enough to wave back and wonder who the hell I was, and then I set off for Matlock, where I was to talk to a mass meeting of mobile librarians.

They were coming from all over the country in their library vans and I had an awful vision of having to stand in the middle of a field and shout at them through a megaphone. But no, they were going to park up and then hold a series of meetings in the Derbyshire County

Council offices. I was to be the light entertainment after lunch and I was quite looking forward to it.

In her later years my mother was a great supporter of the Derbyshire mobile library service.

'I don't know what I would do without them.'

She never took out a book in her life, but the librarian on her route very kindly agreed to ripen her green tomatoes on his dashboard as he drove around the county and she thought he was absolutely wonderful.

'I always give him half a dozen for his trouble.'

I thought they were absolutely wonderful too. They had all the vans lined up in the car park, getting on for fifty or so, some more or less what you would expect, others the last word in sophistication, with lifts for the disabled and playing areas for the children.

I did a tour of them all and tried to pretend I wasn't hurt when they didn't have copies of my books on board.

Librarians have it made when it comes to dealing with authors. If your books are on the shelves they take you straight to them.

'There you are.'

If they don't stock them, have never stocked them and wouldn't even dream of wasting their money on them, they smile and lie in their back teeth.

'You're very popular. Your books are always out. We've got a waiting list as long as your arm.'

The conference drew to a close and the vans began their long journey home, to the South Coast, the West Country, some having only to pop over the Pennines, others taking the tortuous route back to East Anglia. They left the car park in a constant stream, one after the other, heading for the M1, and passers-by stood with their mouths open at the sight.

'I don't know. You wait for hours for the mobile library and then thirty-seven come along all at once.'

I followed them for a while and then, on impulse, doubled back to have another look at Matlock. One of the first things I came across was a large photograph of myself in the window of the Firs Bookshop.

I took it in my stride. Hardly glanced at it. One gets used to these things after a while. Just a quick sideways peep to make sure they had my hair colouring right and that the smile was winsome enough and yet not over the top.

I was just trying to remember what on earth had happened to that shirt I was wearing and whatever possessed me to buy it in the first place when I smashed into the rear of the car that had just pulled up short in front of me.

The driver was out of his seat in a flash. He was one hell of a size and he sort of unfolded out of his Volvo like a well-oiled action man. He was wearing a pair of those camouflage trousers that are designed to make you almost invisible in the jungle but don't half stand out when they are advancing towards you in the middle of Matlock town centre.

From his number one haircut right down to his big black boots he was road rage incarnate, and he was tapping out a tattoo on my window. I pressed a little black button and the passenger window immediately eased its way down.

I stared at him through the glass for a moment and then pressed another button and the driver's window gaped open. A bullet-shaped head came through and joined me in the car.

'Are you all right?'

His voice was gentle and concerned. I had thought as I watched him striding towards me that I might fake a broken rib or two – a little simulated whiplash right now might save me a great deal of pain in the long run. But he seemed genuinely concerned about me, his face as troubled as a face can be when it's topped off with a haircut like that.

'I'm fine, thank you.'

'Are you sure?'

'Yes, really.'

His face broke into a great big grin and his haircut panicked and hung on for dear life.

'Let's have a look at your car then, shall we? See what the damage is.'

I had come off worst. He had one of those towbars sticking out from the back of his car, the sort they use for pulling caravans, and it had buried itself deep into my bumper, with the result that both ends had flirted off and my car now looked as though it was wearing a droopy moustache.

His Volvo was comparatively unscathed. His towbar had buckled slightly and his bumper had a cute little dimple that might look rather attractive in a certain light.

'I'm sorry. I can't think what I was playing at.'

'Ah, don't worry about it. I can knock that out in a few minutes.'

We decided to leave it at that. What with the excess on the insurance it wasn't worth the trouble of claiming. I apologized again but he wouldn't hear of it.

'Life's too short,' he said.

We shook hands and he went his way and I went mine. My way was backwards, into a vacant parking space. The bumper was now dragging on the road, and so I yanked it off and slung it over the back of the empty seat, one end in the passenger well.

A man who had been watching us closely during all this came over to have a word with me.

'If you want a witness . . .'

'How do you mean?'

'He never even looked. Backing into you like that.'

'He what?'

We leaned against the car together, my photograph smirking at me from the bookshop window as he explained.

'He was reversing into here.' The man kicked

my car tyre to show me what he meant by here. 'Never even looked to see if there were owt coming up behind him.'

My witness scribbled his name and address on the back of an envelope and went on his way. I jumped in the car and the bumper gave me a warm welcome and then belted me across the left ear. I screwed up the envelope and dropped it in the passenger well. What the hell. Life's too short, isn't it?

Back at home there was a tape recorder waiting for me on the kitchen table. At that moment I would have given anything to see instead a great big steak and kidney pie with new potatoes, green beans and one or two sprigs of that long thin broccoli that seems to be all the rage down at Marks and Spencer's nowadays.

It would be nice to come home to a piping hot meal once in a while, I thought, instead of having to roll up my sleeves and start from scratch. But then I switched on the tape recorder and heard Aileen's lovely voice and knew I would rather come home to her any day of the week.

'Guess what. Helen's got the afternoon off from the surgery, so she's picked me up and we've gone shopping. I'll be back about half-past six because she's on call tonight. Hope your day went well. Love you.'

So she would be in capable hands. Our doctor has a good eye when it comes to a bargain. She helps Aileen with the colours and the sizes and is always ready to offer that all-important slice of psychology.

'Of course you can afford it.'

She would also be on hand with expert medical advice when Aileen ruptured herself hauling her carrier bags out into the car park.

I extracted the wok from the cupboard and began to chop up a chicken, a couple of cloves of garlic, ginger, spring onions, peppers, celery, sweetcorn. That's the trouble with Chinese cooking, it's all stir-fried in a couple of minutes – as long as you've spent a couple of hours on the preparation beforehand.

The chefs on television have it all too easy. The ingredients to hand in bite-sized bowls, minced by minions and laid out in the correct order. Not a pot to wash and not a single cat in sight. They ought to try it in our house. A studio audience would be a doddle after cooking for years in the presence of four critical cats.

'Oh hell. He's getting the wok out again.'

Aileen bought me the wok for Christmas, together with a stainless steel cleaver and hardwood board. For my birthday she bought me an asparagus steamer. She really knows how to spoil a guy.

The cats hate to see the wok come creeping out of the cupboard. They know the bottle of soy sauce is likely to follow hard on its heels and they can't stand soy sauce at any price.

'He'll ruin that chicken.'

They can't stand the sizzling and spitting

either. What was wrong with the good old-fashioned beef and two veg? Done in the oven as God intended. You knew where you were with that.

In the old days they would sit, two of them either side of our chairs, looking up appealingly, catching odd bits of rogue beef in mid air. Every now and then a lump of coarse horse-radish would slip through the security net and have them flat on their backs, coughing fit for their lungs to burst. But it was a small price to pay and the offending morsel could always be rinsed under the tap and then you could hardly tell the difference.

Best of all were the scrapings from the meat dish, together with the leftovers and surplus gravy. That was really living. But have you ever tried licking out a wok? No wonder those Siamese cats always look as though they've just eaten something that didn't agree with them.

But the cats brightened up considerably when they saw the prawns I had bought to go with the avocado.

'He doesn't muck about with them.'

I had to muck about with the avocado. It was as hard as a rock and I should have left well alone, but it had lain in the fruit bowl for over a week now and I just assumed it would be ready for eating.

The cats moved in for a closer look. All except Tigger, who wouldn't dream of doing anything so vulgar. She stayed aloof, sitting with her paws buttoned up tight together, over by the fire in the corner.

The avocado took the edge off my cleaver as I sliced it in half and then I had the job of removing the stone. It was as though it had been set in concrete. I stuck a knife in and wiggled it about, but this one was going to need major surgery.

I dug deep and twisted hard and the stone shot out like a bullet. It flew across the kitchen, clipped the ceiling light and then dropped like – well, like an avocado stone, I suppose.

Tigger was minding her own business, filing that claw on her left paw, the one that's always given her trouble, ever since she was a kitten. She was just slipping the claw back into its sheath when the avocado stone smashed down on the top of her head.

The effect, as they say in the adverts, was shattering. Her legs folded up underneath her and she fell over and got up, only to fall over again, and then she staggered about on the kitchen tiles like a heifer in an abattoir.

I picked her up and her eyes rolled and she seemed to pass out. I didn't know what to do. The kiss of life perhaps?

'Where am I?'

She played the scene to perfection. It was just like an old movie. She even gave a polite cough to suggest there might be a hint of consumption.

I took her up to my office together with half a dozen prawns. You would be amazed at the healing properties half a dozen prawns possess. They ought to be on prescription.

After a while she curled up in my chair and fell fast asleep. It's not really allowed during the day, but there were special circumstances and Tigger is not one to let a special circumstance go by without giving it her full attention.

The noise downstairs was horrendous as three small cats belted an avocado stone around four skirting boards. If ever an avocado stone paid for its sins, this one did.

It was my fault really. Fancy starting off a Chinese meal with avocado and prawns. Ken Hom would ask for his wok back if he ever found out. I replaced the two halves in the fruit bowl to give them a chance to ripen and then picked up the colander in which I had rinsed the prawns.

Empty. Not a single one left. I looked round accusingly at the cats. Thermal was over the other side of the kitchen. He had the avocado stone trapped under the table and his rear end swayed from side to side as he moved in for the kill.

William, who should have been acting as his right-hand man, had been sidetracked. He does tend to get sidetracked, does William. He was staring closely at a tiny spider who had decided to climb up on top of the biscuit barrel. William doesn't know it's rude to stare and the spider was beginning to realize that coming up here probably hadn't been such a good career move after all.

Little Chap was sitting over by the breadbin, licking his lips and washing his face. He strolled over to join me and sat down by the colander.

'Any more of those? They were very pleasant. Made a nice change.'

He was a very happy little chap indeed, until I shouted at him. His sense of belonging is still paper thin and he just went to pieces.

They tell me that out in the park he's known as the Lion King. Large dogs think twice before taking him on and then don't. One that thought twice and then did was still licking his wounds a couple of weeks later and has since developed a nervous twitch that turns into an all-enveloping shudder whenever he approaches the park gates.

But here in the house Little Chap has found himself a bolt-hole. No need to be aggressive or to sleep with one eye open, he can crash out wherever he chooses and be perfectly safe. Everybody is pleasant to him and food is delivered at regular intervals, on saucers and on time, and if he feels like a snack in between meals he has only to throw back his head and holler:

'Fooooood.'

And now he'd gone and done something terribly wrong and blown it all. He knew he would eventually – he always did. He wondered what it was he'd done this time and he couldn't think of anything, but that nice man was shouting at him so it must be something very serious.

Instead of making a break for it he simply

gave himself up, laid his chin on the draining board and tensed his abject little body, miserably waiting for the inevitable blow to fall.

I patted him on the head and found him a small prawn that had got itself wedged in a hole in the colander. He stared at my peace offering for a moment, thinking it might be a trap, and then began to chew it in slow motion as I lowered him to the floor.

William shouted at him to come and have a look at his spider and I picked up my cleaver and set about a red pepper. Well, life's too short, isn't it?

Chapter 8

The birds woke me even earlier than usual this morning. I think the tall one has a cold. His voice seemed huskier than before and his heart wasn't in it. He had managed to cough his way through only the first few bars of Rossini's *Barber of Seville* before the short one cut in with his latest mobile phone impression. He has been practising Call Waiting for some time and he's just about got it right. The tall one seemed quite happy to hand over the reins and I took a sip of last night's whisky and water and huddled under the duvet, listening as the short one went on and on.

Last night's whisky doesn't taste quite the same in the early hours of the morning and I needed a cup of coffee. Aileen stirred beside me, unduveted and naked as the day she was born, but in much better shape. I sat up and admired her various curves and curlicues for some time until she shivered gently and reached for the duvet.

I covered her and eased myself out of bed. The short one had turned round and was staring in at me through the rooflight, so I automatically pulled in my stomach and puffed out my chest and then felt rather daft. I thought for a moment that I might dial 1471, ring him straight back and tell him to bugger off, but in the end I decided to ignore him and go and make that cup of coffee instead.

The cats decided to ignore *me* as I pushed open my study door. Backlit by the light from the hall I must have cut a ghostly figure as I crept, cup and saucer in hand, towards the table in the window. Tigger opened just the one eye and then quickly closed it again.

'Don't look, chaps. He's stark naked.'

Thermal decided to chance a peep. After all these years he still hasn't worked out how I do it. He'd love to be able to strip off every now and then, on hot summer days and after he's slept too long by the radiator. He spends hours searching his undercarriage, looking for the zip, but so far he hasn't found a thing. That's not quite true – he has found a thing, but he's still looking for the zip.

He came over and joined me at the table and we stared out across the park together. There were lights cutting through the dark, dozens of them, pinpricks at first, strobing through the trees, then growing in stature as they came closer.

Thermal was transfixed. He sat on the table with his back to me, staring out of the window, every muscle on red alert, his two little ears standing to attention, framing the scene for me like a couple of bookends.

I tried to make out what was going on. What looked like a huge spaceship emerged from the gloom, then came to rest in the centre of the park. It was as though I were sitting in on the opening sequence of *ET*.

'ET go home.'

'*Pardon?*'

'It was a movie. The hero had a look of you about him.'

'*Did he?*'

Thermal preened at the thought. I hope to God he's not around the next time they show the film on television.

A flotilla of smaller craft began to surround the mother ship. There must have been over fifty of them, and then as the daylight began to thread its way through the trees and the mist decided it had better things to do with its time, a splash of red and gold lettering solved the mystery.

The Moscow State Circus was with us once more and raring to go as usual. They don't hang about. As Thermal and I sat idly drinking our coffee, me from my cup and Thermal from my saucer, an enormous marquee was raised higher and higher until it was as tall as my house and able to look down on the trees.

Dozens of caravans huddled close round and a series of smaller tents rose as though they had been instantly inflated. A generator burst into life and the marquee suddenly filled with light, turning the sombre dark wine of the canvas into a vivid scarlet red.

By six in the morning everything was in

place, as though it had always been there. A strongman emerged from one of the caravans wearing only a pair of underpants that he had obviously borrowed from a much smaller man. He attached a hosepipe to a temporary cold water tap and waited while the water decided to shift itself.

Thermal and I shivered at the thought and then the strongman's rather stunning young assistant joined him, wearing an even smaller pair of pants and a bra so tiny that at first I thought she had it on back to front.

The water eventually decided to appear and the two performers shared a bar of soap as they hosed each other down in a scene that was wonderfully erotic for six o'clock in the morning. Thermal wasn't all that impressed, but then he didn't have the binoculars.

'How about a spot of breakfast?'

'Just the two of us?'

'Yes. Be like old times.'

Silently we crept from the room. Past William, who was flat on his back and snoring gently, fast asleep on the hearth so that he would be in position for chimney duty the moment he woke up. Past Tigger, who had both of her front paws draped over my Compaq laptop, her head resting neatly on the disk drive.

Past Little Chap, who normally preferred to sleep in the cellar, but who had Velcroed himself to the radiator for the night in order to extract every last drop of warmth. Had it been switched on he would have really felt the benefit.

They don't all four usually sleep together like this. Must have had an important meeting last night. Maybe it had dragged on and on and they'd had a few drinks and decided to stay the night. I would ask Thermal about it over breakfast. I like to be one step ahead.

But first I had to read aloud a selection of interesting bits from the *Daily Telegraph*. This is a service I once provided exclusively for Aileen's benefit, but over the years Thermal has become used to hearing me drone on over the breakfast table and so as soon as he has had a perfunctory nibble at his saucer of tuna chunks he comes over and leans heavily against my ankle, listening intently. Even though Aileen was still fast asleep in bed I had to give him at least a taste of the ritual before he would even think about going out in the courtyard for his early morning run.

Huddersfield Town football club were top of Division One for the first time since I moved here and the Pope had apologized for the behaviour of all the other Popes before him. It's becoming all the rage, this apologizing for the sins of our forefathers, and I can't help thinking it's rather silly. It means absolutely nothing, except to a handful of politically correct half-wits, and I strongly object to the government apologizing on my behalf for the behaviour of my ancestors in days gone by.

I wasn't there, it wasn't me, I didn't do it and what's more my great-uncle Jack, who was there, didn't know any better at the time. Before long the powers that be will be insisting that Florence Nightingale's descendants apologize for her not having used penicillin during the Crimean War and King Alfred's lot will be forced to apologize for that time when he burned the cakes, especially to those who were unfortunate enough to get lots of little black bits stuck between their teeth.

I can get quite heated about these things but Thermal wasn't interested. I can tell by the way he purrs. He ticks over for most of the time, it's become a habit with him. Even when he's fast asleep he sounds like a well-bred getaway car parked round the back of the Midland Bank – a Mercedes or a Jaguar XJS or some such model that has been regularly serviced at a properly appointed garage.

But the moment his interest is aroused he steps on the gas and his 4.2 engine leaps into action, rattling a fading bodywork that would feel much more at home on an elderly Citroën 2CV.

I combed through the paper, from the front page to the business section, where I paused for a moment, marvelling at how the *Daily Telegraph* manages to fit in so many photographs of attractive young women among its rather dull reports of the doings of the CBI and Alan Sugar. There were five of them today. Three posing with a mobile phone, one smiling and not looking where she was going while driving a car and a financial adviser who was wearing an ultra-short skirt, stiletto heels and a rather supercilious expression. Then I found the sort of thing I was looking for.

'Listen to this, Thermal.'

His ears tuned in to the excitement in my voice and his paw hovered over the accelerator pedal in anticipation.

'It says here that over two thirds of the world's production of Benedictine is drunk in the pubs and clubs of Burnley.'

Well, you could have knocked him down with a feather. It shook me, I can tell you – it's not often you come across a piece of vital information like that in the newspapers. They are usually packed full of the more trivial stuff such as the greenhouse effect, world recession and pink being the new black.

'Just think of it, Thermal. We live within spitting distance of the place where they drink more Benedictine than anywhere else in the world.'

He thought about it as he went back and sorted through the massed ranks of tuna in his saucer. He knows I slip a vitamin tablet in among the chunks every morning and his first avowed intent is to find and destroy it before it can do him any good.

I read on. Apparently during the First World War a battalion of Lancashire soldiers known as the Burnley Pals were camped near the Benedictine monastery in France and immediately fell in love with the sickly sweet liqueur that the monks turned out in such huge quantities. It kept out the cold, they found, and made the war seem that much shorter, so after the conflict was over they made sure that they took a plentiful supply back home to Burnley with them.

And the tradition lives on to this day. Burnley is the only place where the drink is sold upside down with the other optics. The Plumbe Street Miners' Working Men's Club stocks Benedictine in three and a half litre bottles and the Plumbe Street Miners' working men knock it back as if there was no tomorrow, in hot water or with lots of ice, as the mood takes them.

I felt intensely proud of Burnley, just as I did when I found out that here in Huddersfield we eat more sliced pickled beetroot than almost any other place on earth.

But Thermal wasn't paying attention. The vitamin pill was proving an elusive little devil and he knew from past experience that the only way to deal with it effectively was physically to get in there among the tuna chunks and sort it out.

So he took a deep breath and plunged in at the shallow end, coming up for air every now and then as he trawled his way through the murky depths. I must get him a snorkel and a spear gun; at least he'll look more professional.

In the meantime I ripped open a packet of cold comfort capsules I'd bought from Boots the chemists. I had a busy week ahead, the high-light of which was to be the first read-through of the play, and I couldn't risk the streaming eyes and running nose that I knew were well on the way.

I suffer from a cold more than anyone else in the world. I have worked on with a broken arm, a broken leg and a broken collarbone, but a common cold immediately puts me out of action and leaves me walking around like a zombie, with my eyes streaming and my brain bouncing around my skull like a boxer on the ropes.

I flipped a couple of capsules out through the foil backing and glanced at the leaflet to see how many I should take.

Two capsules to be taken with a drink every four hours up to a maximum of four doses in twenty-four hours.

Simple enough. I could handle that. I washed down the first two capsules with the remains of last night's whisky and took another glance at the leaflet to pass the time. Apparently there could be side effects on occasion and I read through the list as I tried to get rid of the rogue capsule that had become stuck to the back of my throat.

Stomach pain, sputum retention, nausea, vomiting, diarrhoea or constipation . . .

Diarrhoea *or* constipation? My God. They were versatile little devils, these capsules.

. . . headache, blurred vision, ringing in the ears, irritability, sleep disturbance, loss of appetite, difficulty in passing urine . . .

I didn't think I would have any difficulty in that direction. I was almost wetting myself right now.

. . . rapid heart rate, shaking, skin rashes and sweating.

I glanced down at my bare chest. There did seem to be a small rash, just to one side of the single hair that has begun to look quite distinguished since it turned a steely grey. But it wasn't all that easy to tell. What with the rapid heartbeat, the shaking and the sweating it wouldn't stand still long enough for me to form an educated opinion.

The list wound up with a mind-boggling get-out clause.

If concerned . . .

Concerned? I'm frightened to death.

. . . or if anything else unusual happens . . .

Anything else unusual? The only things they haven't mentioned so far are gangrene, ectopic pregnancy and rigor mortis.

. . . talk to your pharmacist . . .

And a lot of good that would do. I knew exactly what Chris Holt, my regular pharmacist, would say.

'And what the hell were you doing in Boots anyway?'

'I was just passing.'

'No. That's what you should have done. Where you went wrong is you went inside and bought something, so don't come round here looking for sympathy.'

I shuddered at the thought, but then Thermal brought me swiftly back to the here and now. He'd found the vitamin pill. He always does – I don't know why I bother hiding them.

His whiskers trembled with disgust as he rolled it around his mouth a couple of times before spitting it out like a bullet. It smacked hard against the fridge door, rebounded, spun round a couple of times, then circumnavigated the fringe on the circular rug like a drunk on his way home from the pub before tottering over towards the pedal bin, where it collapsed belly up on the floor. Thermal stood up, had a good long satisfying stretch, and then gave the vitamin pill a sharp clip round the earhole as he passed it on his way out of the back door.

I didn't really know what to do with the day. No more script changes until we started shooting and then it would be a case of rewrites on the hoof. Tomorrow I would be in Leeds for the read-through of *Lost for Words*. The entire cast, a crew of some fifty hardened professionals, the director, producer and executive producers, would all be there along with Aileen and myself.

The thought of being trapped in a room while the actors spoke my words for the very first time was both frightening and intensely exhilarating. A book is very much a private affair. I'm never there when the reader decides to skip a couple of pages or puts it down in disgust. I can kid myself that they savoured every word, laughed like a drain and cried their eyes out, and then went straight back to the beginning and started all over again. But tomorrow there would be no escape. I would be able to hear the disdain in the actors' voices, watch the despair in their eyes as they exchanged desperate glances with one another:

'How did I get myself mixed up in this load of old rubbish?'

'Oh what the hell – at least it's a job.'

Simon Gray once described the art of the playwright as an unnatural pursuit and he had it dead to rights. I was thinking I might end it all and leave a suicide note on Aileen's tape recorder when the kitchen door opened and in she came, hair rumpled with sleep, staring in vain at something she had clasped in her hand.

'I trod on this on the stairs. What is it – a penny?'

She pushed a small coin under my nose.

'No, love. It's a five-pence piece.'

Her face lit up.

'Oh goody.'

And off she went to pop it in her purse, in the compartment she reserves for fives, tens and twenties. What a nice start to the day. Hardly out of bed and she was already fourpence to the good. I felt a surge of love run right through me and decided to put off committing suicide for the time being and put on the kettle instead.

The five-penny piece also reminded me of a change I had had to make in the script. We had brought the story up to date, which would save a lot of trouble. Only twelve years had passed since my mother's death, but in that short time an awful lot had happened.

We would have needed a fleet of twelve-year-old cars, with the appropriate number plates, and the cameraman would have had to avoid shooting any passing traffic. Satellite dishes would have had to be removed and road signs checked against a twelve-year-old Highway Code.

In such a short time the nurses' uniforms would have evolved along with the everyday clothing of the cast. The beer on sale in the pub, television sets, kettles, newspapers, books – costumes and props would have had to check everything.

They have to do it all the time of course, but it would be much easier to bring the action up to date. It wouldn't make a scrap of difference to the story so that's what we had done. The only flaw in the script was that my mother's house was still priced at £19,000, so I popped up to my study and with a few taps on the computer keyboard I whipped the value up to £45,000, and then I sat back and rather wished I'd held on to it for another twelve years.

I had passed William and Little Chap on the stairs as I went up to my study. They came charging round the first bend in harness, then split at the last minute, one either side of me, before skidding to a halt on the second landing.

'*What about breakfast then?*'

'Shan't be a minute.'

That wasn't what they had wanted to hear and William gave a deep sigh and settled down for the duration. Little Chap decided to fill in the time by having a good scratch.

Tigger had still been fast asleep on my laptop, so I lifted her head from the disk drive and gently slid her little body over towards the printer. She isn't getting any younger, and beneath her silky hair I could feel the hard knots that the dreaded arthritis has been busily weaving in her flanks.

Every morning I give her a full body massage. I work my thumbs slowly over her shoulders and then down the length of her spine before bringing my fingers into play on her stiff little haunches. It's become something of a ritual and it's usually about a quarter of an hour before she decides that enough is enough and I am dismissed until the same time tomorrow.

When we reached the kitchen Thermal had returned from his early morning stroll and had joined the other two in their noisy demand for a full English breakfast.

'*Fooo-oood.*'

It looked like Bakewell cattle market in there, with Aileen stranded in the middle of the floor, not daring to move in case she trod on the three indignant little bodies that milled around her feet.

I led her safely to the table and sat her down with tea, toast and marmalade.

'*She always gets served first.*'

'*She sleeps with him, you know.*'

'*That accounts for it then.*'

I fed the cats, Thermal for the second time in

an hour, and as soon as they had sorted out what was what and whose was whose I left them to it and went over to the park for a closer look at the circus.

The tap-dancing squirrel was already up and dressed and perched on the very end of a slim branch that bobbed gently under his weight as he surveyed the tented village. As a kid he had often dreamed of running away to join the circus and now a circus had run away and joined him. Happy days.

The big top dominated the scene and I peeped in through a flap and watched as a well-organized team filled the vast space with a stage, seats and scaffolding, shouting at one another in at least seven different languages.

Outside the smaller tents and caravans, ancient and modern, were more people, all of them loudly eloquent in foreign tongues you don't come across all that often in Huddersfield. Scouting about ahead of me were two young girls, about fourteen or fifteen I would guess, on their way to Greenhead College and speaking in a tongue that you don't often come across in Moscow.

'Ow about us comin' here tonight?'

'We can't afford it.'

'We can, we've got six pound twenty between us.'

'No, we haven't.'

'Yes, we have.'

'No, we haven't. I've got five pound twenty and you've got a quid.'

'That's the same thing.'

'Oh no it isn't.'

'Tis.'

'Tisn't.'

They carried on their way, still debating their financial situation, and I wondered where they would be in ten years' time. The one who was hanging on to her money would probably be a high flyer with the Halifax Building Society while the one who was trying to screw it out of her would be making a small fortune on the Monday open market.

It must have been thirty years or more since I last walked round a circus. That was back in Chesterfield, at Stand Road, Whittington, where Roberts Brothers came once a year and fly-posted the town.

I would have had Sally and Nick with me, one hanging on to each hand, buzzing with excitement as we walked round the animal cages after the show. There were lions and tigers, Arab stallions and a moth-eaten old camel who would spit at you if you came too close. There would have been elephants and monkeys and donkeys and performing seals and that's what was missing here in Greenhead Park.

Not an animal in sight. It's for the best, I know. I have never felt comfortable watching the poor beasts being put through their paces on my behalf, and yet as the human performers limbered up outside their tents and tended to their equipment the atmosphere just wasn't the same. Too antiseptic. More like a gymnasts' convention than a circus.

And then I spotted one of our four-legged friends. Not one of the big cats and certainly not a wild cat, but more than welcome nevertheless.

Little Chap high-stepped his way across the damp turf, stopping dead in his tracks every now and then to sniff the air and listen. He's an absolute poser when it comes to sniffing and listening. He likes to give the impression that he's a direct descendant of an old Red Indian guide cat who could pick out a buffalo at thirty miles. His ears swivel in all directions and he sticks his nose up in the air to such an extent that he looks more like a direct descendant of Kenneth Williams.

For what seemed like ages he stood there, balancing on three legs, his right front paw hanging limply in mid air, suggesting that his Indian role model had been as queer as a coot. Then he hopped over a couple of guy ropes and slipped silently down on to his stomach as he scrambled under the rear of a small tent.

Almost immediately he came out through the front door, this time draped lovingly over the shoulder of the young woman I had seen taking an impromptu shower earlier in the morning. She was wearing a thin robe and probably little else and she took him over to introduce him to her partner, who was lifting weights by the side of their caravan.

I had a vision of Little Chap ending his days in Vladivostok, so I nipped over to explain that he was my cat and that I lived over there. I pointed to Little Chap, working my way through the age-old pantomime routine that we always bring out when we are talking to those poor unfortunates who are not able to speak our language. I tapped myself on the chest and pointed over towards my house.

'My cat – lives over there.'

I think they understood. They patted him and they stroked him and whispered sweet nothings in his ear. Little Chap was enchanted. He hitched himself higher and higher until his paws were hanging down the woman's slim back and his head nestled beneath her long blond hair.

'Take no notice, madam. I have never seen this man before in my life.'

Chapter 9

I had forgotten that I was supposed to take the car in for a service, but Perry's made it easy for me. They insisted on driving us to the railway station because it looked like rain and promised to have the car ready for when we got back from Leeds.

I quite like taking the car in for a service. I have a chat with everybody and then tour the showroom, sitting in brand new Jaguars that I can't afford, revelling in the smell of wood and leather. Then I have a cup of coffee and read the *Yorkshire Post* and if it's raining somebody takes me home.

Far cry from the old days when Jim Swallow, God bless him, kept my ancient Lancia alive, with a mixture of old-fashioned expertise, a collection of second-hand bits and pieces and the odd prayer here and there.

Picking it up afterwards is a different story. Perry's bill always comes to about twice as much as I paid for my first car, but then Sharon smiles at me from behind her desk and it seems well worth every penny. On the way home the car purrs with pleasure and all the ashtrays have been emptied and I want to carry on until I reach Edinburgh.

The train was going to be late, the announcer told us, in a wonderful accent that had started out in a Barbados kindergarten and then come over here to a finishing school in Huddersfield. Ten minutes approximately, he said.

Not really long enough to walk down to the waiting room for a cup of tea and so Aileen and I settled ourselves on a bench and waited. After a minute or so a young man joined us and sat down next to Aileen.

He had a mobile phone stuck to his left ear and he seemed to be waiting for someone to come to the phone at the other end, so he just sat there, not saying a word. Aileen smiled at him and he smiled back.

Then he sat up straight, uncrossed his legs and spoke into his phone.

'I'm going to miss my appointment.'

Aileen turned towards him.

'Oh, I am sorry. It should only be about ten minutes. That's what they said on the Tannoy. Maybe they'll make it up.'

The man glanced at her and carried on with his phone call.

'Could you do me a favour?'

'If I can,' answered Aileen helpfully.

The man inched away from her, along the seat. He hadn't far to inch. About an inch or so, I would guess. I tapped her on the arm to gain her attention. She shook me off – she was talking.

The young man had the phone tucked into his chest by now and was almost whispering.

'Any chance you could ring them for me?'

Aileen was only too happy to oblige. She reached into her handbag and took out her mobile phone.

'Here. You can do it yourself. Just dial the number and then press the top left-hand button.'

She was about to hand it over when the man stood up and wandered across to the newspaper stand. Aileen watched him go in amazement. How rude!

'He wasn't talking to you, love. He was on his mobile. You couldn't see it.'

She flushed with embarrassment. She hates it when she misjudges a situation.

'Why didn't you say something?'

'I tried.'

Twenty minutes later the train still hadn't arrived and the young man came over once again, hovering uncertainly in front of the bench.

'Could you do me a favour?'

Aileen looked at me for help. History was repeating itself. But before I could say anything the young man went on.

'Could I take you up on your offer, only my phone's gone dead and I haven't any change?'

Once more she dipped into her handbag and

offered her phone, this time explaining why she had made the mistake. He apologized profusely and said there was no way you could tell. He moved out of earshot while he made his call and afterwards came and sat down and they chatted away together as though they had known each other for years.

I borrowed his *Daily Mail* and shared the next few minutes with Lynda Lee Potter. I know when I'm not wanted.

In Leeds he walked with us as far as the Queen's Hotel and then excused himself, racing off through the traffic towards the ever-growing business district with its clutch of buildings, ancient and modern, that have amazingly embraced each other like old friends.

The newfangled brick melts in with the old-fashioned stone in a way that I would never have thought possible. The new kids on the block have about a week to flex their muscles and show off their charms before yet another boy wonder rises from the dust, to take over and catch the eye in a space that one never noticed was there in the first place.

The beauty of these buildings must come as quite a surprise to some first-time visitors, especially those who have decanted from the M62 on to the M621 and then made for the Dark Arches and Granary Wharf. As they swing around the left-hand bend on their way towards the Hilton Hotel they will have cut their sight-seeing teeth on a miserable Portakabin of a building, squatting on a piece of unkempt land behind a tatty old fence. A sign will tell them that this is the home of the Leeds College of Architecture.

It always reminds me of a plumber I know, whose wife can't get him to mend the leaking tap in the bathroom.

Thank goodness the Queen's Hotel can't see it. This is one of those wonderful old railway hotels. Some aren't looking so wonderful these days, but the Queen's remains as solid as ever. Hugely impressive but not at all pretentious, like one of the old Yorkshire wool barons – rich as Croesus, but can't be doing with any fuss.

We had a little time on our hands, and so we popped inside, settled down with a large pot of coffee and snuggled up together on a deep, comfy settee. I produced the *Daily Telegraph* from the soft leather briefcase that I had bought for Aileen's birthday and then stolen off her a week later.

I took out my pen and folded the newspaper in half and then half again, so that we could get a clear run at the crossword.

The man opposite leaned towards us across the small table and waited, motionless, until he was sure we had noticed that he was leaning towards us across the small table, waiting, motionless.

'Tell you something you won't know.'

'What's that?'

He produced his own copy of the *Daily*

Telegraph and laid it on the table, facing the back page towards us so that we could see what he was on about.

'The quick crossword. The answers to the first two clues always make a phrase or a saying when you put them together.'

Aileen leaned forward, across the table, towards the voice.

'Yes. My favourite was "De Gaulle" and "keeper".'

The man's face fell.

'You know about it then.'

Aileen hadn't seen his face fall.

'Yes. This morning it's "lettuce" and "pray".'

The man snatched up his paper.

'Bugger. I haven't even had chance to look at it yet.'

So, having completely ruined his day, we finished our coffee, said a fond farewell and headed off in a taxi towards the Yorkshire Television Centre in Woodhouse Lane.

The place was packed and at first I thought we must be late, but a glance at my watch told me that we had made it with a few minutes to spare. There were eighty-odd people milling around, fifty or more from the production side along with a cast of over twenty actors, all of them drinking coffee or fruit juice and looking very much at home.

Aileen instinctively moved towards the buzz of conversation. I tightened my grip on her arm and held her back.

'Would you like to go to the toilet before we go in?'

'No. I'm fine.'

She took a step forwards and I yanked her back.

'Let me put it another way. I'm going to the toilet, are you coming?'

She thought about it for a split second.

'Yes. I think I desperately need to go to the toilet.'

We found a his and a hers. She went into hers and I went into his. I lit a cigarette and leaned against a radiator.

What had I started? All the money involved and all those people out there. Soon they would be reading my lines and there would be only one person to blame for a script that didn't quite stand up – the writer.

Thora Hird had just completed a play by Alan Bennett and Pete Postlethwaite was being courted by all the big names in America. Who the hell did I think I was, exposing my soul like this? It would be like walking naked down Regent Street.

The door opened and Aileen strode in.

'Ready?'

There was a rustling noise from one of the cubicles. The sort of rustling noise you make when you are minding your own business, sitting on a toilet seat in a gents public lavatory and you suddenly hear a woman's voice. I put my fingers to my lips and whispered:

'You shouldn't be in here.'

'Neither should you. Come on – let's get cracking.'

I stubbed out my cigarette in a tinfoil ashtray that had gone a long way past its retirement date. It winced and went a funny shape.

'I'm terrified.'

Aileen came over and settled herself on the radiator.

'Look. Thora loves it – she has done from the start.'

'I know but . . .'

'And Pete Postlethwaite can pick and choose his parts as he likes. He chose this.'

'Yes but . . .'

'Keith Richardson thinks it's wonderful and so does Alan Bell. They wouldn't be doing it otherwise.'

In the cubicle a plastic seat shifted slightly and then a toilet roll began to whirl merrily around, as they do when you are trying not to make a noise.

I took a deep breath.

'OK. You're right. Let's get going.'

Aileen gave me a kiss on the cheek as I opened the door for her and then, as it slowly closed behind me, a broad Yorkshire voice rang out from behind the cubicle door.

'Good luck.'

As it happens we didn't need any. We slipped unnoticed into the throng and helped ourselves to coffee. Gales of laughter swept over from the far corner where a small crowd was gathered

138

in a circle, heads bowed as though they were admiring the pattern on the carpet.

'Thora's over in the corner.'

Aileen and I have taken her out on many an occasion. Leave her alone for a couple of minutes and you have to fight through a whole army of well-wishers to get back to her side. She's like a magnet. Once, in a very smart restaurant, the waiters spent a good half-hour waving starters, main courses and puddings under unresponsive noses, in a vain attempt to entice the other diners back to their tables.

'She's very approachable, isn't she?'

'Yes – but I think she'd like to start her soup now.'

Today she was in her element. Holding court in her wheelchair, surrounded by her fellow professionals, she was telling them how she was first carried on stage when only a few weeks old. Over the next month she would bring the story up to date. Only eighty-six years to go.

I had been looking forward to meeting Pete Postlethwaite and he was just as I had wanted him to be. Down to earth, no nonsense and as far from a luvvy as you can get.

Some years ago I was introduced to one of my celluloid heroes, a man who specialized in tough northern roles. I had watched him on television for years, playing hard-bitten policemen, jobbing builders, that sort of thing – if you wanted a bluff town councillor, honest to a fault, here was your man.

And there he sat, poncing about on a settee in

Brown's Hotel, holding a china cup between thumb and forefinger, little finger pointing at the ceiling while he wittered on about how he had always been miscast, in a voice like Donald Sinden on speed.

But Pete could have walked straight from the set of *Brassed Off*. He has the most wonderful face, with cheekbones as high as those of an American Indian. Someone once said that they weren't cheekbones at all – they were shoulder blades that had been put in the wrong place.

Penny Downie, from the National Theatre, was to be Aileen for the next thirty days or so. It was a smaller part than she was used to playing but she had seen something in the role and wanted to do it. She and Aileen were huddled together, sitting at a small table in another corner. They were getting on like a house on fire.

Someone offered Aileen a cigarette that was a little shorter than the brand she normally smoked. She lit it about half an inch away from the end and was then very surprised to find that it wasn't working. She tried to light it again, and once more it failed to function. Penny guided her hand towards the cigarette and we had lift-off. Here endeth the first lesson.

It's much easier for actors to play fictional characters. They can flesh them out and make them their own, but real people bring along extra baggage with them and this has to be sorted and sifted until a fine balance is achieved.

The blindness was going to be a problem

for Penny. We have all seen actresses stumbling about in B movies, arms flailing out in front of them like punch-drunk boxers. More recently I saw one who had the arms just about right, but who moved hesitantly through the film as though, underneath her crinoline skirt, she had filled her nappy about a fortnight ago and it was now hanging down around her knees.

Keith Richardson called us all together, settled us down and introduced us to one another, and then the read-through began. I am not very good at names, but voices stay with me for ever and as the story unfolded many of them became flesh.

As the chemist I heard Norris, Derek Baldwin's salesman sidekick from *Coronation Street*, played by Malcolm Hebden. The mother from the comedy series *Watching* came to life as the wonderful Noreen Kershaw played the part of Margaret.

Coronation Street reared its head once more as Anne Reid read Gloria. She left the show years ago, but to a lifelong fan like me the voices of the past never fade. These days I can enjoy her in Victoria Wood's *Dinnerladies*.

Director Alan Bell took notes but I just listened and it wasn't half as painful as I thought it would be. Three quarters of an hour later it was all over. We'd had some good belly laughs, the odd gulp whenever Pete and Thora handled one of the sadder moments and a smattering of applause at the end.

During the reading we had seen our two main characters come together as mother and son. They were getting on well, and although Thora had all the best lines, Pete didn't mind. His job was to be the catalyst, to hold the whole thing together, and he had done it wonderfully well considering that he was playing the part of a rather boring man.

Afterwards Thora went straight to work recording voice-overs with Alan Bell and David Whiteley, the sound recordist, while the rest of us took care of a cold buffet. Every now and then a head would pop round the adjoining door and bawl at us.

'Shut up.'

We would shut up and listen as Thora strutted her stuff.

'Do you want to be buried, Mum – or do you want to be cremated?'

'Oh I don't know, love. Surprise me.'

Thora was to keep working at a cracking pace throughout the shooting of the film, a punishing schedule that would have taken it out of a much younger woman. She was on set first thing in the morning and still at it late in the day, even though there were times when she was not at all well.

Everyone fell in love with her and she loved being involved. Even on her one day off, when we all expected her to have a lie-in and recharge her batteries, she arrived on the set well before breakfast.

'Do you mind if I watch?'

She hates not being in the thick of it. She just loves company, and after a gruelling day's work she would grab the make-up people, the dressers or anyone she thought would be good value for money and take them out to dinner at the noisiest Italian restaurant in town. Then, back in the Marriott Hotel, she would work on her lines, before waking Pete in the early hours of the next morning.

'Are you going to take me down for breakfast or what?'

Meanwhile Penny was still keeping an observant eye on Aileen. Pete had insisted on escorting my wife to the toilet.

'I'll wait and take you back.'

'Don't worry. I know the way now.'

So he'd left her to it. She memorizes every step and takes great pride in being independent. We watched her negotiate her way back through a pair of double doors and then tentatively ease her way down a wooden ramp, feeling for the handrail.

Penny watched her every step, making mental notes, while I remembered a New Year's party at the home of our friends Alison and Paul. We had left about two in the morning. Others had stayed on.

The next morning a couple arrived to collect their car.

'I did enjoy talking to that redhead last night. You know – the author.'

143

'Yes,' said Alison. 'Didn't she do well, considering that it's not her house.'

She was greeted with a blank look.

'How do you mean?'

'She's registered blind.'

'Well, I'll be blowed. I had no idea. I saw people offering her a hand, telling her what the food was on the table, filling her plate and all that, but I thought she was just pissed like the rest of us.'

We spoiled ourselves and took a taxi back to Huddersfield. I have a problem with taxi drivers – I need to talk to them. I find it physically impossible to sit in the back of a black cab and ignore the person who's doing all the work. They probably just want to sit there and think beautiful thoughts but stuff that, I have my needs and I need to talk.

Of course it doesn't help when the taxi driver hails from one of the more remote villages of Pakistan and I can understand only one word in every twenty-five he utters – it doesn't make for a meaningful exchange of ideas.

As far as I could tell, this one was having trouble with his daughter and that worried me. I watched a television programme not long ago and apparently, in the more isolated regions of Pakistan, they have their own way of dealing with troublesome daughters. They beat them to death.

Maybe I had it all wrong. I thought he had asked me if I had any children. It threw me for a moment because I had just asked him whether he was starting his shift or about to finish it. Anyway I told him I had one of each.

'A son and a daughter.'

I was about to add that I also had four step-children, but the word daughter launched him into a diatribe that lasted for almost half an hour, until he pointed at the sign for Huddersfield at junction 24 on the M62.

'No – the next one.'

And he was off again. The muscles on his neck stood out in knots and his face in the rear-view mirror seemed contorted with uncontrolled anger. Maybe he was just telling me that it was no business of mine whether he was starting his shift or finishing it, or that his daughter had just qualified as a doctor and he was very proud of her.

But I doubt it. Aileen said afterwards that maybe it was simply his natural way of express-ing himself, but there was more to it than that and it disturbed me. I wanted to be able to find out if I was right or wrong but his machine-gun delivery continued to defeat me and he was still at it as we pulled into the back lane.

William was sitting in the gutter, staring down the grate, and I pointed him out to the driver and asked if he would be careful not to run over him. He pulled the taxi to a halt within a foot of William's backside. Whether he'd understood what I'd said I shall never know. He had his daughter on his mind. I know she was on mine.

I paid him and off he went, still muttering to

himself. Aileen marched up the path with her front-door key stuck out in front of her. She gave a little jump in the air and all the outside lights came on. I must have the electronic eye lowered.

I went over to William and told him to come in. He gave me a look which told me to push off.

William is into grates. Just as in the house he spends most of his time peering up the chimney, listening to the birds as they warm their bums on the chimney pot, once outside he spends hours and hours peering down the grate in the back lane.

He once spotted a small rodent and the thrill has stayed with him ever since. He sits in the gutter, still as a garden gnome, head bent in total concentration as visiting cars try to manoeuvre round him, parking almost on his tail.

Every now and then he springs into action, his paw diving down through the bars as he sees something moving in the murky depths. I have done a few basic sums and reckon that since his front legs are roughly six inches long and the grating is some four feet deep, whatever lives down there is more than likely to die of old age. They probably think he's waving to them.

'He seems a very friendly cat. Must go up there and have a chat with him some time.'

Aileen and I sat and drank coffee, discussing how the read-through had gone at Yorkshire Television. There had been a feeling about the place that we had something special. Everyone had read the script beforehand and they were even more enthusiastic now that a little life had been breathed into the pages.

We talked it over for an hour or so and then I went up to my study and came back into the real world, to phone my daughter Sally in Brighton, to see if she was happy and to tell her I loved her.

Chapter 10

I should have known it was going to be one of those days. I had set it aside as a writing day, no interruptions. Aileen was going to field the phone for me but it burst into life long before she surfaced.

Paul Wolfenden is a lot like me. He has to share things and if there's no one else around he shares them with me, on the phone. We were once a double act and when you have died on stage together as often as we have you form a bond which allows you not to worry whether the other one is awake or not.

I can hardly remember a thing he said. I was busy juicing two grapefruits and a conference pear at the time. I love my juicer. Aileen bought it. I said we didn't need it, but now I don't know how we managed without it all these years.

I added a kiwi fruit. I had never juiced a kiwi fruit before and Thermal sat hypnotized as a rather unhealthy-looking green liquid came dripping out of the other end. Tigger is frightened of the juicer – she's frightened of anything that you have to plug in and switch on – so she sat out in the hall, peeping round the door. William had popped out to check on his drain, and so it was just me and Thermal and Paul on the phone.

He told me several jokes, but I can only remember the last one. I can only ever remember the last one anyone tells me. I'm very bad at remembering jokes.

'I said, "I like your perfume." She said, "Yes, it's a new one. It's called Tester." '

Paul said that perhaps I might be able to use it in a book. I said no, I couldn't do that – it would be cheating.

He rang off. He's a busy man and he had lots of other people to annoy, so Thermal and I settled down to our breakfast of rabbit and chicken in jelly and a bowl of crunchy nut cornflakes. I had the crunchy nut cornflakes.

Tigger put her head round the door.

'Have you finished with that thing?'

'Yes, come on in.'

She had a sniff at the rabbit and chicken in jelly and her eyes watered. It does pong a bit. Aileen can't bear to be in the same room and Tigger is allergic to it.

I fixed her up with a saucer of last night's left-over leg of pork and went back to my cornflakes. Thermal was outraged.

'Excuse me!'

'Sorry.'

I filled him a saucer of pork, all cut up into tiny chunks, and added a dollop of sage and onion stuffing to make him feel wanted.

'I should think so.'

We ate in silence, until Tigger produced one of her Walker's barbecued beef and onion crisps from in between the Japanese tea cups. She shared it with Thermal and they crunched away in stereo until the back doorbell went berserk and had both of them hiding behind the rubber plant in the far corner.

We have had a stand-in postman for the last couple of weeks or so, while our regular is away on holiday. This one seems averse to shoving things through the letter box and always rings the bell. At first I thought it a rather charming way of introducing himself, especially when he told me that he had bought one of my books for his father.

'Last Christmas that was. But I don't think he's even opened it yet. He doesn't read as much these days – not since he went deaf.'

I was going to ask him to elaborate on that but then decided to let it pass as there are more productive ways of going mad. Since that first day he has had me out of the shower and running down three flights of stairs on more than one occasion. He must be under the impression that I spend the whole day wearing nothing more than a bath towel.

'He reminds me a lot of Gandhi.'

Today, however, I was fully dressed and it took him by surprise.

'On your way out, are you?'

'No. I'm working.'

'Where's that then?'

'Here.'

'What at?'

'Writing.'

'Oh. You're still dabbling then.'

He handed me my mail, nothing larger than a sheet of A4, and I asked him if he wouldn't mind just shoving them through the letter box in future. His face fell and he trooped off across the courtyard, doing a passable impression of a wounded fawn.

'Miserable old sod, that one.'

I was once talking at a charity dinner, seated on the top table with a whole bunch of people I had never met before. *Diana's Story* had just been voted the most popular serial on Radio Four's *Woman's Hour* over the past fifty years and I was justifiably proud. I had beaten Tolstoy and Jane Austen into second and third place respectively. (Neither of them has rung to say well done. I couldn't be like that, it's not in my nature – it depends on the sort of person you are, I suppose.)

It was being repeated on the radio at the time and the lady on my right told me how much she was enjoying it. A solicitor on my left cleared his throat.

'Are you still dabbling with the writing then?'

'Yes. Are you still dabbling with the law?'

He was rather hurt and went to great lengths to explain that one didn't dabble with the law. It was a very serious business.

'It's not a hobby, you know.'

*   *   *

I was about to close the back door when something moved out from under the hedge by the
rockery. It was probably the toughest-looking cat
I have ever laid eyes on, and I've seen some
belters in my time. We have one down the lane
called Denton who's as hard as nails, and my
mother once had a cat called Horace. He was
short of one ear and one nostril when he first
planted his bottom on my mother's back door
step and she wondered whether she should take
him in.

'Somebody must be missing him.'

I tried to imagine the sort of person who could
possibly be missing Horace and failed miserably.
My mother went to have a word with him.

'I think he's a bit deaf in his left ear.'

'He hasn't got a left ear.'

'He's got a lovely smile though.'

And he had. He also had great dignity, which
is more than you could say for the monster who
was now shambling his way towards me across
the courtyard. He could have been mistaken for
a rather dishevelled hyena.

My first thought was to lock all the doors and
draw the curtains and pretend that Aileen and I
had taken the cats and gone off to Cornwall for a
fortnight.

We had plenty of food in the freezer and a
huge stock of cat litter in the cellar. We had
enough down there to sandblast the Town Hall
twice over. We could hide until he had gone
away and want for nothing.

And then I had another look at him. He was a big cat, there was no doubt about that. You could have thrown a saddle over him and entered him for the 2.30 at Chepstow.

But a second glance told me that all might not be well with him. His coat hung loosely about his body like a cape, as though he had tossed it carelessly over his shoulders on the way out of the house and not even bothered to do up the buttons.

As he settled down to a crouch, he took it in stages. First he thought about it for a while and then he seemed to be explaining to each limb exactly what was expected of them.

It was as though his legs had never done this before. As though they couldn't remember whether they were supposed to bend forwards or backwards and it was some time before they managed to arrange themselves neatly, tucked away underneath him and out of sight.

His shoulders stood out through his coat like the pommel on a hunting saddle and his eyes wouldn't meet mine. One thing was for sure – he could do with a good meal.

Back in the kitchen I picked up Thermal's half-empty saucer of rabbit and chicken in jelly, topped it up from the tin and filled another saucer with milk. As I went out to feed him it occurred to me that perhaps I should have brought a whip and a chair along with me.

'*Easy now. Down, boy. Back – baaaack.*'

Close to, he looked enormous. Even with his bottom still glued to the stone flags he was taller than any two of mine put together.

'There you are, boy. Try that.'

He rose and lumbered towards me. Despite his obvious problems he was still an awesome creature. He had little tufts of hair sticking out of his ears. Did we have wild lynx in this country?

He came to a halt and sat down once more, a little way off, eyeing the two dishes suspiciously.

'It's all right.'

He would be the judge of that. He'd been caught like this before. Once I was out of the way he would come and have a closer look.

I decided to leave him to it, but as I turned Tigger came striding out through the open door and made straight for the two dishes. First she gave the milk a proprietorial lick and then she made a brave attempt to nibble the chicken and rabbit.

The other cat slithered across the flagstones on his stomach like a sniper and I feared for her life. He'll tear her limb from limb, I thought. But then she has always had a remarkable way with other cats, however fearsome. Over the years she has sorted out any number of Thermal's enemies for him. Cats she can handle – you don't have to plug them in and switch them on. The old fellow seemed to recognize this and so he just plonked himself down by her side and waited patiently until she had completed the tests. She stood back.

'I think you'll enjoy that.'

'Sure you've finished?'

'Please. Be my guest.'

And with that he tucked in, the plate travelling along in front of him and across the courtyard. He came back for the milk and mopped it up with a tongue the size of a loofah, then looked around for more.

I emptied the remainder of the tin into the saucer and stood back, but the cat was still wary of me. Tigger reassured him.

'It's all right. He's harmless.'

He took her word for it and the food disappeared as though it had been thrown down a coal chute.

Tigger smiled indulgently.

'Let me show you the accommodation.'

And with that she escorted him down the cellar steps so that he could have a look round.

She was at it again. Mother Theresa was alive and well and living in Huddersfield. This was how we had acquired Arthur, William and Little Chap and enough was enough. I really didn't fancy turning the house into a hospice once again.

I followed them at a safe distance and peered in through the cellar window. Tigger jumped up on the cane chair with the Dunlopillo cushion and began to demonstrate its qualities.

'I think you'll find it's very comfortable.'

The newcomer thought about it for a while and then opted for the sheepskin blanket on top of the boiler.

'Old bones, you know.'

Tigger was most understanding. She waited until he had made himself comfortable and then, leaping up on to the old stone table so that she could watch over him, she settled herself down on a pair of my soft leather gardening gloves. They're very cosy – they've hardly been used.

A national newspaper had asked me to write seven hundred and fifty words on my mother, to be printed the week before *Lost for Words* was televised, and they were prepared to pay me in real money.

I rather liked the idea of being paid to write my own publicity, but it was proving to be hard going. I had already written about her in two of my books, in a television play, in more magazine articles and for more radio programmes than I care to remember. I didn't want to repeat myself. I wanted a fresh approach and so far I had run into a brick wall.

Bits and pieces of my life with her kept coming back to me, but not one of them had the legs to run to seven hundred and fifty words.

I remembered Betty Brothwood's, the chemist on Chatsworth Road in Chesterfield. She had a huge set of scales in the corner of the shop, especially for weighing babies, and they gleamed with brass. They were magnificent, as far removed from an ordinary set of scales as one of the old coach-built prams is from a modern pushchair.

The babies were laid on a pure white fluffy blanket, so as not to favour either sex, and Betty Brothwood herself would come out from the back of the shop and supervise the whole operation. I think it cost a penny.

But not for me. The butcher's at the end of Heaton Street was that bit nearer and a penny cheaper, so my mother would order a pound of stewing steak and half a pound of tomato sausage and ask them if they would mind weighing Deric for her while they were at it.

'Give him up here then.'

Not that I remembered of course. My uncle Len told me. He said that for the first eighteen months of my life I weighed in at one and sixpence a pound. What I do remember is making sure that a few weeks after my daughter Sally was born she was laid on the pure white blanket in Betty Brothwood's chemist's shop.

Several other fragments of my past offered themselves for consideration, but most of them were rather sad and not what was wanted at all, so I sat and stared at my laptop for all of an hour.

Aileen had gone out. Just after nine o'clock a car had arrived and whisked her away to North Yorkshire, to present the prizes at one of our few remaining grammar schools. So much for manning the phone – or the front doorbell for that matter.

Compared with its mate on the back door, the front doorbell is a proper little gentleman. It merely clears its throat a little and then enquires politely.

'Do excuse me, sir. I'm so sorry to bother you, but someone has just assaulted me with their forefinger.

Do you wish to come down and have a word with them, or would you rather I simply gritted my teeth?'

However restrained its performance it has never yet failed to drag me out of the deepest coma and as usual I obeyed. When I pulled the door open there were three large women standing on the step.

'Sorry we're late, love. He forgot to pick us up.'

They didn't tell me who *he* was or who they were, they just pushed past me and hung their coats on the hall stand. Underneath they were wearing aprons and two of them had an armful of dusters and a bucket each full of aerosol sprays, while the third one dragged a chubby little vacuum cleaner behind her. It had a face painted on the front and reminded me of one of those things the council use for sucking out the drains.

It was the cleaning ladies from hell.

'I didn't know you were coming.'

If I had known, I would have been up there in North Yorkshire with Aileen.

'We told your wife one day this week – we couldn't be sure which. She said that would be all right.'

'Yes, well . . .'

To their credit they didn't muck about. They wore thick leather belts with holsters and they fired Pledge from the hip. Thermal had followed me some way behind and he was caught by a stray burst of Ajax Liquid the moment he put his head round the hall door.

'Sorry, puss.'

I picked him up and we stood back as this monstrous regiment of women moved into the lounge. They half closed the door behind them and then there followed a short pause before the radio burst into life, an expert hand whipping the dial through more stations than I ever knew existed before it came in to land on Radio Two.

Abba were about halfway though 'Waterloo' and it must have been some surprise to them when they were suddenly joined in harmony by three raucous voices and a badly tuned vacuum cleaner. They must have known they had competition because they immediately turned up the volume to the point where the brass lamp on the hall table began to have a fit and tried to throw itself over the edge.

Thermal and I were halfway up the stairs when William flew past us. He sat down on the first landing, breathing heavily. He was suffering from shock and smelled faintly of Pine disinfectant.

'It suits you, William.'

'Thank you.'

For the next five hours or so the three of us moved around the house like a pack of gypsies. At first we took refuge back in my study. Thermal opted for the peace, quiet and total stillness that can be found only in the bottom drawer of my desk. I yanked it open and he jumped inside. It's the deepest drawer and contains several translations of my books in

German, Italian and Dutch. His likeness appears on all of the covers and I like to think he thumbs through them once I have shut him in.

William sat and stared up the chimney, listening to the cooing of the pigeons as they warmed their bottoms on the cowl at the top. I sat and stared at my computer, listening to the muffled snores that issued from the bottom drawer of my desk.

Apart from the distant drumming of the hoover down in the bowels of the house we had roughly an hour of peace and quiet before the cleaning ladies from hell began to climb the stairs, and very soon they had us surrounded once more.

They started off in Aileen's study before moving out into the hall and I listened to the bits and pieces of conversation that were shouted from one room to the other.

'I'm taking my own cakes – none of that bought rubbish.'

I thought of my mother's baking and of the days gone by when I would have given anything for her to have brought home a flip-top box, full of that bought rubbish from Henstock's.

'And I'm going to get a proper dress – one like those big dinner ladies wear.'

Long dresses, I finally worked out, the sort that posh ladies wear when they go to big dinner dances.

'It's not a cheap do. Mind you, talk about pricey, have you ever been to one of them motorway service stations? The prices! We set off early and stopped for breakfast. We had bacon, egg, sausage, tomato and fried bread, twice. The girl rang it up on the till and said how would you like to pay for it and my husband said how about monthly instalments.'

I was beginning to enjoy myself when the door burst open and the three of them charged in.

'Don't you worry, love. You won't know we're here.'

William had anticipated their coming. He must have smelt the Pine disinfectant as it worked its way across the landing and he'd just managed to squeeze himself down by the side of my walnut bookcase when he was caught by a badly aimed volley of Pledge, right behind the left ear. And if he's no better by this time next week I'm taking him for counselling.

I quickly unplugged my computer and tucked it under my arm. That's the advantage of having a laptop. In theory you can work anywhere.

In theory, that is. In practice I can't do anything of the sort. I set up my little box of tricks on the table in the dining room and stared at it for ten minutes, trying my best to look intelligent. I'm not very good at that either. A thought struck me, and I bounded up the stairs, one at a time, towards my office.

The women had completely cleared the decks. All my movable possessions were piled high on the long conference table in the window and they had somehow managed to tune my television set to Radio Two. I didn't know you could do that. Frank Ifield was belting out his once famous rendition of 'I Remember You'. It took me back because I remembered him, as it happens. It was like walking into a time warp.

One of the women was busily polishing my desk and I was instantly ashamed to see, from the virgin imprints, where my letter rack, table lamp and any manner of other bits and pieces had once stood amid the thick coating of fag ash and dust.

'Excuse me.'

'Of course, love.'

'Forgot something.'

I bent down and pulled open the deep bottom drawer, struggled a bit, and then plucked from it a small white cat who had gone absolutely rigid with fright. I tucked him under my left arm and with Thermal staring straight ahead, looking for all the world like one of those wrought-iron animals you might find stuck on the top of a weather vane in a Cotswold village, I marched confidently from the room.

Aileen rang to say that all had gone well. The head teacher had taken her out for lunch and there she had met an old schoolfriend. They were in the hotel now, chewing over old times and she would ring me later to tell me what time she would be home.

I didn't tell her about the invasion of the bleach people. They had gone through her study like a dose of salts and nothing would be quite where it should be. She needed to have everything to hand, where she could reach out, touch and find it, but we could sort that out when she came home.

'What's that noise?'

The vacuum cleaner had just clattered past my door on its way to the kitchen, which they had decided to leave to last.

'It's the television.'

'Don't forget your deadline.'

'I'll switch it off.'

I had pulled a hundred words from out of somewhere or other, read them through, and then tapped a key on the computer and despatched them to wherever it is they go when you tap that particular key. I didn't ever want to see them again.

There was another tap, this time on the window pane, so I moved the rubber plant to one side and saw Tigger, high on her hind legs, belting the living daylights out of the other side of the double glazing.

I had forgotten all about Tigger and her new-found friend in the cellar. I let her in and she let me know what she thought about me, in no uncertain terms. I couldn't quite make out what she said but the general gist of it seemed to veer towards my being inconsiderate, uncaring and idle soft.

Right, I thought. I'll show her who's uncaring. I stripped the last of the meat from the leg of pork and piled it high on a saucer. There was enough to have made a tasty supper for all three of them but we were talking Christian values here. The old cat down in the cellar deserved a break, so I filled another bowl with water and went off to give him a treat.

He hadn't moved, still fast asleep on the sheepskin blanket, even though I had barged in through the door and cursed under my breath when I cracked my knee on the Black and Decker workmate. I didn't want to wake him, no point in that, so I placed the two dishes on the floor where he couldn't fail to notice them and crept out as quietly as I could.

I was halfway up the stairs when something told me to go back and have another look at him. This time I padded softly across the stone floor and moved in as near as I dared. He was all curled up, with one paw wrapped around his face, covering his nose and both his eyes. It's a pose that always gets me. Thermal sleeps like that and he looks so cute, though I would never dream of telling him.

And so did this old fellow. With his tail tucked in between his back legs he seemed about half the size he was before and I was pleased he had found a safe haven where he would be warm and well fed.

I still didn't realize he was dead. He didn't look dead. Then I looked again. I felt his body and it was as warm as toast, but then he was lying on the boiler. I looked to see if there was any rise and fall in his body, but no, he wasn't breathing. I lifted his head and let it go and it fell down on to the blanket.

I sat for a while on the workmate and watched him, half expecting him to wake at any moment. At least he had had the comfort of a full belly and the warmth of the boiler.

There was a cardboard carton from Bibliophile Books on the floor, waiting to be torn up and tossed into the green wheelie bin. I picked him up and placed him in it. He fitted perfectly, so I closed the lid on him and went upstairs.

An hour later I took a spade and buried him in the little cardboard coffin, on the spare ground by the side of the house. Over the last sixty minutes his body had turned icy cold. At least the last few hours of his life had, in all probability, been far happier than much of what had gone before.

Back in the cellar I cleaned the spade and then trooped up the inside stairs to the ground floor. I had hardly known the cat but its death had affected me, leaving me flat and downcast, and so did the fact that the cleaning ladies from hell had called it a day and gone home, but not before locking the cellar door from the inside.

I banged and shouted for a while, but it was no use. They didn't have to wait for me to pay them, the agency sent a bill along later. They had probably thought I'd disappeared so that I wouldn't have to give them a tip.

'He's a tight devil, that one.'

So I began to clean out the cellar while I waited for Aileen to come home and a couple of hours later it fairly sparkled. But not nearly as brightly as my wife did as she told me about her day. Then I told her about mine and she laughed like a drain until I came to the bit about the stray cat.

I cooked us a meal and afterwards we had coffee while I read out loud a selection of edited highlights from the *Daily Telegraph*. The answers to the first two clues in the quick crossword were 'dupe' and 'hitter'.

Aileen decided to have an early night but I had to stay up and work on the article, even if it meant toiling away until daybreak. I stared at the blank screen for over an hour. My calculator told me that the going rate of pay worked out at fifty pence per word and of course the publicity would be worth its weight in gold.

Around two in the morning I was still staring at a blank screen and I knew that it wasn't going to get any better. So I flexed my fingers and typed three short words.

'Oh, sod it.'

And then I went off to bed. At least I had the satisfaction of having earned myself a steady one pound fifty, even if it was going to disappear down the drain when I pressed the delete key first thing in the morning. Ah, well. Easy come, easy go.

Chapter 11

One quick flip through the film schedule had told me that Thora wasn't going to have much time off for sightseeing. It would have been a punishing thirty-odd days for an eager young beginner still running on neat adrenaline, never mind a woman of eighty-seven who hadn't been looking at all well lately.

But there she was, on the set, in Clinton's card shop in Huddersfield, at half-past seven in the morning, having set off from the Marriott Hotel in Leeds at half-past six, before which she had already been given the once-over by the make-up artists and then fitted out in a bright green coat and red woolly hat by the dressers.

She looked rather frail as she sat in her wheelchair, thumbing through her script, mouthing the words quietly to herself. Shooting was to start with scenes sixty-seven and sixty-eight before the crew nipped smartly over to the other side of town to shoot two earlier scenes, numbers eight and nine.

Of course a film is always shot out of sequence, so whenever you read that an actor has *grown* into a role, it's more likely that they were in there to start with, then they grew out of it, grew back into it and then faded slightly in the early stages which were filmed later when they were beginning to wonder what the hell the movie was all about.

But Thora and Pete knew what it was all about and Alan Bell had the two-page scene wrapped up in no time at all. Thora had to be helped out of her wheelchair, but from the moment she was on her feet she became the consummate professional and immediately turned into my mother before my admiring eyes.

I had experienced the same feeling during the making of *Wide-Eyed and Legless* and nowadays, whenever I write about my mother, or even when I think back fondly to the old days, it's Thora's face that I see in my mind so that now and then I have to dig out some old photographs of my mother in order to hoist my memory back on to an even keel.

Nick and Sally have suffered from the same experience. As, inevitably, the mental picture of their mother fades somewhat, so the more they see Julie Walters in their mind's eye. It's all quite understandable, but nevertheless rather unnerving.

I slipped out through the shop doorway for a much needed cigarette. After the script is done and dusted the writer's role is very much on the edge of things.

I wanted to be there to make sure the feel of

the script was coming over, and there would be the odd time when I would be needed to write a bridging scene, or to rewrite a few lines that weren't coming across as well as expected.

Ruth Holden, who was playing Nellie Elliot, had a line that needed watching closely. After she hears that my mother has had a stroke and that Mrs Corey is looking after her, she pushes past Pete with the words:

'That's *all* you need when you've had a stroke.'

Which tells us that she doesn't think much of Mrs Corey. Whereas with a slight change of emphasis –

'That's all you *need* when you've had a stroke.'

– she would tell us that as far as Nellie is concerned, Mrs Corey is up there alongside Florence Nightingale.

As I stuck the cigarette in my mouth a lighter was immediately shoved under my nose, from over my right shoulder, complete with half-cocked thumb.

'Thank you.'

I bent towards the lighter and an eight-inch sheet of flame shot up and singed both my eyebrows and that rather cute little curl that hangs down over my forehead on a good hair day.

'Sorry.'

The smell of burning was quite overpowering and I rubbed hard at my hair before I lost the lot. I turned and saw a man in a brown raincoat, tall and thin and completely without shoulders, like a telegraph pole. He was staring proudly at his cigarette lighter which he cupped fondly in his hand.

'Has a mind of its own, does this. You can't tell it a thing.'

I sniffed up at my eyebrows and they smelt awful, so I sniffed at them again, as you do.

'That's all right.'

He had a lump of cotton wool sticking out of his left ear. Not just any old lump of cotton wool, this was one of those huge wodges that you might find tucked in the top of a bottle of aspirins – the ones that keep on coming for ever and ever when you pull them out. It poked out of his ear and then hung down to where most people would have had a shoulder.

He nodded towards the shop.

'What they doing. Making an advert?'

'No – it's a film.'

He seemed disappointed, until he caught sight of Dame Thora through the window.

'I know her, don't I?'

'Thora Hird.'

'Oh aye. Now what is it that she's in?'

'*Last of the Summer Wine*?'

'That's it. And I know him and all, don't I?'

'Pete Postlethwaite.'

'Oh aye. Now what was it he was in then?'

'*Brassed Off*?'

'Oh aye. So what they doing here, then?'

'Making a film called *Lost for Words*.'

He thought for a while.

'Oh aye. I've seen that.'

'No. We're just filming it now.'

He nodded wisely.

'Ah well. It's all repeats these days, in't it.'

At that moment a smiling Thora came trundling through the shop door in her wheel-chair and following hard on her wheels was her double, Dorothy Arnold, dressed in an identical coat and hat. The man in the raincoat swallowed hard as his eyes went from one to the other. A woman standing by his side nudged him.

'You were right about the repeats, love.'

I escaped back into the shop, but there was only the one way out and he was there waiting for me long after the film crew had left and I couldn't find an excuse for hanging about any longer. He seemed to have adopted me.

He stuck by my side until we reached the Midland Bank.

'I have to go in here.'

He came in with me, so I had to draw some money out of the machine that I didn't really need.

'Look, I really must be off.'

He walked with me as far as the car.

'When will it be on telly?'

'I'm not sure – around Christmas, I should think.'

We stood there, not knowing what to say.

'Hope your ear gets better.'

He tapped the cotton wool hanging like a dwarf's beard from his left ear.

'Oh this. A cotton-wool-bud-related incident,

that was. Dangerous things, cotton-wool buds. Burst my eardrum.'

I loved the 'cotton-wool-bud-related incident'. It was like a Ministry of Health handout and it made the last half hour almost worthwhile.

'What did you do, shove it in too hard?'

'No, not me. I were asleep. It were my mother. She creeps up on me and cleans out my ears while I'm having a nap. Always has done – ever since I were a kid. I didn't know owt about it until I woke up.'

I popped back home to pick up Aileen. She had been working late into the night and had decided to ease herself gently into the new day. She was sitting at the kitchen table, eating a bowl of cornflakes with her nose up against the television screen, watching one of those daytime make-over programmes.

They were making over a suburban garden and they had to have it finished off by the time the husband came home from work at half-past five. Why they don't give themselves more time and do the job properly I shall never know.

It would be interesting to have another look at some of those *Challenge Anneka* projects, where they were given twenty-four hours to build an indoor riding centre, or a classroom for disabled children. I would like to see how the wallpaper has fared after all this time, especially the one with the contemporary pattern of pale-blue chickens and the odd-looking eggs that they had to hang long before the plaster had dried

172

properly. It would probably look rather pretty now with its bas-relief bubbles and its elegant border of green mould.

Today a team of designers were transforming the garden by applying a coat of paint to anything that had the decency to stand still long enough. They had already whipped through all the colours of the rainbow and were now working with some shades of this, that and the other that I can't ever remember having seen before.

Three of them were attacking a small fence, painting each paling a different hue, and Aileen was shouting at them, as and when the cornflakes permitted.

'For God's sake sand it down first.'

They took no notice of her, so she upped the volume.

'At least give it an undercoat. The paint'll just run off the first time it rains.' She didn't know I had joined her until I picked up the tea towel to wipe a rogue cornflake from the television screen.

'You have a look. Is that emulsion they're using?'

I had a look.

'Looks like it.'

'How silly.'

She switched it off.

'Not a patch on *Ground Force*.'

I must admit we do rather like watching *Ground Force*. It's more fun than the others and Aileen has always had a soft spot for Alan Titchmarsh, ever since she worked with him at a literary luncheon, while I tend to sit back with a glass of red wine and concentrate most of my attention on Charlie Dimmock, the blonde lady with the wonderful nipples.

The cats were out in the garden as we left the house. Thermal was deadheading the roses – he's very good at it and getting better all the time. The other cats can't understand his horticultural obsession. They are into the more traditional feline pursuits such as hunting, shooting and fishing, although I must admit I can't remember the last time they shot anything.

They are also heavily into the preservation of territorial rights. First thing in the morning Tigger likes to check all the hedges, sniffing at almost each and every leaf with the utmost dedication.

It's rather like a wine tasting. She sniffs delicately at first and then, gulping in the tell-tale evidence, she swishes the aroma around the back of her throat.

'Mmmm! Small short-hair kitten, female tabby with a slight limp in her left back leg. Passed through the hedge at around 6.37 this morning, probably on her way to do her paper round.'

Sometimes she jumps back in alarm, her eyes crossed and running with tears.

'Yuk! Denton – and he's been eating garlic again.'

But Thermal takes his deadheading just as seriously and his commitment to the cause is a lesson to us all. His interest in roses started last summer when a kamikaze wasp took a deep breath, plucked up the courage, and dive-bombed him from behind.

Thermal wasn't having that. He chased it all over the garden and then watched as it settled on the petals of a geriatric rose that had but a few short hours to live.

He moved in silently and belted both rose and wasp with a crisp right-hander. Whatever happened to the wasp we shall never know, but the rose gave a deep sigh and disintegrated immediately, its petals falling gracefully, showering Thermal until he looked like a bridesmaid at a posh society wedding.

That small moment changed his life for ever and since then he has kept a close eye on the roses. He moves through the garden tapping every one from inexperienced bud to fully grown adult. His disappointment on those occasions when they merely lean back and roll with the blow is more than compensated for when the older ones collapse and rain petals down on his head.

Once he's sorted out the smaller bushes I go and fetch the kitchen steps for him. They are on castors and I push him around the garden as he tackles those that would otherwise be out of reach.

I waved the two cats goodbye, opened the car door for Aileen, then bent and lifted William out from under the back wheel. As I carried him out of harm's way and sat him on the wall he gazed back longingly over my shoulder at his unattended drain.

'We'll be gone in a minute, then you can go back.'

He seemed to understand, but as I climbed into the car Thermal came stalking out of the gate, bristling with indignation.

'We'll be back by lunchtime, then I'll get the steps out for you.'

He relaxed and forgave me.

'Thank you.'

'My pleasure.'

'Have a nice time.'

The film crew had moved down to Byram Street and taken over Neaverson's china shop, opposite the parish church. I parked the car and we walked back through a tight little band of sightseers who were having to make do with gawping at the sound engineer since it is almost impossible to see in through Neaverson's modernistic windows.

Inside they were rehearsing a rewrite of scene nine and I experienced my first dialogue cut. Since this was Penny Downie's first appearance as Aileen I had wanted to show the audience that she was blind without going over the top. No white sticks or anything like that, just Pete describing each ornament as she picks it up. At the same time he would be telling her about the strange way in which my mother had bought her house.

DERIC: So she gazumped herself by £5,000 in as
 many seconds.

Aileen picks up an ornament and is puzzled. She runs her hands over it.

AILEEN: Still. It could all turn out for the best in the long run, couldn't it? What's this?

DERIC: It's a frog. It's got a sort of hat on. It's just the family home gone for ever. She's been there for almost forty years, you know.

Aileen is still puzzled by the ornament.

DERIC: It's carrying a set of golf clubs and a fishing rod.

Aileen grimaces and puts it down in disgust.

Of course I knew that the props buyer was going to have a bit of trouble finding a china frog with a sort of hat on, who just happened to be carrying a set of golf clubs and a fishing rod, but I was prepared to compromise. I had already combed the gift shops of West Yorkshire and I knew exactly where I could lay my hands on a pair of youth-hostelling rabbits who were wearing khaki shorts and Doc Martens while carrying a haversack apiece and sporting a couple of stout walking sticks to assist them on their cross-country stroll. They'd be just the job.

But we cut the lines anyway. They weren't really needed, and Sita Williams was worried that the script might run a few minutes over time. The commercials are sacrosanct.

* * *

For the moment we were surplus to requirements. The china shop was already packed solid with people who were busy doing proper jobs such as lighting, directing and acting, so we popped outside and left them to it.

As we mingled with the crowd of onlookers we were joined by a couple of ladies in blue overalls who seemed very excited by the whole business, except that they had their backs to us and were staring across the road at the parish church.

'What is it, a wedding?'

One of the crew had a word with them, explaining the situation, and they listened to her with faces as blank as two sheets of A4 paper. But they thanked her anyway and when another friend joined them they were able to fill her in with the necessary details.

'Who's getting married then?'

'Simon Armitage apparently.'

'What – the poet?'

'Must be.'

'From Marsden?'

'Yes, that's the one. That's why this lot are all here.'

She gestured dismissively over her shoulder at the crew who were now beginning to wrap things up. But the women waited on, shuffling from one foot to the other while making sure their Sainsbury's carrier bags remained upright and alert. Occasionally they glanced at their watches. It wouldn't matter if they were a few minutes late for work.

'You'd have thought he'd have got married in Marsden, wouldn't you?'

'Mmmm.'

'Maybe she wouldn't have it. Put her foot down. Who is she anyway?'

'Some model, I shouldn't wonder.'

There was a communal sniff of disapproval.

'All the same, aren't they?'

I took Aileen Armitage by the arm and guided her back to the car. The women were framed in my rear-view mirror as I pulled out into the traffic, still staring across at the empty church. I just hope that Simon lives happily ever after, with his Naomi or his Kate or whoever she is – he's a nice lad.

Women of a certain age have always proved a rich vein of material for me. After a talk I gave in Sheffield a doctor's receptionist told me the story of a rather refined old lady who had been asked to bring in a urine sample so that they could send it away for tests.

She was back later that Monday afternoon carrying a small brown-paper bag and, shielding it with her body from the others in the waiting room, she produced from it a delicate little vinegar bottle in finest mock Wedgwood, with a tiny cork stopper in the neck.

She liked things to be nice, she told the receptionist.

On the Saturday morning she was waiting outside as the surgery opened for business.

'Sorry to bother you, but do you think I could

possibly have my vinegar bottle back? Only we're off on a trip to Fountains Abbey tomorrow and it's part of my picnic set.'

I've never really enjoyed a plate of fish and chips since.

Straight after lunch I set to work. I had deadlines to meet and the fading light had driven the film crew back to the studios in Leeds. I must have sat at my desk for a couple of hours or so and while I was away in another world the cats had drifted into my office and quietly spread themselves around the room.

By the time I came back to reality my shoulders ached and my legs were freezing, tucked away as they were under the desk, in the pigeon-hole between the two sets of drawers.

I unscrewed the top off my insulated jug of coffee and poured myself a cup, then lit a cigarette, swung my legs out from under the desk and dangled them in the gulf stream of hot air that flows directly between the Valor living flame and the radiator on the wall behind me.

The weirdest sight greeted my eyes. The sun had come out to play once more and I was surrounded by a herd of multi-coloured cats.

There was a red one over by the fireplace and a bright blue one lying flat on his back on the table in the window. Another red one, of a slightly more crimson hue this time, was fast asleep on that bit that sticks out from the book-case and there was a green-and-yellow-striped tortoiseshell just below him, stretched out on the carpet.

For a moment I wondered what sort of cigarette I was smoking and decided that Dunhill must have started putting some of that funny stuff in them.

'Aileen, come and look at this.'

Which is a pretty stupid thing to yell to a woman who can't even see her hand in front of her face. She appeared from out of her study.

'What?'

'The cats. They're all sorts of colours. Thermal's gone blue.'

A look of horror passed across her face. Had he stopped breathing? Should she give him the kiss of life?

'It's the stained-glass windows, love. The cats have each picked out a different spot of sunlight and now they're all the colours of the rainbow.'

As the sun shifted its position in the sky, the cats shifted their position in the room, seeking out fresh pastures in which to soak up the warmth. Tigger moved a foot to her left and instantly turned a bright emerald green. Thermal, half in the sunshine and half out, swopped his electric blue duffle coat for a pair of tailored jogging pants in a rather fetching shade of pale lilac.

It was as though I had been transported to an *Alice in Wonderland* world where anything was possible, especially when William glared at me through a pair of deep green eyes that clashed awfully with the orange tips of his whiskers. He had looked so much better before Technicolor arrived, back in the old black and white days when cats were cats and not some sort of mobile fashion accessory.

Then Thermal shifted his position once more, this time slipping into a little pale pink number with adjustable shoulder straps and matching bootees.

I gave Aileen a running commentary on the changing scene but it was still some time before it dawned on me that we now had four cats and not just the resident three.

'Hey, Little Chap's back.'

'Is he?'

'Yes. He's the red one over there by the bit that sticks out from the bookcase.'

We went over to have a closer look at him, to see what sort of state he was in this time and as I drew nearer all the redness drained out of him. It was a strange experience, as though the Technicolor cat had been beamed up by Scotty, and I realized that to witness the full psychedelic effect one had to view the scene from a certain angle, like sitting over there at my desk.

He was knackered as usual but as I turned him over, this way and that, he didn't appear to be any the worse for his latest expedition. Thinner, yes, but otherwise all in one piece. Odd bits of fur here and there were hanging on by a thread, but that was pretty good going for Little Chap.

Aileen was waiting anxiously for my verdict.

'Is he all right?'

I turned him over and had another good look underneath.

'Yes. He seems to be fine.'

Unconscious, but fine. William came over to give me a second opinion. He sniffed here and he sniffed there, and then he sniffed there again and that seemed to touch a nerve with Little Chap. His eyes shot wide open but it took a little time for them to warm up.

First there was a deep vacant space as though there was nobody at home and the answer-phone had been switched off. Then as the wheels in his brain began to turn and the pulleys in his memory began to do whatever it is that pulleys are supposed to do, a little light began to dawn and his head began to move like the gun turret in a Sherman tank.

He saw Tigger and then he saw Thermal and then he felt William's cold nose as it closed in on him once more, just to make sure. Then he leaped to his feet and saw me kneeling above him and he threw back his head.

'*Foo-oo-oo-ood.*'

Aileen relaxed. We could rebuild him.

Chapter 12

I was in the front line, fielding the phone for Aileen, when Annie Ashurst rang me around half-past ten in the morning. If the name doesn't immediately ring a bell, allow me to fill you in.

Annie is that wonderful woman who romped away with the *Mastermind* title in the very last programme of the TV series, and she's a very good friend of mine.

Me. The man who not only failed each and every examination he ever took in his life, but who also once scored a perfect zero in woodwork at the Manor Secondary School in Chesterfield. It's a record that stands to this day.

Annie is a feisty, multi-talented lady – the breadth of her knowledge is mind-bending. She's also a cricket fanatic and under the pseudonym of Sara Craven she writes best-selling romances for Mills and Boon, always to the accompaniment of a roof-lifting barrage of hard rock music.

She also is the proud possessor of a tongue so cutting that it could probably pass a woodwork examination all on its own, no problem.

You don't mess with Annie, but as a friend she is truly loyal and at times extremely useful. If you are ever stuck for an answer in the middle of a family quiz, what better than to sneak out into the hall, pick up the phone, and have a one-to-one with the winner of the *Mastermind* title? Slightly dishonest, I agree, but it works for me.

She wanted to talk to Aileen but it really wasn't on just then. That's why I was fielding the phone.

'Can she ring you back, Annie? Only she's talking to her computer at the moment.'

Annie quite understood.

'I often talk to mine. I say, you stupid wanker, what the bloody hell do you think you're playing at?'

Life has been much easier for Aileen since she dispensed with the keyboard and began to dictate straight into the computer. They make quite a team, the two of them. They spend hours together, chatting away happily, but if someone happens to barge in on her unannounced or the phone suddenly rings, then the computer goes into a mad panic and a whole stream of gibberish appears on the screen.

She has to shut it down in an orderly manner. She leans forward and breathes into the microphone.

'Go to sleep.'

The computer doesn't argue. It's probably glad of the break and I like to think that somewhere deep inside this highly intelligent lump of machinery, a tiny piece of software has a good long stretch and then manages to grab a quick five minutes while the going's good.

When she's ready to start work again Aileen leans forward once more.

'Wake up.'

Sometimes the computer takes a little time to obey the command, but before long the two of them are back on the same wavelength.

'Sorry about that, Aileen. I was on the toilet. Just downloading a few megabytes. Now then, what can I do for you?'

So I answer the door and look after the phone for her and most days I'm up and down like a jackrabbit. Friends want to know why I don't simply leave the answerphone on and deal with the calls later, but I can't do that.

There was a time, long ago, when I wanted to hide behind the settee whenever the phone burst into life. It was bound to be either the Gas or the Electricity Board threatening to send in the heavies if I didn't cough up immediately – either that or the Midland Bank asking very politely if I would be kind enough to pop in for a quiet word.

But things have changed since then and nowadays, apart from the odd special offer from a double-glazing firm who just happen to be in my area, the news is generally good, ranging from the extremely pleasant to the downright exciting.

So the moment I hear the answerphone begin to clear its throat I'm off down two flights of stairs to listen in and find out who's on the other end, and then since I'm down there anyway I might as well take over and have a word with them.

My granddaughter Katie rang ten minutes after Annie to tell me about her trip to London Zoo. Katie is seven years old going on thirty-five.

'I was very disappointed in the giraffes.'

She had especially wanted to see the giraffes.

'They weren't as tall as I expected.'

I heard her mother's voice in the background. It was a voice under pressure, a voice that was trying to keep an eye on things while at the same time pulling a load of wet clothes out of the washing machine.

'That's because they were a long way away, Katie.'

'They were smaller than the gorilla.'

The voice butted in once more.

'Because they were a long way away.'

'The gorilla was very nice.'

I managed to get a word in.

'You liked the gorilla, did you?'

That's the sort of stupid remark grandfathers make to their offspring once removed. Of course she liked the gorilla – she'd just told me. I don't get enough practice at this sort of thing.

'Yes, he smiled a lot, but the giraffes were very small.'

Sally's voice passed by on the way to the

tumble dryer. It had gone up a couple of notches on the Beaufort scale.

'Because they were over the other side of the field. You tell her, Dad.'

Stuff that. She's their kid. Grandfathers are there to be loved, not to give lectures.

'What else did you see?'

She gave me a quick rundown on all the other animals and then went through the menu in the coffee shop, item by item.

'So you had a good time?'

'Yes. Apart from the giraffes.'

The next call was from Alan Bell, the director of *Lost for Words*.

'Are you thinking of coming over today?'

I hadn't. The day before I had spent a full eight hours hanging around a garden centre, watching the longest scene in the play wither before my eyes.

Thora was supposed to wander along a rack stacked with packets of rose fertilizer, picking up each identical packet, reading the identical instructions on the back of each packet as though she were seeing them for the first time, which in effect she was, with her befuddled mind.

She would then move on to a shelf stacked with identical packets of slug pellets and do exactly the same. I was trying to show how this fragile mind of hers had deteriorated, that she remembered very little from one moment to the next.

But during the early script conferences it had

been suggested that I might make more of this and at the time it had seemed rather a good idea. Thora, on seeing the packets of slug pellets, each decorated with a large picture of a big black slug, would be frightened and recoil, being reminded of the slugs she imagined were invading her house and making her life a misery.

'Little devils.'

Pete would rush over and comfort her, explaining that the packets didn't really contain slugs, but the poison to kill them, and this would give her an idea. 'Poison,' she would mutter thoughtfully as Pete led her away.

But it didn't work. This wasn't the way it had really happened. Her mind at that time wouldn't have stretched to such an idea and it detracted from the main point of the scene.

Added to that, the packets of slug pellets seemed to take over the whole set. They had been brilliantly concocted out of boxes of cornflakes, disguised and decorated with a huge black slug who sneered out at the world, daring anyone to mess with him.

'*Come on, punk – make my day.*'

They had a cartoon quality about them and although they had been a considerable investment in time and ingenuity, they just weren't right.

The extra business also denied Thora the space to do what she does best. As I wrote the scene I had closed my eyes and watched her doing it over and over in my head and I knew she would be wonderful. With just a twitch of her nose and a raised eyebrow she would examine each packet closely before putting it back and reaching out for another. It's impossible for Thora to be boring and the repetition would establish how far her understanding had deteriorated.

But the new business had intruded, allowing time for her to examine only a couple of packets, and the point was missed. From that moment on nothing seemed to work. My lines came out forced and wooden and I just wanted to run away and hide.

So I had decided to give it a miss today, but Alan thought differently.

'We're shooting the party scene in your mother's old house. Be handy if you were there.'

Andrew Sanderson had recreated my mother's lounge in the studios at Leeds and I was looking forward to seeing it. He and Josh Dynevor, the location manager, hadn't been able to get into her first house in Chesterfield, so they'd had to make do with peeping in through the windows and then let their imagination tell them how the room might have appeared some twenty years earlier.

And they had it just about right. It was uncanny. The brick fireplace, the French windows and the general layout of the room they would have seen, but the bric-à-brac, the furnishings and the general feel of the house were spot on. I half expected my mother to put her head round the kitchen door.

*   *   *

I joined a group of extras who were watching Thora run through a scene with Anne Reid and Keith Clifford. Between takes the conversation around me always seemed to come back to who the extras had worked with in the past and what they had lined up in the near future.

'Of course I've worked with Thora before. On *Last of the Summer Wine.*'

'Yes, I've done a couple of those and I've got an *Emmerdale* coming up shortly.'

Peak Practice, Heart of the Matter and *Heartbeat* were all tossed around in a cavalier show of one-upmanship. *Coronation Street* and *Brookside* zipped in and out of the conversation until I felt I had been beamed down into some sort of Yorkshire Hollywood.

One of the extras had held the door open for Kevin in the Rover's Return and apparently the whole scene revolved about this seemingly innocent action. Maybe he was right. Kevin wouldn't have been able to come in if he hadn't.

Another of them chipped in with an *Inspector Morse* appearance and that shut everybody up for a while. In between bouts of looking smug he quietly sang to himself, snatches of Nat King Cole's 'Let There Be Love'.

' "Laurel and Hardy / *dum dum* / Sparkling champagne." '

I knew there was something wrong with that somewhere but I couldn't think what it was and I worried about it all afternoon.

A kindly soul tried to include me in the conversation.

'You done anything lately?'

'Not a lot.'

'It seems to come in runs, doesn't it?'

'Yes.'

He picked up a script from a nearby table.

'Who's the writer? Not Alan Bennett, is it?'

There was a small snort from down the line.

'Nah.'

The man with the script riffled back through the sheets of A4 until he came across the title page.

'Deric Longden.'

The snorter snorted once more.

'Never heard of him.'

My friend came to my rescue.

'Probably some kid. They've got a good cast for him, though. Worth keeping an eye on.'

I promised I would do just that and went off to the toilet where I twirled around twice like Superman and immediately changed back into the writer.

We broke for lunch and everyone trooped off to the canteen, with the exception of Dame Thora. She wasn't at all well, and the thought of being hauled about in her wheelchair once more was too much for her, so she had her lunch brought to her on the set. It consisted of three cream buns which served as her starter, main course and pudding. I grabbed a cup of coffee, pulled up a footstool, and kept her company.

We talked about how, some three years ago in the Huddersfield Hotel, we had sat down over dinner with Aileen and discussed how we were going to adapt the book for television. During the intervening years several people who had a good track record in the medium, been there and done that and knew better than I did, had told me that it wouldn't work.

'Not enough story. Too little action.'

But I had Thora, and I knew we could make it work. Ever since she played my mother in *Wide-Eyed and Legless* I was sure that, with Thora's interpretation of my mother's generous and eccentric behaviour, we could turn it into a winner.

We didn't need car crashes, multiple murders or lurid rape scenes. It's the small moments in life that stick in the memory. People can come through a war and put it all behind them, but they never forget a hurt inflicted when they were nine years old and vulnerable as hell.

What I did need, however, was a structure, and that was a long time in coming. It had to be tighter than the book, and it wasn't until eighteen months later, when I decided upon a flashback through a series of old photographs, that the play began to take shape.

Those photographs were on the mantelpiece behind me now as I sat talking with Thora. There was me in my little white bootees and my little white angora coat and bonnet, with my rosy pink cheeks artificially coloured in and my lips touched up to perfection with a bright red lipstick by Rimmel. I have often thought that I reached my peak on the day that photograph was taken and it's been downhill ever since.

Then there was my mother as a beautiful young woman on a day out in Blackpool, with the tower in the background, wearing a coat that long since went out of fashion and then came back in again quite recently.

Nuzzling up to this was a photograph of Thora taken just a few days before, with her looking for all the world the spitting image of my mother in her later years.

Slotted in between these three were several photographs of Pete as a small boy, first in short trousers and then as a teenager in football boots, charting the progress of my life from the little white bootees to the photograph of my wedding to Aileen, as posed professionally by Pete Postlethwaite and Penny Downie. You could hardly see the join.

Thora had thought it over and decided to save the cream bun with the chocolate icing for her pudding – it seemed to be the right thing to do. You can't go having a cream bun covered in chocolate as a main course.

I sipped my coffee and listened to her. That's the way a conversation with Thora usually goes. At first there is a certain ebb and flow and then the duologue becomes a monologue and I never mind a bit. She's far more interesting than I am and I could listen to her for hours, and often have.

As she talked I began to take in the room about us. The sideboard just like my mother's, the battered but comfortable settee, the blue and white cups and saucers laid out on the table. I knew without looking that if I turned them upside down the word *Empire* would be stamped underneath.

'It's a very good make is Empire. You want to have those valued after I'm gone.'

A sewing box – hardly used. On the dresser a row of suspicious-looking Toby jugs all lined up, as though for an identity parade. A tea trolley fashioned out of a metal so shiny bright that it was enough to give the brass trivet an inferiority complex.

As Thora talked of her early days in show business my mind went back with her, at least part of the way, to the time when I was a little lad sitting at my mother's feet in this very room, listening to her read my father's letters from Louth in Lincolnshire where he was stationed in the Fire Service.

'He says he loves you very much.'

He probably did. He just had a funny way of showing it.

It was the weirdest feeling. Never mind that the set had an open end from where an off-duty camera stared down gloomily at our feet, or that without the saving grace of special lighting the trees and houses through the French windows were obviously painted on to a vast backcloth.

For a short while it was all very real, until one by one and two by two the cast and crew began to drift back on to the set, the extras sticking together in a tight little bunch.

'Did I tell you about when I was in *Woken-well*?'

Pete Postlethwaite was fed up to the teeth. He had cut short his lunch break to give an interview to a couple of journalists up from London for the day. He had wanted to talk about the play and they had been asking him about the house where he'd been born in Warrington.

'Did it have an outside toilet?'

'What the hell's that got to do with anything?'

This unfortunately is the lot of any actor who happens to have been born up here in the north. Did your dad work down the pit and did he keep pigeons?

'No. He was a barrister.'

'He'd have had a whippet though, wouldn't he?'

Pete is a star and a good man to have around. Steven Spielberg says that without doubt he is one of the four best character actors in the world and we were lucky to have been able to grab him for the whole of one of those rare months when he wasn't hard at work in the United States.

His concentration is total, but he always has time for the younger members of the cast and loves nothing better than a pint with the crew in the nearest pub.

While we were filming I had to pop over to Rochdale to talk at a conference of hospital broadcasters and in the bar beforehand I had several drinks with a total stranger who worked as a stunt co-ordinator in the movies.

Now coming across a big-time stunt co-ordinator in Rochdale is amazing in itself, but we also found that we had Pete in common. This man had spent a week with him, driving around in a small van on location in Africa. He thought Pete was the bee's knees and talked of little else for the best part of an hour, but even Mr Postlethwaite was upstaged when Henry arrived on the set.

Some actors prefer to drift in quietly, unannounced, but Henry was the master of the grand entrance. He strode proudly through the spaghetti mass of wires and cables as though he were on his way up to collect his Oscar, back straight as a ramrod, his red lead and collar marking him out as the sort of cat who could always be relied upon to turn in a sound performance.

His handler slipped him off the leash and parked him on the back of my mother's settee. He took in the scene around him as Allan Pyrah and Dave Carey tried out a few dummy shots with the camera.

'*Bloody amateurs.*'

I could imagine him sitting up late into the night, working on his moves with the script laid out in front of him.

'*Now what is my motivation when Dame Thora drops me four feet on to a solid concrete step?*'

His handler whispered into his ear.

'Sit.'

And so he sat and then never moved a muscle

for the next fifteen minutes. At drama school he had received a special commendation for the quality of his sitting and it was a skill that had come in very handy throughout his short career.

You get involved in a lot of sitting when you are playing the part of a cat. But he hoped that future roles might stretch him even further so that eventually he could introduce his famous dead mouse routine or maybe do that fancy dribbling thing with the ping-pong ball. He was also planning to take fencing lessons.

I had been very careful when writing the cat into the action. Cats can't act – end of story. But then, of course, that was before I met Henry, so how was I to know?

We did need a cat. My mother could talk to it, letting the audience in on secrets that she would never tell me. There were also several funny bits and pieces that I didn't want to lose.

My mother regularly washed Whisky in the kitchen. She would lather him up in one sink and then rinse him off in the other.

'This double drainer's been a blessing.'

Whether the cat thought it a blessing or not I shall never know, but I remember he always looked downright miserable as she stood him on the draining board and towelled him down before fluffing him up with the hair dryer. Every now and then, for a special treat, she used to hoover him.

I knew we couldn't expect a stand-in cat to put up with all that sort of nonsense, it would run a mile, so I had written the scene so that Henry would be able to do just that.

Scene 11. Interior of Mother's old house – kitchen – day.

Deric's mother is about to wash the cat in the kitchen sink. It's full of foaming liquid. She wears rubber gloves, one yellow, the other pink, and she has the cat trapped on the draining board.

MOTHER: It's no good grumbling. If you made a better job of it yourself there'd be no need for this.

The doorbell rings and, as she turns towards the sound, the cat makes a break for it.

MOTHER: Whisky – come here. Oh damn it.

Pulling off the rubber gloves as she goes, she exits towards the kitchen door.

MOTHER: Take me ages to catch him again.

Cut to hallway.

We had shot the scene earlier in the week but of course the RSPCA would have had our guts for garters if we had plunged Henry head first into the sink, so we'd stuck him on the draining board and let Thora have her wicked way with him.

She soaked him and lathered him, rubbing bubbles into his important little places, but would he jump off? Would he hell. He loved every minute of it.

199

'I think you've missed a bit, Thora. Just under my armpit, left front.'

Take after take we tried again. Thora was just about as wet as the cat.

'Do my tail again, Thora. Run it through your fingers. Slowly. There, that's right. Oh God, that's wonderful.'

In the end Alan Bell had to sit Henry on a tea towel that hung over the edge of the draining board. He placed a man strategically, down by the side of the sink unit, and then as Thora began to lather the cat once more the man yanked the tea towel and Henry, wondering why his feet were suddenly disappearing from underneath him, finally called it a day and leaped to the floor.

If ever I have the opportunity to work with Henry again I shall write him a scene where he has his split ends seen to and his ears pierced.

Today, however, it was his sitting skills that were called for. With a huge red bow slung around his neck he was required to sit on a pouffe for as long as it took my mother to show a bevy of would-be buyers around her house.

He must have learned a lot sitting there. It was like a masterclass. Anne Reid and Keith Clifford were wonderful, and when the widower from North Wingfield, played by Eddie Caswell, walked on to the set I could hardly believe my eyes. He was a dead ringer for the bloke who came to look round the house all those years ago.

Bemused by all the bustle and further embarrassed by the scrutiny of all the women in the room, he hesitates and then apologizes.

WIDOWER: I seem to have picked the wrong time.
MOTHER: Not at all. No. Is your mother not with you?
WIDOWER: No. (*Beat*) She's got her leg up again.
MOTHER: You don't have to tell me about legs. I've got one myself.

Henry sat perfectly still on his pouffe and took it all in, making mental notes of Thora's immaculate timing. He could build on that in a few minutes when it came to his big moment.

And he did. As Pete entered and then moved towards the settee, Henry shot off his pouffe like the born athlete he undoubtedly is, bounded across the carpet, leaped up on to the settee and then scooted over the back and out of the room.

Another shot in the can, another day's work well done. He called for his driver and without a backward glance departed from the set.

'Probably pop in tomorrow to have a look at the rushes.'

I smiled all the way home. Alan Bell and his team had lifted the scene straight from the page and breathed life into it. Everything had gone like clockwork and the previous day's shoot in the garden centre, with the help of a little early editing and the disappearance of the slug pellets, didn't look so bad after all. Now if I could only get this damn tune out of my head, all would be right with the world.

' "Laurel and Hardy / *dum dum* / Sparkling champagne." '

I must have sung that line a hundred times between Leeds and Huddersfield. I knew Laurel and Hardy had no business being in there, but no matter how I tried I couldn't come up with the original words.

I messed around with a varied combination of cuckoos, larks and doves but I still hadn't worked it out by the time I arrived home.

Aileen had laid the table and opened a bottle of white wine. She was already two glasses ahead of me.

'I thought it was red.'

It didn't matter as it happened. I had planned to cook a couple of steaks but they were still buried deep in the freezer. Aileen took the news philosophically, as you do when you've already had a couple of glasses of white wine.

'Never mind. Let's have some pasta – and there's that leftover chilli con carne in the fridge.'

I kissed the top of her head. That was it!

' "Chilli con carne / *dum dum* / Sparkling champagne." '

Over dinner I told her how clever she was and as always she wholeheartedly agreed with me. Then I told her all about having lunch with Thora and about the extras and about Henry the cat and how, with just another little tweak here and there, we could rescue the scene in the garden centre and she beamed and was ever so pleased for me.

Some days you just can't go wrong, can you?

Chapter 13

I sometimes worry about myself. There are times when I wonder whether I might be losing it. My mind, I mean.

I had made an overnight trip down to Bournemouth where I spoke to some very nice people in the Pavilion, but then as I prepared to point the car north for the long journey home I found that the automatic gears had gone on strike and had decided to stay put in P for parking.

Jiggling about didn't do much good and neither did a bout of strenuous yanking and so, having worked my way through my extensive knowledge of all things mechanical, with special reference to automatic gears, I resorted to switching the engine on and off several times and suddenly there was a click and we were back in business once more.

On the way home I stopped off at a Little Chef for a quick cup of coffee, a free newspaper and to experience the unalloyed pleasure of hearing the one-sided conversations of people nattering away on their mobile phones.

They were all company men and women, two of them sitting at the same table, each ignoring the other, reporting their whereabouts to some suit at headquarters.

'I'm in his outer office now. Hope to get in to see him before lunchtime.'

As I sipped my coffee – the Little Chef's coffee is going downhill, by the way, they'd even managed to burn the water this time – as I sat there and sipped and winced and looked around me, I wondered if those brandishing their mobile phones realized that in most cases they are merely a modern refinement of that row of bells in the big house, the ones that used to be slung high above the door in the servants' quarters.

'*We want you. Now.*'

It was fun to try to work out the status of each of these mobile phone-a-philes. The smug little man bawling out instructions from behind the potted plant was bound be the Butler and there was the Housekeeper over there, her eyebrows dancing with frustration as she listened to a string of miserable excuses trotted out by one of her minions on the other end.

We didn't seem to have the Cook with us, as far as I could see, but the Downstairs Maid had obviously made a pig's ear of the dusting and she was getting a right telling off. I don't think she'd said a word in the past ten minutes.

Over in the corner a young man, who just had to be the Boots, was squirming in his plastic seat, his polyester suit shiny with embarrassment as its owner was told for the umpteenth time to pull his finger out.

I was feeling a right little smart-arse as I climbed in the car and switched on the ignition, but that lovely glow of self-assurance faded somewhat over the next twenty minutes as I sat there and jiggled and yanked and switched the engine on and off.

My imaginary domestic staff filed out of the Little Chef one by one and then roared off out of the car park in their Escorts and Mondeos with not a care in the world. I was right about the Butler by the way – he had a black Lexus with a personalized number plate.

All of which didn't help me one jot, and I was just about to call the AA when my foot accidentally brushed against the brake pedal and there was a little click and it was all systems go once more.

The next morning I decided I had better get my gears sorted out. For the time being a gentle tap on the brake pedal would bring them into play but it was obviously only a temporary measure and things were bound to go from bad to worse.

The lovely Sharon was behind her desk and Mark the mechanic came out to have a word with me. I sank into the deep leather chair and told him all about the trouble I'd had in Bournemouth and at the Little Chef.

'. . . but I've found if I tap the brake pedal it seems to work.'

Mark waited patiently for me to carry on but there wasn't any more to say.

'That's it really.'

He settled his right shoulder against the nearest wall and took a deep breath and I saw in his eyes a look that I have seen quite often over the years. It's known as the 'we've got a right one here' sort of look and I would recognize it a mile off.

'How long did you have your previous Jaguar?'

'Three years.'

'And how long have you had this one?'

'Three months.'

He took a deep breath.

'And in all that time you never realized that you have to press the brake pedal to release the gears?'

That's when I first realized I must be losing it.

'I can't have.'

'You must have.'

He took pity on me.

'Give me the keys and I'll go and have a look at it.'

I handed them over, squirming in my leather chair. I smiled at Sharon.

'You won't tell anybody, will you.'

'Yes, of course I will.'

Mark returned a few minutes later, waving my dipstick in the air as though he were about to conduct the Huddersfield Choral Society.

'When did you last put any oil in?'

Now I had him there.

'Yesterday afternoon. At a Shell station just outside Oxford.'

I bet not many of his customers can pinpoint their movements quite as accurately as that. I thought he would be impressed.

'Pity you didn't think to screw the cap back on the oil tank.'

He took me to have a look at my car. My lovely 4.2 engine was a disaster area. It reminded me of when the *Amoco Cadiz* split in half and 50,000 tons of crude oil made straight for the beaches of Brittany. There was oil everywhere, smothering the engine and the underside of the bonnet.

'It must be all over your garage floor.'

'I didn't see any – I reverse out.'

Mark stuck his hand down by the radiator and I half expected him to come up with a mucky-looking seagull that was going to sue me for every penny I'd got. Instead he produced my missing oil cap.

'That's something anyway.'

He spent ages steam-cleaning the engine and blowing it dry, then he dried the spark plugs on a cloth and put them back. The engine purred into life.

'You've been lucky.'

I didn't really want to be that lucky ever again. I don't think I have ever felt such a prat in my life – well I have, but we won't go into that at the moment.

On the way out I had another chat with Sharon.

'You won't really tell anybody, will you?'

'No, of course not.'

So the whole episode remains a close secret between the three of us, Sharon and Mark and me – plus half the population of Huddersfield. It's nice when you know you can trust people.

At least I had the car back in time to make a start on my list. As a result of the filming we were getting a little behind with the nuts and bolts of life, those small insignificant jobs that don't matter at all until you string half a dozen of them together and find that life doesn't run so smoothly any more.

I called in and signed something at the accountant's. I have no idea what it was, but Roger Armitage had told me to call in and sign it – so I did.

He also told me that he'd been at a conference over the weekend and when they returned from lunch they discovered that someone had gone and stolen three laptop computers from the meeting room.

As they left to go home that night they found that they had also had three cars stolen from outside the hotel. One of his colleagues had a solution.

'They want their hands chopping off.'

Another colleague chipped in.

'It doesn't work.'

'How do you mean?'

'My wife works for the Social Security. She had to refuse benefit to a man with no arms – so he head-butted her.'

I left the car where it was and walked the fifty yards across to Sainsbury's. It's not something I would normally do but they say exercise is good for you and I thought I would give it a try.

There were two dogs tied up outside. One of them was a big black mongrel and the other a posh-looking poodle with a pedigree as long as your arm.

The poodle was attached to the railings by an exquisitely plaited lead that would have had Gucci stamped all over it had their designer decided to take a sideways step into dog accessories.

The hair was definitely by Vidal Sassoon and you have to admit that he does give a damn good cut, no matter what his own hair looks like. This dog would have been quite at home on the catwalks of London, Paris or Milan, but he did look a bit daft tied up to the railings outside the Huddersfield branch of Sainsbury's.

The mongrel, however, had been secured to the railings by a tatty piece of string that had been called upon to tackle one job too many. I say secured – the piece of string had been draped on the floor quite near the railings and wasn't attached to anything other than thin air. But the dog didn't know that, he was too busy wagging his tail and rolling his eyes at all who passed him by, collecting pats on the head until one feared that he might suffer brain damage.

I see him around town quite a lot, sometimes in the company of a small Irishman but more often than not out walking on his own. I assumed he must be with the Irishman today – he was hardly likely to have tied himself up to the railings, however loosely.

He's a good dog and he knows his way around, especially when it comes to traffic lights. He stops at the pavement edge and looks first left and then right and then left again. Then he marches straight across the road whether there's anything coming or not. At least you know where you are with him.

We had a few words and a lick and a pat. He did the licking and I did the patting. I wiped my damp hand on his coat, which was what had brought me over to have a look at them in the first place.

While the pedigree poodle was all dressed up like a dog's dinner, it was the mongrel who was wearing the brand new tartan jacket with the shiny plastic straps and the two little sleeves that stretched down over his haunches as far as his knees.

There's democracy for you. However lowly born, you can still reach for the stars, even if they do turn out to be tartan with plastic straps.

'You look very smart.'

'*Thank you.*'

*   *   *

I can usually nip round Sainsbury's in a matter of minutes, but they'd had a refit while I was away and I couldn't find a damn thing. Neither could anyone else. We should have been roped together and taken on a guided tour.

It took me ages to find the small Atlantic prawns and the coley steaks. They were where the white wine used to be but at least they were on offer, and so I bought six packets of each.

Fortunately the tins of tuna were where the mince used to be and the mince was where the tuna used to be, so that worked out all right. An assistant filling shelves tried to point me towards the cat food but couldn't think for the life of her where it might be, so we teamed up and spent a very pleasant half hour in each other's company. She's married but he works away a lot, so who knows where it might lead?

We chatted for a while longer as she tidied up the Kitty Treats and then we each went our separate ways, she clutching an empty cardboard box to her heaving bosom and me coquettishly swinging a hundredweight and a half of Sainsbury's own brand cat litter. And they say romance is dead.

I don't bother buying cat food any more. Well, I do – it's just that nowadays it seems to consist of small Atlantic prawns, coley steaks, mince and small tins of tuna in brine.

I am beginning to think I spoil my cats. When they first move in they will mop up anything I put in front of them and I am able to clear out all those tins of cat food that have worked their way to the back of the cupboard over the past few months, the ones that had the long-term residents turning up their collective nose.

'I don't think so – do you?'

'Wouldn't touch it with a bargepole myself.'

Even Little Chap is becoming more sophisticated. When he first arrived he would plunge his head deep into a saucer of mixed leftovers and emerge looking grateful. But then I was stupid enough to give him a tin of Sainsbury's tuna in brine and ever since then he has stalked upstairs first thing in the morning to discuss the day's menu with me in my office.

'Ah. Just the man I was looking for.'

In a few short months he has become the Ainsley Harriott of the cat world and it's driving me mad.

'I thought perhaps a chicken leg with a side salad. And do we have any feta cheese by any chance?'

The trouble is that I am already the proud owner of a Persil-white Keith Floyd and a tortoiseshell Delia Smith and I can't be doing with any more.

Thankfully, William is still going through his Ryan Giggs period at the moment and is no trouble whatsoever. He dribbles a lot but that's about it.

Every now and then I put my foot down. I open a couple of anonymous tins and plant the contents on the kitchen floor.

'There you are. It's either that or nothing.'

The trouble is it's usually nothing. They sit in a

line, a good foot away from the dish, not even deigning to look in the right direction. I can pick them up and move them a foot nearer the saucer and yet when I let go of them they are still sitting where they were originally, a good twelve inches away. I don't know how they do it.

I have tried leaving it there all day, until it looks totally inedible. But it's no good. I have never been a leader of men and as far as my cats are concerned I am merely a private in their personal Catering Corps.

On the way home I called in at the bank to sign something they wanted me to sign and then popped in to the solicitor's to sign something else. Next it was up to see Jayne, my dentist. Apparently one has to re-register every fifteen months nowadays, and I was sitting in the waiting area, catching up on Maureen Lipman's column in *Good Housekeeping*, while an elderly couple decided on which day to make an appointment for a check-up.

'We'll be at your mother's on Wednesday.'

'Thursday then.'

'York Races. What's wrong with Tuesday?'

'Oklahoma.'

'Oh aye.'

I was just thinking that they were going to have a hell of a job to get back from Oklahoma in time for her mother's on Wednesday when the man opposite me put aside his copy of *Woman and Home* and came over and sat down beside me.

'You write about your mother. Don't you?'

'I have done, yes.'

'Well, you could be writing about mine.'

He went on to tell me that his mother was always complaining about her false teeth. She had a rough bit sticking up on her top plate.

'I call in and see if she's all right every lunchtime. We have cold meat and pickles and just recently she's gone on and on about her teeth. In the end I'd just about had enough. I said I didn't want to hear any more about her blessed teeth. I told her to pop up here to the dentist's. I told her they'd have it sorted out for her in five minutes flat. But she never did.'

'What happened?'

'Well, yesterday she never mentioned them at all and so as I was leaving I asked her if she'd been up to the dentist.'

'And?'

'She said no, she hadn't. She said she'd done 'em herself on the front step.'

As I arrived home I took a good long look at the front step. Solid York stone. One hundred years old and curved at the top edge. Just the right shape for sorting out a bolshie top set.

Then I had a good look at Thermal. Aileen was worried about him.

'He doesn't seem too well.'

He hadn't bothered with his breakfast that morning. He'd decided to have a lie-in and I had taken him up a saucer of tuna just before I left.

'*I'll have it later if you don't mind.*'

'You all right?'

Roughly translated his symptoms seemed to suggest a cross between irritable bowel syndrome and morning sickness. But then he does put it on a bit.

'We'd better take you to the vet then.'

He didn't think so. Apparently what he needed was the top off the milk and just a smidgen of that salmon pâté Aileen and I had had for supper the night before. His mother used to swear by it.

I had left him dozing in front of the fire, but if he had managed to keep it up until now then perhaps he ought to see the vet.

There were two other cats there when we arrived at the surgery, both of them tucked up behind the bars of their portable cat baskets. An enormous Alsatian sat by the side of a little old lady who could have passed for either its owner or its lunch.

Over by the fireplace there sprawled a small round dog who seemed to have been put together by a committee, and something even more compact rustled inside a flat cardboard box that shook ominously on the knee of a teenager who wore a purple anorak and a vacant expression.

I couldn't think what he could possibly have in a box so square and flat. Perhaps it was some sort of snake, all curled up like a Danish pastry. I shuddered at the thought and Thermal dug his claws into the back of my neck and held on for dear life.

He won't have anything to do with a cat basket. He lay wrapped around my shoulders, his hot breath riffling my left ear while one of his back legs poked into the one on the right-hand side. I leaned forward a little and shuffled him up a notch.

'Thank you very much.'

'My pleasure.'

He hadn't wanted to come and I still wasn't too sure it was necessary. Aileen said he had slumped in front of the fire all day, just taking the odd trip over to his litter tray and back again whenever the urge came upon him. But since that was all he ever did during the first few months of the year she wasn't too worried about him. It wasn't until he politely declined the offer of a prawn-cocktail crisp that she was sure something was amiss.

He has been known to lie and cheat for a prawn-cocktail crisp. I wouldn't put it past him to maim and kill. And so here we were, taking our turn in the waiting room.

I had begun to suspect he had a temperature and if he hadn't, then I had. It can get awfully hot when you have a cat wrapped round the back of your neck. He whispered in my ear.

'She won't use that glass thingy, will she?'

'She might have to.'

'You won't look, will you?'

'Of course not.'

He gets most embarrassed when they take his

temperature. Sitting there with a thermometer sticking out from under your tongue is one thing, having it sticking out from under your tail is another matter altogether.

The Alsatian whined piteously and the smaller dog looked across with undisguised contempt.

'Wish he wouldn't do that. Not with all these cats around. Lets us down, it does.'

The young man in the anorak was in and out of the consulting room in a flash. He still had the vacant expression but he had left his box behind with the vet and I wondered what she would be able to do for a sick snake. I wouldn't even know where to stick the thermometer.

The nurse consulted her card index and called in the next patient.

'Major Bowden.'

I waited for the Alsatian to make a move but it was the smaller dog who rose to his feet. He marched in, not waiting for his owner, back straight and head held high. All that army training, I suppose.

Thermal and I were the last to be called and the vet gave him a thorough going over.

'Don't look.'

'I won't.'

She gave him an injection and he was very brave. Then she felt him all over and he enjoyed that. She's known him since he was a kitten and they get on very well.

'Keep an eye on him, but I don't think there's much wrong.'

I was waiting for Thermal to get dressed when

a fully grown rabbit burst into the consulting room, from the private office round the back. He did an about-turn when he saw us, skidded on the lino, and his feet went from under him. Then he crashed into the skirting board and I bent down and picked him up while he was still stunned.

'Perhaps he was frightened by the snake.'

The vet looked bemused.

'The one in the box.'

Thermal didn't talk to me all the way home. I think he was ashamed of me. But how was I to know that the vet had been out in the country all day? How was I to know that she hadn't had time to eat? How was I to know she'd ordered a pizza?

'You won't tell Aileen, will you?'

But Thermal just licked his sore bum and snorted. And after all I've done for him.

Chapter 14

The next day I drove over to Horsforth and once there began looking for St Joseph's Residential Home. Earlier in the week, while the crew were filming in Seacroft Hospital, I'd had the devil's own job finding out where they were.

I know the outskirts of Leeds like the back of someone else's hand and I went round and round in circles before I eventually worked out what the temporary signs were all about.

When Yorkshire Television are filming *Heart of the Matter* they hang discreet little signs here and there, on lampposts and telegraph poles, each bearing the single word *Heart* and a small stumpy arrow. That way the caterers, the crew and the cast can find their way to that day's location.

I didn't know about this at the time and although I saw lots of yellow signs with the word *Lost* emblazoned upon them I didn't take any notice – they just seemed to be telling me what I knew already – and by the time I arrived at the Seacroft Hospital I was just about ready to book myself into the psychiatric ward. On the way home I pinched one of the *Lost* signs and it now has pride of place on my bookshelf. It seems to sum up so much of my life.

St Joseph's was an enormous old house set in its own grounds, and standing in its car park was the usual fleet of enormous television vans, pulled up alongside the caterers who had been busy serving breakfast since six-forty-five.

I sat in the car and examined the call sheet for the day. From the outside the home looked more than capable of accommodating the entire aged population of a small to medium-sized town, Harrogate, for instance. But we were going to have to make it look fully occupied with just three extras. The call sheet specified two elderly lady residents and one elderly man. They were going to have to nip about a bit.

In one stark line the call sheet also announced the acting debut of a fresh and youthful new talent.

Kitten at unit base – 1200 hours.

I imagined this small ginger kitten twisting and turning in his sleep last night, forever glancing at his alarm clock.

'Please, God, don't let me sleep in.'

His first job would be to walk in through an open door and his second, in a later scene, to jump off the bed and walk out again. He'd probably been practising for weeks and would be very nervous. This sort of chance doesn't come along all that often.

'Rolf Harris might be watching.'

I just hoped he didn't catch a glimpse of the call sheet. While the elderly ladies and the elderly man were listed as extras, they had the kitten listed under props.

After a nourishing bacon sandwich and a decent cup of coffee I went into the home and found Thora and Pete busily rehearsing a scene with Noreen Kershaw and our two elderly lady residents.

Although it was still early, with a definite chill in the air, Thora and Pete had already been out filming an earlier scene in which my mother suddenly sees the nursing home through the car windscreen.

They are supposed to be driving home from the garden centre. My mother is downcast, with no life in her face, and Pete is attempting to cheer her up. Suddenly she sees a large house on the other side of the road. It's the one she's been trying to tell him about ever since the stroke robbed her of any recognizable form of language.

MOTHER: Spongo.

Deric's eye follows the line of her finger. We see a sign: Springbank Nursing Home.

DERIC: That's Spongo!

A car pips them and Deric sets off again. His mother turns to him.

MOTHER: Spongo.

She stares down lifelessly at the dashboard.

MOTHER: Ready. So ready.

In the finished product the scene brought tears to the eyes, especially to mine. And yet it was filmed at just after seven o'clock on a cold spring morning with the car window rolled right down, and by a camera mounted on a steel frame strapped to the outside of the vehicle.

At that time in the morning the eighty-seven-year-old leading lady had already been up for a couple of hours and then been driven out from Leeds before passing through the hands of wardrobe and make-up. On top of that the writer had handed her only five short words with which to paint the depth of the scene. Two Readys, two Spongos and a So.

And she had done it as only Thora could have done it, with the possible exception of my mother herself.

Now she was sitting on a cane chair in a light and airy conservatory. St Joseph's Residential Home was probably even older than Thora and yet it was playing the part of Springbank to perfection. You can't beat experience.

Alan Bell was due to shoot the scene in which my mother is about to be shown over the home by Noreen Kershaw, who is playing the part of Margaret.

In any biographical story of this nature there are bound to be scenes which bring back painful memories. Most of them would be pretty obvious to the viewer, but some are less obvious than others and this was one of them.

Not only was I about to 'put my mother away in a home', an action which left me running on empty for the next twelve months, but I was also acutely aware of how nervous she was. How she wanted to make a good impression.

By that time she could hardly string two sensible words together. When she was with the family, with Sally or Nick or Aileen or me, she could relax and laugh at herself, poke fun at herself, and then we could all settle down to the tedious task of trying to work out what the hell she was on about.

But here she was, setting out on yet another journey into the unknown and she wanted to prove herself. To show that she had dignity and was a woman of substance.

She had been quiet in the car and I knew she was working on some sort of opening statement, some casual remark that would convince Margaret that they would indeed be lucky to have my mother as a resident in their home. She muttered away under her breath and put on her gracious face, which we always referred to as her Queen Mother look. So I left her to it.

We had sat in the hall for a few minutes, as Pete and Thora were doing now, waiting for Margaret to come and show us around. Every now and then we caught each other's eye and smiled nervously. She didn't want to talk. She was saving herself for the big moment.

Then Margaret appeared, ignoring me as she should. She went straight to my mother and sank down on her knees before her, taking both of her hands in hers.

'Mrs Longden. I've been looking forward to meeting you.'

My mother took a deep breath and then went for it, smiling her tight little Queen Mother's smile. Here it was, make or break.

'Yes, well it will have.'

She was so proud of herself. I could feel the relief flooding through her whole body. She'd done it. A whole sentence and she was sure it made sense. They wouldn't think she was some sort of idiot now. Not after that.

Alan Bell shouted action and Pete and Thora began to play out the scene. Noreen entered down a long hall, quickened her pace, and kneeled in front of Thora.

'Mrs Longden. I've been looking forward to meeting you.'

I began to wish I had spoken to Thora beforehand, to explain the state of my mother's mind at the time.

Thora smiled a sweet little smile, rather like that of the Queen Mother, and then, as if she were knighting Noreen for services rendered, she took her voice slightly up-market towards posh.

'Yes, well it will have.'

I went out to the car for a cigarette and a think. I had some tissues on the back seat.

That was scene ninety-nine and from there we went straight into scene one hundred and four. They both took place in the conservatory and it would be easier to film them back to back rather than shift out the great mass of equipment and then lug it all back in again.

I was getting used to this business of shooting out of sequence. It made sense, of course, but I had often wondered how the actors coped. For instance, in a single morning Thora might have to take my mother's character on past the stroke to a point where she is beaten down and living in a confusing world that doesn't understand her any more, and then straight afterwards play her as an energetic and eccentric old lady who has a wonderful way with words. They were to film the stroke itself the following Wednesday afternoon.

It was a strange world that I had entered. That afternoon we would shoot the scene where Margaret takes my mother to show her Mrs Wibberley's room, so that she can see what can be done with a little imagination.

My mother falls in love with the room and Margaret and Pete become worried.

'Of course, this is Mrs Wibberley's room.'

But my mother doesn't understand and they almost have to drag her out. She wants that one. They take her across the landing to show her the room they have in mind for her. It's more like a hospital ward, bare and without frills and my mother wants nothing to do with it.

'Na. Crap. Ward – is a ward.'

Then Margaret calms her down and begins to paint a picture with her hands, showing her how it will look when it's furnished with all my mother's own belongings and gradually she draws her into the game.

The next scene is a dissolve. Time has passed and we see her in the room, nicely decorated, with her own bits and pieces all around her. The photographs are there on the sideboard along with so many of the other personal things we remember from her old house.

When it came to shooting the scenes Alan Bell filmed them in reverse order, simply because it would take the designers the best part of a day to furnish the room, but only twenty minutes for them to shift all the stuff out again.

That way, while the crew were busy filming in the conservatory, they could spend the whole morning arranging the props and then whip them all out again in the time it took Thora to change her costume. There would be little or no waiting around, and time was of the essence.

Perhaps somebody should have explained all this to the kitten. He must have spent hours in bed last night studying the script and now they were telling him that he was going to have to jump off the bed and walk out through the open door before he had even had a chance to come into the room.

It's a lot to ask of a kitten who hasn't done this sort of thing before and he panicked. First of all he jumped down off the counterpane and hid under the bed, and it took a whole posse of highly paid technicians to persuade him to come out.

They began by appealing to his better nature and then, when they discovered he didn't have one, they went under the bed after him, offering him handsome bribes, such as the corner of a ham sandwich, the top off a mayonnaise bottle and a kick up the backside. One of the crew told me that he'd had much the same experience while working with Dustin Hoffman.

Eventually the kitten got bored and wandered out. His handler grabbed him, sat him down and explained the situation in detail, and for the next five takes he jumped off the bed right on cue and just out of range of the camera.

Finally Thora managed to steer him in the right direction. He trotted down the length of the bed and hopped on to a coffee table. This wasn't in the script but we were prepared to let him wing it as long as he stayed in shot.

Then he disappeared under the bed once more and someone suggested that it might be kinder to have him put to sleep. Fortunately the camera was still running as his head emerged from under the counterpane. He paused momentarily, the frill of the bedspread framing his face so that he looked uncannily like the religious leader of some small Arab state. Then he was off across the carpet and out of the door.

It's not often you come across a kitten who has graduated from the method school of acting and this one had certainly been worth waiting for. By the time the furniture had been cleared and we were ready to shoot the scene before the one we had just shot, the kitten had worked out his motivation and had another surprise up his sleeve.

All he had to do was to appear in the open doorway, showing no sign whatsoever of the fact that his handler had just given him an almighty shove up the backside, and then march into the room.

This took a bit of doing and for the first few takes he stopped in his tracks and turned round and glared at her.

'Who the hell's the actor here, you or me?'

Alan Bell left the two of them to sort it out. He has an acid tongue when it comes to working with human beings but when it comes to working with kittens he's a pussy cat.

'Action.'

This time the kitten came mincing round the door frame, more John Inman than John Wayne. He took two strides into the room, sat down, stuck his right back leg high in the air and began to lick his bottom outrageously.

'Cut.'

I think with a following wind and a bit of luck he might make it. There's a lot of talent there. With the right management and the right parts, who knows?

Let's just hope that Rolf Harris is watching when the film comes out.

*   *   *

We should have known. There is an old saying, never work with children or animals, but as far as I am aware no one has ever issued a warning about working with pottery.

In an earlier scene Penny Downie had been called upon to examine a china figurine. It was one of my mother's treasured possessions and the script asked for Thora to stroke it fondly, her fingers tracing the buttons on the shepherd boy's jacket, before handing it over to Penny.

Penny doesn't know that the head is loose, my mother having stuck it back on with the help of a matchstick and a great blob of Bostik.

As Penny lifts the figure up close to her eyes the head falls off and lands on the carpet.

MOTHER: It does that.
DERIC: They all do that.

It seemed an easy enough scene to shoot. With actors of Thora and Penny's calibre, a quick rehearsal and one take. That should do it.

But nobody had thought to rehearse the shepherd boy. We had to have a close-up of his head as it fell to the floor, bounced about a bit, and then lay still on the patterned carpet.

It took ages. For the first few attempts the head went straight under the sideboard and then the crew began to experiment with variations of back spin and side spin.

'Stick your fingers in his eyeballs and give him a flip.'

With practice they got closer and closer, but

every time, as the head landed on the carpet, it would give one final death twitch and roll out of shot.

'Oh, sod it.'

You try it. Grab a camera, put your eye to the viewfinder, and then drop a shepherd boy's head on the carpet. Now try to keep track of it as it lands. See what I mean?

It seemed to take for ever. Eventually the head was hurled to the floor in disgust and it must have realized it had pushed them too far. This time it did a nosedive, got its right ear caught in the tufted pile and lay where it had landed, absolutely knackered.

'Cut.'

Today we had to do it all over again, an echo of the previous shot. As my mother had her final stroke she would sweep the shepherd boy from the table and the ornament's symbolic fall would save Thora the trouble of taking a swallow dive herself. She's way past doing that sort of thing and it was a very small rug.

However, this time the figurine had to fall intact, come apart on impact, and then both the head and the body had to finish up close enough to each other so that the two of them would stay in the frame.

I left the crew to it and went for a cup of tea. I was getting wiser by the minute. I knew that after the first few abortive attempts a collective mutter would run round the room.

'Who wrote this bloody stuff?'

No point in telling them that it looked easy enough on paper. Much better to keep out of the way for a while.

It was a long, long while. I popped back every now and then and peeped round the door. They were getting nearer. At least the head was staying in the same room as the body. Best go and have another cup of tea, they'd get the hang of it eventually.

They were still at it when I left. I had rung Aileen and arranged to take her out for a meal. By the time I got home it would be too late to start cooking and over the past few weeks we'd had enough takeaway pizzas to last us a lifetime.

I was going to say goodbye to everyone, but as I walked up the corridor towards the set I heard Dave, the camera operator, shouting 'Sod it!' and I changed my mind. It's not that I'm a coward, I just don't like any unpleasantness.

Aileen was all dressed up and waiting for me to check her make-up.

'Well?'

We decided to calm down the bronzer a little, from an extremely healthy-looking Pocahontas to a more acceptable Gwyneth Paltrow.

'That's better.'

'Sure?'

'You look lovely.'

And she did. Black suits her flame-coloured hair wonderfully and once she had swapped the navy blue tights for a pair that matched her outfit she looked like a million dollars.

'Thanks.'

'My pleasure.'

We had a meal at the Birkby Lodge Hotel and I can highly recommend it. Not only because the business has been lovingly fashioned out of a wonderful old hall, with fantastic food and friendly service, but also because Gary, one of the owners, is an accomplished underwater hockey player.

I know. That's what I thought when he first told me. I asked him if he'd ever tried underwater table tennis or maybe deep sea ballooning, but apparently underwater hockey is for real.

They call it Octopush and it's played all over the world. They use a specially weighted puck and wear face masks, extra large fins and snorkels. Gary's so keen he goes training three nights a week, in Dewsbury, Miles Platting and Batley.

'The goal is ten foot wide and we have two refs.'

Perhaps everybody knows about it except me. Aileen said she thought she had heard of it before, but then she is the woman who once took part in a blind archery contest at county level and was disqualified for planting all of her six arrows in her opponent's target, so what does she know?

She also thought that it was the year of the buffalo in the Chinese calendar. I was sure it was the year of the rat and Gary suggested it might just be the year of the snake.

I can't for the life of me remember why it was important at the time or how it had come up in the first place, but it had and it was and on the way home Aileen was trying to work it out backwards. She counted out the years on her fingers.

'Rabbit, Gerbil, Hamster.'

Or something like that. Then I had a brilliant idea. We had just passed a Chinese takeaway, so I turned the car round and went in to consult the experts.

A pretty young Chinese girl was on duty. She looked about fifteen so she was probably twice that and married with three kids.

'Excuse me. Sorry to bother you, but I'm trying to settle an argument. Could you tell me what year it is in the Chinese calendar?'

It was late and she smiled a tired smile that told me she had already dealt with more than enough plonkers for one night.

'You wan menu?'

'No, I just wondered if you could tell me what year it is.'

'Wha year?'

'Yes.'

The inscrutable smile became a little less scrutable.

'Wan moment plis.'

And with that she disappeared through a curtain of plastic strips and within seconds it sounded as though World War Three had just broken out in the kitchen. Voices were raised to fever pitch and at one point a man's face poked out between the plastic ribbons for a good long look at me. Then there came an unnerving silence, eventually broken by the girl's delicate steps as she hurried to put me out of my misery.

'Sorry keep you.'

'That's all right.'

'Cook says year is 1999.'

'Thank you very much.'

I thanked her again before I left. She said it was no problem and took the weight off her feet by leaning against the counter, waiting for the next prat to come prancing in through the door. To those in the trade it's all part and parcel of that troublesome hour between midnight and one in the morning.

Aileen asked me how I had got on.

'Apparently it's 1999.'

She was still laughing by the time we got home. Maybe it's the year of the hyena.

Chapter 15

Tigger was on guard by the laundry basket. She sits there for hours, waiting for the washing to begin. Then she insists on sniffing each and every garment before it is hurled deep into the bowels of the washing machine. It's a sort of feline quality control and she's very good at it.

She doesn't sniff them on the way out as she has become allergic to Sainsbury's meadow-fresh fabric conditioner. It makes her eyes water and she says she can't taste her tuna for days afterwards.

While Aileen held out a lace-trimmed pillow case for her to sample I took Kealen and Claire to the upstairs kitchen to show them the ropes. They had offered to look after the house for us while we were away for the weekend and I knew it would be in safe hands.

They would also be cat-sitting and here one or two doubts were poised at the back of my mind. So I tried to make everything crystal clear.

'Thermal and William like the tuna in water, but Tigger prefers the smaller tins in brine. They're the tins on the second shelf and she has smaller portions than the other two – if you give her too much she won't touch it. They all have their own likes and dislikes, and so I've marked the tins of cat food with an indelible pencil: with a "TH" for Thermal and a single "T" for Tigger. William's are marked with a "W".'

Kealen turned this information over in her mind.

'Let me see now. Thermal is the white one, isn't he?'

I wondered for a moment if I should mark each of the cats with an indelible pencil, but decided it would be going a little too far.

'The coley steaks go in the microwave for three minutes and then I let them stand for a while. The cats prefer them hot, but not too hot. So I blow on them and then I . . .'

At this point I glanced at Kealen and her eyes were telling me that once I was out of the way these blessed cats would eat whatever they were damn well given and be grateful for it.

To be on the safe side I had written out a long list of instructions, but there were one or two other things that I needed to point out, for instance that Thermal liked to sleep in my office and that I always left him a midnight snack on my desk, just to the right of the letter rack. Also that I changed their water daily – using the filter tap in the kitchen, not the ordinary tap.

The more I told them the dafter I felt, but I just couldn't stop myself. I mentioned in passing that Tigger slept on the fax machine in Aileen's office and asked them not to draw the curtains, otherwise she wouldn't be able to see the cars going past in the night, and that William liked to sleep in the kitchen, with his chin hanging over the edge of his feeding bowl, to save time in the morning.

I had filled two sheets of A4 paper with instructions and, as Kealen skimmed through them I watched her eyebrows going up and down like a pair of Venetian blinds.

'How long are you going for?'

'Just the weekend.'

She passed the sheets over to Claire. Claire has a way with words – she clubs people to death with them.

'What about their ballet lessons?'

We had only been driving for a couple of miles when Aileen pushed back her seat and settled down for a nap.

'Sorry about this.'

'That's all right.'

She can't cope with the bends as we drive through Flockton and on towards the M1. Because she can't see where we are going they tend to make her feel dizzy and sick.

'I'll just have five minutes.'

That means I've lost her for the next ninety miles. Once she has dropped off she could snooze her way through a multiple pile-up, but somehow she always manages to wake up just two miles short of the Leicester Forest East service station.

'What about a cup of coffee?'

No matter how hard I try I have never been able to smuggle her past that point and it's becoming an obsession with me. Once, for one glorious moment, I thought I had cracked it. I played one of the relaxation tapes she'd brought back with her from an aromatherapy session, all pan-pipes and water music, trickling streams and babbling brooks. Another half mile and I would have done it. But just before we reached Leicester Forest East she shot up and snapped back the seat.

'I need to go to the toilet.'

But today I was in with a chance. We were going to Stratford-upon-Avon which meant turning off the M1 and on to the M42, several miles short of Leicester Forest East. Let's see if she could sort that one out.

Did I tell you that Nick and Lisa now own a restaurant cruiser which they have moored on the Avon at Stratford? Well, I should have done. It's called *The Countess of Evesham* and it's rather like the Orient Express with water wings, all brass fittings and deep rich wood.

They have had it for almost three years now and they cruise up the river and back for three hours, lunchtime and evenings, serving up great food and wonderful scenery.

They've survived a complete lack of experience and several great dollops of really bad luck, not least the disastrous floods of Easter '97 when Nick spent twenty-four hours up to his waist in water, hanging on to his business for grim life.

Now they have it down to a fine art and I couldn't be more thrilled for them. I always wanted a son with a restaurant. What could be better than to be the father of mine host, sitting at a table in a quiet corner, being plied with fresh food and fine wines?

Aileen and I were there the week they opened and on the way down I told her that I would insist on paying my way. 'They can't afford to give free meals away, not at this stage.'

But knowing how generous my son is, I knew I was in for a stiff battle.

As we boarded I took him to one side.

'Look, Nick. I insist on paying.'

He escorted us both to our table.

'You bloody well will,' he told me. 'We can't be doing with any freeloaders, not at this stage.'

Aileen slept like a baby all the way there. Her nostrils quivered slightly as we whipped past a Little Chef on the A46, but it obviously didn't have the pulling power of the Leicester Forest East service station and so, after a bit of a sniff and a brief nostril-to-nostril consultation the two of them decided it wasn't worth waking her up. She slept on while they kept a lookout for something a little more enticing.

Just outside Stratford we passed a hitchhiker sitting on the grass verge. He had propped himself up against a tree and had a rough cardboard sign leaning against his knees.

KID.

He didn't look much of a kid to me and it was

a mile or so further on before it dawned on me that he must have been trying to get a lift to Kidderminster. I wouldn't have picked him up anyway. You can't nowadays, can you? The men might mug you and the women might claim to have been raped, although there's a better than even chance that it could be the other way around.

And to think of the chances I've taken in the past. A young man who I thought was ill – he certainly wasn't drunk – who I now realize was out of his mind on drugs. A teenage girl who wobbled along on stiletto heels that were high enough to have given her vertigo and who asked if she could sit in the back, where she promptly whipped off her mini-dress and pulled on a pair of jeans and a T-shirt that she had tucked away in a plastic bag.

'Me mam thinks I've been out with our Glenys.'

It's a shame. I've learned a lot from hitchhikers over the years, not least that if you lend them any money you never get it back. But I think even I would have made an exception for a girl I read about recently. She was standing on the hard shoulder of the A1, holding up a large well-printed sign.

I HAVE CHOCOLATE.

You couldn't say no, could you?

The boat was filling up nicely by the time we arrived and Aileen woke as fresh as a daisy.

'Did I snore?'

'No.'

'Good.'

She's never got over waking up from a deep sleep at a set of traffic lights in Droylsden one Sunday morning. A cyclist was leaning on the car door, staring in at her through the passenger window. I tapped her on the knee.

'What?'

'You had your mouth wide open and there's a kid looking in at you.'

Ever since then she's managed to organize her subconscious so that she sleeps with her mouth fashioned into a tight little rosebud. It looks ever so cute and I'm glad I didn't tell her that the kid had probably never even noticed.

She also had the top three buttons of her shirt undone and the view was truly stupendous. It had kept me going for the past fifty miles, but it was almost the end of the kid on the bike.

When we set off he wasn't concentrating and we took him with us. He was trapped between my car and the car on the inside lane, and as we both slowed down to let him out, he shot forward and was almost emasculated by a couple of wing mirrors. He didn't seem too upset about it at the time. I know it's a price I would willingly have paid myself.

The boat was full and the passengers seemed very happy and relaxed as we set off out of the marina. Everyone except me, that is. I was due to talk to the assembled company for forty minutes on the return trip and already I was beginning to panic.

An Evening with Deric Longden. That's what it said on the menu. Nick hadn't had the space to print the full title of the event.

An evening with Deric Longden, together with a full supporting cast of a thousand mallards, hundreds of swans and various other waterfowl, all of whom will be performing cute little tricks right outside your window as he talks.

That's not to mention the locks. I knew I was going to have difficulty in holding the guests' attention and I had anticipated the problems that might be presented by the ever-changing scenery, but hadn't thought for a moment about the locks.

I never have to worry about passing through locks when I am about to perform in some distant outpost of the Hilton Hotel chain. As long as the microphone is working properly and the audience are pointing in roughly the right direction, I can usually hold their attention, whatever else the gods might throw at me. But locks?

I had my first taste of what was in store for me in the canal lock, and that was before we had even hit the river. The huge gates were opened wide and in we sailed. There were only a few inches to spare on either side of the boat and half a dozen swans, who had decided to come along for the ride, wisely stayed up near the pointy bit at the front where they would have a little more room.

The water rushed out of the lock and the boat descended, or rather the walls seemed to grow to a great height all around us. The diners sat at their tables, staring out of the windows and sipping their first drink of the evening. Then a woman up near the pointy bit became rather agitated.

'The swans, they're going to be killed!'

Of course they were in no danger whatsoever. They knew what they were doing. They would just get swished about a bit as the swell of the water carried them this way and that.

'Let's have a spot of fun with 'em.'

'Go on then. You first.'

One of the smaller swans made a dash for it, the length of the boat, from pointy bit to blunt bit, flapping his wings in sheer terror.

'Please help me. I am but a poor swan about to be crushed to death.'

The others joined in the flurry of wing flapping, hardly daring to look.

'Help him. He can't swim.'

The swan put on an even better performance on his way back towards his mates, this time incorporating his famous broken-wing impression that always goes down so well with the tourists.

Then, once they had wound us up, they turned their elegant backs on us in disgust, bobbing up and down majestically until the gates were opened wide enough to let them out on to the river.

My heart fell and my confidence came out in

sympathy. How the hell do you compete with that? Aileen, of course, hadn't seen any of this.

'Let's go up front for a smoke.'

I joined her and did my best to paint a picture of the Avon for her as we cruised past the Royal Shakespeare Theatre and Holy Trinity Church.

How Mark manages to produce such wonderful food from his tiny galley I shall never know. He's an excellent chef and a qualified skipper and you don't get many of those to the pound. He's also a brave man. He had duck on the menu, so Nick was the skipper today, up on top, taking us safely through the locks and keeping a weather eye open for protest groups of marauding mallards.

After the starter and main course we moored up at Lullington for a while, so that we could stretch our legs while Nick turned the boat around.

Lisa introduced me to Scruffy, the local duck. The name is appropriate – she's a bag lady of a duck whose feathers don't try hard enough. They each have a mind of their own and seem to be in a state of continual dispute with one another.

Scruffy shuns the bright lights of Stratford, preferring the quiet of the countryside. But she likes a bit of company every now and then and as soon as the boat docked she jumped on board and settled herself above the hatch, quacking a raucous welcome to each and every diner as they made their way off the boat.

She went missing last year and then, much to Lisa's relief, just as they thought they would never see her again, she reappeared with a line of five little ducklings, one of whom Nick bravely saved from the attentions of an angry swan.

Scruffy has been eternally grateful ever since and she loves him dearly, which is at least something, since the swan also remembers him and lays siege to his private parts whenever she sets eyes on him.

The light began to fade as we set out on the return journey and my spirits started to rise. Maybe I would get away with it after all. Then the floodlights came on and lit the river banks with magic. Performing mallards waited until they were highlighted in a convenient cross-beam before sticking their heads in the water and their bums high in the air.

I got away with it, just. Mainly because the *Countess of Evesham* was full of decent people that night, who tried hard to pretend that there wasn't a swan peering in at them through the table window, that we weren't rising spectacularly in yet another lock and that there was nothing funny at all about that mallard who was mooning at us. He was just being rude and we shouldn't encourage him.

So I kept it short and then afterwards they were all able to relax. As we returned to the basin, with Holy Trinity Church gloriously flood-lit behind us, the birds were beginning to settle down for the night.

The ducks were plastered all along the river bank, miles of them lined up like shuttlecocks, six inches apart, and the latecomers were belting up and down the river looking for a space.

'I was there last night.'

'Bugger off.'

The swans had their own special island, dozens of them reclining graciously under the delicate umbrella of a weeping willow.

It was all so beautiful and I began to relax as well. I had got through the talk without being lynched and signed an awful lot of books afterwards. Liz, the head waitress, brought me a large whisky and suddenly I felt very hungry. I could really have enjoyed my dinner now.

We sat up talking most of the night and the next morning I woke with a thumping great headache and a small white cat fast asleep on my chest.

'Come on, Bart, give us a break.'

She's a strange cat. Nick found her wandering alone in Dubai and brought her home with him when he came back from the Emirates. He named her after Bart Simpson and then found out later that she was a girl. Her hobby is sitting on your chest and staring blankly straight in your face. It's quite unnerving, she never blinks. I picked her up and plonked her on the bedside rug.

'Stay there. I'm going for a shower.'

It's not possible for her to sit on your chest while you are having a shower so she just sits on the bath mat and stares, but not necessarily straight in your face.

'Stop staring, Bart. It's rude.'

If Dougal from *The Magic Roundabout* had been a cat, then Bart could have played him to perfection. She's a mobile mop of white silky fur with no discernible legs and no undercarriage, just two enormous black eyes that seem to see straight through you.

'I shan't tell you again.'

The bathroom door swung open and Lisa marched in.

'Is Bart bothering you?'

'She just keeps staring at me.'

Lisa bent and scooped up the cat from the bath mat.

'How many times have I told you? It's rude to stare.'

My beautiful daughter-in-law then draped herself all along the side of the bath.

'What do you fancy for breakfast?'

'A slice of toast will do.'

'We've got bacon and eggs.'

'No, it's all right. Just toast and coffee. Be fine.'

I soaped a bit here and I soaped a bit there and listened intently as Lisa told me how Bart had this very bad habit of wandering into the bathroom and embarrassing their friends. She tapped the cat on the nose.

'And it's very naughty.'

She stood up and made for the door, then turned with the cat staring back at me from over her shoulder.

'Right then, just toast and coffee?'

'That'll be lovely.'

'Come on then, Bart. Let's get cracking. And for goodness' sake, stop staring.'

She tapped the cat on the nose once more as they went out.

'I don't know where you get it from.'

I think I do.

Chapter 16

We were home by lunchtime and the cats were strung out in a line on the garden wall waiting for us. I told Aileen and she went over to say hello.

But they jumped down and marched up the drive ahead of us, ignoring us completely, dodging under our vain attempts at back-scratching and meeting our fond greetings with a stony glare.

Once inside Thermal went straight into the lounge and jumped on Kealen's knee, purring like an outboard motor, while Tigger gave a great big stretch and then curled herself up around Claire's feet. William marched stiffly into the kitchen and lay down on the floor with his chin resting miserably on the lip of his empty dish.

It's always the same if we leave them for more than a few hours.

'Stuff you, then.'

But Aileen isn't one for confrontations and she dug deep into her handbag. We had saved them a sausage each from the Little Chef on the way home and as William was the nearest he got first choice.

After a few moments the other two drifted in from the lounge, like Bisto kids sniffing the air, and then they began purring and rubbing round our legs. We stuck it out for as long as we could, but eventually our resistance crumbled. Still, it's nice to be wanted for yourself, isn't it?

I left Aileen to unpack and nipped over to Roundhay Park in Leeds. Earlier in the film schedule we had shot a scene in Greenhead Park, almost opposite my study window. Thora and Pete were seated on a bench and Thora was telling him that she wouldn't sell up her house and come to live with him.

MOTHER: I don't think so, love.
DERIC: Why not?
MOTHER: Oh, I could write you a list as long as your arm. I've done it, you know, four sisters – one after another. I finished up hating our Jessie.

The scene took a long time to set up and the light wasn't all that promising and so while they were hanging about I went off to help find a suitable site for the last shot of the day.

Rather than spend time going all the way over to Chesterfield, the props department had decided to bring Chesterfield over to Huddersfield and they had a huge sign in the back of the van.

Welcome to Chesterfield. A fine market town.

All we needed now was a straight stretch of road with a soft grass verge in which to plant the sign and within minutes we could shift Chesterfield forty-five miles up the M1 to Yorkshire.

It took longer than I thought it might, but eventually we found a spot that would fill the bill, on the Brighouse road into Huddersfield.

And it worked very well indeed. After the scene on the park bench was all done and dusted, Pete would come up here, drive down the road, see the sign, glance at his watch and look worried.

Unfortunately between the planting of the sign and the shooting of the scene a lot of other drivers would see the sign, glance at their watches and look worried.

They had just left Brighouse on their way to Huddersfield and now here they were, on the outskirts of Chesterfield. Maps would be pulled out of glove compartments and brows furrowed.

By the time I had got back to Greenhead Park the scene on the bench was already in the can and Aileen was none too happy. She had worked as my script associate all the way through the writing of the play and knew exactly what I had in mind for every line of every scene.

'Alan asked Thora to break down and cry at the end of the bread and butter line.'

And that wasn't what I had in mind at all.

The scene finishes with my mother springing a surprise on me.

MOTHER: No. I've made up my mind. I've found a place. One of them residential homes. You've got your own room and they look after you very well. And you can have as much bread and butter as you want.

They get up to leave.

DERIC: But there's no need . . .

MOTHER (*interrupting*): I can't remember what it was called offhand.

Deric goes back to the bench for her handbag.

DERIC: We're noted for our bread and butter, you know. They come from miles around.

Cut to interior of church hall.

On the surface the whole point of this scene, in fact of the whole play, is that each of them wants what is best for the other. The subtext, however, is a different matter altogether.

Deric has already spent fifteen years nursing his first wife until her death two years ago and now, just as he has begun to forge a whole new life for himself, it looks as though he is going to be saddled all over again, this time with the burden of caring for his mother at first hand.

Because he loves her dearly he is prepared to take her in and look after her and he continues to make this quite clear. But in his heart of hearts he hopes that she will insist on going into a residential home. It would take the pressure off him. After all he couldn't blame himself, could he? He had done his level best to persuade her. And it was what she wanted – wasn't it?

At the same time his mother knows full well that she can't live on her own for much longer, but she dreads the idea of giving up her independence and retiring into a communal home. Yet she is determined not to be a burden on her son and turns down his offer again and again. However, if he continues to push her for much longer – who knows?

It's a drama that is forever being played out in family after family, right across the land.

'You've got your own room and they look after you very well. And you can have as much bread and butter as you want.'

That last sentence, however daft it sounds, was meant to show how difficult it was for her to come up with anything really positive about the prospect of living in a home, and Deric realizes this. She was being brave in spite of everything and if she had broken down and cried at that moment, then the game would have been up and there is no way that he could have ever let it happen.

I know, because I was there.

But Alan Bell thought differently and he was very excited about the way Thora had responded to his direction.

'There won't be a dry eye in the house.'

'But I don't want them crying at that point.'

'Just wait until you see it.'

'It's going to make Deric look an absolute bastard.'

I had become quite used to referring to myself in the third person. I switched easily between Deric, Pete and Him.

'You'll love it when you see it.'

But I didn't. It was too much, too early, and fortunately the producers agreed with me and insisted that we do it all over again.

These things happen. Right at the end of the film Thora is in hospital, unable to communicate in any recognizable way, and Pete is sitting on the edge of her bed. Two young nurses, wonderfully played by Jennifer Luckcraft and Katisha Kenyon, are examining a photograph of my mother taken in Blackpool when she was a young woman. I had brought it in so that they could see that she was a real person with an interesting past and not just a bag of bones in a hospital bed.

NURSE 1: Who's this? Is it her daughter?

DERIC: No. It's my mother. When she was young.

NURSE 1: Really? I love that coat. They're in again, aren't they? I was looking at one just like it in Next not long ago. Couldn't afford it though.

Nurse No. 2 enters and glances over her colleague's shoulder.

NURSE 1: Mrs Longden. When she was young.

NURSE 2: Where was this taken?

DERIC: Blackp—

NURSE 1 (*interrupting*): It's Paris. There's that tower, look.

DERIC: She travelled a lot.

Mother has no idea what is going on. Nurse 2 sits on the edge of mother's bed and shows her the photograph.

DERIC: Modelling, you know.

Mother recognizes herself and is pleased. But she has no idea what is being said.

MOTHER: Dobbie.

NURSE 2: And you were a model in Paris?

MOTHER: Oh merrily.

NURSE 2: Wow. And did you mix with all them famous painters?

MOTHER (*nods seriously*): They came at it.

NURSE 2: Wow.

NURSE 1 (*taking the photo*): I love that coat.

She lays the photograph wistfully on the bed.

NURSE 1: Course it's how you wear 'em, isn't it?

As the two nurses talk, the camera closes in on the photograph.

Cut to interior of mother's new house.

The next scene takes us back, through the photograph, to the beginning of the play, to where Pete is sorting through my mother's meagre possessions. He takes out her purse, glances inside, and then produces a few coins.

'Didn't pay much, did it? Modelling.'

I had been very proud of this smooth transition from past to present, but Alan added a personal touch of genius to the scene. As the photograph was laid on the bed he closed in on Thora's hand and we watched it slowly move across the counterpane until it gently covered her son's.

In that one wonderful moment he had shown that although she had no idea of what was going on, she knew that something had changed and whatever it was, it was working in her favour.

It was absolutely right and it was Alan's doing, not mine. There wasn't a dry eye in the cutting room as we ran the scene over and over again.

We reshot the bench scene in Roundhay Park in Leeds to save time. The crew were filming nearby and given a handy tree, a stretch of grass and a wooden bench, one park can be made to look very much like another. This time Thora simply gave Pete a wistful smile at the end, a brave little smile that said everything that had to be said. No lace handkerchief and no tears.

To this day Alan and Thora still think they had the scene right first time. Pete didn't and I didn't and more importantly the producers didn't. You win some, you lose some, but I'm glad we won that one.

*   *   *

On the way home I had some shopping to do. Man the hunter, stalking the aisles of an out-of-town Tesco in search of fresh food.

They had grapefruit on offer, buy two and get one free. I bought twelve of them and completely filled my basket, so I swopped it for a trolley the size of an articulated lorry and the two of us ploughed our way across the store.

I added a huge bag of over-ripe pears for juicing with the grapefruit and congratulated myself on the fact that with my trolley already half full we now had enough fruit juice to see us through the next six days.

Cat litter was also on offer. It came in a thumping great gro-bag of a thing that was full of wood chippings and would take two men to lift it, always assuming, of course, that I was one of the two men.

'Let me give you a hand.'

He must have been eighty. It would now take three men to lift it, always assuming that he and I were two of the three men.

'No, it's all right, really. I can manage.'

'You take that end.'

I took that end and he took the other, but it was jammed against the shelf above and we had to shuffle a load of stuff sideways and then out into the aisle before we could even make a start.

We pushed the bag over on to its side, and then with knees and stomachs and thighs and at least one rather delicate crotch, we pulled it outwards and lifted it skywards and then dumped it in the trolley.

It landed on the grapefruit and pears with an ominous squelch and it occurred to me that I might have achieved a personal best. I was already juicing the fruit before I had even left the store. Then a trickle of wood chippings filtered out of a torn corner of the bag to add a distinctive, sort of crunchy quality to the sticky mixture. Mmm, yummy.

I couldn't think what had possessed me to buy such a monster, but never mind. It would see me out. I could top up the cats' litter trays for many years to come and never have to leave the house. And if there were any left over I could always insulate the loft.

The old man was leaning against the shelf, breathing heavily, but quietly content with the past few minutes of his life.

'Bet you can't guess how old I am?'

Oh I hate it when they say that. If you get it spot on they are sorely disappointed and if you go over the top they are downright offended.

'I'm afraid I'm not very good at that sort of thing.'

'Go on. See if you can guess?'

So while I was down on my knees, clearing the aisle and restacking the shelf, I had a guess, and then took away the number I first thought of.

'Sixty-seven.'

He beamed. He had glanced in the mirror before coming out that morning and could well understand my making such a mistake. He pushed himself away from the support of the shelf and stood there straight-backed, rocking gently on his own two feet.

'I'm eighty-six. And I've never had a terminal illness in my life.'

We met up again a few aisles further on. Man the hunter had now added a twelve-pack of Andrex toilet rolls to his trolley and was in danger of becoming seriously overloaded. If I had been out on the road the police would have asked me to pull over.

I hauled the trolley over towards the more exotic sauces and concentrates. Whenever I run out of ideas I select a jar at random and then read the recipe suggestion on the label. This time it was Patak's Original Balti Curry Paste and I was making a note that I now needed plain yoghurt, tomatoes and eight ounces of chicken, when I heard the old man grumbling down by the pasta sauce.

'Foreign muck.'

I edged my way towards him.

'What are you after?'

'HP sauce.'

It was up at the far end of the aisle. I had passed it as I turned sharp left at kitchen rolls and had noticed that they were clean out of the fruity variety. HP sauce, that is – not kitchen rolls.

'Come with me.'

So far he had only the one item in his basket.

'Did you know that's balsamic vinegar you've got there?'

'It's all right, isn't it? They didn't have any Sarson's.'

'I'm sure they have. Let's have a look.'

We strode on through the retail jungle, man the hunter and his ancient sidekick.

'Bet you can't guess how old I am?'

'Eighty-six.'

The disappointment flooded his face.

'You told me back there.'

'Oh that were you, were it?'

I sorted him out with the sauce and the vinegar.

'Right. That's me done. I'll stop off for some fish and chips on my way home.'

I still had the jar of balti paste in my hand and I checked the recipe to see if I needed anything else.

'My brother used to mess about with all that sort of stuff. He were a devil for that pasta rubbish.'

A tremor of revulsion ran the length of his spine.

'Have you ever tried it raw? It's horrible.'

I had actually. I once bit into one of those multi-coloured shell-shaped things. It was horrible.

'He swore by it. Healthy living and video exercises every morning and he only lived to be seventy-nine. That Jane Fonda's got a lot to answer for.'

The traffic on the M62 was at a standstill and the boredom on the way home was only slightly relieved by random thoughts of a seventy-nine-year-old man doing exercises to a Jane Fonda video.

The car stopped in front of me was suffering badly, with steam pouring out from under the bonnet. A young woman in her mid-twenties jumped out of the driver's seat and tried to delay the inevitable by pouring a small bottle of Malvern water into the radiator.

It wasn't really up to the task. This wasn't part of the job specification. When the bottle left the factory it had been led to believe that it was destined for better things than this. Smart dinner parties with the chattering classes, perhaps, or working hand in hand with some thrusting young executive, forever on the move. Anything but this – and as she poured the water into the radiator it went all weak at the knees and turned into steam at the very thought.

While the young woman obviously wasn't born to be a motor mechanic she had certainly been born to wear jeans and as she bent and puzzled over the radiator a dozen pairs of eyes watched her closely as the traffic began to move.

I was the first to offer help, but by the time she had settled herself in the driving seat there were about nine of us milling around. Four of them set about man-handling the car from fast lane to hard shoulder, while the rest of us held back the traffic to make sure her path was clear.

I pulled over in front of her while she used my mobile phone to ring the RAC and then, having made sure she was going to be all right, I gave her a wave and eased myself back into the traffic.

We would have done it for anyone, of course, but a good bum doesn't half speed things up.

The balti chicken was a great success, even though I say so myself. I had spiced up the stir-fry with flesh from the grapefruit, and the rice was light and fluffy. The naan breads were just about perfect, despite the fact that they looked more like a couple of heavily muscled odour-eaters.

I wish I could say the same for the cat litter. I had hauled it in from the car and dragged it down the cellar steps, leaving a tell-tale trail of wood chips behind me.

After I had swept it up I emptied each of the three personalized litter trays from upstairs, together with the all-comers' communal skip in the cellar, then washed them out and dried them off, refilling the whole bunch of them with the sweet-smelling wood chips.

I showed Thermal my handiwork. He had a good sniff and then backed off.

'*What the hell is it?*'

'They're natural wood chips.'

'*What was wrong with the other stuff?*'

'I thought we'd try something new.'

'*We?*'

'Well, you – and the others.'

But they wouldn't go anywhere near it. William jumped in his tray, had a quick nibble and then jumped out again.

'*Tastes funny.*'

'You're not supposed to eat it.'

Tigger took one look and ran out of the room. I couldn't think what could be wrong with it and I was just about to ask Aileen for a second opinion when the doorbell rang.

It was Mrs Cartwright from down the road. She took up most of the doorway and, backlit by the outside light, her shadow painted the mosaic tiled floor a solid black until eventually it ran out of puff and gave up, over by the combined boot-scraper and umbrella stand.

'I'm fed up to the teeth with them,' she blustered. 'They're forever in my garden. They camp there all afternoon like a bunch of boy scouts.'

I promised to do what I could – though I didn't know what I could do. Confiscate Thermal's Swiss-army knife perhaps, or threaten to readjust Little Chap's toggle if ever he set foot on Mrs Cartwright's lawn again?

'I can't keep them on a lead, you know.'

'Well, if I catch them at it once more, I'll set the dog on them.'

She stormed off down the path. I managed to keep a straight face until I had closed the door tight behind her and shut myself in the kitchen.

Set the dog on them. Have you seen her dog? No, of course you haven't – that's a silly question. It's one of those miniature white poodles. He's had his middle shaved like a belly dancer, wears a couple of pairs of sculpted plus-fours and has a stringy little tail with a great big furry bobble on the end.

I know it's not the dog's fault and I know that, despite being made to look a right Charlie by their owners, some of these poodles are very tough little devils indeed. I suppose they have to be, looking like that – but not this one.

His name is Buffy and he's still suffering nightmares from having once barked at Tigger in what he supposed to be an aggressive fashion.

'I beg your pardon. Are you addressing me by any chance?'

'Woof.'

He never knew what hit him. One minute he was poncing down the path like a Vivienne Westwood model and the next he was upside down in the catmint with a very sore nose and an ego to match.

It's the catmint of course that draws the cats over there, time after time. There are acres of the stuff, completely surrounding a huge sunken lawn that hosts a rustic bird table and an old stone birdbath and is at all times covered with the crumbs of at least four loaves of bread with the crusts cut off, for those older birds who have lost their teeth and are afraid of heights.

And it's the ideal spot for my four furry ornithologists to spend a sunny summer's afternoon. They lie on their backs, soaking up the sun and breathing in the catmint.

'Hey, man – this is the real stuff.'

Buffy glares fiercely from the other side of the French windows, his mouth opening and shutting silently as he yelps at them from behind the safety of the double glazing.

'Yeah. Roll me another joint. That dog over there's beginning to look damned attractive. Just love those cute little pyjamas.'

They rarely catch a bird. About once a year they come across an ancient sparrow, an old-age pensioner complete with Zimmer frame, who just happens to be studying a pamphlet on euthanasia at the time, but generally they are far too stoned on the catmint to give a damn about anything as active as hunting, shooting or fishing.

I wish I had trained them properly, but it's too late now. They are set in their ways, even when it comes to a change of cat litter.

I thought of Henry and wondered how Thermal might have turned out if I had been more forceful with him when he was a kitten.

'Who's Henry?'

'He's an actor. He has to sit still for ages and then jump over a settee when his trainer gives him a signal. Then he has to jump off a sink.'

'What's the money like?'

'Pretty good.'

'I could have done that.'

'No, you couldn't. You would have run off and hidden in the scenery. Anyway – you're the wrong colour.'

'That's racial discrimination, that is.'

'Don't be ridiculous.'

'I could have you for that.'

But I don't think I need to worry. One word

from me and the police will have him for being in possession of catmint with a street value of over twenty-three pence. They'd lock him up and throw away the key.

It's a tough business, show business. Even if you do sleep with the writer.

Chapter 17

Next morning the birds burst into song at six o'clock on the dot. They don't know that we put the clocks forward a couple of months ago and by rights I should have been enjoying an extra hour's unbroken sleep.

The trouble is that now I wake up at five o'clock on the dot and simply lie there in bed, waiting for them to get ready for their early morning session, while they clean their teeth, wash their hair and shave their legs or whatever.

Mind you, I don't think this pair have started shaving anything yet. They are just a couple of kids. The long one and the short one have disappeared, flown off to the exotic east, Cleethorpes or Skegness or somewhere, to enjoy the sun and the sand and the donkey rides.

The newcomers are at that awkward stage, teenagers who think that pretending to be bored out of their skulls is somehow interesting.

'*Coo . . . ool.*'

That's about all I get out of them and one day soon I'm going to climb up there on the roof and give them a good kick up the bum.

No more imaginative mobile phone impressions and no more selections from the best of light opera, just a monosyllabic rap that goes on and on until I feel like chewing the duvet.

'Hey man – like wow.'

I should have taken the short one under my wing when I had the chance and encouraged him to extend his repertoire. He could have had a crack at the fax machine and the whistling kettle. He might have made it on television.

'When I return, Matthew, I shall be – a smoke alarm.'

However, there is one bright spark on the horizon or, to be more accurate, on the other side of the third tall chimney pot on the main roof, the one with the twisted cowl that's neither use nor ornament. I haven't seen him yet but I imagine he wears glasses. He's not one for joining in and he waits until the others have packed away their gear and moved on to their next gig.

He is still only in the rehearsal stage, you understand, but he's working very hard on a more than passable rendition of 'You can't touch me, I'm part of the union'. We'll have to wait and see if he has the staying power, and then of course he's going to need that all-important lucky break. But with a little more practice and a decent backing group he could turn out to be the best of the bunch.

On our way over to the studio Aileen and I stopped off at Wakefield to see Goldie Armitage.

She's a much loved friend of ours, but nowadays it's not a trip that we take lightly.

She is in a nursing home, just as my mother was, and going through pretty much the same living hell that Thora would be painfully recreating in a church hall over in Leeds at this very moment.

It wasn't always this way. Goldie was once the life and soul of any party, with a voice like a gravel pit and an endless fund of risqué stories that would curl the hair of the uninitiated.

She also had an indomitable spirit and a laugh that could strip wallpaper at fifty yards. Goldie was the sort of person who brought something extra into the lives of all who knew her. And then she had a series of strokes.

'I wonder how she'll be today?'

It was a question hardly worth the asking. Nowadays she can do nothing for herself, she has to be fed and dressed and bathed and her conversation has been whittled down until it is little more than a grunt. We rarely understand what she is trying to say to us and I'm sure she has no idea what the hell we are on about.

And so we all smile at one another until it hurts and we are all so bloody jolly until Goldie, who has more sense than the rest of us, cries at the awfulness of it and then we are all so solemn. We adjust her pillow and massage her shoulders and tell her stories about her old friends. She doesn't understand, but we tell her anyway.

Last year Aileen and I drove her to a writers'

week at Swanwick, in Derbyshire. She had been going there for donkey's years and she would be among old friends who would remember her as the woman she was and not have to start from scratch.

And it all worked out very well. Carol, her carer, took the brunt of the load and we all pitched in, her wheelchair burning up the corridors and leaving scorch marks on the grass.

She tired towards the end of the week, but still her face lit up at seeing so many faces from the past and with the intelligent use of her eyebrows, the odd grunt here and there and an extremely dirty laugh, she attempted a strangled conversation with all and sundry.

One morning we were sitting quietly at a table in the Vinery, soaking up the sunshine and indulging in a death or glory battle with the writers Mary Wibberley and Jolante to see who would be first to complete the *Daily Telegraph* cryptic crossword.

This isn't fun, it's war, and it's been rumbling on for as long as I can remember. Once upon a time Goldie was one of the foot soldiers, but today she was merely an observer, her wheelchair pulled up close as she stared into the middle distance.

I have to read the clues out loud to Aileen and Mary does her best to irritate us.

'Oh, we got that one ages ago.'

Mary is very good at irritating people, she's been doing it for years, but she kept quiet as I read out the clue to thirteen across.

'. . . and it's six letters.'

Aileen worked at it in her head, Jolante scribbled something in the margin of the newspaper and I tried to look intelligent. And then from Goldie's wheelchair there came a deep robotic growl.

'En-ig-ma.'

I went as cold as ice. Mary took it in her stride.

'You were quick there, Goldie. Beat the lot of us.'

I shall never forget the look of joy on Goldie's face that morning. For one moment she had cut through the fog. She shuffled in her chair and bent over towards us, listening intently as I read out clue after clue. We held some of the answers back in the hope that she might double her score, but that was it for the day.

I took her back to the nursing home the next morning. She was tiring fast and the novelty was wearing off. As we zoomed up the M1 the effort of trying to shuffle words into some sort of order was too much for her and as a result I found my own sentences getting shorter and shorter until they almost vanished into thin air.

'Meadowhall.'

'Mmmm.'

I think she was glad to see the back of me. To be tucked up in her own bed and safe in her own mind where she wouldn't have to make the effort.

'En-ig-ma.'

Was it a one-off or did she understand more

than we ever realized? And if so, had I ever discussed anything in her presence that would have hurt her? I tried not to think of that. God, I hope it never happens to me.

Aileen and I were both wrapped up in our own separate worlds as we drove away from the nursing home. She had known Goldie for a lot longer than I had and now she closed her eyes and dipped into the past.

'You all right?'

'Yes.'

I seem to have spent half my life moping around nursing homes and hospitals. It's like being on a roller coaster that is barely moving. The highs and lows come around at their own pace, the lows in the shape of misery, pain and humiliation; the highs in a sort of glory that makes life worth living.

I couldn't close my eyes – I was driving – but a couple of snapshots from the past came to life and mingled with the brake lights and the broken exhaust pipe of the car in front.

An aristocratic old lady sits up in bed, having her nails painted by a delightful young nurse who admires the birthday cards on her locker.

'Do you know how old you are today?'

The old lady considers the question for some time.

'I had it written down somewhere, but I've lost it. I must be all of seventy-six?'

The nurse dips a small brush into a bottle of

clear varnish and gently takes hold of the woman's thin hand.

'You're a hundred and two.'

A warm smile crosses the old lady's face and she looks down on the pert little pony tail that is bobbing about under her nose.

'Don't be ridiculous, my child. Nobody lives to that age.'

Another time, another nurse – this one barely twenty. She stuffs a bedpan under the sheets and then lifts an old woman whose body seems to consist entirely of small bones sticking out through a covering of grey parchment.

'There you are, Doris.'

The woman's nightdress is open to the waist, exposing a thin flat breast straight out of the *National Geographic* magazine. I look away so as not to embarrass her, but she doesn't seem to know I am there. The nurse glances at her watch.

'You sit still, Doris. I won't be a minute.'

My eyes are drawn to her once more. She sits high on the bedpan, her back surprisingly straight as she stares after the retreating nurse. Then she murmurs softly to nobody in particular.

'My name is Mrs Rowley.'

I found the church hall by the usual method of driving around the outskirts of Leeds several times and then getting lucky. The television vans were parked on the street outside, and so I slipped into the small space between them and then slipped out again when they told me to bugger off.

One of the crew took pity on me and guided me to a spot right outside the front door where Aileen and I waited in a rather dismal porch for a break in the shooting.

This was a small, intimate film. The daily call sheet detailed the actors required for each scene. Pete and Thora – Pete and Gloria – Pete, Thora and Man – Pete, Thora, Margaret and Stunt Kitten.

More often than not the scenes would be two-handers, but today was the nearest thing we ever got to a remake of *Ben Hur*.

Along with Dame Thora we had Ruth Holden as Nellie Elliot and Dinah Handley as the Do-Gooder, together with a dozen whist-playing extras and a thousand Marks and Spencer's prawn and mayonnaise sandwiches playing themselves.

Or not as it turned out. This was a Granada/Yorkshire television production and at the time of shooting Marks and Spencer were suing Granada because of comments that had been made in a recent documentary, and there was no way Granada were going to give them free advertising time for their prawn and mayonnaise sandwiches. The props department had been busy producing a whole stack of fake labels that were to be stuck on to the Marks and Spencer packets, transforming them at a stroke into prawn and mayonnaise sandwiches made by the hitherto unknown firm of Field and Dunster.

The sandwiches took the switch in their stride and behaved like real professionals, glad of the chance to do a bit of proper acting for a change, but the packets weren't quite so versatile and remained absolute little sods to open.

'Cut.'

All over the room the whist players were struggling with their triangles of plastic and cellophane, ripping the things to pieces, while at the main table Dinah Handley was having the devil's own job in her attempt to release Dame Thora's prawn sandwich into the wild.

Scouts were despatched to buy more supplies until there wasn't a prawn and mayonnaise sandwich left in the whole of Leeds and the Field and Dunster labels were running out fast.

'Action.'

'Damn it.'

'Cut.'

It wasn't until someone had the bright idea of easing back the little tags in advance that the scene began to take some sort of shape.

NELLIE (*to Do-Gooder*): They usually make 'em themselves, you know.

DO-GOODER: Maybe *they* do – but I had my Red Cross this morning and then there's the St John's Ambulance as soon as I've finished here. They're not cheap, you know.

MOTHER (*to Nellie*): What did she say they were?

DO-GOODER (*pouring tea*): They're prawn and mayonnaise.

MOTHER (*to Nellie*): You don't put prawns in a sandwich.

DO-GOODER: Field and Dunster do. They're very nice. Try it.

Deric's mother takes a tentative bite.

MOTHER: I've never been very keen on seafood myself. Apart from fish.

NELLIE: You eat crab. And we had that lobster in Blackpool.

MOTHER: And those.

NELLIE: You like cockles and mussels.

MOTHER: I like shrimps as well.

NELLIE: There you are then.

Deric's mother takes another bite, a more confident bite this time.

MOTHER (*to Do-Gooder*): It's very nice. Thank you. (*Confidentially*) It's just seafood I'm not so fond of.

Thora's timing of that last line was absolutely brilliant and I could sense the assembled company trying hard not to applaud.

'Cut.'

And then they applauded. All through the filming of the play Thora's timing had been an object lesson to any aspiring actor. We should have invited all the drama schools and charged admission.

'Action.'

This time Thora had to change the mood entirely. She took another bite of her sandwich, then reached out for her cup of tea. The cup swung loosely in her grip for a moment before slipping from her grasp. The camera closed in as she suffered her second stroke – in the background the extras looked on in horror.

MOTHER (*barely audible and unclear*): Jessie. (*Long pause*) Jessie.

This time there was no applause. It was far too real. This was something I had written, but had never witnessed. The details of my mother's stroke had come to me second hand and now it was happening before my eyes.

A couple of years ago Thora's husband Scotty had suffered the same fate while Thora was in another room and I wondered how she felt at this moment.

'Cut.'

She was helped into her wheelchair and brought over to where Aileen and I were propped against a table, surrounded by a regular army of prawn and mayonnaise sandwiches. She leaned over and pinched one, took a bite and then studied my face at close quarters.

'It hurts, doesn't it, love?'

After a pint in a local pub with Pete Postlethwaite, Aileen and I went over to Roundhay Park for a series of newspaper interviews with a band of journalists who had come all this way to talk to Thora and Pete, but who were prepared to put up with us in the meantime.

That afternoon we would be filming in a chemist's shop nearby and so a small corner of the park had been turned into what looked like a mobile holiday camp, with personal caravans for each of the leading actors, specialist trucks for make-up and wardrobe, and most essential of all, a couple of portable toilets with roller towels that actually worked.

There was a huge chuck wagon providing exceptionally good food in the circumstances and a single-decker bus cum dining car in which Aileen and I had been parked up at the far end.

I am not very good at showing off. I have always believed that the only compliments worth having are those that come from someone else, but today I was determined to let the journalists know that *Diana's Story* had recently been voted the most popular serial ever in the fifty-year history of the BBC's *Woman's Hour*. I was proud of the award. I had written the book and read the serial myself and so why not?

A journalist from a national paper plonked herself down on the other side of the table. She took out her shorthand notebook and I took out my own trumpet and prepared to blow it.

'How's Thermal?'

'He's fine.'

'And Tigger?'

'She's very well.'

'I was very upset when Arthur died.'

'Yes, it was very sad.'

I put away my trumpet for the time being. From the other tables I could hear Penny talking about her previous work at the National Theatre. Pete was saying nice things about my script and Thora was starting from scratch with tales of her early days in provincial rep. And here was I – talking about my cats.

We discussed Frink's untimely death, which brought tears to the journalist's eyes, and then we moved on to the time when Thermal had been stoned out of his mind on home-made damson wine.

It was all very pleasant, but of course not a word would appear in the newspapers and I was determined to take the next interview by the scruff of the neck and point it in the right direction.

At a signal from the publicity people the journalists played musical chairs and this time we found ourselves in the company of the sort of man who wasn't about to take prisoners. He was tough and hard and jaded from years of show business interviews. He clicked a button on his portable tape recorder and leaned across the table, this time directing his questions at Aileen.

'How's Thermal?'

'He's fine.'

'And Tigger?'

'She's very well, thank you.'

We did have our moment of glory later on. In *Wide-Eyed and Legless* Aileen and I had walk-on parts as the guest speakers at a literary luncheon. The audience would have needed a pair of binoculars to spot us as we climbed on to a stage in the far distance, but as far as we are concerned it was the highlight of the film.

But there would be no chance of us doing a Hitchcock this time around. The scenes were too tight and too intimate and the last scene of all was being acted out right now, in the chemist's shop.

I peeped in through the window and watched as Pete and Malcolm Hebden ran through the two-handed exchange. There was hardly room enough to swing a packet of soluble aspirins and yet, as the two men eased themselves into the scene, all the necessary paraphernalia seemed to recede and then disappear.

The camera, the lights and the overhead microphone faded into the background, together with the spaghetti junction of wires and cables strewn across the floor. There is something sublime about watching two such excellent actors turn a couple of pages of script into a moment of real life.

And then it was all over. Thirty-one days of intensive graft and that was that. The film would now be edited and then join the rest of us in the long wait for transmission.

Out on the pavement Aileen and I had a smoke and a chat with Malcolm Hebden, who seemed like an old friend since he appeared in our kitchen several times a week, playing the part of Norris in *Coronation Street*.

David Whiteley, the sound recordist, had his box of tricks parked by the shop window as he checked through his script.

'Just the two answerphone voices to record back at the studio and we're finished.'

He glanced across at us.

'Why don't we get Deric and Aileen to do them while we're all set up?'

If I'd known I was to play the part of Colin on the answerphone I would have given him a damn sight more than four lines. I would have built the whole play around him. In every scene the phone would have rung at a crucial moment and there would have been Colin on the answerphone, a man of mystery.

And I certainly wouldn't have given Aileen twice as many lines as I had. Just for a moment I wondered if we might switch parts; but then common sense prevailed and after a quick rehearsal I had to admit that Aileen had been born to play the part of Mrs Bushell from the Guide Dogs.

We had about five minutes to rehearse. I could read from the script but of course Aileen had to learn every word off by heart, so we sat in the car while I read her part out loud to her in my best Mrs Bushell voice.

'Do it properly.'

'OK.'

She had it off pat in no time at all and we were ushered into the chemist's shop to put the final touches to the film. I cleared my throat and thought of the microphone as my friend.

'Aileen – it's Colin here . . .'

'Try it again.'

'Aileen – it's . . .'

'And once more.'

All in all I thought five takes was pretty good going. Colin is quite a complex character, even if he is only ringing Aileen to tell her that a spare part for her computer has now arrived, and I hope that my voice held the subtle hint of an unhappy childhood and a fairly healthy sex drive.

Aileen carried off her Mrs Bushell in a single take.

'That was brilliant, Aileen.'

Some you win and some you lose, but if I have my way that director will never work again.

Back at the studio they gave a small drinks party so that we could all say goodbye to one another. Thora had had the afternoon off and arrived looking every inch a Dame of the British Empire.

Aileen and I kept close to executive producer Keith Richardson. As usual he was smoking like a chimney and we were working on the theory that nobody was going to ask the boss if he would mind putting it out.

Dorothy Arnold was already there when we arrived. Without her wig and matching ensemble she looked nothing at all like the woman who had been Thora's double for the past thirty-one days. She had a photo album under her arm and she came across and shared it with us. The pictures traced her career in the music hall from way back and showed her wearing a series of rather racy frocks or, more often than not, nothing more than a fan and a couple of tassels. On some she was without the tassels and hadn't quite been quick enough with the fan.

After a while she sat down with Thora and together they thumbed through the album. I wondered what Thora would make of it. She is known for her dislike of bad language and sex on television and remembered fondly as the presenter of *Songs of Praise*.

Page after page went slowly by and then finally Thora handed the album back.

'Well there's one thing certain, love, they are never going to ask me to double for you.'

Wish I had written that.

Chapter 18

The film was due to be televised in October and Transworld had re-jacketed the paperback of *Lost for Words* to coincide with the transmission date.

When the book was first published the cover sported a photograph of me and my mother, which was then replaced by one of Jim Broadbent and Thora Hird when *Wide-Eyed and Legless* was televised.

Now the cover took on yet another life with a photograph of Pete and Thora sitting at my mother's kitchen table. By now the poor book must have been as confused as those Marks and Spencer's prawn and mayonnaise sandwiches over in Leeds.

Then the powers that be decided to hold the film back until Christmas, hoping for a larger audience, and bookshop customers all over the country must have been as confused as the sandwiches and the book itself when they read that *Lost for Words* was now a major television film.

'Don't ever remember seeing that.'

It turned out to be rather a smart move. We

sold out long before Christmas and the book had to be reprinted.

Meantime back in Huddersfield life continued much as before. Aileen had been buying suitable Christmas presents throughout the year and now she couldn't remember where on earth she had put them. Apparently many of these suitable presents were from me to her, so I wasn't allowed to help her look for them.

'Surely if I'm supposed to have bought them for you, then it won't matter if I know what they are?'

'It'll spoil the surprise.'

I knew there was something wrong with that but I couldn't for the life of me think what it was, so she put my mind at rest.

'It'll be more fun if you find out on the day.'

Of course. That was it. Sometimes I'm a bit slow on the uptake.

At least I'm allowed to do all the Christmas shopping, write over three hundred Christmas cards and put up all the decorations, so don't anybody go thinking I'm henpecked.

In fact I am really rather well organized these days and I had it all done and dusted at least ten days before Christmas. All, that is, except for a few bits and pieces in the dining room, a touch of tinsel here, a little holly there, and I was sorting them out on my hands and knees when Thermal came running into the room.

'*Little Chap's back.*'

'Where is he?'

'He's unconscious in the cellar.'

I followed Thermal down the cellar steps and wondered what sort of condition our occasional cat would be in this time. You can only go on burning the candle at both ends for so long and by now Little Chap must have just about the shortest wick in Huddersfield.

At least he had made it as far as his basket. His front end was all tucked up neatly, his head resting on the cheap tartan car rug that the cats had taken over after it had shrunk in the wash and almost disappeared.

But his rear end hadn't been quite so lucky. It looked as though someone had thrown him at the basket from a great distance and missed, and his haunches sprawled half in and half out, his two hind legs spreadeagled across the central heating boiler.

For the umpteenth time my heart fell and I wondered if he had been in some sort of accident, but as I tried to tuck his rear end gently into the basket he started, then quickly scrambled to his feet and threw back his head.

'Fooo-oood.'

He'd been gone for quite a while and we were happy to have him back again. After he had downed a couple of saucers full of nourishing Whiskas and another half-full of semi-skimmed milk, he joined me among the baubles on the dining-room floor and immediately took a large chunk out of Frosty the Snowman's head.

'That wasn't very nice.'

Frosty and I have been together now for some thirty-five years and I had promised him that this year he could stand under the flowering cactus in the window and be a special feature.

But he didn't look quite the same now. He tried to smile but it doesn't come easily when a cat has just bitten off half your face, and I could tell that he was disappointed. So I still stuck him under the cactus, but turned him round with his back to us so that he was staring out of the window.

'Now we can see your sack properly.'

He didn't say anything, but he's not daft.

Little Chap's social skills still require a lot of work. He gave a passing thump to a recently retired fairy and then went and sat under the dining table and began to scratch all those parts that even a Russian gymnast would have had trouble in reaching.

Whenever he returns from one of his journeys into the unknown he brings with him a whole lorryload of fleas and he seems quite happy to have them aboard.

'*A flea isn't just for Christmas, you know – it's for life.*'

The others sit and stare in amazement as he bites and scratches, furks and gouges. This is his hobby, this is what he is good at, and over the years he has turned himself into a master craftsman.

Nevertheless I can't be doing with it under my dining table and I was just about to sort him out when Aileen appeared wearing her satin robe and a half-baked expression.

'Little Chap's back,' I told her.

'I know. I could hear him scratching. He woke me up.'

I made her a cup of tea and poured a drop in a saucer for Thermal. He took a delicate sip and then frowned.

'You've forgotten the sweetener.'

Aileen took a sip from her cup and grimaced.

'I know. I've forgotten the sweetener.'

But I hadn't forgotten about Little Chap. I usually manage to get hold of him as soon as he thumps in through the cat flap. He's the only one who will have anything to do with the flea powder. The others run a mile. Thermal even takes off first thing every morning, the minute I pick up a can of deodorant. They have been spoilt rotten. They prefer to go private, demanding either a little drop of Tiguvon on the back of the neck or a small dash of Program as part of a calorie-controlled diet.

Little Chap isn't as fussy, mainly because he has no idea what is going on and his ignorance has enabled me to clear out most of the cans of old flea powder from the back of the cupboard. If I brush him for a moment or two he disappears into a world of his own – his mouth falls wide open and his body relaxes to such an extent that at any moment I almost expect one of his legs to drop off.

At this point I reach out for the can of flea powder and the other cats take cover behind the sideboard, doing their best to warn him of the oncoming danger.

'Look out! He's behind you.'

But a little scrub at the base of his tail will make sure that Little Chap stays safely tucked away in Never-Never Land and before long I can hear the fleas coughing and spluttering.

'My chest feels just like sandpaper.'

'There's a lot of it going about.'

But this time the hole in the canister was all bunged up and so I had to improvise. I massaged Little Chap with my knee while I poked the hole free with the thin wire stalk of a Christmas tree bauble. It took a bit of doing but in the end it worked a treat, so I gave him a practice squirt and then sat back on my heels to admire my handiwork.

He had a broad white line right down the length of his back and his tail. One moment I was dealing with an affectionate, albeit flea-ridden, moggie and the next I was the proud owner of a small but beautifully marked skunk.

He couldn't believe it. He stood up, took one look at himself and sat down again.

'What on earth have you done?'

Well, how can you explain to a cat that you have just sprayed him with a can full of artificial snow?

I couldn't believe I could have been so stupid. I made a grab for him so that I could put matters right, but he was off down the cellar and out through the cat flap before you could say Jack Frost.

It didn't take long to find him. We don't have all that many skunks in Huddersfield and Sarah, my neighbour, was surprised to see one sitting on her kitchen window sill.

The good thing about Little Chap is that he doesn't bear a grudge and I'm sure he will forgive me eventually. I'm not so sure about the small herd of albino fleas who were unfortunately caught in the crossfire.

Sarah pushed him under the hedge to me and I caught him on my side as he came up for air. Sarah peered through the hedge to see if all was well.

'Have you got him?'

I hoisted Little Chap up on my shoulder. He looked ridiculous.

'Yes, thank you.'

'Good. I'll go and get on with my Christmas decorations. Have you finished yours yet?'

'Not quite,' I told her. 'But I've made a start.'

That afternoon I went out to buy a copy of the *Radio Times*. Ever since I can remember the Christmas double issue has been one of the highlights of the festive season. As a teenager I would pounce on it the moment it dropped through the letter box and work out a programme of things not to be missed.

This time I bought the *TV Times* as well and took them both for a cup of coffee and a toasted teacake.

I think they enjoyed it, but for me it was something of a disappointment. I went straight to 23 December, hoping to see photographs of Thora and Pete and maybe a few kind words, but we weren't even listed.

I shuffled through the other thirteen days to see if we had been moved sideways for some reason, but nowhere was there any mention of *Lost for Words*.

The coffee had gone cold and the toasted tea-cake had lost all confidence in itself and become listless and morose. Even the two magazines seemed to suspect there was something wrong, so I tried to cheer them up.

'Must be some good reason for it, I suppose.'

But my heart wasn't in it. I had added a note to all my Christmas cards – '*Lost for Words*, 23rd Dec. ITV' – and now I looked like an idiot.

I took the two magazines home with me, but left the coffee and the teacake sitting miserably on the restaurant table. I could feel their eyes boring into the back of my neck as I pushed open the door, but thought it best not to look round.

The 'good reason' came later that afternoon in a phone call from Keith Richardson and it was quickly followed by a call from Sally, who wanted to know what on earth had happened.

'You're not listed anywhere.'

'No, I know. The people down at the network found that we would have been scheduled right opposite Dame Judi Dench and Billy Connolly in *Mrs Brown* on BBC1, so now we're going out on January the third.'

For the next half hour or so we had one of those talks. You know the sort – one of those talks when somebody who loves you very much takes logic by the scruff of the neck, bends it in half, and then goes searching for all the reasons why what has just happened is really for the best.

'Lots of people would be going out to parties that night.'

'That's true.'

'By the third of January they'll have had enough and they'll want to put their feet up and stay in and watch television.'

'Yes, that's very true.'

'I think it's brilliant news really.'

What was really brilliant was having a daughter like Sally, especially when she told me about her Christmas present for Steve. She'd wanted it to be a big surprise.

'So I bought him a load of weightlifting equipment. One of those bars with a huge selection of weights that you screw on either end. I wanted it to be a big surprise, so I asked them if they would mind gift-wrapping it for me so that he wouldn't know what it was and they said they would be delighted to and it took them ages and they made a really good job of it. But then I tried to pick it up and I couldn't even lift it off the counter and I realized that there was no way I was going to get it home on the bus.'

So Steve had to go into Brighton and fetch it himself. She's a lovely girl. She's a lot like me.

*　　*　　*

Christmas was going to be a quiet affair. Aileen's daughter Annie was coming up from London with her brother David and we were going to laze about and do as little as possible.

Our doctor, Helen, had invited us to one of her wonderful parties that go on and on for ever and we were really looking forward to that – until her husband John rang and told us it was off.

'Is there anything wrong?'

'No. We just can't be bothered.'

I think that's wonderful. I would have invented some complicated story that involved Aileen having contracted a mysterious and highly contagious disease that required her to lie in a darkened room over the Christmas period.

I would be ever so sorry and hope that it hadn't screwed up everyone's plans over the festive season and Aileen would be furious with me and then have to spend the next couple of months explaining her miraculous recovery to all and sundry.

But John and Helen just couldn't be bothered and everyone understood. I have a lot to learn.

As 3 January crept ever closer a number of previews began to appear in the national newspapers. Without exception they were encouraging to say the least.

. . . *but you will have to wait until after Christmas for what is arguably the pick of the crop on any* channel, ITV's Lost for Words. *The schedulers ummed and aahed about where to put this little gem, and eventually settled for a post-hangover slot, January 3.* That was the *Sunday Times.*

I didn't let it go to my head of course. I merely glanced at the article and then put it aside, then picked it up and merely glanced at it once more while I was in the bath and then again later, sitting on the toilet. I merely glanced at it as I washed the pots, before taking the paper out with me into the garden, spreading it out on the paving stones so that I could glance at it every now and then as I weeded the rockery.

Nick rang a little later.

'Have you seen that wonderful piece in the *Sunday Times?*'

'I glanced at it.'

I have lost count of the number of writers, directors and actors who say that they never ever read their reviews, and just maybe, tucked away among that formidable army, there might be the odd one or two who are actually telling the truth.

But reviews matter to me. I want people to like what I have done, and I was increasingly delighted as both the tabloids and the broadsheets joined together in singing our praises, giving rave reviews to Dame Thora and Pete.

I already had a video of the film, but watching your work go out live always adds an extra edge. So on 3 January we settled down early with

Coronation Street and mourned the passing of Alf Roberts along with eighteen million other like-minded souls.

We put Chris Tarrant on mute for half an hour, which I always think is for the best, and worked our way through the *Daily Telegraph* crossword until he had stopped being silly and gone home.

For once I wouldn't have to talk Aileen through the scenery, the action and the quiet bits, she knew it backwards. So we snuggled up on the settee in her study and for the first time in my life I sat and enjoyed the adverts.

No one had told me that the play was to be sponsored by HSBC Midland Bank in their Great British Drama series. My mind went back to all those Friday mornings long ago, when I would hang around the front door of their Chesterfield branch, waiting to cash a cheque to pay the wages, trying to spot a cashier who didn't know me and who would be less likely to say that the manager would like a word with me in his office.

The Midland were very patient with me. They could have pulled the rug out from underneath my feet at any time, but they gave me a lot of rope and eventually we finished up all square. Then a few years ago they invited Aileen and me to cut a ribbon and declare open the refurbished branch of the Midland Bank up here in Marsh, and now here they were providing the wrap-around commercial for the play. It's what they call a happy ending.

Which is hardly what we had in the play. As it drew to an end I could barely see the screen for tears. Thora and my mother have become inextricably linked in my mind over the past few years, through two films and many happy times together, and as her hand moved slowly across the bedspread and covered Pete's it was as though I was losing both of them at once.

Sometimes when I think of my mother I see her with Thora's face and have to fish out some old photographs, and even then it's hard to separate the two. They have almost merged and become one. Not long ago I found a note I made many years ago after calling in to see my mother, just after my father had died.

She was sorting through some leaflets from the DHSS.

'I'm a single parent now.'

Her eyes lit up at the thought of an extra allowance.

'I don't think they'll wear it, Mum.'

'You don't?'

'No. Not when your son is in his early forties and married with two kids.'

As I ran the moment over in my mind I could see my mother's lovely and ever hopeful face, and yet the words came through loud and clear in Dame Thora's voice.

Or was it the other way around? I don't suppose it matters. The two of them are locked together in my memory for ever and they couldn't be in better company.

The next morning I bought all the papers and read the reviews and we couldn't have done a better job if we had written them ourselves. Thora and Pete received a whole bunch of rave notices and there was even the odd pat on the back for the writer. Teletext carried seven pages of viewers' comments, all of them singing our praises. And then the news came through that we had captured an audience of over twelve million and I sat down and tried to imagine what twelve million people would look like if they were all bundled together in one place. The best I could do was to close my eyes and imagine Wembley Stadium on Cup Final day, and then multiply it by one hundred and sixty.

Of course there's always one, and this time it was Robert Hanks in the *Independent*. He didn't like the play at all and he ended his review with a rather smart-arsed comment that must have seemed awfully clever at the time.

'. . . *this was as cheerful and life-enhancing as rouge on a corpse's cheeks.*'

A little over the top, I thought, and just a mite clumsy. I would have written, '. . . *as rouge on the cheeks of a corpse.*'

But then he was probably in a hurry to meet a deadline at the time and heaven forbid that anyone should think I can't take a bit of criticism. If he didn't like the play then he had every right to pan it. That's what he is paid for and if ever we should meet I shall tell him so. I shall give him a broad smile and shake him by the hand and then bring my right knee up sharply into his groin.

Postscript

Whenever I have a bout of the flu my mind drifts sideways into a fantasy world. My son-in-law Steve has the same problem. He worries about broccoli.

I worried about the bedside rug. It seemed frightened. All alone and vulnerable on the bedroom floor, it trembled slightly, its pile standing on end, and so I rolled it up and hid it in the bottom of the wardrobe where it would be safe from its many predators, any of whom can turn the life of a bedside rug into a living nightmare.

As I struggled back between the damp sheets my head swam and my body quickly heated itself back up to the two hundred degrees centigrade at which I had simmered gently for the past few days.

My chest pounded, as did the small white cat who happened to be sitting on it at the time.

'Stop it, Thermal.'

Later Aileen brought me a cup of tea and the evening paper, then settled herself on the side of the bed.

'I think you're sitting on Tigger, love.'

'Sorry.'

A rather flat tortoiseshell cat crawled up from between the sheets and laid her head on the pillow beside me.

'Are you all right?'

'Just give me a minute.'

Aileen stroked her better.

'Are they all here?'

'Three of them. Thermal's asleep on my chest and William is in charge of my genitalia.'

But as soon as Aileen left the room all three of them followed her. It was time for their dinner and dinner can be a most exciting meal when Aileen is in charge. She is never quite sure which tin she is opening and her offerings over the years have ranged from Whiskas tuna and chicken to Del Monte's pineapple chunks in syrup.

I sat up and drank my tea, thumbing through the *Huddersfield Examiner* until I found the Denis Kilcommons column. He's a good man, is Denis. Once wrote a cracking thriller called *The Dark Apostle* and today he was writing about me.

Apparently the video of *Lost for Words* had just been released. Denis knew all about it, which is more than I did. I picked up the phone and rang Nick in Stratford.

After a long conversation with a woman in Bridgnorth who told me to keep well wrapped up and take plenty of liquids I had another go at ringing Nick, this time dialling a number which bore a much closer resemblance to his.

As I waited for him to answer the phone I

couldn't help thinking how pleasant the woman in Bridgnorth had been, especially since her husband had just left her for a girl half her age and now she'd broken out in this rash.

Nick was really excited about the video and promised to comb the shops in Stratford first thing in the morning to see if they had it in stock.

'Only I can't get out of bed at the moment and it would be nice to know.'

'You leave it to me.'

I have nice kids. He also told me to stay well wrapped up and to take lots of liquids.

The next morning the fever had gone and all was well with the world. The little bird on the roof had woken me at just before six with a brand new reggae version of 'Lady Madonna' and I lay in bed and listened with a wonderfully clear head to his entire repertoire before sadly coming to the conclusion that he was tone deaf.

I dozed on and off for the next three hours, not wanting to move in case I set him off again. Then the phone rang. It was Nick on his mobile.

'Hi, Dad. I've been to W. H. Smith's and they've got a shelf full and now I'm outside Our Price. They had five and they've sold four, so I bought the last one.'

'Oh, that's terrific.'

He hesitated.

'Just one thing. They haven't put your name on the cover, just Thora's and Pete's.'

I reached out for the *Examiner*.

'They have. There's a photo of it in the paper. It says *by Deric Longden*. Up near the top right-hand corner.'

He hesitated again.

'Just a minute.'

I heard a short spell of heavy breathing as he tucked the phone under his chin, and then a scratching sound before he came back on the line.

'You're right. They'd stuck the price ticket over it.'

I told you I was famous.

A SELECTED LIST OF FINE WRITING
AVAILABLE FROM CORGI BOOKS

LEATHERFACE

Leatherface is the sobriquet earned by John Neville, the highwayman who haunted the Dover Road. This story is seen through the eyes of a young boy, with romantic notions of taking to the pad himself. Swashbuckling action is set against city taverns and roadside inns, and played out amongst rogues, the Bow Street Runners, cheats and gamblers — not forgetting the Drury Lane actress, Royall Demarest, and the notorious pickpocket, George Barrington, both of whom come under Leatherface's strange spell.

ERNEST DUDLEY

LEATHERFACE

Complete and Unabridged

LINFORD
Leicester

First published in Great Britain

First Linford Edition
published 2008

Copyright © 1958 by Ernest Dudley

British Library CIP Data

Dudley, Ernest
    Leatherface.—Large print ed.—
    Linford mystery library
    1. Historical fiction
    2. Large type books
    I. Title
    823.9'12 [F]

    ISBN 978–1–84782–300–7

Published by
F. A. Thorpe (Publishing)
Anstey, Leicestershire

Set by Words & Graphics Ltd.
Anstey, Leicestershire
Printed and bound in Great Britain by
T. J. International Ltd., Padstow, Cornwall

This book is printed on acid-free paper

'Stop, damn ye! or I will
blow your brains out!'

'Gentleman' Harry Simms
(*Educated at Eton,
Newgate and Tyburn*)

1

All this that I am going to relate happened long ago. Yet so much of it remains in my mind that it might have been only yesterday. The image of that strange man whose name became a legend of his time remains as vivid as if he had just ridden out of my life, the way he did that grey dawn, to stand silhouetted black and forbidding against the pale sky before vanishing from my ken forever. And the faces of those others whom I met so briefly, yet in such dramatic circumstances, come back to my mind still so that I might have left them but a few hours ago I can see again the red hair like a flame of the girl at the Fox Inn, and the blood runs warm again in my old veins at the memory of her embrace; and my gaze once more meets the dark eyes of Royall Demarest glancing at me meltingly from the darkness of the coach, as it races through the night along the Dover Road.

I can hear the sanctimonious whine of Mr. Fisher's voice, and feel again the bitter sting of old Lord Deal's sharp tongue.

In my imagination I am once more pacing the gently rolling deck of the packet where the fantastic adventure all started. In the distance ahead the harbour lights of Dover were beginning to twinkle against the haze that softened the whiteness of the cliffs stretching as far as the eye could see on either side of the town. The sea-gulls dipped and wheeled around our packet, their harsh cries loud above the creaking of the sails and the vibration in the rigging. The steady breeze bellied out the crackling canvas, and from somewhere came the sound of the sailors' voices singing a sea-shanty.

A murmur of conversation rose from the passengers gathered on the deck, their faces all turned expectantly towards the shore. I stood a little apart from the groups around me, my own mind full of all I would have to tell them at home of my visit to Paris, and my journeyings. I fancied how my father and mother would listen to me all interest and nods and smiles; or I could picture myself gazing out from my bedroom window dreaming over all that I had experienced during the brief time that I had been away. It was a favourite habit of mine to sit at the window for a while before going to bed and stare at the road, winding past, white in the moonlight until it disappeared in the darkness towards Rochester. I always loved that, especially in the summer when I could have the windows open to the scents of the dusk that crept over the garden. Little could I foresee then as my thoughts winged homeward that I would have so much to re-live again in my imagination that would quite outshine my stay in Paris.

A scrap of conversation obtruded itself on my musings and I turned to see a round-shouldered, elderly man with a heavy enamelled complexion and his claw-like hands bedecked with rings. This was Lord Deal. He was the centre of several passengers, smiling at him syco-phantically and weighing what he had to say as if his words were minted gold in wit and wisdom. Close beside him stood a huge, simply dressed man with a broad, scarred face, Jack Morgan, the Champion of England, Lord Deal's protégé.

The present topic under discussion was some highwayman called Leatherface, the news of whose execution at Tyburn had reached Calais before we had sailed that early morning, and had provided the passengers with a never-ending source of gossip and speculation.

For the past two or three years my youthful imagination had been fired by the stories of the exploits of this highwayman they called Leatherface. Of course, I was only a boy, but to me it seemed dreadful that this vital, daring individual who had become a legend of the road between London and Dover, along which he had ridden with such dash should ride no more. So, at the mention of his name by Lord Deal I found myself unconsciously edging towards the latter and the circle of people about him. Then, as if weary of their chatter, or aware of my proximity, he turned and fixed me with a questioning smile. I can still see those enamelled features,

4

the rouged lips drawn back over the black stumps that were all that was left of his teeth, as he said: 'And what are your sentiments concerning this Leatherface's end?'

I stared at him, not only taken aback by his sudden interest in my opinion, but because I was embarrassed by my ignorance of the full meaning of what he was saying.

'Do you think,' Lord Deal said, his tone a little sharpened at my stupidity, 'that he richly deserved his fate? Or would you rather he'd made a bold escape from the noose?'

'To be hanged by the neck must be very terrible,' I said, managing to find my tongue, and I added impulsively: 'They do say he only robbed, he never killed anyone.'

'So,' Lord Deal's grin was now full of derision, 'you think that not wicked enough to merit hanging?'

I saw the faces of his companions bent upon me with severe expressions and one portly man with a pair of sharp eyes sunk in his fleshy face, said: 'I don't know what the youth of to-day is coming to. A

5

desperate scoundrel who — '

He broke off as Lord Deal turned towards a mild-looking man, dressed soberly in parson's black, who had been hovering on the edge of the group, and stabbing a talon-like finger which flashed with the jewel that beringed it at me, he said: 'Here's a young rake who requires all your prayers if he's to be saved.' The clergyman blinked first at Lord Deal and then at me, as the other continued. 'He thinks that this rogue they hanged at Tyburn was hard done by.'

'I was only saying, sir — '

But I was interrupted by the clergyman who had turned to Lord Deal, and said in mollifying tones: 'No doubt a tender-hearted lad, my lord. It is not unpraise-worthy,' he looked at me with a gently reproving expression. 'If we sin,' he said, 'then we must pay the penalty. We must expiate our crime in this world, so that we may receive forgiveness in the next.'

But I was not to be deterred from speaking up in the defence of someone who could no longer defend himself. 'They say he gave to the poor,' I said.

6

While Lord Deal's watery eyes flickered contemptuously over me, the plump-faced man mimicked me. 'They say,' he said; 'I don't know what you young scamps are thinking of. Hero-worshipping a tawdry villain — '

The rest of his remarks were lost in a fit of coughing, and as he buried his purpling face in a white silk handkerchief, the clergyman diplomatically took the opportunity to change the subject. 'The evening breeze blows fair enough,' he said to Lord Deal. 'By the grace of God it bears us safe to harbour.'

Lord Deal nodded absently, his thoughts elsewhere, as if he had realized that there were matters more important than idle gossip to claim his attention. He turned away, Jack Morgan who had remained solidly silent all the time, moving close by his side. Their departure was a signal for the rest of them to break up, all except for the parson who gave me a sympathetic smile, his features pale and bloodless beneath his black hat.

'It was a Christian thought of you,' he said, 'to feel a pang of sympathy for that malefactor.' He glanced in the direction of Lord Deal and the others who were straggling across the packet's deck, and I heard him say under his breath: 'He that is without sin among you, let him first cast a stone.'

Encouraged by his demeanour, I could not resist saying: 'After all he must have been very brave.'

The parson nodded slowly, then his expression became saddened. 'If only he had exhibited his courage in a worthier cause.'

I could think of no answer to this, and we stood there for a moment without saying anything. The sea-gulls wheeled and cried above, the ship creaked and rolled gently, and the voice of the sailors reached us in their rhythmic chant. I had turned my glance away from the dark mournful figure beside me. The lights of Dover were appearing brighter against the shadows of twilight which had begun to colour the smooth sea with purple. A deprecatory cough brought my gaze back to the parson.

'You are travelling alone?' he asked.

I took the note of interest in his voice for that of curiosity at the fact that I was, in fact, without any companion on board. It was a question I had become quite used to ever since I had left my home near Rochester, on my journey to visit an aunt, my mother's sister, in Paris. I said as much to the clergyman, and he listened with interest, as if quite absorbed by my account, and this I found quite flattering. 'I am proceeding straightway to London by the coach,' I said, and added by way of explanation: 'My parents have been visiting London while I have been away. I shall be going back to Rochester with them.'

He nodded understandingly. 'Perhaps I shall have the pleasure of your company on the coach to London.' Then he paused, and mumbled to himself. 'Would we were safely there,' was what I thought I heard him say, and I looked at him in faint surprise.

'Surely, sir, you have no fears for the journey?'

He did not answer me for a moment, but fixed his eyes on me, and now it struck me how dark and probing they were. They reminded me of one of the masters at the school I attended in Rochester, and who seemed for ever peering at us as if to discover what wickedness we might be up to next. No doubt, I thought to myself, a clergyman might be expected similarly to be on the look-out for wickedness in others.

He was saying solemnly: 'I have taken the liberty of observing you. Plainly you are a resolute young man.' His voice tailed off, and I waited for him to continue, while he hesitated as if about to impart some confidence to me, yet uncertain that it would be wise to do so. Then, apparently making up his mind, he said: 'I am almost persuaded to seek your help.'

I was so surprised at the notion that he should think I could be of any assistance to him, that I found it difficult to make any reply. While for his part he seemed to regret having committed himself so far, and as if for something to say, he inquired my name, and when I told him imparted to me the information that he was the

Reverend Mark Fisher.

'I must confess,' he said at last, 'to feeling a trifle apprehensive regarding the coach-journey tonight. I have a trinket from Paris, a small present for my wife.'

I could not help wondering what a parson would be doing journeying to Paris, but it would be impertinent of me to ask; and I decided that perhaps it was in connection with some religious business to do with the increasing number of those more timid who, alarmed by the as yet mutterings of the revolutionary storm over France were thinking it prudent to seek sanctuary this side of the English Channel.

'If I should be robbed of it,' Mr. Fisher said, and then once again his voice faded away.

'Who could rob you?' I said.

An apprehensive shiver passed through his frame. 'The Dover Road is lonely, it will be dark, and we should be at any highwayman's mercy.'

A picture of a figure swinging from a gallows flashed across my mind; I had never been to Tyburn to witness a felon's execution, but once on a journey from Rochester to Gravesend I had seen a cross-road gibbet in the dusk of a winter's evening, from it dangling a manacled shape off which the carrion birds had flown as our coach clattered past.

'Surely,' I said, 'no highwayman will ride that way since the example of Leatherface?'

Mr. Fisher did not appear to be reassured. 'I do fear,' he said, his voice was decidedly timorous, 'that even though he no longer terrorizes the night, another undaunted will emulate his crimes.' His expression was full of anxious indecision. And then he said: 'But I must not repeat foolish tales.'

I was so intrigued by this cryptic observation that I could not resist asking him what he was going to say. He regarded me carefully for a moment, and then glanced round to see that he was not overheard. But the other passengers nearby seemed too interested in the approaching lights of Dover Harbour, now brighter every minute. Mr. Fisher took my elbow, and spoke into my ear.

'You have not heard, then, how at Tyburn he boasted that his ghost would haunt the road and still ply his trade.'

I stared at him in frank amazement. I had heard the tale when first I had come aboard at Calais. Several of the passengers had been talking about what was supposed to have occurred at Tyburn. How, just before the noose tightened round his neck, Leatherface had shouted out to the crowd that his ghost would continue to ride the road he had ridden with such notoriety and profit, before his capture. But it seemed to me incredible that a clergyman, of all people, should take the story seriously. He must have read my thoughts, for he said hurriedly: 'Foolish nonsense, of course. It is the prospect of meeting one of his kind in the flesh that affords me anxiety.'

He looked at me expectantly, obviously awaiting me to say something, only my mind was too engrossed with the notion of Leatherface's phantom to scent what was expected of me. I believed in ghosts no more and no less than anyone else. Although, nevertheless, the idea of

Leatherface returning to continue his exploits in phantom shape had caught at my imagination and I could not help turning over in my mind what it would be like to encounter the wraith of that colourful individual. Then Mr. Fisher's look became more penetrating, and it dawned on me what he was waiting for me to say.

'Why not let me take your wife's present,' I said accordingly, and saw him smile slowly.

'You have read into my very thoughts,' he said, 'that was the favour I had in mind to ask you.'

I nodded understandingly. 'Should we be held up,' I said, 'it is unlikely that anyone would imagine me to be carrying any valuables.'

'I had gauged your spirit truly,' the parson said, 'you are as keen-witted as you are brave.'

I gave him a confident little shrug. It seemed to me there was not so very much to be brave about. I felt certain that the journey to London would be completely without untoward incident. I was about to suggest to him that he handed over the trinket that was a present for his wife, there and then, when I saw that he had turned away and once more the anxious look marred his features. I followed the direction of his gaze and saw someone close to the ship's side, clutching tightly at a stick.

It was a blind man whom I had helped to guide earlier when we were a little way out of Calais and he was tapping his way round the deck, and in danger of tripping over a coil of rope left carelessly in his path. He made a stooping figure, ill-dressed and his eyes, deep-sunk and shadowed by bristling brows were as expressionless as the windows of a deserted, empty house.

'We will remove ourselves,' Mr. Fisher said in a low voice, and to my surprise tinged with some amusement, he led the way to the starboard side of the ship where he took up a position in the lee of the deck-house. 'Blind men have sharp ears,' I thought I heard him say.

We were screened from the notice of any nearby passengers; and as he beckoned me closer, the parson delved into an inside pocket of his rusty black coat. I watched while he fumbled with something and then very nervously he brought out a white lace-edged handkerchief which was wrapped round some small object. He unwrapped the handkerchief to reveal a large, gold brooch. He said that he hoped it would please his wife, and I said that I was sure it would. He wound the handkerchief round it most carefully and securely, and was about to hand it to me when he gave a sudden start and drew back quickly.

2

I turned to see what Mr. Fisher was staring at. 'I thought I heard something,' he said to me over my shoulder. But there was no one there. 'All this talk about highwaymen is making me quite nervous.'

'Do you let me take it,' I said, 'and you will rest easier in your mind.'

His hand was trembling as he gave me the wrapped-up handkerchief, and I placed it in the inside pocket of my jacket. 'I will guard it with my life,' I said lightly.

'Indeed,' he said with perfect seriousness, 'I have no wish for you to run any risks for the sake of a mere trinket.'

I gave him a reassuring nod as we left the lee of the deck-house, and made our way along the deck, while the canvas bellied out more strongly above us, and the rigging vibrated in the freshening breeze that had newly sprung up. Mr. Fisher muttered a warning in my ear that

I should not breathe a word to a soul about what had transpired between us, which I thought was an unnecessary warning, for, of course, it was the last thing I should do.

There was an air of excitement amongst the passengers at the prospect of stepping once more on English soil. I could feel a tingling in my veins myself at the knowledge that I should within a very short while be on my way home.

Mr. Fisher began asking me conversationally about my visit to Paris, and I recalled the shops and the playhouses and the bands playing in the streets, how full the city seemed to be of carriages and sedan-chairs, with fine gentlemen and fair creatures wearing most bizarre clothes and strange and wonderful wigs, some of which towered several feet high, shaped like gardens full of birds, or some eastern temple.

'They take great pains to ape the latest fashion there,' the parson said, and added with a little sigh: 'Would that church-going were equally *à la mode*.'

I could not help a certain feeling of

guilt at this observation, since I myself had not attended church while I had been in Paris; or at least not to worship. Mine had been a two weeks' stay, and though the numerous places of interest to which my aunt had taken me included, of course, the great cathedral of Notre-Dame, I had not attended a service there. However, I was able to please the parson, I thought, by my description of the famous place. I waxed eloquent about the fantastic beasts and demons, the gargoyles and strange creatures which looked down from the towers and the cathedral-roof; and the three superb entrance-gates, the doors veined with cunningly wrought-iron, and the statues and bas-relief all aglow in azure and vermilion, greens and yellows, against a background of gold, and the portals of the Last Judgment and of the Virgin, glittering and glistening with the message of salvation and damnation. And within the great shrine, where its imposing columns broke and curled into graceful gothic capitals of floral motifs and leaves, with on every hand the rich silks and gildings, paintings and brocades, golden images, carpets and pictures. I recalled my aunt telling me how for the *Fête-Dieu*, it would be transformed into a garden of flowers, and on Whit Sunday doves, to which lighted wicks of tow were fixed, fluttered about, until, their feathers all burnt, they fell to the floor. And, of course, the marvellous rose windows of medieval stained glass.

I could not refrain from teasing Mr. Fisher a trifle when describing how while everywhere priests and canons hurried to and fro, and choir-boys with their incense, among the bigots, beggars and loafers, lurked pickpockets and thieves. 'They said that cheats and cut-purses were everywhere abroad,' I said. 'It was not safe to venture off the main streets, especially at night. George Barrington, himself, they said, had descended on Paris, to ply the trade which had made him so notorious in London.' And I gave Mr. Fisher a sideways glance, smiling a little to myself at his uneasy expression. 'Yet I never saw a cheat or thief,' I said, 'that I could tell by his looks.'

'Wickedness is not always apparent in

the faces of God's creatures,' he said, shaking his head sadly. 'It is only when the beholder peers into their hearts, that evil may be seen.'

As we came amidships I saw Lord Deal again, with Jack Morgan towering over him. It occurred to me that the latter's face betrayed his profession without any doubt. Yet, as we drew nearer, and I looked at him closely, it seemed to me that his eyes were unexpectedly gentle; not so were Lord Deal's, which glinted at me as he said waspishly to Mr. Fisher: 'And have you dinned some proper notions into his young skull?'

The parson glanced at me, then back to Lord Deal and made a deprecatory movement with his hands. 'To be sure, my lord,' he said, 'his notions arise from an excess of high spirits.'

But my attention was fixed upon Jack Morgan. For I decided that here was an opportunity which would enable me to boast to my school-fellows that I had actually shaken the hand of the Champion of England. Accordingly I adopted an expression composed of admiration for the prize-fighter and respect for his lordship. One of the most important topics of the hour in Paris while I had been there was the fight staged in a field on the city's outskirts between Jack Morgan and an Irishman called the Dublin Butcher, and whom he had beaten over eighty rounds. It was from this victorious expedition that he was now returning. 'The news of your victory went all around Paris while I was there,' I said to Jack Morgan. 'When next will you be fighting in the ring?'

The prize-fighter glanced at Lord Deal, who nodded, and then he stepped forward and held forth his hand. 'Pleased to make your acquaintance, young sir,' he said, while I gazed with wonder at my own hand which had completely disappeared in his.

'Is it true,' I said, 'that you pickle your hands in brine to toughen them?'

He nodded. 'It is an old prize-ring trick.'

'I have put up my fists several times with other boys,' I said. I was thinking of a bully at school who had bested me on each of two encounters, which had much galled me, and it was certain we should meet again. He was taller than I and weighed much heavier, and nothing made my blood boil more than to witness someone else being bullied, or to be bullied myself. 'But I fear I am not all that skilled,' I said, as a further idea took shape in my mind.

'So long as you hold your left hand straight before you.' Jack Morgan said, and almost automatically he stepped forward with his left foot, assuming a fighting stance.

'The boy's receiving a lesson from the Champion no less,' Lord Deal said to Mr. Fisher, and I thrilled at the prospect of being able not only to boast to my school-fellows that I had shaken hands with the great man, but that I had actually been instructed by him.

'Remember to tuck your chin well behind your shoulder,' Jack Morgan was saying, 'as you lead with your left.' I nodded and out of the corner of my eye I could see several of the passengers, amused interest on their faces, draw close in anticipation of witnessing a demonstration of his art by the prize-fighter, and I was already beginning to bask in the reflected glory of the moment, when there came a sudden interruption.

'My snuff-box,' Lord Deal said, and at the agitation in his voice Jack Morgan and I turned at once towards him. He was going through his pockets, his pencilled eyebrows drawn together in a frown of dismay. 'I had it,' he was saying, 'and now it's gone.'

Mr. Fisher, with a shocked expression, had moved towards him. 'Perhaps you have dropped it? Let us look around the deck before someone should step on it.' All of us stood back, and searched the immediate vicinity of the deck, while Lord Deal, muttering to himself, searched through his pockets yet again.

'I remember, my lord,' Jack Morgan said, 'you took a pinch of snuff only a few minutes since.'

'I do not see how I could have dropped my snuff-box,' Lord Deal said, 'and not noticed.'

'Someone might have kicked it aside,' I

said, with a glance in the direction of the scuppers. But Lord Deal was not listening, instead he was glancing at those around him, his watery eyes narrowed with suspicion. 'Someone might have picked it up, more likely,' he said.

'Surely, my lord,' Mr. Fisher said, wringing his hands, 'you don't suggest that anyone would wilfully make off with it?'

I turned to him quickly; an earlier incident had jogged my memory. 'The blind man,' I said, 'could he have heard it fall?'

'Blind man,' Lord Deal said, his mouthful of rotten teeth opening and closing with a snap, 'who is this?'

I explained to him about the presence on board of the blind man, to whom I had earlier given a helping hand; and Mr. Fisher confirmed how he had been in the vicinity a short while previous to our again meeting Lord Deal, and my conversation with Jack Morgan. 'And I did remark,' the parson said, with a glance at me, as if warning me not to refer to the matter of his present from

Paris for his wife, 'that those who are without sight are often compensated by more acute hearing.'

The words had barely left his mouth when I heard the faint tapping of a stick, and spun round to see the very creature we were discussing approaching us. The others followed my gaze. 'We could ask him if he had heard your lordship's snuff-box fall,' I said quickly in a low voice.

Lord Deal's eyes became hooded for a moment, and then he dug his fingers into Jack Morgan's arm. 'Do you step deliberately in his path,' he said.

The prize-fighter nodded understandingly, while Mr. Fisher drew in a little hiss of breath so that I thought he was about to protest, but if it was in his mind, he decided against it, as Jack Morgan with elaborate pretence stepped backwards into the path of the approaching figure. The blind man, apparently unable to forestall the collision, banged straight into him, his walking-stick dropping with a clatter to the deck. With well-simulated surprise the prize-fighter swung round, grasping the other, who seemed about to stumble and fall, apologizing to him profusely.

But the blind man appeared not in the least put out, and I quickly picked up his stick and put it in his hand, while Mr. Fisher stepped closer to inquire after his welfare. The blind man assured him that he had suffered no harm, though he commented, a whimsical smile touching his lips beneath his blank eyes, on the rock-like stature of the other party to the impact, whereupon Jack Morgan grinned a trifle shamefacedly. Then, saying he remembered my voice from the previous occasion when I had helped him, he thanked me for giving him his stick and off he went in the direction of the cabins, and a wave of compassion for him swept through me.

Jack Morgan faced Lord Deal, who had been watching the scene with silent scepticism. 'Blind as a bat, my lord, I'll wager.'

'Sadly afflicted,' Mr. Fisher said, shaking his head, 'most grievous.'

Still Lord Deal said nothing, but continued to gaze speculatively in the direction of the tap-tap of the stick upon the deck, until it had gone.

3

We had sailed into Dover Harbour on the quickening breeze of that late summer's evening in 1776, just as the port began to withdraw itself deep between the enfolding arms of darkness stealing down from the white chalk cliffs on either side. There followed all the bustle and commotion of disembarking; the shouting of the sailors; the furtive little boats that clustered round our vessel like flies about a honeycomb. Their rascally-looking crews were, I was told, all smugglers offering to transport any passenger's dutiable goods, such as cognac or lace secretly to shore, there to be restored safely to the owner who would have boldly cleared the customs.

At length, Mr. Fisher and I had disembarked and we made our own way through the customs without hindrance. I may have been slightly nervous that the parson's trinket might be found on me, not that it was of any dutiable value, but because I knew its owner would be painfully upset by the discovery. We sought out the Royal George Inn nearby and found it crowded, mostly with passengers from the packet, all clamouring for food and refreshment preparatory to retiring for the night, or setting off on horseback or by post-chaise, or by the Flying Hope coach for their respective destinations.

As Mr. Fisher and I went through the noisy bar-room into the coffee-room, I glimpsed Lord Deal, together with Jack Morgan, and just for a moment I thought I caught sight of the blind man, solitary in a corner, though I could not be sure of it. I made a good supper of steak, cooked over a sea-coal fire, and coffee; my appetite had been very much sharpened by the sea voyage. Mr. Fisher appeared as gloomy as ever and still seemed too nervous to do more than peck at his food.

Every now and again I would catch his sideways glance towards my pocket wherein I carried his precious present for his wife, wrapped in the white lace handkerchief. Once or twice while we sat there he passed his hand across his moist brow, complaining the air was thick, and that it made his head swim. It was true that the rich fumes of cooking, and wine and tobacco-smoke which permeated the atmosphere did not help to make the surroundings tolerable. But for my part I was too hungry to notice, and when my appetite had been satisfied I became vastly intrigued by the scene around me. The comings and goings of the travellers, the bustle and shouting of servants as they answered the demands made upon them for a bed for the night, with hot water for a wash; or a meal; or tankard of ale, or a bottle of wine.

I commented upon Mr. Fisher's poor appetite and he heaved a wistful sigh: 'In truth I don't anticipate enjoying a morsel of food or a wink of sleep,' he said, 'till we are safe in London.'

Presently I followed him out of the coffee-room into the bar-room, it was now nearing nine o'clock when our coach, the Flying Hope, would be setting off for London. As I glanced round the still crowded place with the large red-faced proprietor guffawing with some guests, I saw no signs of Lord Deal or Jack Morgan. The blind man, too, if it was he I had seen there, had left the solitary corner and was gone. I assumed that he had been met by someone who would take him under their friendly wing. Mr. Fisher and I passed out into the courtyard, and I took some gulps of air as I gave a look up at the night sky, clear and full of stars. The air was not much fresher than that in the Royal George, what with the smell of fish and the stench that came from the many vessels drawn up alongside the nearby quay mingling with the smell of the hotel stables.

In the light of lanterns we saw our coach stood ready for flight with four full-blooded chestnuts, obviously anxious to be off. Ostlers hissing like steaming kettles were giving the finishing touches to the animals; and in a dim doorway I saw the figure of the coachman drawing on his gloves, while he joked with the guard at his side, who would be accompanying him. Servants were pushing luggage into the boot of the coach, while others clambered on to the roof and arranged the valises and portmanteaux there.

Mr. Fisher and I made our way to the coach to see that our luggage was safely stowed. I easily picked out the travel-stained portmanteau which my father had used for so long which he had loaned to me. Mr. Fisher saw that his bags were safely aboard, and then turned to the coachman who had appeared out of the darkness, chewing a piece of sweet-lavender, and carrying his long-lashed whip. Behind him the guard was bearing a fearsome-looking blunderbuss. Mr. Fisher gave one of his nervous coughs.

'The road to London,' he said to the coachman, 'passes through some desolate places, does it not?'

'That it does, Mr. Parson,' the coach-man said. 'Proper lonesome it grows, a wilderness, you might say.'

'But you keep a good speed, all the time, do you not?' The anxiety in Mr. Fisher's voice was very apparent.

The big coachman adjusted the button of his coatcollar, and I could see by his face that he was not unused to these sort of questions from timorous-minded passengers.

'A fine spanking pace, Mr. Parson,' he said, and I fancied that he gave me a conspiratorial wink as Mr. Fisher nodded with relief. Once again I felt irresistibly impelled to tease him, so apprehensive did he appear of the journey. And so I asked the coachman slyly:

'You travel fast uphill as well?'

'Like the wind, young sir.' And then, with an ominous change of tone the big man added: 'That is, except for one or two stretches of the road. Very desolate they are, not a living creature for miles.' He turned to Mr. Fisher, 'only the wind wailing through the trees, like ghosts.'

The parson drew in his breath in a little hiss of fear. 'And are you obliged to slacken speed?'

'Only natural, horses being no more than what God made them.'

I shot a look at Mr. Fisher; he was obviously working himself up into a fine state, and encouraged by the sight I said: 'And such a spot would be just where a highwayman would choose to lurk?'

'Couldn't choose better,' the coachman said nonchalantly, shifting his sprig of lavender from one corner of his mouth to the other. 'But there, Mr. Parson,' he said with a complacent chuckle, 'you don't need to be frightened no more by the gentlemen of the pad.'

'Why not?'

'The rascals will be scared off the road since Leather-face danced on the air at Tyburn, that's why.'

'Quite,' said Mr. Fisher, but I could tell he was not completely satisfied. 'All the same you will whip your horses as hard as you can, even uphill?'

'As though the devil himself were after us — saving your reverend's cloth.'

There were footsteps and voices behind us, the waspish voice of Lord Deal snapping at some servant who had aroused his umbrage. In the light of the lanterns I saw him advancing, Jack Morgan inevitably by his side. The coachman had seen them. 'Lord Deal,' he said, 'and Jack Morgan himself, the Champion of England. Didn't I tell you,

Mr. Parson, you'll have no cause to worry on this journey? And Jack Morgan's aboard, you'd be safe against a score of highwaymen.'

After Lord Deal and Jack Morgan learned we were to be companions together in the Flying Hope, Mr. Fisher asked after the missing snuff-box. Those watery eyes became venomous slits once more as Lord Deal shook his head. 'No news of it, I fear. I complained to the captain of the vessel, much good it will do me. It's gone, and there's an end to it.'

Mr. Fisher murmured sympathetically, and I said something to the same effect, but Lord Deal had turned away to supervise the stowing of his baggage, leaving Jack Morgan to mutter to Mr. Fisher: 'Worth £5,000, that snuffbox was,' he said, 'had it off an Indian prince at faro. Easy come, easy go.'

The prize-fighter shrugged his massive shoulders and turned to the coach, while I was staring after Lord Deal, my eyes wide with incredulity. To lose five thousand pounds, and with such philosophical calm, impressed me forcibly.

There came a fat wheezy voice out of the shadows, and a short, tubby figure emerged into the light of the coachlamps. The newcomer's face was round and smooth, and wreathed with a smile. It was only his small eyes set a shade too close together and which lingered briefly upon each one of us which gave me the impression that he was not so ingenuous as he appeared to be.

'I fear I stayed over long on my supper, but the beef steak was that excellent.' He paused and smacked his lips reminiscently. 'We are fellow-passengers?'

'All bound for London, sir,' the coachman said from behind us.

'Allow me to introduce myself, my name is Josiah Ellis.'

The stranger appeared suitably over-awed at the presence of Lord Deal, while he expressed his admiration for Jack Morgan, commenting appropriately upon his prowess in the prize-ring. Lord Deal turned to the coachman inquiringly. 'Do we wait upon any other passengers?'

'Only one, my lord, a lady.'

I could not fail to notice a flicker of

interest in Lord Deal's expression, while Mr. Ellis observed that the landlord had informed him that a lady was resting upstairs, preparatory to setting out for London, and the coachman added that her luggage was already on the coach.

'It's a lady's privilege to keep us waiting,' Lord Deal said with a little snicker.

'Perhaps the time of departure has slipped her memory,' Mr. Ellis said, and there was a tinge of impatience in his tone as if he, at any rate, was all for being off.

'The landlord will have made it known to her,' Mr. Fisher said, whereupon Mr. Ellis muttered something about the possibility that the landlord might have been over-busy and had omitted to remind her. It occurred to me to offer to go back to the inn and see what was detaining our passenger. The servants were preoccupied over the luggage which still remained to be put aboard, or one of them would have been sent; instead I hurried off, and edging my way through the crowded bar-room once again, I sought out the landlord, his red face now redder than ever, and perspiration shining on his brow. I explained that I was looking for the passenger who was to travel on the Flying Hope, and he announced that she must still be in her room where she had been resting, though he said he had sent a servant up to warn her that the coach was waiting, and that only recently. I said I would go up and advise her that the coachman would be growing impatient; the Flying Hope was proud of its punctuality. He nodded somewhat absently, his attention taken by a guest banging on his table and shouting for another bottle of wine. Over his shoulder the landlord directed me to the room, and I went up the dark staircase.

The light from the oil-lamp burning over the first-floor landing reached no further than the first door or two. I went to room number five, which lay along the passage, and in a pool of darkness, since the next lamp was several feet away, and knocked gently on the door. There was no reply. I knocked again, louder. Still there was no answer. I wondered if the lady had fallen asleep. Plucking up my courage, I turned the handle and pushed against the door. It creaked open and I stepped gingerly inside.

The room was in darkness and it was impossible to see more than the very faint outline of the four-poster bed, though the curtains were drawn open, for I could see the glimmer of the white pillows. I stood perfectly still, listening, but there was no sound, its occupant had gone. I called out softly, but no one answered. I was about to turn back towards the door when I heard a faint creak of floorboards behind me. I stood still on the threshold of the dark room, and felt a faint tinge of panic which swung me round on my heel, to call out: 'Who is it?'

A dark shape seemed to materialize out of the shadows of the passage, and a voice answered me with gentle reassurance.

It was Mr. Fisher.

4

'Forgive me, I had not meant to make you jump,' Mr. Fisher said, and while I continued to feel annoyed with myself for having shown that I had been startled for no reason, he added: 'I followed after you to help find our missing passenger.'

That made me smile a little to myself in the darkness; it was much more likely that he had come after me in order to keep an eye on his precious brooch. Perhaps he had feared that someone lurking about the inn might bang me over the head and make off with it.

'She must have gone,' I said.

He blinked at me in the gloom. 'How strange that one of us did not pass her.'

It had occurred to me that it was curious that I had missed her on the way up to her room; and then I wondered if perhaps there was another way out which she had taken. I said as much to Mr. Fisher, and he thought this was a likely

41

explanation. 'We could continue along the passage, and discover for ourselves,' he said. 'She may have mistaken the direction in the dark.'

After we had passed the second lamp we rounded a corner and there ahead of us were some stairs leading downwards. Mr. Fisher stood by me, looking at a faint glow of light below indicative of a door which led outside. I hurried down the stairs, pausing when Mr. Fisher pleaded with me not to be so impetuous. He caught up with me, picking his way carefully in the darkness, down the steep flight of stairs, and we gained the door together.

It opened on to a narrow alley beyond which lay the inn yard. The moon was rising above the rooftops, flooding the scene with a pale light, so that we could see the coach with the ostlers and servants, and the coachman impatiently flicking at the air with his whip. The guard was already in his place, his blunderbuss together with half-a-dozen horse-pistols, ready loaded to hand. As we came into the courtyard I saw Lord Deal with Jack Morgan and Mr. Ellis beside him, bowing to a lady who was obviously the missing passenger.

She wore a deep blue velvet cloak with a hood over her head, and turned as we approached and smiled her apologies to us, 'I am so sorry to have caused you such trouble, I lost my way in the inn, which explains why I have delayed you.'

Her voice was very soft, and in the light thrown by the lanterns, she struck me as being young with a heartshaped face and dark eyes, though I couldn't tell what their colour was beneath her hood. Lord Deal introduced her to Mr. Fisher and then to me as Miss Royall Demarest, adding that she was the young actress whom he had not long since witnessed playing at Drury Lane. While I stared at her most vastly intrigued, for I had never met an actress before, though I had been to the playhouse at Rochester on several occasions, Miss Demarest turned and got into the coach, the rest of us following her.

The horses were stamping their hooves and shaking their heads with impatience, so that their harness chinked and rattled. The ostlers slammed the coach-door upon us, and collected the coins thrown to them. The coach lurched as the coachman mounted to his seat, the guard rang out his posthorn loudly and we heard the coachman's voice and the crack of his whip, and we were on the move.

Lord Deal sat in a corner facing the way we were going and opposite Miss Demarest, and I sat between him and Mr. Fisher, with Mr. Ellis opposite me and Jack Morgan in the other corner. The inside of the coach was musty, reeking of old leather and horses, so that Miss Demarest's perfume was welcome to my nostrils. The six of us sat silently at first, for though Lord Deal, Jack Morgan, Mr. Fisher and I were all acquainted with one another, the addition of two strangers to our company could not fail to introduce a feeling of caution amongst us.

If you were wise you did not exchange confidences quickly with fellow-passengers, or allow yourself to be led into conversation, for fear of betraying useful information to someone who might be in league with the highway-men. There was hardly an inn or posting-house which did not harbour a spy in the pay of some worthy of the pad, whose secret purpose was to supply intelligence of what sort of valuables a passenger might be carrying, and where they might be disposed, among the baggage or upon the person.

So the crooked streets of Dover with the friendly lights in the windows had fallen behind us to be swallowed up by the night, while the coach swayed and creaked, Lord Deal and Miss Demarest and Jack Morgan and Mr. Fisher holding on firmly to the leather slings to save them from being jostled against their neighbours. The horse's hooves beat out their steady drumming on the road, the wheels rattled, and the interior of the coach caught the light that was reflected back from the lamps, and from the moonlight that turned the road into a white ribbon. While now and then as the road dipped into a hollow between the woods and fields, a mist eddied past us, a hint that autumn was not far away.

Presently Mr. Ellis produced a capacious canvas bag, which had been hitherto concealed in the folds of the ample coat in which he had wrapped himself. From the bag he took a meat-pie, then another, which he ate with much smacking of his lips, while I watched both amused and amazed by his appetite. He reminded me of one of the boys at school who seemed to be for ever eating cakes and sweets.

'I could see you do not mean to starve,' Lord Deal said in that waspish tone of his. But if Mr. Ellis detected the sarcasm in the remark, he affected not to notice it, for his face beamed in the gloom.

'I own I am inclined to cosset my stomach,' he said.

Now Lord Deal began to gossip with Miss Demarest about the playhouses in London. I heard the young actress say that she had been appearing with players at theatres in Canterbury, Tunbridge Wells and then Dover. Now she was returning to London to appear again at Drury Lane in David Garrick's company, together with the famous Mrs. Bellamy. I was fascinated to hear her talk of such notable names so casually, so that I found it extremely difficult to pretend not to be listening. Finally I exchanged one or two words with Jack Morgan, but his iron chin began to sink on his broad chest. Mr. Fisher in his corner next to me folded his hands nervously and had nothing to say, though from the corner of my eye I could see his lips moving, no doubt in prayer. Presently Miss Demarest and Lord Deal fell silent, and leaned back in their corners; Mr. Fisher's lips became still, even Mr. Ellis's jaws ceased their munching, and he sank back with a sigh of repletion and soon he began to snore.

Through the window I glimpsed the shadowed trees and hedgerows as they raced past, beyond them fields stretching away into the woods and beyond them the purple and blackness of the horizon. The coach swayed and lurched, the coachman's whip cracked, every now and then he would cry out to urge his cattle onwards. I could see Miss Demarest's eyes gradually flutter and close, her lashes thick and black on her cheek, and then her small chin fell forward, and her pale features were lost in the shadows of her hood. Despite the fact that one of the windows was open several inches, for there was a decided nip in the night air, the atmosphere of the coach was becoming more and more close, the aroma of its interior and that of Miss Demarest's perfume commingling, and I began to nod myself.

We had been swaying and rattling for some two hours, and I had been waking with a start, to doze off again, when a sudden shout from the coachman awoke me violently and I almost jumped out of my skin. Simultaneously with the sound of horses' hooves slithering on the road, the coach jerked to a halt. The sudden stop to its career pitched Lord Deal, Mr. Fisher and myself forward so that I found myself half smothered in Mr. Ellis's coat, while I could hear those waspish tones raised querulously on my left, and a fearful whimper on my right.

I was the first to extricate myself and while Mr. Ellis was grumbling that any of his refreshments which still remained in his canvas bag must have been ruined; and the others were sleepily demanding to know what might be amiss, I scrambled over Mr. Fisher towards the partially-opened window and lowering it hastily, poked my head out. The radiance of the moon had driven the stars from the sky, and there at the side of the road, on the edge of a pool of shadow thrown by a huge tree whose branches hung low, was a menacing figure astride a black horse, a pistol glinting in either hand. The horseman's face beneath the shadows of his cocked hat was completely blotted out, and as he urged his horse into the centre of the road, his pistols still aimed unwaveringly in the direction of the coachman, the moonlight gleamed for a moment with a macabre effect across his face, and I realized that it was entirely covered by a black leather mask. As my heart began to race I heard the coachman choke incredulously.

'Leatherface — '

And then the guard's voice, quavering with fright: 'But it can't be — it's his ghost.'

In the taut silence that followed, the voice of the dark, sinister figure on the horse answered with a strange, hollow rasping tone from behind his mask: 'Ghost or no ghost, keep your blasted nags quiet, or I'll shoot them down and you after them.'

His words reached us in the coach like the strokes of doom, and over my shoulder came a gasp of abject terror from Mr. Fisher, a nasal snarl of fury from Lord Deal. Then there was a laugh, mirthless as a tomb and as hollow-sounding from behind the leather mask, which sent an ice-cold shiver through my veins.

'Yes, that's who it is, Leatherface's ghost.'

5

As I stared at the horseman, his attitude was relaxed and casual as if he had stopped merely to ask the way, with only the glint of his pistols and the black leather mask to betray his trade, I heard Lord Deal's shrill tones in my ear: 'What is the damned guard doing? He is armed, why hasn't he shot the poxy rogue down?'

'Fainted from fright most likely,' Jack Morgan growled, and indeed remembering how his voice had shaken with fear when he had spoken, it seemed apparent to me that the guard had been rendered incapable of taking any action by this sudden appearance of Leatherface, whether he was wraith or reality.

'Probably in the scoundrel's pay,' Lord Deal said, and I threw him a quick look. I knew it was sometimes the case that the very people who were responsible for the safe arrival of the coach had themselves been discovered to be in league with the highwayman.

'But if he is a ghost — ?' I started to say, only for Lord Deal to interrupt me with a contemptuous snort.

'Empty a barrel of shot into him,' he said, 'and you'd soon see if he was a ghost.'

I felt Mr. Fisher sway against me, uttering a low moan, I turned to see him rolling his eyes heavenwards, and for a moment I thought he was going to faint. Jack Morgan was scowling and looking as if he would have loved nothing more than to burst out of the coach and throw himself at the dark figure, there in the moonlight; while Mr. Ellis was murmuring reassuring words to Miss Demarest. And then I heard the coachman recover his powers of speech, and blurt out: 'How can you be Leatherface, you were hanged at Tyburn?'

Again that hoarse laugh from behind the mask which sent chills crawling under my scalp and down my spine. 'What did I tell them,' the figure on horseback said, 'even with my head in the noose?'

'Why, that you would — '

'That my ghost would still haunt the road, and take my tolls; and here I am true to my dying speech.' His tone became brisk and business-like, still with that biting edge to it as edging his horse nearer, his pistols still pointed at the coachman, he said peremptorily: 'Get down, and your friend with you,' adding to the guard as if he was biting off each word: 'And if you should even think of reaching for that piece of old iron you've got there, you're a dead man.'

Cursing under his breath, the coachman descended from his seat, the guard quietly following suit, and Mr. Fisher gave another long-drawn-out moan. Mr. Ellis, leaving Lord Deal to comfort Miss Demarest, offered the observation that the highwayman was neither Leatherface, nor his apparition come to operate in his stead, but some other masquerading as the notorious highwayman. I turned this possibility over in my mind while Jack Morgan growled that if only the villain wasn't armed he would soon settle his hash.

'Everyone out,' and the pistols gleamed, and Mr. Fisher pulled my arm. I stood aside and he fumbled at the door-handle, and then opened the coach-door. He half fell out on to the road, recovered himself, while Miss Demarest, preceded by Lord Deal who turned to her attentively to help her step down, took her place beside him.

'This is most alarming,' she said tremulously.

'I do own I prefer to observe such scenes enacted on the stage,' Lord Deal said, whereupon she played up to him.

' 'All the world's a stage,' ' she said, affecting a lightness in her voice. ' 'And all the men and women merely players.' '

I hesitated at the door of the coach, and I could feel the eyes that glittered behind the slits in the mask boring into me.

'Get out.'

I glanced back at Mr. Ellis, who thereupon indicated that I should obey the hollow rasping command. 'We had best do as he says,' he said reluctantly, and as there came a deep-throated grunt from Jack Morgan, I, too, stepped on to the road.

'May you rot in hell, you're no more Leatherface's ghost than I am,' Lord Deal was saying.

'Who then do you take me for?'

'I take you for an impudent masquerader.'

'I've been accused of many things, but never before of impersonating myself.'

'It's Leatherface, all right,' the coachman said. He and the guard, who I could see was visibly trembling and giving wistful glances in the direction of the coach where his blunderbuss and other firearms lay, stood next to Jack Morgan.

Without altering the aim of his pistols, Leatherface kicked his feet out of the stirrups, and swinging a leg over his horse's lowered neck, he landed lightly on the ground. He seemed to tower above the rest of us as he advanced, a casual swagger in his walk, his spurs clinking musically. He was dressed in a black velvet suit, and his riding-boots were of elegant cut and most highly polished. Against the white of his cravat at his throat his long angular chin was all that showed of his face beneath his mask. A hopeless groan escaped Mr. Fisher, and I turned to him. 'It will be all right,' I said. 'No harm will come to you.'

But Mr. Fisher continued to moan quietly to himself. The highwayman paused a couple of yards away from us, and surveyed us, his head tilted arrogantly on his shoulders, which were as wide as a barn-door. 'You may heed the boy's counsel, parson,' he said. 'So long as you are not rash enough to make a false move.'

'I wouldn't do that,' Mr. Fisher said quickly, and for a moment I thought he was about to fall to his knees in an attitude of supplication.

'I am reassured,' Leatherface said, without being able to keep a note of contempt from his tone.

'We are all of us humble, innocent souls, sir,' Mr. Fisher said hopefully. 'None of us of any account at all, sir, only the poorest of God's creatures.' But the other's glance fastened on Lord Deal, who stood there his enamelled face contorted with frustration and rage, and I caught the flash of one of the rings on his fingers. I fancied I could see the smile of greedy anticipation grow beneath that leather mask.

'You sing too small,' he said in answer to Mr. Fisher's plea. 'Everyone is someone to somebody, if only to their mother.' His gaze travelled from Lord Deal to Miss Demarest. 'Your face is so shadowed by your hood,' he said, 'I cannot tell what it looks like.'

'If it will help you to change your mind and allow us to resume our journey,' Miss Demarest said, and let her hood fall so that the moonlight filled with light the cloud of dark hair that fell about her shoulders.

'Let us make speed with your business,' Lord Deal said, a snarl of impatience twisting his thin rouged lips, 'we are anxious to resume our journey.'

It occurred to me that the object of Lord Deal's urgency was to hurry the highwayman in the hope that in his haste he might make a false move which would give Jack Morgan a chance to settle him.

Without his pistols he would stand little hope against the prizefighter. But Leatherface made it apparent that he did not intend to be hurried. He continued in his nonchalant vein, though I imagined that all the time he must have had one ear cocked against the sound of anyone approaching along the road.

'The picture you make quite charms me,' Leatherface said, replying to Miss Demarest, 'almost enough to dissuade me from — ' He broke off suddenly, and appeared to be staring at her with fresh interest. 'But surely I have seen you before?'

She returned his attention with a steady look. 'One should feel flattered, one supposes, to be recognized by anyone, even such as you. Was it Drury Lane?'

He shook his head thoughtfully. 'No, it was the playhouse at Bath.'

I was incredulous. 'You mean that you dare to venture into a playhouse?' I said, and as those eyes behind the slits flickered over me, Royall Demarest gave an exclamation.

'It was there I first set foot upon a stage,' she said. 'I well remember, it was Mr. Desborough's company.'

Leatherface nodded. 'I had seen him often at the Smock Alley Playhouse in Dublin,' he said conversationally, for all the world as if he and the actress were entered into some gossip of the town.

'The play was *The Tempest*, and I was Miranda. 'We are such stuff as dreams are made on' ' she quoted, ' 'and our little life is rounded with a sleep.' I do think they are my favourite lines in all the plays.'

'They have a pretty sentiment,' Leatherface said, and then suddenly his head shot up in an attitude of listening. Instantly each one of us stood as if transfixed. I had not heard anything, but then my ears were not so tuned to catch the faintest warning on the breeze as were those of that strange, looming figure before us, taut and alert.

And then I, too, caught the distant sound of hooves proceeding from the direction of Dover. I heard Mr. Fisher give a sigh. 'The Lord shall deliver us out of the hands of our enemies.'

'Don't count your chickens yet,' Leatherface said, still without any sign of haste in his speech or about his movements. I wondered whom it might be approaching; there was not another coach running from Dover at this hour, it was most probably a post-chaise engaged by someone wishing to travel more privately, or a rider on horseback. I could not distinguish whether there was one horse or more, nor could I catch the rattle of wheels.

Leatherface rapped out a word over his shoulder to his horse which was quietly cropping grass at the side of the road, and the animal raised its head and merged into the shadows of the tree from which it and its rider had first appeared. 'Stay all of you where you are,' he said to us, once more his pistols glinting menacingly. Then to my surprise he gave a nod in my direction. 'You there.'

Mr. Fisher gave a gasp of apprehension, as if now the presence of his precious brooch was about to be revealed. While the others watched wonderingly I stood before the great dark figure, my throat dry, and my heart hammering, though I did my best to ape his nonchalance and indifference to danger. He did not keep me long in suspense, before disclosing what he had in mind. 'Listen,' he said over my shoulder to the others, 'so long as you do as I order, no hurt shall touch him.'

'A hostage, eh?' Lord Deal said.

'You have a sharp perception, old fox.'

I heard Jack Morgan growl something, and I half-turned to see Mr. Fisher nudge him nervously to be silent. 'All of you get back into the coach,' Leatherface was saying. 'And you, coachman, if our traveller stops to ask you if you require help, fob him off.'

'What do I say?'

'Any excuse so long as he suspects nothing. Use your wits. Your ribbons have tangled. A stone in one of your nags' hooves.'

The coachman muttered in acquiescence, and the guard nodded his head. Leatherface flourished his pistols again. 'The rest of you will play up to him; I'll be watching and listening.' He jerked his head towards the blackness beyond the massive tree. 'If any of you should try to play me false, I'll shoot the boy without compunction.'

'We'll do as you say, of course,' Mr. Fisher said nervously and obediently made for the coach.

'Or you'll be needing your prayers for another soul tonight,' Leatherface called after him mockingly. 'Back inside with the lot of you.'

The sound of hooves was now plainly distinguishable as that of a solitary horse. It was nearing us quickly and at any moment would be topping the rise in the road some hundred yards back along the road we had come. The others followed Mr. Fisher, there was nothing else they could do but obey their orders. Leatherface held us all in the hollow of his hand. He left no doubt in anyone's mind but that he would carry out his threat to shoot me down in cold blood, if any attempt was made to trick him.

I watched while Mr. Fisher in his nervous haste forgot his manners to the extent of starting to climb into the coach before Miss Demarest, only to be unceremoniously hauled back by Lord Deal. For my own part the hammering of my heart eased, and although my mouth was still dry with fear I managed to pluck up enough courage to glance at the sinister figure beside me, and as if to excuse Mr. Fisher's behaviour say: 'I am not frightened of you.'

Leatherface might not have heard me, his attention being concentrated on the coach as the others crowded into it and slammed the door, while the coachman and the guard, who had been warned not to go near his blunderbuss or his other arms, pretended to be giving their attention to one of the horses' harness. Then I felt a bruising jab in my ribs as one of the pistols was stuck into me and harsh tones filled my ear: 'So you're not afraid of me, eh?'

My heart was hammering fast again, and now I could not speak but only shook my head defiantly.

'What's your age, damn your eyes?'

'Sixteen,' I said, though I could barely force out the word.

'And if you want to live to burn your next lot of birthday candles, not a poxy squeak out of you,' Leatherface said through his teeth. And prodding me again with his pistol, so that I felt he must have cracked a rib, he urged me swiftly into the darkness beneath the branches of the tree.

6

We had no more than a few seconds to wait before the horse and its rider came into view. Overhead the wind sighed through rustling leaves, and I felt the tall black figure beside me tense, and his pistol dug deeper into my side. As the solitary traveller drew nearer to our coach, it could be seen that it was a man, who slowed up, calling out in a rough voice, like that of a farmer, if there was anything amiss. I saw him peering at the coachman and the guard with curiosity, and for a moment my heart stopped beating as the coachman hesitated before making his answer, then I thought I caught his glance in our direction and he found his voice.

'All's well,' he said, 'thank you kindly.'

A sigh hissed in my ear and the pressure of the pistol against my ribs eased somewhat. The guard muttered something to the effect that one of the traces had snapped but it would hold, and the horseman seemed satisfied by this explanation. He spurred his nag forward, and trotted speedily past us, a sturdy figure, well-mounted, and the drumming of the hooves died away.

I could sense Leatherface turn his head to watch the danger receding. I stood slightly towards his left in front of him while he held the pistol in his right hand across his body. His other firearm he had stuck into the top of his breeches underneath his black velvet coat. As he turned to follow the horseman out of sight I caught from the corner of my eye a glint of moonlight seeping through the branches which glinted on the silver and steel of his other pistol.

It was then that I was filled with a sudden daring, and my heart in my mouth I reached out with my right hand and closed my fingers round the wooden stock. My movement altered my position slightly enough, but Leatherface's pistol was no longer stuck in my ribs, it pointed harmlessly behind my back. Even as I wrenched his pistol free in that moment when Leatherface's attention was distracted, he swung round with a muttered imprecation. But my movement was as swift as his and he found himself looking down the twin barrels of his own pistol.

'Don't move,' I gasped, my voice hoarse with excitement and he let the pistol in his other hand hang by his side.

I had never fired a pistol before, my experience of firearms was limited to my father's fowling-pieces, one of which I had used under his tuition, when accompanying him during my holidays on game-shooting expeditions in the woods and meadows surrounding the house where we lived. I had proved myself not an entirely unsuccessful shot and added my share to the bag at the end of the day's sport. I had many times watched with fascination my father, or his friends handling the pistols which they invariably took with them whenever they set out on a journey away from home. I had listened to my father argue with his cronies about the respective merits of the Birmingham-made pistols and those manufactured by London gunsmiths, or comparing English pistols with those made on the Continent. And from observation and questioning I felt confident that I knew enough about frizzens and flashguards, breeches and pans effectively to fire the twin cannon-barrelled pistol whose steel and silver furniture now glinted so dangerously in my hand.

But if I expected Leatherface to be impressed by my bold action and the menacing attitude I struck I was profoundly disappointed. 'Shall we return to the coach?' was all he said, as casually as if our circumstances were as they had been before, and he no longer held the whip-hand over me, but on the contrary it was I who had him at my advantage. But I was not to show that I was nonplussed by his nonchalance.

'Don't move,' I said, through tightly-clenched teeth, hoping that my grim-set features and hard tone would impress him that I was not to be trifled with. But all that happened was that the eyes behind the mask of shiny black leather twinkled, and I could see the shadow of a smile playing about the sides of his jaw.

'That was careless of me,' he said quietly, 'and you are to be complimented on the dexterity with which you took advantage of my momentary lapse.' He made as if to raise his own pistol at me.

'Drop it,' I said.

'Why, you poxy young cub.'

'Do as I say,' I said, my voice rising, 'or I'll fire.' He lowered his own firearm but he did not drop it, instead he gave a little chuckle. 'I shall count three, and if you haven't dropped your pistol, I swear I will fire. One,' I counted.

'Fancy yourself a bold young cockerel, eh?'

'Two.'

'Who can turn the tables on Leather-face.'

Again he chuckled. 'A pity for you, however, that what you are pointing at me so menacingly happens not to be loaded.'

I caught my breath sharply, and was about to lower the pistol in my hand when I fancied I saw a mocking gleam behind the mask. 'I don't believe you,' I said, 'it's a trick.'

He only shrugged his broad shoulders.

'Call my bluff then,' he said, 'by pulling the trigger. Of a certainty if you're right you will blow me to perdition. You are too near to miss.'

I stared at him trying to discern from that expression-less mask that blotted out the face, whether he was lying or not, while at the same time I tried to pluck up sufficient courage to pull the trigger. Despite the note of conviction in his voice I still harboured the suspicion that he was bluffing me. My impulse was to throw a quick glance at the pistol I held to try and gauge in the darkness if it was, in fact, charged. But I dare not, since to do so would betray that I half-believed at any rate what he said. Secondly, since I had in fact never even seen or handled a double-barrelled pistol before, the mechanism might be such that I would not be able to ascertain whether it was charged or not. Over and above all these thoughts that crowded my heated brain was the overpowering knowledge that I could not shoot him down in cold blood.

'Rot me, if you don't look positively dangerous,' he was saying.

Made desperate by his mocking tones I jabbed the pistol at him. 'I tell you I will shoot.'

'Better let me have it.' He held out his hand in such a cool, audacious manner as if I were some humdrum shopkeeper from whom he had purchased some item. My grip relaxed on the pistol-butt so that the barrels tilted downwards, and a moment later the pistol had changed hands once more.

'I couldn't do it,' I said lamely.

'I am glad to hear you express such lofty sentiments,' he said.

I glanced up at him. 'Though had you been in my shoes you would have shot me in cold blood,' I said.

'Indeed I should,' his tone once more a brutal rasp, 'but then I am a professional villain.'

Why, it flashed across my mind, should a highwayman be carrying one firearm that was unloaded? Then I decided that perhaps it was because it helped him to look that more awesome. An idea occurred to me, and I said: 'Then why did you not shoot me with your other pistol?'

The shadow of a smile flickered underneath his mask once more. 'Why waste powder and shot when it's not necessary?' He must have caught the deflated expression on my face because he added: 'Or perhaps it was because I possess a warped sense of humour.'

'Was that why you pretended to be a ghost?'

He gave a shrug. 'I pretended nothing; it was fostered by the tale that had got abroad concerning me.'

'So all that about your being hanged at Tyburn was rumour?'

He did not answer for a moment, and I experienced the strange impression that had not his hands been engaged with the pistols he would have fingered the cravat about his neck. The eyes glittered balefully, the lines of his jaw seemed to grow more gaunt. He flourished the pistol in his right hand, indicating me to precede him and threw a word over his shoulder to his horse, which followed after us. We stepped out on to the road, and once more I felt the pistol stuck into my ribs.

As we returned to the coach, with the coachman and the guard eyeing us narrowly, I noticed that the great banks of dark cloud had appeared in the sky in the direction of London. And the wind had quickened and carried more of a chill with it. Leatherface ordered me to take my place alongside the coachman and the guard and rapped out to those inside the coach to come out again. Mr. Fisher was the first to appear, followed by Mr. Ellis, whose jaws were moving and who brushed away from his chins the crumbs, no doubt, of another pie with the back of a hand. He was followed by Jack Morgan and then a moment or two later Lord Deal stood at the doorway of the coach, his thin lips drawn back from the black stumps of his teeth, as he called out: 'Miss Demarest has fainted. We have been trying to revive her.'

Leatherface came a few paces nearer, as Mr. Fisher muttered that it must have been the excitement which had caused the actress's indisposition, to which Mr. Ellis swallowing the last morsel of food in his mouth, concurred.

'Fainted, eh?' Leatherface said. 'We'll soon see about that.'

'What do you propose to do?' Lord Deal asked him, still at the door of the coach as if to bar the other's entrance.

Something made me glance in the direction of Jack Morgan, and I thought I detected that there was a tenseness in his attitude, which started a question-mark buzzing at the back of my brain. Leatherface's pistols moved threateningly so that Lord Deal could do nothing else but stand aside, and slowly, his face twisted with a snarl he took his place with the rest of us. All of us were watching the towering black figure who stood at the door of the coach. His pistols still trained on us, Leatherface spoke into the coach. 'In a faint, eh, Miss Demarest? Let's see if this bat I pulled off the tree will cure you.'

I heard Mr. Fisher give a gasp of horror as something flipped into the coach. I had not observed Leatherface take anything from the tree while we had been underneath it, but whatever it was that had fluttered from his hand was immediately followed by feminine screams. Miss

74

Demarest appeared at the door and half-stumbled out, so that for a moment I thought that she would fall on to the road. 'Take the horrible thing away.'

'I thought it would revive you.' And Leatherface gave that hollow rasping laugh, as Miss Demarest recovered herself and hurried to join us. As she did so an object fluttered to the ground, and Leatherface bent quickly and caught it up on his pistol end. It was a black handkerchief.

'Two can play at counterfeit,' and Leatherface pushed the handkerchief into his pocket. 'I have met a similar ruse a score of times; even an actress of your talents could not shine in such a hackneyed rôle.' He turned to rake each one of us with his gaze. 'And now the play-acting's over, let's to business.' A moan rose from Mr. Fisher, and Leatherface held him in his glance momentarily. 'I shall not detain you long,' he said with mock sympathy.

'You'll pay for this,' Lord Deal said.

'On the contrary, it is you who are going to pay.'

I could almost hear Mr. Fisher's teeth chattering, as he managed to say: 'Have mercy on us. I am only a poor, poor parson.'

'Then to relieve you of the little you have will fetch you that much nearer heaven,' Leatherface said. 'Just a small contribution for my collection plate.'

Shoving the pistol in his left hand, the one presumably which was unloaded and which I had returned to him, into his coat-pocket he took off his hat and threw it on to the ground in front of him. 'Do all of you now fill it with your money, your watches, your jewels.'

As Mr. Fisher uttered another moan I caught a look that passed between Jack Morgan and Lord Deal, and once more my nerves tingled with the thought that the two of them had hatched some scheme aimed at turning the tables on Leatherface. What was in their minds I could not anticipate, but I stood and held my breath. I had forgotten the presence of the parson's brooch in my pocket and I was equally oblivious of the agonized look that Mr. Fisher was casting in my direction.

'I swear I carry nothing of any value,' I heard Mr. Ellis say.

'What about the ring on your finger?'

'It is of only sentimental value, worth barely a few shillings.'

'Add its weight to the hat,' Leatherface said remorselessly. 'All is grist to my mill.'

I watched Lord Deal take a bulging purse from his pocket, and weigh it in his hand, so that the chink of coins sounded clearly. He leaned forward and threw the purse but it fell at least a yard to the side of the hat. Leatherface muttered irritably and out of the corner of my eye I saw him step forward and bend to pick up the purse. But my full attention was taken by Jack Morgan.

This I knew was the moment he had been awaiting; and then with the swiftness of light he lunged forward.

7

Despite the force of Jack Morgan's onslaught, Leatherface, bent as he was about to pick up the purse, stood his ground, giving a grunt of surprise. For a moment I thought he was going to collapse beneath the sudden impact, but some sixth sense must have warned him so that he twisted aside in time to avoid the prize-fighter's full weight. But the pistol in his right hand was jerked from his grasp and clattered to the ground. The other pistol was still in his coat-pocket. The one he had dropped was the one, I recalled, which had been loaded; though, of course, Leatherface might have changed them over after I had returned him the unloaded firearm.

Even as the other pistol hit the road, Mr. Ellis moving with surprising agility, jumped forward and kicked it well out of reach. Jack Morgan had closed with the highwayman, but was not able to manœuvre himself into a position from which he could get in a blow. The coachman had jumped down from his seat, followed by the guard carrying his blunderbuss, though he had no chance to use it at that instant, for fearing of peppering the wrong man.

I saw Jack Morgan manage to free one hand from Leatherface's smothering clinch and grab the pistol which still protruded from the other's pocket. Lord Deal shouted out triumphantly, but I realized that Jack Morgan had made the same mistake as I had made in the darkness of the tree. 'It's no good,' I shouted out impulsively, 'it's not loaded.'

My warning must have taken Jack Morgan by such surprise that he glanced in my direction, and with a sudden twist Leatherface tore himself free, and ran for his horse. Mr. Ellis had dived for the pistol which lay at the side of the road, but by the time he had picked it up and taken aim, Leatherface had flung himself into the saddle. At the same moment that Mr. Ellis fired, the guard, prompted by a shout from the coachman, let loose his blunderbuss with a tremendous report. But either his aim was too hasty or Leatherface's luck was holding unconscionably well, but at any rate the charge must have missed him. The deafening explosions from both blunderbuss and the twin pistol-barrels, as Mr. Ellis pulled the second trigger, caused Mr. Fisher to jump, clapping his hands about his ears.

'Perdition,' Lord Deal said, as Leatherface urged his horse along the road Londonwards. The guard had dashed to his pistol-chest on the coach and was brandishing a pistol in each hand ineffectually, realizing that it would be useless to fire them. The target was well out of range, a fast-disappearing smudge against the distant shadows, with only the receding clip-clop of horse's hooves echoing at us mockingly. While Mr. Fisher moaned that he was deafened and Lord Deal gave his attention to Miss Demarest, inquiring if she had been upset by all the excitement, Jack Morgan grumbled loudly to Mr. Ellis at his failure to hold Leatherface. He was still holding the pistol, and Lord Deal turned to him commiseratingly. 'If only it had been charged,' he said, 'you could have taken a pot at him.'

'He had the devil's luck,' said Mr. Ellis.

'At any rate,' Miss Demarest said, 'he was forced to leave his booty behind.' Lord Deal had already retrieved his purse, and Mr. Ellis was now picking up Leatherface's hat from which he took his ring which he had thrown into it. 'You will keep it as a memento,' Miss Demarest said to him indicating the hat, and Mr. Ellis smiled at her.

Lord Deal said to Jack Morgan: 'You also have a souvenir,' and I saw Mr. Fisher who had been standing next to the prize-fighter give a start as he caught sight of the pistol the other was holding. Lord Deal noticed the parson's expression of alarm at being so near the pistol, and pointed out that it was perfectly harmless, since in this case it wasn't charged.

As Jack Morgan began casually to examine the pistol, indicating that it was double-barrelled and commenting on its fine workmanship, and I moved closer to take a view of it, Lord Deal asked me how was it that I had come to know it was unloaded. I began to tell him what had transpired between Leatherface and myself; and soon the attention of all was turned upon me, as I described my attempt to hoist Leatherface with his own petard. I found myself blushing at the murmur of admiration which rose from my listeners, and Miss Demarest's gaze was fixed on me, most bright and attentive. Mr. Fisher also directed some complimentary observations at me, then glanced with interest at the pistol in Jack Morgan's hand.

'Is it really quite safe?' he said, doubtfully.

'Safe as houses,' the prize-fighter said, 'or I would have been able to take a shot at Leatherface myself.'

I noticed Mr. Fisher eye the pistol again with increasing curiosity. Lord Deal had also observed his interest, his enamelled face creased in one of his thin-lipped smiles. 'Take it Mr. Parson,' he said, 'it won't bite you.'

Mr. Fisher hesitated, stretched out a

nervous hand, then his fingers closed round the butt. He held it up, and bent his gaze upon it nervously fingering the steel and silver furniture and murmuring admiringly at the foliated engraving on the upper part of the breaching. Growing more bold he began fingering the trigger. 'This is the device that fires the charge?'

'If there was any charge to fire,' Lord Deal said.

Mr. Fisher now held the pistol firmly by the butt and his finger curved round the trigger. Jack Morgan and Lord Deal watching him with patronizing smiles as gently at first, then more firmly he squeezed his finger. There was a sudden report. Mr. Ellis, in whose direction the twin barrels happened to be pointing, ducked with an exclamation, and then, while the rest of us stared first at Mr. Fisher, then at the smoking pistol incredulously, Mr. Ellis moved forward and quickly took it from the parson's trembling hand.

'The shot just shaved my ear,' he said on a somewhat aggrieved note, while Mr. Fisher swayed moaning and his eyes closed, against Jack Morgan. He seemed to be under the impression that he himself was mortally wounded, and continued to wail to that effect, while I observed Mr. Ellis remove the charge from the second barrel, as if to make plain there should be no more risk of an accident, and then I turned to give my account to Lord Deal, Jack Morgan and the rest how I must have been fooled deliberately into accepting that the pistol was not charged.

I explained my inexperience in the matter of firearms, and how, in the darkness of the great tree I might not have been able to tell whether the pistol was loaded or not. Miss Demarest, who listened with the others, seemed to agree, together with Mr. Ellis and Jack Morgan, that under the circumstances I was not to blame for having been deceived. But I fancied I caught a narrowing of Lord Deal's watery eyes, and I received the impression at the back of my mind, and which was to prove of more significance later, that he was not altogether satisfied with my explanation.

Presently, however, we were all settled in the coach once more, Mr. Fisher having at last been convinced that he was completely unharmed; and all of us thankful for our escape from our perilous encounter, and the coachman was cracking his whip and we were off again for London.

The looming banks of cloud which had appeared on the pale night-sky horizon had spread rapidly, a chill wind had risen, causing us to wrap our cloaks or topcoats around us more snugly and to close the coach windows tight. So that very soon the atmosphere within was thick with the now familiar odour of leather and the sweat of horses, mingling with Miss Demarest's heady perfume.

Miss Demarest, Lord Deal and Jack Morgan lay back drowsily, while Mr. Ellis's plump jaws moved rhythmically, so that I could imagine he was enjoying some repast in his dreams. Beside me Mr. Fisher sat quiet, his hands pressed together as if in prayer, his eyes in his pale moist features tightly shut.

As for myself I did not feel sleepy, my

brain wakefully alert, a score of pictures were spinning round inside it, all of them holding that tall dark, swaggering image, whom I had last seen bent low over his horse disappearing into the night. Once more I could see the glitter of his mocking gaze behind the leather mask; I could hear the harsh rasping voice. I was recalling the heart-stopping moment when I thought I had held him covered by the twin barrels of his own pistol, and I felt increased wonderment at the nonchalant calm with which he had faced me. I recalled the chill that had swept through me at the knowledge that he would have shot me down without compunction, destroyed me in cold blood if I had called his bluff. Whereas I had faltered at the prospect of pulling the trigger against him.

We could not have been more than about two miles this side of Canterbury when the storm broke. The lightning-flashes illuminated the inside of the coach with awesome brilliance, the thunder cracked and rumbled overhead and in a moment a deluge of rain smote us. The commotion shook my fellow-passengers into wakefulness. Mr. Fisher coming to with a start, crying out that he was shot, and looking round sheepishly as he realized that he had been dreaming of the incident with the pistol.

The coach pushed on resolutely, though now and again one of the horses would whinny with fright as an extra searing arrow of lightning zigzagged down the sky. And the coachman's voice could be heard urging on his animals or cursing the elements. The storm started Jack Morgan off reminiscing about the time when he had milled with a coloured prize-fighter, Negro Pearce, at Shrewsbury; and I listened, while the others began to nod once more, to his account of how he and his opponent took the fight to forty-five rounds although the pair of them could hardly see each other for the rain, and a vast puddle had filled the middle of the ring. With typical modesty Jack Morgan said that if the coloured man hadn't slipped at the end of the forty-fifth round and struck his head, he might not have lost, so remarkable was his recovery on account of the reviving rain-storm.

And then while the coach thrust onwards through the blackness illuminated by the lightning-flashes, Mr. Ellis awoke again and took part in the conversation turning it upon the subject of Leatherface. Mr. Ellis seemed to possess not a little knowledge concerning the highwayman, which was explained by his reference to the fact that he was a Londoner who had been on a business-trip to Dover. It seemed that Leatherface had been born John Neville, and though his parentage was wrapped in obscurity, he had when a mere boy been a member of a gang of youthful criminals who skulked about the alleys and dark, noisome courts of St. Giles, London.

He had become notorious as a footpad, who, when imprisoned had made sensational escapes. Then he had disappeared from the London scene, some saying that he had fled to Ireland, others that he had taken service with one of the mercenary armies on the Continent. At any rate, it was rumoured, Mr. Ellis went on, that he had received a gunshot wound in his face, so disfiguring him that he had been prompted to wear the leather mask by which he had subsequently become notorious. At this, Miss Demarest, who had also been awakened, and had been listening to Mr. Ellis, shuddered with revulsion, while I felt my blood curdle, as I remembered that towering figure, whose face was completely obscured. I could not help but wonder what horribly mutilated flesh lay behind that mask of shiny black leather.

It was Lord Deal who had also been jogged out of his sleep by the continuing storm, who raised the query respecting the rumour which had reached to Calais as we were leaving on the packet, that Leatherface had met his fate on the gallows. If it was indeed he who had danced his jig on the air at Tyburn, who was it, Lord Deal wanted to know, that they had recently encountered back along the road?

'It was certainly not his ghost,' Jack Morgan said, 'I found him solid flesh and bone for certain.'

'No doubt about it that Leatherface was hanged,' Mr. Ellis said. 'I myself was among the multitude that thronged at Tyburn to witness his execution.'

'You saw him on the gallows?' Miss Demarest said, her voice low with horror.

Mr. Ellis answered her in the most casual tones, as if such a gruesome scene was something of everyday occurrence to him. 'He made a brave show, jested with the hangman, and as was reported did indeed tell the mob how his ghost would continue to haunt the Dover Road.'

His words seemed to fall upon us with silent awe; I puzzled over Mr. Ellis's first-hand revelation. If he had actually seen him die, how could Leatherface have held us up but a short time since. An eerie silence had laid its chill fingers on us, and I was about to ask what explanation Mr. Ellis had in mind, when there came a loud, ominous crack, followed by the sound of splintering wood. Suddenly the coach lurched to one side and came to an abrupt standstill, while above the buffetings of the storm, the voice of the coachman cursing and shouting was blown wildly down to us, as we stared at one another, our faces white in the gloom, and now full of alarm.

8

It was the nearside wheel which had gone. The wooden inside of the iron rim had cracked and two of the spokes had splintered, no doubt as the result of striking against some projecting boulder or loose chunk of rock that had lain on the road. Jumping to my feet I was first out of the coach and stood beside the coachman and the guard, the rain dripping from their soaked hats and greatcoats, as they inspected the damage, cursing at such ill-luck. The rain pelted down and drove against us in squalls, clouds of white steam rose from the horses pawing impatiently and twitching and starting as the lightning flashed and the thunder rumbled. We were joined quickly by Mr. Ellis and Jack Morgan who were drawing their collars up under their ears and their hats over their eyes against the squalls. Lord Deal stuck his head out of the coach to inquire in his waspish voice what was amiss, and on being informed, asked querulously how far distant they were from the next inn.

'There's the Fox,' the coachman said, 'just as we come into Canterbury, and that's two miles or more.'

'Far enough to have to walk,' Lord Deal said, 'on a night like this.'

Lord Deal was joined at the coach door by Mr. Fisher, and consternation showed upon their faces at the prospect of having to quit the shelter of the coach, and find their way through the storm on foot. The coachman asked Lord Deal and Mr. Fisher if they too would get out of the coach so as to lessen the weight on the broken wheel, and they obeyed though hardly with alacrity; and then Lord Deal made much of persuading the coachman to allow Miss Demarest to remain behind on account of the driving rain, and since her light weight could be of little consequence.

By now the coachman and the guard having examined the damaged wheel more closely thought something might be done to repair it temporarily, if only enough to enable us to reach the Fox Inn which he had spoken about. Encouraged by the prospect that we might save ourselves having to trudge through the storm, Jack Morgan, Mr. Ellis, and I also did my best to help, joined in with the coachman and the guard with all the cord and rope available and managed to bind the wheel, so that it would be secure enough for us to continue our journey a short distance. Hopefully we clambered back into the coach and reassured Miss Demarest that all would be well. The coachman and the guard walking at the head of the horses and the repaired wheel wobbling and bumping so that at any minute we feared it might collapse, so presently the Flying Hope limped up to the Fox Inn.

Beyond the low-built inn could be made out the shadows of houses and buildings and beyond them rose the towers of Canterbury Cathedral against the lightning-filled sky. Within the Fox Inn all was a haze of tobacco-smoke, and steam rising from the clothes of a score of other travellers who were sheltering there.

Hot broth and steaming punch was being served, as Lord Deal, followed by Miss Demarest and the rest of us led the way to a table in the corner, close to where a fire of logs had been lit. A pert-faced young woman, red-haired and with impudent eyes, attended us, and Lord Deal ogled her and she laughed at him teasingly as she set down broth and other refreshment before us. The coachman and the guard had been left to deal with the matter of the Flying Hope's broken wheel.

While our requirements were being brought by the red-haired wench, with Mr. Ellis demanding something more substantial than broth, we set about drying our cloaks and overcoats which had got damp when we had quitted the coach at the time of the accident. After we had settled ourselves in our corner before the refreshment, full of conjectures concerning when we should be able to take to the Dover Road once more, I felt a tug at my elbow, and glanced round to meet the gaze of Mr. Fisher, who was sitting next to me. The attention of the others was for a moment distracted and he spoke to me from the side of his mouth: 'I must speak with you alone.'

It was apparent by his tone that he anticipated that I should think of some pretext which would get us away from our present company. It was obvious that he was merely anxious for the safety of the present for his wife which he had entrusted to my care, and it was on the tip of my tongue to whisper back that he had no need to worry on that score for I could feel the pressure of the wrapped-up handkerchief in the inside pocket of my jacket. Then it occurred to me that it was the sight of my overcoat placed with the others airing before the fire which had aroused Mr. Fisher's fear. No doubt he was afraid that I had carelessly put his precious brooch in my overcoat. I was touched somewhat by the frown that drew the the parson's pale brows together and grasped at an opportunity, which at that moment presented itself, to set his mind at rest.

It was Miss Demarest, who wanted to know what sort of progress might be made upon repairing the coachwheel. I had been able to observe the actress now in the brighter illuminations of the inn and thought how enchanting she was. She appeared much smaller without her hooded cloak and the impression I had of her was that she a small and childishly alluring creature. Her eyes were fixed on me so brightly as if inviting me to allay her curiosity that I was prompted to offer to go and ascertain what the situation was. I felt a discreet nudge from Mr. Fisher which indicated to me that he imagined it was for his benefit that I had made the suggestion to Miss Demarest. She was so full of admiring gratitude as I stood up to go out that I could not help but blush a little.

'I will accompany you to the door,' Mr. Fisher said quickly, 'and take a breath of fresh air.'

And making a great to-do to the others about the stuffy atmosphere of the inn, he followed me out and we stood by the door leading to the street. Glancing about him cautiously Mr. Fisher whispered the question I had been expecting. 'My wife's little gift? You still have it with you safe and sound?'

'Safe and sound,' I said to him, tapping against my inside pocket where I could feel his present safely reposed.

He gave a nod of thankfulness. 'It was only that I feared that you may have left it in your other coat.'

It was as I had thought, and I made it very clear to him that I would not remove the brooch from where it lay now, until we reached London and I would return it to him.

'And I shall be thankful when we do come to our journey's end,' he said, wringing his hands.

'We shall, and safely,' I said, and I watched as, muttering to himself, he went back to the noise and bustle of the room we had left, and I thought that he made a pathetic, if not particularly edifying spectacle, and it puzzled me that a clergyman could be so timorous and concerned so much for his own safety and that of material possessions. Then I recalled that the item he had entrusted to me was intended for his wife, and that

was why he attached tremendous sentimental importance to it. Out in the dark
courtyard, I found that the violence of the
storm had lessened, the rain threw itself
against the Fox Inn in only fitful squalls,
while the lightning was less frequent and
further away, as was the grumbling of
thunder. It looked as if the storm had
passed overhead, and was now heading in
the direction of the coast.

The smell of stables was strong in my
nostrils, and from somewhere in the
darkness I could hear voices, I fancied I
could hear the coachman, and the
banging of hammers. Puddles glistened in
the centre of the courtyard, and I looked
about for a way to escape the mire. I had
gone but a few paces when from the
shadows came the scrape of a horse's
hoof and the faint jingling of a bridle. It
was a black horse that stood there, and as
I peered at it, another dark shape
materialized beside it. Dark and towering.
A voice spoke to the horse very quietly,
but it was loud enough for me to
recognize it so that it stopped me in my
tracks. There was no mistaking that harsh,

rasping tone. Involuntarily I called out. 'Who's there?'

The tall figure was motionless, I could feel those eyes on me which I had last seen glittering behind the leather mask. A chill hand laid itself on my heart and I wished fervently that I had bitten back the words before they had escaped my tongue. What I ought to have done, I realized, was to have moved on as if I had not noticed that there was anyone there at all. I could have retraced my steps quietly to inform Lord Deal and the others of my discovery, and left it to them to act as they thought best upon my information. Now it was too late, and yet even as these thoughts flashed through my mind, I experienced the emotional conflict arise within me: one half of me was not all that anxious to see that figure, so still and silent, apprehended.

While I stood there indecisively the figure emerged to the edge of a pool of light cast by a nearby lantern. There was no doubt in my mind as my eyes took in the black velvet suit, pausing for a moment at the white cravat, who it was.

Then I recollected the rumour of which Mr. Ellis had spoken, how the man who called himself Leatherface had suffered a disfigurement to his features in the wars abroad. I was preparing my imagination for what I thought might lie behind the leather mask. But it was no mask that my gaze now encountered, nor any scarred or mutilated face. Instead, the dim light shone on a gaunt, saturnine visage. High projecting cheek-bones, deep lines which ran down on either side from a huge hooked nose jutting out from heavy craggy brows beneath which those familiar black eyes glinted at me with their mocking light. A strange sensation of mingled wonder and gladness filled me at the evidence which quite disposed of Mr. Ellis's rumour. However the aspect before me may have been ravaged by dissipation and the vicissitudes of his notorious career, it was whole and complete, not even scarred by a pock-mark. Impetuously I was about to offer some comment to the effect that this rumour about him was false, and then it struck me that it may not have sounded very polite.

'Have we not had the dubious pleasure of meeting somewhere before?' And as I opened my mouth to say something the harsh, low tone went on. 'Keep your voice down.'

'I — I know who you are,' I said lamely, for that was all I could think of by way of reply.

'Indeed,' he said, calmly, 'but I had guessed as much. Which is why I thought it best to warn you.'

'Warn me?'

'That before you shout it out to the house-tops, you had better know what I know about you.' I could only gape at him in astonishment. A flicker of lightning forked across the distant sky to the accompaniment of a growl of thunder, and in the greenish reflection the gaunt haggard face twisted in a faint grin. I could not for the life of me imagine what his remark was intended to convey, and would have asked him to explain himself, only he turned coolly on his heels, saying over his shoulder: 'You had best follow me.'

I did not move, for I could not see why

I should, but still without turning his head, he said: 'For your own sake do as I say.' There was something in his voice which I could not deny.

I followed him through the darkness to a small door at the side of the inn. It opened silently to his touch, and I went in after him, closing the door behind me. We were in a passage that was as black as pitch. The sounds of the travellers in the parlour came to me faintly as if through heavy closed doors. Leatherface was moving along the passage and I could do nothing else but follow him. He led the way through another door, which he held open for me. It was a small, gloomy room lit only by the light of a lantern outside which streamed through the windows. I could see that it was barely furnished, with a wretched palliasse in one corner and appeared as if it might have been occupied by an ostler.

'You said you knew something about me?' I said as he closed the door.

'Quite a coincidence,' he said, ignoring my question. 'That we should meet again so soon.' His expression became grim.

'Had it not been for Jack Morgan,' he went on, 'I should by now have put many miles between us.' And then he said that which made me stare at him again, my mouth agape. 'While you would be that much lighter of the item you carry for the so-called parson.'

'How did you know — ?' I started to say, and then broke off. 'So-called parson?' I said, echoing him.

'An excellent actor,' Leatherface said, 'almost as good a player as Miss Demarest, or the blind man aboard the packet.'

My head began to reel, I found it impossible to grasp the full impact of what he was saying. All that I could do was foolishly gasp out questions.

'A spy in my employment,' he said calmly. 'Ferrets out all he can about travellers taking the Dover Road.' I felt like shaking my head, to clear it of the mist of perplexity that befogged it. 'I give my employment to several such as he, at Calais as well as Dover; that way do I glean intelligence about any traveller worthy of my attention.'

'He isn't blind at all?'

'Much use he'd be to me if he were.'

I recalled the tap-tap of the stick on the deck of the packet; how I had helped the man who had, as I'd imagined, been so dreadfully afflicted; I remembered how he had so cunningly avoided the trap set for him by Lord Deal and Jack Morgan, and had contrived not to give himself away. And then my thoughts pinned themselves upon someone else much nearer to me, to whom I had given my help and who, only a few minutes ago, I had spoken to so reassuringly, and unconsciously my hand touched my coat over the pocket wherein lay the brooch.

'Mr. Fisher,' I said, 'is not a parson?'

'His name isn't even Mr. Fisher.'

'Then who is he?'

The gaunt, craggy features creased in a thin smile. 'Why, George Barrington, of course,' Leatherface said. 'The pick-pocket.'

9

He was lying, was my first thought, lying so that he might trick me into some evil matched to his own design. I stared at him in plain disbelief, but he might not have noticed or heeded, for he went on to say: 'I am not unaware how I am indebted to you, Jack Morgan might have shot me dead.'

I regarded him coldly. 'And a fine fool I looked when your pistol went off accidentally afterwards.' He raised a beetling eyebrow questioningly and I explained to him what had happened when Mr. Fisher, as I knew him to be so named, had pulled the trigger. 'It's all very well to laugh, but I shouldn't be surprised if I'm not suspected of deliberately stopping Jack Morgan from firing at you.'

'I told you what a good actor he is,' Leatherface said. 'George Barrington knows as much about pistols as the best of them.' Then as if he had only just heard what I had said, he looked at me sharply. 'Suspected?' he said. 'You think that?'

He seemed amused, and I decided not to pursue the matter any further. Instead, I said: 'Anyway, why should you be interested in this trifling brooch Mr. Fisher, or George Barrington, as you say he is, asked me to take care of?'

'If I tell you,' he said bluntly, interrupting me, 'that the so-called present for his so-called wife is in fact Lord Deal's snuff-box.'

'Snuff-box? The one he lost on the ship?'

'Barrington filched it from him.'

I was convinced now that he was lying. Whatever his purpose was I could not tell, but that he was lying I knew. Had I not seen the brooch wrapped up before my own eyes? 'When I took it,' I said, 'I saw that it was a brooch.'

'Barrington married,' he was smiling to himself. 'He and the gentle state of connubial bliss would go as well together as oil and water.'

But now I was not listening to him. I

went on triumphantly. 'And,' I said, 'it has been in this pocket all the time.'

As I made to indicate the pocket, I saw his glittering eyes fixed on me and I suddenly realized he was out to snatch the brooch from me when I produced it. Now I knew what was behind his attempt to blacken poor Mr. Fisher. It was as plain as anything to me, his aim was to trick me into revealing the brooch to him, and it flashed through my mind that perhaps the item with which I had been entrusted, which trust I had almost been deluded into betraying, was more valuable than I had guessed, more valuable than Mr. Fisher guessed. Some special significance about it, was there, which made it so desirable to Leatherface?

He laughed, and I knew that he was reading my thoughts. 'If you still do not believe me, why not look for yourself? I vow I will keep my distance.'

I hesitated, looking at the gaunt face, with the nostrils of the great hooked nose drawn into the lines running down on either side of it, so that his teeth gleamed in a wolfish smile. Then I moved away, ostensibly to the pool of light cast through my window the better to see and, feeling his smile upon me all the while, I pulled the knotted handkerchief from my pocket and started to unwrap it. He watched me without moving. At last I had the handkerchief open, spread there in the palm of my hand.

'Did I not tell you?' Leatherface had mistaken the look of astonishment on my face. 'It is the snuff-box.'

I was shaking my head stupidly. 'There is nothing at all.'

He was at my side in a moment. 'Pox take the cunning swine,' he said through his teeth, staring at the empty handkerchief lying white and open in my hand.

'I don't understand,' I said. 'I saw him, I tell you, I saw him wrap the brooch and give it to me.'

'Barrington owns the nimblest fingers in Creation. You thought he was giving you the brooch, but he substituted the snuff-box for it. Then, suspecting that my spy had observed his trick, he later chose the moment to filch the snuff-box back from you, leaving the dummy handkerchief in its place.'

I was completely overcome with dismay as the truth of his words sank in. Mr. Fisher wasn't Mr. Fisher, the parson after all. He was George Barrington, cleverest and most notorious of all the light-fingered gentry who were waxing rich on the results of their dangerous art, practised in London and Bath, in Paris and Edinburgh, in any city in Europe, where the gulls were wealthy enough for the fleecing. I tried to recollect the sequence of relative incidents as they must have transpired aboard the packet, commencing from when Mr. Fisher, as he called himself, had first urged his acquaintance upon me. Was it before or after he had appropriated the snuff-box for himself? Had he singled me out as his dupe and then satisfied that I was an all unknowing, suitable accomplice, proceeded to brush close against Lord Deal? The first few questions started a whole surge of them spinning round my brain.

Why hadn't Leatherface robbed me of the snuff-box which he knew I carried on me, when he had me in his power in the darkness while we were waiting for the lone traveller to pass? After all, a five thousand pound haul would have been amply rewarding, no need for him to trouble with the rest of the passengers' belongings. Then, it occurred to me that such action, concentrated solely upon the snuff-box would have suggested to the inquiring mind the presence of an accomplice; the blind man on the packet might have leapt to someone's musing. And then I could not fail to wonder why Leatherface had not appeared to have given any reflection to revealing the identity of his accomplice to me. Why should he not have felt fearful that I should pass on to the proper authorities the intelligence with which he had supplied me? I looked at him, quite out of my depth. 'What shall I do?' I said helplessly.

'Nothing, except what I tell you.'

'You mean I am to keep silent, so that you can make another attempt to steal it?'

'That is a matter about which you need not bother your young head.'

I stared levelly at him, while I tried to

111

marshal my senses, to assemble my imagination to deal with the tortuous circumstances in which I found myself. 'Aren't you afraid I shall denounce you?' His eyes narrowed, I thought, but they never left my face. 'Or do you think I'm too soft-hearted?'

'I think you would not be so foolish.'

'Foolish?' And then it came to me what he must be driving at. 'You said just now you knew something about me.'

'Nothing very serious,' he said lightly. 'Simply that you yourself are his accomplice.'

'Accomplice?' I was horrified. 'What do you mean?'

'I mean that you face starker danger than I.' In my agitation I was fumbling with the handkerchief in my fingers. 'I fear you have let yourself drift into somewhat deep waters.' He grinned again. 'Pray allow me to bring you to shore. Suppose you are rash enough to denounce me, and I deny your accusation, declaring myself to be another person entirely?'

'But you are Leatherface.'

'Can you prove it? When thousands saw me swing at Tyburn?'

That was what Mr. Ellis had said, I recalled, and I continued to stare at him nonplussed. Without his leather mask which completely blotted out his face, and against that proof at Tyburn, who would allow himself to be outweighed by my denunciation of him as the notorious highwayman? Would not anyone choose to think that he was merely a masquerader? I hesitated.

'I should brush your accusation away as a horse-tail does a fly,' he said.

'I still cannot see,' I said, and I knew that I sounded on the defensive, 'how I could appear blameworthy for that of which I am entirely innocent?'

'Permit me to enlighten you,' he said and paused. A distant mutter of thunder came to us in that gloomy room; in the dim light he looked for all the world like a picture I had stored up in my mind of some denizen out of hell, looming up at me there in his black velvet suit, I fancied I could almost smell fire and brimstone. 'You admitted that over the matter of the pistol,' he said in his rasping voice, 'you fancied you might be suspected of being in league with me.'

'That is only a faint notion I had,' I said, interrupting him strenuously. 'I may be quite mistaken.'

'And again you might not.'

'But you have just vouchsafed me the information that you are dead, which for my part, removes that fear.' And this time there was a triumphant ring in my tone.

'You keep your wits razor-sharp,' he said, and his thin smile was edged with bitterness at the corners. 'All the same, supposing I informed Lord Deal how, mistaking me for Leatherface you had sought me out, and offered me his lordship's snuff-box which you had helped Barrington to steal?'

'You would not dare attempt such a bluff.'

'Not if your parson friend, in whose company you have been mostly, was found to have the booty on him?' he said suavely. 'As would prove the case were he searched.'

'Would you deliberately snare me in a web of lies?'

'I and my kind deal in such commodities, they are our stock-in-trade.'

'You would see me degraded and disgraced?'

'To save my own skin, I would see you hang.' And I gasped, horrified at the deadly menace behind his reply. 'Do not distress yourself unduly.' He smiled. 'It may never happen.'

A squall of fury and frustration shook me so that the perspiration started on my brow at his attitude, his nonchalance and certainty of himself, his complete control of the situation. I had the feeling that I was no more than his puppet at a fair, forced to dance whichever way he pulled the strings. 'And all the time you aim to obtain the snuff-box for yourself,' I said in a burst of anger, for that was all I could think of to say, so helpless did I feel. And then I broke off, listening. He had heard the sound, too. Someone was outside the door by which we had entered, and the next moment my name was called in that nervous voice which had become so familiar to me.

Footsteps scraped, a hand fumbled at the catch. 'Now's your chance,' I said sarcastically over my shoulder as I swung round.

There was no answer.

I heard the click of a latch and turned back to see a door on the other side of the room which I had noticed before, closing silently. I recollected that Leatherface had not been carrying his persuasive double-barrelled pistols and doubtless he preferred to await a more favourable moment, when he was armed, to deal with George Barrington. The other door now opened and the dark, parsonical figure appeared. He gave a gasp as he saw me standing there, then staring at me, he drew closer.

I felt as if I were dreaming in the shadowy room from which Leatherface had just silently vanished, and into which had now entered the individual in whom I had implicitly believed, and who it transpired was an impostor, who was in fact a notorious pickpocket. I could hardly credit it, I would have brushed Leatherface's revelation aside, had it not been for the damning proof of the handkerchief. Proof enough that whether he was Barrington or Fisher, he had tricked me to serve his own ends.

'It is as dark as the bottomless pit,' he said as he peered at me. 'I thought I heard you talking?'

'I — that is, I was talking to myself.' I felt sure he would see through my lame excuse, he would sense something in the atmosphere that would warn him that the game was up; but he did not appear to detect anything amiss.

'A habit in which I must confess I myself sometimes indulge,' he said. 'I was beginning to wonder where you had got to.'

'The coach isn't ready?'

He shook his head. 'Nor will be for another hour. I just thought I'd come and find you, and make sure that you were safe and my — ' he hesitated ' — and my wife's little brooch.'

'I lost my way,' I said.

'I did the same, it is such a rambling

sort of inn. So ill-lit, I should not wonder if — ' He broke off and glanced nervously at me again. 'I must cease giving way to irrational fears.'

'What were you going to say?'

He hesitated before finally answering. 'Only that I shouldn't be surprised if this were one of those inns which shelter highwaymen.' I gave such a start that his dark eyes widened, and I thought his gaze became more penetrating. I felt angry with myself that his words should so obviously have taken me off my guard. 'You have found no reason to suspect such a possibility?'

Involuntarily I had glanced towards the other door in the shadows, and then feeling his eyes fastened upon my face, I returned my gaze to his. 'I'm sure it's no such place.' I tried to make myself appear calm.

'You don't think,' he said, running his tongue over his lips, 'that Leatherface himself may be under this very roof?'

I swallowed convulsively. I felt certain now that he suspected something, per- haps was even insinuating that he knew about Leatherface and myself.

'You are trembling,' he said, and sounded as though he was full of concern.

'It's just that I feel a trifle cold. I may have caught a slight chill.'

He nodded sympathetically and made a move towards the door. 'Let's go back to the others, where you can get warm.' I followed him out into the dim passage, where he faced me suddenly. 'You've convinced me that I'm imagining things,' he said.

We made our way back, my mind seething with conjecture and foreboding. While it still seemed to me impossible to believe that the shrinking, stoop-shouldered individual ahead of me was the infamous George Barrington and not Mr. Fisher, anxious for the safety of the trinket he'd brought for his wife, at the same time I recalled how Lord Deal had lost his snuff-box directly after he had been standing close to the so-called parson. So now I became convinced that he was indeed the infamous cut-purse; and here I was just behind him, apparently all innocence and not knowing who he was and that the stolen snuff-box lay in his pocket.

Looking back on it now, I cannot imagine how I kept those emotions which were overwhelming me hidden beneath a calm exterior. But I did remain outwardly casual, though my ears sang with Leatherface's sinister warning. What was I to do? To whom could I turn who would believe me against his cunning story? Or again how could I hope to outmatch George Barrington's wily boldness, if I took it upon myself to accuse him? Would it not be best, I wondered anxiously, to accept the advice I had been given in the dimly-lit room I had just left, and remain silent? After all, I told myself, it need not concern me that one scoundrel was out to rob another. Then I recalled that the prize in question was the snuff-box which belonged to neither. It was my duty, I well knew, to help Lord Deal recover his property. And then, supposing I did remain silent, and one or both of the criminals were later caught, was it not likely to be revealed how I had held my tongue?

Looking back on it, as I say, I know, of course, that I should have sought out Lord Deal there and then, and informed him of everything, throwing myself upon his understanding. Was it then that I was so much under Leatherface's menacing spell, and so much persuaded that he would reach out and destroy me if I did confide in anyone else, that I could not think clearly? I believe it must have been that, and that at the time I was fully convinced that my only hope of defeating both the rogues, while at the same time clearing myself of any suspicion of being implicated with one or the other or both of them, was to strike out for my own.

My mind was much more composed as we joined the others. Miss Demarest was not among them. Mr. Ellis, I think it was, mentioned to me that she had complained of feeling wearied and that she had retired to a quieter room, there to rest until the coach should be ready.

Then it was that an idea came to me, a bold scheme formed itself in my mind as if I had been inspired; and so a few minutes later, slipping away and directed by the smiling red-haired maidservant, found me knocking on the door of the room where Miss Royall Demarest was resting.

10

In answer to my knock, Miss Demarest said for me to come in. Feeling a trifle nervous, I opened the door and stepped into the room. A log fire burned with intermittent bursts of flame in the fireplace, lighting up and throwing the shadows of the tall chair-backs grotesquely over the walls and heavy ceiling-beams. A lamp glowed brightly on a table in the corner, and the heavy curtains were drawn close against the night; and that elusive but recognizable perfume which Miss Demarest affected filled the room.

I stood hesitantly in the doorway, gazing towards the long, low couch before the fire on which Royall Demarest lay. She smiled at me encouragingly, it seemed, as wondering why it should be that having determinedly set out to seek her help, I should now feel so reluctant in approaching her.

'Close the door.' Her voice was soft and inviting and I obeyed her, shutting the door quietly behind me, and then I stood there, looking down at her, and for a moment her beauty took my breath away. She had left her travelling-cloak with the coats and cloaks of the others, drying out before the bar-parlour fire. She wore a dark travelling dress of some clinging material. Her hair was lustrous, clouding about her shoulders, and in the flicker of the firelight her eyes were large, like shadowy pools. Her mouth was soft and generous. I stood there wondering what strange feeling it was which was causing me to lose sight of the object of my visit, so that my thoughts were filled with the invitation which seemed to be written across her mouth.

She was just a girl, no more than that, so I could not comprehend why suddenly the sight of this one feminine creature should have made me overpoweringly aware of her existence. It was the excitement of the evening, perhaps, which I had experienced. And she was an actress. Though she looked so young and fragile, yet I knew she must be years older than I in knowledge of the ways of the world. She appeared so cool and self-assured, and how long the silence lasted I could not tell, but when she spoke again she gave the impression that she had noticed no awkwardness on my part.

'I thought it more restful to couch me awhile until it is time to resume our journey,' she said. She spoke in an extravagant way which I imagined all actresses spoke, and which I thought was fascinating. Her lips were parted in a little smile, so that her teeth gleamed white in the firelight.

'They say the coach will not be ready for an hour or more,' I said.

She nodded absently. 'It was growing unbearably stuffy and noisy with the others.'

I made as if to draw a chair close, when the flutter of her hand stopped me. She patted the couch beside her and made room for me to sit beside her. 'There is room here.' She spoke lazily, and I sat down gingerly after some hesitation, my senses somewhat muddled, but whether by the nearness of her beauty, or her heady perfume I could not tell; and I wondered how I was going to broach the subject I had come to discuss.

She leaned back, and it seemed to me that she was somehow very close. Then her fingers lightly touched my hand. She watched me through half-closed lids, and I saw that her dark eyelashes were thick and spiky, heavy with make-up. 'You have about you an air of slight preoccupation,' she said, a faint gleam of amusement in her eyes.

'I wanted to ask you, please, if you would help me,' I said and I could not save myself from stammering a little.

'I am most suitably flattered,' she said, and I was not sure if there was not a mischievous flicker in her eyes. 'I should like to help you, if you think I could do so.'

I had leaned forward in my earnestness. 'I — I'm afraid it's to help me to tell a lie,' I said.

She raised herself up, so that her heart-shaped face was closer to mine, and the sweet perfume of her hair made me feel so thankful that I was sitting down. If I had been standing at that moment I am sure my knees would have given way.

'One so frank-seeming as you,' she said, 'engaging in deception?'

'It is urgently necessary for my plan.' I tried desperately to sound calm and collected, and I could not resist wondering how Leatherface would have appeared so suave and masterful, so saturninely cool and compelling, he who was used to the company of actresses and pretty women's melting glances, so that she would not realize the effect her nearness was having on me. 'And,' I said, 'you would have to tell some lies for me.'

Her eyes were shining straight into mine, and I was reminded of how I had found her glance bent upon me in the darkness of the Flying Hope. 'This more and more intriguing grows,' she said in mock whisper. 'Is it huge falsehoods that you'll require of me? Or little lies? Untruths black, or white?'

'Only small lies, really.' I was praying that she was not laughing at my seriousness of manner, which must manifest my inexperience. 'You see, it's for someone else's sake.'

'Whose?' she said, teasingly. 'For what temptress do you the primrose path of prevarication intend to tread? Or do you prefer I should not know?'

I hesitated for a moment, but only for a moment for each time I stared at her dumbly, I found my attention was diverted from my plan. 'It isn't anyone like that,' I said. 'You see — ' I broke off and pleaded desperately. 'You won't tell them, or anyone else?'

'I vow to hug your secret, here.' She suddenly took my hand tightly in her own and cupped it over her rounded breast. I felt the rapid rise and fall of her tightly smooth satin bodice, and such tremors of exhilaration coursed through me that I had never experienced before. I could not think what I should do, my mind was spinning so; and then I managed to draw my hand away and I forced myself to speak.

'Lord Deal,' I said.

'Lord Deal?' Her elegantly pencilled eyebrows arched in surprise. 'I confess I had imagined he could safeguard himself, without the sacrifice of your integrity. Now, had you said that timorous friend of yours, the parson — '

'That's where you're wrong,' I began to say, then I stilled my tongue in time to prevent my revealing Mr. Fisher's real identity.

'Is not Mr. Fisher your counsellor and friend? He appears to hold you in no slight esteem and,' looking into my eyes, 'I do not wonder. But Lord Deal is nothing more than a wicked old rake. You could not have failed to observe the manner in which he looks at me.'

'I want to alter his opinion of me,' I said glibly.

'Whatever that is,' she said quickly, 'I should not allow myself to be persuaded by it.' Her eyes were searching my face, her mouth was close to mine. I could hear my heart pounding so loudly I felt sure she must hear it too. 'What is it you have in mind? It is not dangerous, I hope?'

'No,' I said. This was the part I disliked, having to lie to her, and my resolution wavered so that I was half-minded not to continue with the undertaking which had formed itself out of the turmoil of my brain. But I felt I could not draw back, I must proceed with determination to achieve success. 'There is little risk; but I cannot tell you more. You must forgive me, but I dare not.'

'You make it all sound so mysterious, so that I am vastly intrigued,' she said, and then a little sigh escaped her. 'I am yours to command.' Her gaze was brilliant. 'What is it you wish me to do?'

'You must tell the others that I have been taken ill and cannot resume the journey to London.'

'You will remain behind, here?'

I avoided answering her. 'Mr. — er — Mr. Fisher already fancies I have a slight chill,' I said. I paused and contrived to smile at her with some show of confidence in myself. 'Could you per-suade him and the others it has worsened to a fever? Could you not pretend you had advised me to retire to bed, until I am recovered?'

'But will not Mr. Fisher require to see

you before he takes his departure?'

'I think it most likely,' I said, knowing full well that he most certainly would, and I went on quickly. 'I could be resting temporarily — er — here — on your couch.'

Making this suggestion brought home to me most forcibly the strange sudden intimacy of our acquaintanceship, so that acute embarrassment and shyness almost swamped me, and I would have been lost, but that if she observed my distress she failed to show it.

'I will go and advise them of the news,' she said. She got up off the couch and I caught the flash of the white lace of her petticoat. She bent, and was taking me by the shoulders. 'You must recline against the cushions. You must act the part if you are to be convincing.'

She pressed me back with a gentle, encouraging little laugh. She stood smiling down at me, the soft curves of her figure silhouetted against the leaping firelight, her hair falling like a dusty twilight about her shoulders. I put my feet up on the couch and as I did so something seemed to take possession of her; her eyes clouded over until they were smoky black, her teeth were clenched tightly together, gleaming white against her mouth, and then she was lying beside me, her arms slipping round my shoulders, her mouth seeking mine. We clung together and I was unconscious of time, or of where I was, of the scheme I had concocted, of everything, but her caress and murmured endearments.

Then, while I strove to collect my spinning thoughts there came a tap on the door.

11

As we listened, holding our breath, there came another knock, and Miss Demarest got up off the couch again, pressing me back as I also made to rise. 'Whoever it is,' she whispered, 'they must think that you have a fever.' Pushing back her hair and smoothing her dress she crossed quickly to the door and opened it.

It was the pert red-haired young woman I had seen in the parlour. I had raised myself to glance over the back of the couch, my thoughts a maelstrom which it seemed would never subside. The circumstances between Miss Demarest and myself had reached a pitch where I knew not what might have happened if we had not been interrupted. It was my first experience of a woman's embrace in the throes of passion and I had been overwhelmed by the urgency and fire of her caresses, so that I had not found it within me to wish to resist her. In fact, I must confess, I had found myself only too willing to return her kisses, once my first clumsy embarrassment had vanished; at the sound of the knock on the door I had been reluctant to let go the warmth and closeness of her body.

But now the interlude had been curtailed my emotions were mixed, a sense of escape flooded back into my being; somewhat shamefacedly it seemed to me that the red-haired wench's appearance could not have been more timely, and had turned my mind back once more to the matter which was to me the most important proceeding of the moment. But I would never forget Miss Demarest, and the memories of her nearness and the abandonment of her passionate embrace would long continue; while I was most tremendously flattered that from among her many admirers who I felt must be far more accomplished than I in such matters as love, she had sought me out, even in my youthful inexperience.

'I had no thought to disturb you,' the young woman at the door was saying, 'but the Flying Hope be ready very shortly.'

I caught her glance in my direction. It seemed to me, or perhaps I was unduly sensitive, which was not unnatural in the situation, or perhaps it was because of the feeling of guilt which nagged at me, that there was a knowing glance in her bold eyes.

'So soon?' Miss Demarest said. It appeared that the repair to the limping wheel had not taken as long as had been anticipated. Miss Demarest then requested the other to ask Mr. Fisher to come up on a matter of some urgency. With another flash of her saucy eyes the red-haired wench went off and Miss Demarest contemplated me most affectionately, while I could only look shy. The spell that had locked us together had been broken by the interruption; and it seemed to me, although it was still just fancy on my part, that the pert-faced young woman had brought some indefinable undercurrent to the atmosphere, as if Miss Demarest and I had been caught out like a pair of scapegrace schoolboys in some furtive act of wrongdoing. Then the so-called Mr. Fisher appeared, all deprecatory coughs and stroking his nose nervously and blinking curiously at me.

'How fortunate it is that the coach is ready so soon,' Miss Demarest said to him, and while he started to murmur some words of agreement, she went on. 'But it is ill-luck for your young friend here, that he should be suddenly indisposed.'

His expression quickened with a sudden and new interest as he wrinkled his brow at me.

'It is the chill I've caught,' I said, by way of explanation.

'Which has, I fear, developed into a fever,' Miss Demarest said, quickly adding her weight to my excuse. 'Nothing serious, you understand, but he is far from well enough to travel.'

She gave her words just the right touch, and I marvelled at the skill and experience which she displayed, acting her part on my behalf. The bogus parson watched me intently, while I passed my hand across my brow as though to wipe away perspiration, which to my surprise did, in fact, dampen my fingers. I knew my face to be still over-heated with the excitement which the suffocating close-ness of Miss Demarest's alluring person had aroused in me, but had not realized it had brought out beads of perspiration also. I was indeed in a fever, but of quite a different nature than that which the black-garbed figure before me imagined. He had taken a few paces the more clearly to see me.

'He must rest in bed until the fever has subsided,' Miss Demarest was saying.

'If you truly believe I should do so?' I said, making a great play of reluctance in my voice, as I appealed to her.

'Do you not agree, Mr. Fisher, it would be much the wisest course?' Miss Demarest said. 'As you see,' with a faint twinkle in her eyes, intended for my private understanding only, 'I have so far persuaded him to rest on the couch.'

The individual whose real name was George Barrington looked at me dubi-ously, and I guessed that he was concerned less with my well-being than with what lay in my pocket, which he had entrusted to my care. Even though it was no precious brooch, but merely an empty, wrapped-up handkerchief, he would still have to pretend for the sake of the lies he had told me that I held his property in my possession. 'I am sure you are right,' he said to Miss Demarest, after some hesitation.

Feigning resignation, I quite enjoyed this little play-acting, I agreed, and then wondered what should happen to my luggage which was still on the coach. I knew it would be best left there, but I thought I should mention it.

'Will you require it with you?' Miss Demarest asked me.

I replied that I thought I would prefer it to go by the Flying Hope, if someone would see that it was kept safely for me at the end of the journey, against my arrival in London. Miss Demarest said that she would see it was cared for and arrangements made for me to collect it. At the same time I gave her a message to convey to my parents, explaining the reason for my delayed arrival, and that all was well with me, and that I should see them on the morrow. All this Miss Demarest most kindly agreed to carry out on my behalf, and then flashing me a smile she went out. She would be but a few minutes, she said.

The so-called Mr. Fisher stared after her for a moment, then closing the door, stood by the couch. He looked down at me, gaunt and black against the firelight so that his sinister appearance seemed to be emphasized in my eyes. Despicable, black-hearted rogue that I knew him to be, common footpad masquerading under the cloth of a respectable God-fearing parson, I looked forward to the realization of my hopes which included the bringing about of his destruction.

'This is most distressing, most distressing,' he said in his false simpering voice. 'But since you are so unfortunately indisposed — er — most distressingly indisposed — '

I picked up what he was driving at behind all his hesitating with as innocent an expression as I could muster up for his benefit. 'I shall no longer be able to take the brooch for your wife,' I said.

'You may be delayed several days,' he said, nodding his head, 'though I trust it will not be the case.'

I felt in my pocket for the handkerchief all wrapped up about nothing whatsoever, and passed it to him, resisting a wilful impulse that took possession of me which was to demand that he unwrap it and show me the brooch that was supposed to lie in its folds. 'I am most grateful to you for your kindness,' he said handling it as if it was the most fragile object in the world. He carefully inserted the wrapped-up handkerchief into a deep pocket inside his coat, which he buttoned up and gently patted the place where it was concealed. He gave a long sigh. 'Perhaps all the worst is past us, and with God's will it should be safe there until I reach London.' He leaned over me, holding out his thin hand. 'No doubt we shall meet again.'

'I hope we may,' I said, without allowing the certainty I felt that we should indeed meet again creep into my voice.

'May Heaven protect and guide you.'

After enduring a further flow of effusive thanks and more blasphemous appeals to the Almighty, the door closed on him. I lay back on the couch, more resolved than I had ever been before to bring the enterprise upon which I had launched myself to a successful conclusion. I began to work out the next move in the desperate game when the latch rattled and Miss Demarest came in.

'The coach will be leaving in fifteen minutes,' she said, regarding me with a melting look, which affected me so much that my heart began to race once more. 'Good-bye,' she said, 'and good luck attend upon you.' She clutched her cloak which she was once more wearing about her, though the hood fell back from the dark, lustrous hair around the heart-shaped face.

'I could not have got so far without your help,' I said.

'I have spun the tale to the others,' she said, 'so that all believe you are truly not fit to travel. They expressed their sympathy with the state of your health, except Lord Deal who had fallen asleep.

He will later learn what's transpired.'

She stood beside me and took my hands in hers, then she said: 'Mr. Morgan is most concerned, and is on his way here to bid you good-bye.'

My face lit up; and at that instant a sudden inspiration seized me. Could I if I tackled him discreetly get Jack Morgan to help me, without his having any knowledge that he was doing so? Then Miss Demarest was bending over me, her white teeth gleaming. 'You must have the same appearance of feverishness that was in evidence for Mr. Fisher,' she said, and ran her hand through my hair, gently ruffling it. The tap at the door did not stay her, and before I realized her intention she had pressed herself close to me and her mouth lingered about mine. She released herself, while I lay back, truly limp from her clinging embrace.

'Now you look the part once more,' she said in a mischievous whisper.

Unable to reply except to nod my head, I watched her go coolly to the door, admit Jack Morgan, who filled the threshold, with a smile at me, as if to say this was not the last we should see of each other. She was gone and Jack Morgan came across to the couch. His wide rugged features were full of concern, and he muttered something, commiserating with my state, while I did my best to play up to him. During the pause which followed his words of hope for my speedy recovery, I silently struggled to devise an innocent manner in which to put my request to him. He was peering at me appraisingly, no doubt considering my appearance to be entirely due to the attack of a feverish cold.

'Mr. Morgan,' I said at last, 'a thought has passed through my mind. I am able to boast about having the honour of the Champion of England's acquaintance — oh, yes, I shall be the most envied person at school — but there is another souvenir of our meeting which I would most like to own.' A questioning look was in his eyes. 'Only that I fear you would not choose to part with it.'

'How can I answer that until I know what it is?' he said, good-humouredly.

I hesitated again, as I looked up into his

face. 'Leatherface's hat,' I said.

He stared at me uncomprehendingly, and then he chuckled. Opening the overcoat he had put on again preparatory to resuming his journey, he brought out Leatherface's black, three-cornered hat. I had earlier noted that Mr. Ellis had passed it on to Jack Morgan, saying that he had no room on his person to carry it and would he take it for himself? Unfolding it and knocking it into shape with one of his huge hands, Jack Morgan then dived into another pocket and pulled forth what I recognized as the double-barrelled pistol, the very one, which I had been fooled into believing was not loaded. I could scarcely credit my good fortune and only just refrained from reaching out to take the gleaming firearm.

'What exciting souvenirs,' I said in a suitably fervent tone. 'Naturally you'll keep both for yourself. You'd never give them away.' I put all that I could into the insinuation, and watched his reaction like a dog cornering a rabbit.

'Notorious highwayman's hat and his pistol,' he said, an expansive smile spreading across his face. 'How a boy who owned such prizes could boast to his schoolmates.'

'Indeed he could,' I said; and then quite unable to control my excitement, I blurted out: 'You mean you will?'

'They're yours,' Jack Morgan said. 'What would a cove who lives by his fists be doing with such things.' I grabbed them eagerly, thanking him with all my heart for his generosity, while he surveyed me quizzically. 'Why,' he said, 'you'll be able to pretend you're Leatherface himself.'

12

Jack Morgan left me on the couch, staring at the pistol and the black hat and pondering his remark for some minutes after the door had closed. Could it be that he suspected my intention? Yet surely that was impossible, no one knew my plan; not even Miss Demarest. Then I reassured myself that Jack Morgan would never have entrusted me with the very devices I required, had he for one moment possessed any inkling of what was in my mind.

I told myself that I must move, and that speedily. There was little danger of anyone coming to look for me now; at any rate, that was a hazard I should have to take. The account of my indisposition would have answered any query my fellow-passengers might have raised, and with Jack Morgan and the bogus Mr. Fisher confirming Miss Demarest's news, it was more than likely that the others had already dismissed me from their minds. The Flying Hope would be on its way very soon, the wheel all mended, and the storm abated, and a fair road to London ahead. I could not refrain from wondering if Miss Demarest still held me in her thoughts. Her ardour could not have cooled so quickly, I tried to think; then I brushed these distractions aside and I stood up and pushed the pistol into my pocket and folded the hat. I must seek out the landlord of the Fox Inn without further delay.

Leatherface himself must be the next object of my attention, where in the dark and rambling inn would I find him? Only, it seemed to me, the innkeeper could help me in that direction, and in order to persuade him to yield up such information to me I would have to rely on all my boldness and capacity to bluff. I opened the door and slipped out into the shadows of the passage. I could hear the murmur of voices which came from the direction of the busy, crowded bar-parlour. I must avoid that part of the inn at all costs, it was just possible that someone from the

Flying Hope, Mr. Ellis, for instance, or Lord Deal, might be there, lingering over a final drink.

I set off in the opposite direction and presently found myself at the foot of a rickety staircase on my left, poorly illuminated by a flickering lamp. The bare wooden treads creaked loudly as I started to ascend and as I held on to the rough banister-rail I moved up through a cloud of cobwebs and dust. I decided against continuing in this direction and retraced my steps. I stood there listening for a moment.

From what I guessed to be the courtyard of the inn came faint voices and a burst of raucous laughter. Beyond this back staircase the passage continued, still ill-lit, so that it was impossible to distinguish substance from shadow more than a few yards ahead. I heard a door open somewhere behind me and men's voices loud at first and then dying away, as if the door had closed on them again, or their owners had moved off. I slipped silently along the gloomy, dusty passage. It was narrow with one turning which I passed, pushing on into what was now utter darkness. Then the passage twisted and a few feet ahead of me was a door partly open revealing a faint edge of light.

I stood outside the door for a moment, wondering if I should enter. A hoarse whisper and the scrape of a tankard reached me from within. There was a chink of what sounded like coins and then a croaking laugh. I nudged the door and it creaked open a few inches so that I could see enough to cause me to recoil back into the shadows. A man sprawled at a table, a huge hand about the bare shoulder of a plump woman at his side, whose fingers stretched towards some coins scattered on the table. Her hair was unkempt and brassy in the light of the hanging lamp, and hung over her coarse, heavily painted face. Her bodice was wide open. The man leaned drunkenly against her and his other huge hand plunged into her bodice, so that she giggled coyly.

In my haste as I backed away my sleeve caught the door, and it swung open wider, creaking loudly. The woman jerked up, tearing away from the man's grasp and fumbling to adjust her bodice. She came towards me and although I stood back in the shadows, the light from the room now caught my face, and I saw her round, protruding eyes peer at me. Hoping that she would not detect the quavering note in my voice, I said: 'I am looking for the landlord, I seem to have got lost.'

A gush of laughter bubbled from her fat throat. 'Why, it's a lad,' she said, over her bare shoulder to the other who remained half-slumped over the table. 'Come to taste forbidden fruit, eh?' she jeered at me obscenely. 'So you want Old Reuben?' She was obviously referring to the innkeeper and I nodded. 'No doubt,' she said, 'he's got some ripe wench for the selling.' I edged along the passage, her sickening laugh following me. 'Where you'll find him in this rabbitwarren, I couldn't tell, and I'm too busy to help you.' The dreadful creature leered so that for a moment I thought she was coming after me. Then there came an impatient shout from the room behind her and she turned back. The door slammed and I made my way to the staircase again, thankful at my escape.

The atmosphere all about me was heavy laden with squalid evil, and it was apparent to even my youthful sensibilities that behind the facade of respectability of the Fox Inn lay a vicious den, sheltering notorious rogues as well as the scum of the alleyways, loose women, the very dregs of humanity. Though I was filled with revulsion, for the dusty air I was breathing seemed poisoned with corruption and vileness, I remained determined to see my scheme through, and because of it forced myself to shrug off the sense of horror that filled me.

My accidental encounter with the brazen wanton could be put to good use; I knew that the landlord's name was Old Reuben, and already my confidence was returning. All I needed, I told myself, was to bluff my way boldly; to speak and act with the voice and manner of one who kept company with the riff-raff who haunted such a place as this. I peered first one way and then the other into the gloom ahead. Then I heard shuffling steps and as I placed myself further in the shadow the lamplight fell across the figure of a manservant who pulled up sharply when he saw me. He was a dirty-looking individual with one shoulder higher than the other. I went towards him quickly and snapped at him in a grating voice which I adopted 'Direct me to Old Reuben, I've been walking around in circles in this black hell-hole.'

'Who are you?' He pushed his face into mine.

'Never you mind,' I said. 'Take me to him or it'll be the worse for you.' He continued to regard me with a crafty look. 'He will see me if you tell him that my business concerns Leatherface.' and I was rewarded to see him start and give a furtive glance over his twisted shoulder.

'Keep your voice down,' he said, but I merely shrugged nonchalantly at him. 'Wait here, I'll tell him.'

He shuffled away, to be swallowed up in the darkness, while I stood there, the cobwebs across my face, the dust in my nostrils, my heart beating wildly, my mouth dry. I knew the danger I faced. If

Leatherface, the last person I wanted to meet if my plan was to succeed was even now with the landlord of this evil place, everything would not only be wrecked on the first shallows my fragile craft traversed, but I felt pretty certain that I should be fortunate to get out of the Fox alive, let alone with a whole skin. I tried to overcome the feeling of alarm that assailed me while I waited; but it was not until the creature reappeared and said for me to follow him, that my confidence came back.

I followed him along the passage which twisted and grew narrower, then descended a couple of steps to a door which the man in front of me opened, and stepped aside for me to enter. I went in and heard the door close behind me. I turned to see where the man was who had brought me. He was not there. The room in which I found myself was large and untidily furnished. It was low-ceilinged with black, crooked beams and was lit by spluttering tallow-candles. There was a table and behind it a long cupboard which ran almost the length of one dark-panelled wall; three or four chairs stood about.

But it was the gross figure in a tall-backed chair before the table who drew my attention. He wore a faded dark-brown coat with worn silver-braid and a grubby cravat stained with the tobacco-dribblings from his long clay pipe. His coat was open so that over the waistband of his breeches his huge belly spilled out. His thick, fleshy nose had been broken and was almost lost in the puffy fat beneath his small eyes. He looked me up and down, before drawing at his pipe and letting me hear his cracked, wheezy voice.

'You were looking for me?'

'If you're Old Reuben,' I said, and I made my tone sound as inconsequential as I could.

'That's me,' he said. His mouth gaped in a toothless smile. 'That's what they call me.' He put his pipe back in his face and drew on it. 'And as for you, you call yourself a friend of Leatherface?'

'We are acquainted with each other.'

'And who would you be?'

'Who I am is of no concern,' I said with an airiness which even surprised myself. 'You give him shelter?'

'Who says I lets any pestilent highwayman rest under my roof?' The small, colourless eyes glared at me, and I stared back at him, while I tried to recall to mind the sort of phrases which I had heard Leatherface use.

'I had news at Dover he would be here,' I said.

'I don't remember him mentioning you,' he said.

'Does he habitually acquaint you with the names of all his spies?'

'Spy, eh?'

'I am on an errand for him,' and I gave my words an impatient edge to them. 'You must know I arrived here on the Flying Hope.'

He nodded, and his eyes searched me for some evidence of my mission. The pistol was hidden inside my pocket and I kept the hat folded in my hand. With a flourish I brought out the pistol, and unintentionally pointed the barrels towards him. He shifted uneasily in his chair and a shadow passed swiftly across his face.

'Point that the other way,' he said, wheezingly. 'I've no time for such new-fangled inventions, no more than I have for the dangerous fools who flash them.'

'It belongs to Leatherface,' I said, and I lowered the pistol, but not too far. I was vastly encouraged by his fearful manner, and my tone became fairly menacing. 'Where is he?'

'He is here,' he said. 'Do you put that thing away.' I thrust it down into my pocket, but kept my hand on the butt. I was seething with excitement mingled with wariness; I realized my performance was so far succeeding, and I gave him a smile that was almost patronizing. He pushed the pipe back between his gums and his eyes flickered over me; greedy, calculating eyes they were.

'You are little more than a whipper-snapper,' he said, his wheezy voice tinged with contempt, and he took out his pipe and spat. 'You shall see him,' and he pointed a dirty stubby finger to the bell-rope near the door.

13

I crossed to the door, keeping my eyes on the man watching me from the chair, and jerked the bell-rope. Somewhere I heard the faint echo of a bell jangling, and then still keeping the pistol half-pointing at Old Reuben, I moved back to the table, looking down at him with a casual air trying to mask my wariness.

'When the dolt who brought you here chooses to answer,' he said, 'he will show you the way.' He spat again, and then turned his attention on me. 'His temper's none too sweet,' he wheezed, and I realized he was harking back to the subject of Leatherface. 'He was caught in the storm, and I believe got the rough end of the stick in some enterprise on the Dover Road tonight.' It was only with difficulty that I refrained from nodding as if to say that I knew all about that. Then I guessed that Leatherface had for reasons of his own not mentioned to the landlord of the Fox that the Flying Hope had been the object of his most recent attention. Therefore, I was not to know that this had, in fact, been the case. 'Spoke little to me, but to say to keep his wench out of his way.' He broke into a thin cackle of laughter, and I had a mental picture of the brazen creature I had encountered a short while since.

'If the game goes against him his mood grows surly,' I said as one who was only too well acquainted with the highwayman's moods. I must have succeeded in the impression I intended to convey, for a sudden anxious glint came into his eyes.

'No need to mention I was so swift to blab to you,' he said.

I gave him the benefit of an understanding smile. 'Rest assured I will maintain a discreet silence.' And I sat myself on the edge of the table, holding the pistol loosely in one hand, and tucking the hat under my other arm. A silence settled over the room, broken only by Old Reuben hawking noisily and spitting. It seemed to me an interminable time before I heard shuffling footsteps outside and the door opened. The twisted figure appeared, to enter with an obsequious attitude, his crafty eyes warning me that a feral cunning lurked behind his pale, unshaven features. The great bulk stirred in the high-backed chair, but I could not catch the look that I sensed Old Reuben exchanged with the other. In his wheezing voice was a growl of impatience.

'You've been long enough.'

'It's the guests, they keep me busy all the time.'

'Has the Flying Hope left?' I said.

The other nodded and informed me how the coach would have reached the other side of Canterbury. For a moment my mind held a picture of Miss Demarest as I had last seen her in the coach, her face shadowed by her hood, but her eyes bright as they looked at me. Old Reuben took his pipe out of his mouth and spat again and the chair creaked as he swivelled his vast bulk round to the creature with the twisted shoulder. 'Our young coxcomb,' he said, 'is here on a matter of business with someone he seems to think has gone to earth under my roof.' His eyes flickered to me and back again to the other, who gave a nod of understanding. 'You had best show him the way.' He paused, and the shadow of a grin passed across his bloated features, though I did not think there was much humour in it. 'We can let him into one of our little secrets,' he said.

I watched with mounting excitement as the other crossed the room and paused on one side of the mantelpiece which stretched beyond either extremity of the fireplace. The woodwork had been carved in elaborate shapes, leaves and acorns. I moved closer so that I could watch the operation which followed, though at the same time I could still see Old Reuben from the corner of my eye, and I still held the pistol-butt in a ready grip. My mind was well enough occupied with the prospect of my encountering Leatherface face to face, which situation I had to avoid if my plan was to materialize, but I kept my wits about me and was determined not to be caught off my guard by the proprietor of the Fox or his sly-eyed minion, who was now running a grubby finger along the carving, suddenly to press firmly. Immediately I heard a faint click from somewhere in the depths of the woodwork, and I could not refrain from a slight gasp as a section of the panelled wall to the right of the mantelpiece slowly swung inwards to reveal a dark cavity beyond.

I had heard many tales of secret panels and hidden passages in the great houses and inns, especially in those parts where smuggling was rife. But never before had I seen the working of such things. However, I contrived to bottle up my excitement at the sinister-looking aperture that had appeared so magically before me. 'Deuced clever,' was all I permitted myself to offer.

A faint cackle of laughter came from the high-backed chair and the flabby belly shook. 'Looks as dark as the inside of a barrel of pitch,' Old Reuben said. 'But you just follow him. He will not lead you astray.'

With a solemn bow of invitation the man who had opened the panel indicated me to step into the secret passage. I hesitated, glancing at Old Reuben. He had his pipe between his gums, and the imitation of a smile cracked his fleshy jowls into deep crevices. 'Follow him. Got eyes like a cat he has. Like a cat.'

Bracing myself I stepped into the opening and followed the man. He had gone but a few paces when there was a click behind me and the panelling closed again. No doubt Old Reuben had seen to it. As the light from the room I had quitted was cut off and I was enclosed by utter darkness, panic filled me. But the footsteps of my guide continued ahead and I followed after him. Once my eyes became accustomed to the darkness I could see his blurred outline just in front of me as he led the way. The ceiling was low and I was forced to stoop uncomfortably for most of the way. The floor was uneven and the sides of the tunnel so narrow that my shoulders brushed the walls. Suddenly the passage turned slightly and here it was so dark that the only evidence I had that the man still remained before me was his laboured breathing and the scuffing of his feet. When a few moments later there was a sudden silence I realized he must have stopped, and pulled up myself in time to save banging into him.

'Where are we?' I said.

He made no answer, and then I could hear the searching movement of his hand along the wall on one side. Suddenly there was a metallic click similar to that which I had heard in the room when the panelling had opened. A square of light appeared in front of us and I followed the sinister, crook-shouldered figure into a dimly-lit place which seemed to be a kind of store-shed. The walls were rough stone and the uneven floor was cobbled. There was one small window high up in the opposite wall through which filtered some light, but whether it was moonlight or from some lantern outside, I could not tell. In one corner was a vast clutter of broken crates and an old wine-barrel. The smell of stables and saddle-leather was strong, and as I stood there peering about me in the semi-darkness, a horse whinnied nearby. I wondered if it was Leatherface's animal.

From the heap of junk in the corner came a sharp scurrying noise and I made out the hurrying shape of a rat, which turned aside and ran along the floor near my feet. My guide thrust out a foot as if to kick at it, but it twisted sharply and vanished. 'Plenty of company here,' he said.

Although the thought of such horrible creatures around me sent shudders down my spine, I gave no sign. 'Where are we?' I said. For answer, he pointed across to what seemed to be nothing more than the blank wall. I stepped forward, thinking there must be another secret door which he had indicated for my notice, and for a moment he was beside me. But he must have taken a pace backwards, for next thing was he had clouted me across the back of the neck with the edge of his hand and I stumbled forward, tripping on a sack of straw and fell headlong to the cobblestones. By the time I raised myself the section of the wall through which we had entered was closing and a cackle of laughter came from behind it.

Blind with fury at my own stupidity, I rushed at the wall with a shout. I threw myself against where the secret door had been, but the part of the wall was as unyielding as the rest of it.

'Make all the row you want.' Even through the wall that divided us I could hear all the gloating in the twisted man's muffled tones. 'You'll just stay put until we decides what to do with you.'

I did not reply, but stood there with my ear against the wall listening until I knew he must be gone. My first impulse was to shout and rant at him to come back, but though the sweat of panic ran down my face, and apprehension of all manner of unknown terrors filled my mind, yet I remained calm enough to realize that Leatherface might be somewhere in the near vicinity. Whatever trap then I had allowed myself to fall into, my circumstances would not be improved by attracting him to the scene of my frustrated discomfiture. It was up to me to find a way out of the predicament as I had found a way into it, alone and unaided, so that I could proceed upon the enterprise in which I had engaged myself, and from which I stubbornly refused to turn back.

14

I stepped back from the wall, implacably unyielding, and glanced around me, bitterly angry with myself. What a fool I had been to imagine I could outwit that gross, crafty toad and his sly-faced minion. In spite of the cool tones I had fused into my voice, my authoritative almost arrogant manner, Old Reuben must have seen through it all and deduced that I was nothing more than an inexperienced impostor. No doubt he had received the impression that I was at least a spy for the Bow Street Runners; or at any rate some other enemy of Leather-face. And I thought I had handled myself well, that I had carried off my bluff most convincingly. It looked as if I was going to pay for my folly, and that dearly, for here I was, caught like a fly in that fat, loathsome spider's web, helpless and left to wait until he chose to devour me.

Another rat scurried about the floor,

and brought me out of my mood of depression and self-pity. This was no way to think, I told myself, and I braced my shoulders. I had to get out of this awful place somehow, and quickly. Every moment meant that the Flying Hope was drawing further and further distant; it was well on the road to London already. And there was much to be done to implement my crack-brained plan, for now I did find myself thinking of it ruefully in that light, and yet I would not in my youthful obstinacy relinquish it. But first I could do nothing until I had found my way out of my present predicament.

The whinneying of the horse came again and set me moving. Carefully, in the gloom I went round the rough wall where the door must be, feeling for some device, which would open it again. But there was nothing, only the edge of the door where it fitted snugly into the aperture. I could come across nothing which might be the spring which opened it. I came to the conclusion that the device whose metallic click I had heard must be on the other side of the door only. For some reason it had not been thought necessary for the door to be able to be opened this side. I stood back in the middle of the room again and looked up at the small window which seemed to me to offer the only hope of escape, and that a remote hope too. The sound of the horse came from beyond the wall in which the window was placed, and it occurred to me that the real reason for its height was not so that it should be out of reach of a trapped fool such as I, but because it opened on to the loft of a stable next door, which in fact held the horse I could hear. The faint glimmer of light which fitfully illuminated my surroundings could be from the moon shining into the loft, or could be the light of a lantern there, or just outside.

I crossed to the corner and my nerves tingled at the prospect of disturbing one or more rats. I pulled out the old barrel and rolled it along until it was underneath the window, where I stood it on one end; even when I clambered on to it my outstretched hand was inches short of the narrow window-sill. I jumped down and found a crate which seemed strong enough to take my weight. I placed this on top of the barrel and carefully balancing myself eventually climbed up on to it. My perch swayed precariously, but I steadied myself by clawing to the rough wall, until I could reach the sill with just one hand and then the other, and gradually eased myself up until my face was level with the window.

It was glazed with a sheet of dirty glass, through which I could dimly make out what was, as I had guessed a loft. Across the other side of it a door opened in to what was presumably the yard of the inn, and it was the pale glimmer of the moon which gave the light which had shown through the window. I could make out nothing else, for the window was as dirty on the other side as it was on mine, which I tried to clear with the corner of my coat-sleeve. I could make out what appeared to be bundles of hay, the rest was shadow and darkness. The window-frame was just about large enough to permit me to wriggle through, and my first thought was to shatter the glass with the butt of the pistol which I had shoved in my pocket. Leatherface's hat was crushed into my other pocket. Then I decided the noise of breaking glass might attract unwanted attention; apart from the proprietor of the Fox, and the man with the twisted shoulder, Leatherface himself might be in the near vicinity. I wanted to meet him no more than the others. And so, the pistol raised, I hesitated before I drove it against the window. Swaying dangerously on my perch, so that I had to steady myself against the wall, I pulled out the hat and wrapped it round the pistol-butt, thinking to deaden the sound, and then began to beat against the glass, more and more strongly until at last it cracked and finally a piece broke and fell with a faint tinkle to the floor below. Now I managed to work the rest of the glass loose and remove the entire window piece by piece. I could not help the faint crack and tinkle of the glass as pieces fell to the floor, but the noise was not so loud. No one disturbed me at my task.

Now I was able to pause and look

through, my view unimpeded, into what was indeed a loft. A large one with bales of hay, and heaps of sacking strewn about the floor. The window was just above the floor-level and I could plainly see by the edge of a shaft of moonlight through the door the outline of a figure stretched out in the straw. It appeared to be a man, and he had heaped the straw up around him and was lying face downwards in it. He lay so still that he might have been dead had it not been for the sound of his breathing which I could plainly hear.

But what with the gloom and the straw which halfcovered the figure lying there I could not make out who it was. That was a matter about which I should soon satisfy myself. Congratulating myself upon having so far succeeded in not awakening the sleeper, I began to ease myself through the window, thrusting the pistol and the hat before me, and pausing every now and then in case the slumbering figure stirred or awoke; but it slept on undisturbed.

I was forced to break away all the remaining jagged pieces of glass before the aperture was large enough for me to squeeze through, and when I had at last accomplished it I eased myself most carefully into the loft, the dust from the floor rising in my face and half-blinding me and it was all I could do to save myself from sneezing or choking out aloud. And all the time my scalp crawled at the notion that some curious rat would appear and boldly poke its snout into my face to investigate who this intruder of the night might be. At last, a deep breath, and with my hands and arms through so that my shoulders could take the weight against the window-frame either side, I wriggled and heaved myself forward. Inadvertently the dangling toe of my shoe kicked against the top of the crate upon which I had lately been standing, it toppled and crashed from the barrel to the floor.

I lay there, half-way through the opening, hardly daring to breathe, my eyes fastened on the sleeping figure. My tension eased and the pent-up breath hissed through my gritted teeth as I realized that even the noise had not stirred that sleep-numbed brain. I uttered a prayer of thankfulness that the barrel had not also toppled over; surely the hollow rumble of that falling about the floor must have awakened the dead? In another few moments I was through and crouching on the loft floor.

While I waited to get my breath back after such energetic contortions, I could hear the stamping of hooves and the sound of a horse in what must be a stable below. The smell of horse-sweat and harness-leather came strongly up to my dust-filled nostrils. Outside and in the loft all was silent except for the breathing of the inert shape in the straw. I rose and cautiously moved towards the figure, which now at a closer glance was that of a man. It was not possible to see his face and most of his body was covered by a blanket, but my heart stopped for a second as I saw that the build seemed familiar, blurred as it was by the straw and the shadows.

Now I could make out the clothes which lay scattered about, the black velvet cloak, the elegantly-cut riding-boots, and near them the spurs glinted. And there, near one outflung hand, lay the black leather mask. The figure still seemed soundly asleep and then, my heart now thudding, I bent and picked up the mask. As I stood there, with the pistol in my pocket again, the hat clapped on my head for convenience in carrying, and the mask in my hand, Jack Morgan's jesting words echoed in my mind: *'Why, you'll be able to pretend that you're Leatherface himself.'*

I could not help a smile in the gloom. Moving with the utmost caution I proceeded to put into action the plan that had all along been in my mind. If I had been deterred from it by recent misadventure, I was now keyed up again with fresh resolve quickened by the instruments of my purpose now so close to hand.

I pulled off my shoes and slowly and quietly pulled on the leather boots. They were too big for me, but no matter, I moved carefully in them. Next the black velvet jacket, which hung on me, for my shoulders were half the width of the owner's. It smelled of horse-sweat and saddle-leather, and a faint indefinable perfume, as if it was used to the atmosphere of women's boudoirs or the scented *salon* of a woman of Society. Next, I fixed on the mask beneath the hat. It felt chill to my heated face, and was also too large for me, but I fixed it firmly enough. Thus accoutred, and unconsciously swaggering in my new get-up I threw a look at the slumbering form and started for the door of the loft which led to the yard. There was the usual half-door, and I knew that there would be no means of descent to the yard that way, no stairs, no ladder; and I wondered if there was a rope by which I could swing down. And then the toe of my boot touched something metallic beneath the straw. I bent and scraped away the straw and found the steel ring of a trap-door. This was a better exit, I thought, I could descend into the stable without the risk of being observed by any prying eyes outside.

I pulled up the ring and silently opened the trap; looking down I could make out the black horse fidgetting in its stall. At the same time I realized that there was no ladder to the stable directly beneath me. I looked round me for the means by which I could lower myself. The loft must have been reached from outside, I concluded, or the ladder hauled up through the trap-door. Then I saw the ladder in the shadows. But I had my own idea, as at the same moment I noted hanging over a beam a rope. I grabbed it and was going to knot it over the beam above the trap when I decided that it was long enough for me to loop it through the ring on the underside of the trap-door, using it as a double line. I paid it out through the opening to the stable floor. Then I sat myself on the edge and began to lift the trap towards me.

My manœuvre would, I calculated, allow me to escape without leaving a trace behind for anyone's benefit. It tickled my imagination to make such a mysterious exit. Provided I was careful the operation was simple enough. I pulled the trap over me so that it rested on my head, then I eased myself down through the opening, lowering myself with my hands which had a firm grip of the edge. The double length of rope was suspended by my side from the ring, and I gripped it between my feet. Soon I hung from the edge of the opening with the trap-door now resting upon my straining knuckles. Without putting any weight on it I entwined my legs around the rope and then let go the edge of the opening with one hand and grasped the double rope. Then I took away my other hand and let the trap drop home. Because of the bare inch or so that it had to fall the sound was even less than I had expected.

I shinned down and pulled one end of the rope until I had it all out of the ring. I threw this into one of the empty stalls and went towards the horse; but before I reached it, there came a sudden sound outside the stabledoor, and chill fingers played a tattoo up and down the nape of my neck. Someone was coming to the stable. Having got so far I could not bear the thought of being stopped now. It would be the end of all my hopes. I clenched my teeth as the stable-door slowly opened. No doubt it was the man with one shoulder higher than the other, or another of Old Reuben's sinister creatures, come to seek out Leatherface; or perhaps by now my escape from the room at the end of the secret passage had been discovered. I thought of trying to hide myself somewhere in the stable, but there was not time enough; I was in the direct line of sight of whoever it was coming in. In another moment I would be discovered, Leatherface would be called, and either way I should be lucky indeed to get out of this trap.

I gripped the butt of the pistol in my pocket, thinking wildly that I might use it as a club in my defence. I stood there trembling, waiting. The door opened wider and the moonlight slanted in and framed on the threshold stood a young woman. The red-haired young woman from the inn. I stepped further back into the shadows, as if it was of any use, I stood no chance of eluding this unexpected vision out of the moonlit night. And indeed my movement brought an exclamation from her, and then a smile appeared on her shadowed face and I caught the brightness in those bold eyes.

'Leatherface,' she said, in an eager whisper and came swiftly towards me, her arms outstretched in fond affection.

15

The sound of his name sent a cold shiver down my spine. I halted in my tracks, a hand flying involuntarily to my face and finding the black leather mask there, which I had momentarily forgotten. From the tone of her voice it was most apparent what the relationship was between her and the man for whom she had mistaken me. Here was a complication which took the wind out of my sails and no mistake, even as I realized that it would be typical of Leatherface's kind to have such a wench as was now moving towards me so eagerly, for his doxy, his light-o'-love. I stood there, like any tongue-tied dolt, numb-headed and vainly railing against the misfortune that should have brought her across my path, just at the moment when the coast had seemed clear. Another few minutes, so I told myself, biting my lip in my dismay, and I should have been far from the Fox, which was well-named enough for was it not a lair for crafty beings, of evil hearts, a place of nerve-freezing twists of fortune such as had now appeared in the shape of this bold-eyed, red-haired creature before me?

I brushed these ruminations aside as swiftly as they entered my head, for my desperate objective now was deadly plain. I must be rid of her and that quickly, and I had to accomplish the manœuvre without revealing to her that I was other than he for whom she took me, in the moonlight and shadow of the stable. It was, I thought, a moment for boldness and to trust to good luck. And so pulling the hat down over the mask I stepped forward and spoke in what I fervently prayed was an imitation of those harsh, rasping tones with which my ears had grown so familiar. 'I told Reuben I was not to be disturbed,' I said shortly.

She was close to me, too close for my sense of safety. Apart from my voice she must realize that I was not of the same stature of the man I was impersonating, attired as I was in his clothes and swaggering boots. And while she might unconsciously be putting down this difference in our height and breadth to some trick of the moonlight, the illusion would not deceive her for long. The implication in what I had said did not make her pause. Her face was in the shadow, but I could see the soft glow of her eyes, the dark lashes curled above her cheeks, the gleam of her teeth. 'Pox take the old devil,' she said, in an impatient whisper. 'I've waited long enough to find you.' I could see the bold gaze narrow, and her voice became gently teasing. 'And since when have you thought my company disquieted you?' There was a faint perfume from her hair, which flamed like fire where a shaft of moonlight caught at it. 'Though I do agree the pair of us together should remain undisturbed for the rest of the night.'

I felt myself go hot and cold, beads of perspiration sprang to my brow as I thought wildly for words to speak which would help to extricate me from this situation fraught with such peril for my scheming and my hopes. 'Luck has been against me,' I said, forcing a snarl to my throat. 'I've no time for dalliance, even with you.'

'Dalliance,' she said, and her mouth curved in a pout. 'That's not the name you gave it last time you topped me. You went into raptures about how soft and loving I was, that my thighs were like columns of alabaster, only much warmer, that my — '

The blood rushed to my face, I felt scarcely able to breathe behind the mask; and it was all I could do to choke out a growl, as if of impatience at her. She broke off, and now her eyes were brighter than before, and sparkling with amusement. 'Do I excite you so much?' she said, and I knew she was deliberately misconstruing my reaction to what she was saying; and now her hands were gripping my shoulders. 'Then why do we wait on a moment?'

I must blurt out something to stop her, and my imagination stunned as it was by her brazenness, contrived to rise to the occasion as with a rush of words, I said: 'I have an appointment, don't stay me, since it will mean a trinket or two for you.' And

I made to push past her. But her arms had slipped round my neck and she was clinging to me so that I was brought to a full stop. 'It will be too late,' I began to say, but she cut me short with a derisive laugh.

'You have a glib tongue. More like you're on your way to some whore's tryst.'

'I have a rendezvous with the Flying Hope,' I said, trying to free myself, yet not using her too roughly. 'Do you hold me further with your talk and I shall never overtake it.' I felt her arms slacken about me and congratulating myself that my ruse might succeed, I held her off and swung her aside. I was almost free of this unexpected interruption to my plan, upon which I had expended so much thought and energy; I was not to be thwarted by this red-haired apparition. An angry exclamation forced me to face her, and now I saw that she was watching me curiously, her eyes wide open in perplexity. She had a round, pretty face that had not yet been imprinted with the coarseness so plainly apparent in the over-painted creature I had encountered during my earlier exploration of the inn. Her neck was short but slender, her long hair fell round her shoulders which arose plump and bare above her dress. There was a half-smile touching the corners of her mouth, but there was a sudden uncertainty about it, and even as I watched, a wariness crept into her expression which made me feel uneasy. I did not care for the speculation in her glance and I turned aside, filled only with the intention of getting to the horse in its stall and recklessly riding off on it, throwing caution to the winds, come what may.

She gripped my arm. 'You have held up the Flying Hope once tonight. Only a fool would attempt it a second time. But if you must, grant me one thing before you venture.'

While I was intrigued by the revelation which she had just vouchsafed that she was in possession of the intelligence respecting the hold-up of the coach, and I wondered what other secrets she held concerning those who preyed along the Dover Road, I tried to puzzle out what might be behind her request. Some stratagem, an inner voice warned me, sure enough.

'What?' I asked, as gratingly impatient as I could.

'A kiss,' she said softly. 'Just a kiss to remember you by.'

Swiftly she moved close and pressed her body to mine. For a moment panic filled me, for certainly, in order to comply with her request, she must demand that I take off the mask; but she did not do so. Her hands stole round my shoulders and she tilted her head back, her eyes glittering brightly at me, her mouth waiting for mine. There was nothing for it but to do what I did, which was to bend my head and while her hot mouth clung to mine, she placed my arms around her waist so that I could feel the soft warmth of her beneath her dress. Her arms slipped back around me and in another moment she slowly took her mouth away.

'I guessed as much,' she said, 'and now I know for certain.' With a quick movement that took my fuddled wits by surprise, she broke away and tore the mask from my face. She stepped back, breathing quickly, but there was a faint smile still playing about her lips. But I could only stand there, eying her miserably. 'An impostor.' I was quick to realize there was no anger and little surprise in her tone, so that I experienced the feeling that she had all along known it was not the man she had first mistaken me for. 'I remember your face,' she said, 'you were with the party from the Flying Hope.' I nodded, there was nothing that I could think of to say. 'And didn't I interrupt you with your actress-friend,' she added, her lip curled insinuatingly.

But I could only stare at her, helplessly. I felt so discouraged that even the notion which had leapt to my mind that I should present my unloaded pistol at her and attempt to bluff her into believing it was loaded and allow me to get away, I rejected. She did not look the sort who would bluff easily. Then she seemed to recall having mentioned the name of the coach, I caught a flicker across her face, as if she had thought of something which puzzled her. It occurred to me that she must be wondering how I had been involved in the hold-up, and what connection it might have with my present situation, which found me rigged out in the garb of the very highwayman who had attempted to rob us at the point of his pistols. These conjectures mingled in my mind with the realization of the utter failure of my whole venture, I stepped towards her involuntarily, and then hesitated as I saw that she stared at me with some defiance. 'What are you going to do?' I said.

'One false move,' she said, 'and of one thing you can be certain, I'll scream for him you're passing yourself off as.' She paused to give a glance upward and then her expression relaxed again in a smile. 'No doubt sleeping off the wine.'

'I took only his cloak and mask,' I said, the words tumbling out pell-mell. 'His hat and this pistol,' I patted my pocket, 'and which is unloaded, did he lose in the hold-up. That was when, he will tell you if he has not yet done so, I helped him escape.' It seemed to me that this was a good moment to indicate that I was not ill-disposed to the sleeping man above. 'It is most urgent,' I went on quickly, 'that I go now in this guise, or all the risk I have taken so far will be for naught.' I spoke desperately, hoping to win her sympathy and, as it suddenly occurred to me that such a turn of Fate was not entirely outside the realm of possibility, her co-operation into the bargain.

'What in Satan's name do you plan?' she said. 'To step into his shoes?' She threw a look upwards. 'To rob your fellow-passengers? For what purpose?'

'There's no time to explain.'

'There's time enough.' She caught my arm once more. 'More haste, less speed, my young cockerel.'

'But I have to overtake the coach, already I am much delayed.'

'As to that, I might help you,' she said, 'for a consideration.'

I did not catch the nuance in her voice, I saw only the laughter in her eyes, which I took to be on account of amused excitement that moved her. My heart leapt. Had I found a friend in her, an accomplice whose guile and knowledge could be of inestimable value to me? How could she help me so that I might make up the time I had so grievously lost here at this inn of dark hazards and evil machinations?

'I know these parts like the back of my hand,' she said as if answering my unspoken questions. 'I could set you on your way so that you could be ahead of the Flying Hope.' She paused, her eyelashes lowered, so that there was a shy expression in her sideways glance which she directed upon me. Still I hesitated; filled as I was with renewed hope and excitement, I found myself unable to comprehend her offer of co-operation. I could not fathom what her motive might be. It could do no harm to tell her, I then decided; since she knew already that I was up to some unlawful game, it might be better to accept her offer rather than provoke her to rage and revenge, which she could easily wreak upon me, merely by warning Old Reuben, or Leatherface, or setting the watch of the city upon me, though it struck me as unlikely that being what she was, she would follow the latter course of action. It was at that moment that I suddenly grasped how much she held my fate in her hands, perhaps my life, leave alone the success of my plan. She had only, as she had threatened at first, to scream and it would bring Leatherface down upon me from the loft like a ton of sea-coals, if not all the inn about my ears. She understood precisely what was passing through my thoughts for she wrinkled her nose at me and nudged me with her elbow.

'Lord Deal,' I said, making up my mind and coming out with it in a typical rush, 'he's lost his snuff-box, worth five thousand pounds it is, and with him in the coach is the notorious pickpocket, George Barrington, disguised in parson's cloth. I know he has it, Leatherface himself proved it to me. But Lord Deal fancies I am concerned in it, I am sure.'

She had listened without a sign of surprise at what I had just informed her, either she knew something about it already from her lover, or she was used to such shady devices and murky tales of cunning and wickedness. I went on to describe how I had sensed Lord Deal's suspicion of me, and perhaps that of Mr. Ellis, over the matter of the unloaded pistol that was loaded all the time. I spoke urgently and she listened as I wound up by saying: 'I must reinstate myself in Lord Deal's opinion and anyone else's by forcing Barrington at pistol-point to return the stolen snuff-box to its rightful owner. That done, I shall reveal my true identity.' I paused breathlessly, appealing to her. 'Do you not agree it's worth the risk?'

'A more crack-pot notion I never heard before,' she said. 'And I wouldn't give a jot for its chance of success.' She saw my woebegone expression and her eyes glowed softly, but whether with reluctant admiration or sympathy I could not tell. She moved closer to me. 'All the same,' she said, and her tone had filled with a tenderness which stirred me strangely, 'it is a game after my own heart.' My blood quickened, I stared at her eagerly. 'I will help you,' she said, 'to the utmost. Though I am but a weak, foolish girl with all of a girl's follies and longings.'

The air was suddenly taut as she sighed languorously and laid her head against my shoulder, and a plump arm reached up to encircle my neck. 'And you would not refuse to help me in return,' she said, her words muffled in my coat. Now her fingers seemed to burn into the nape of my neck as she dragged my face down to her.

I wanted to struggle free, get away, yet some power sapped my will so that I could not raise my head. I told myself that there was nothing for one to do, but give way to her imperious demands, that if I attempted to thwart her now, to brush her aside, the passion which racked her would turn as swiftly to fury. That with all its dangerous consequences I dare not risk. Yet was it this alone which made me so unresisting, so weak? And if it was because other emotions were clamouring within me so that my head reeled like a drunken fool's, was I to be accounted so blameworthy for my lack of will, the weakness that invaded every nerve and muscle of my limbs?

With her arm tight around my waist,

and pressing herself close to my side, she urged me out of the shaft of moonlight wherein we had clung so desperately together and into the shadows. I sensed what was in her mind and while one part of me fought against the overpowering urgency that throbbed through her so manifestly, the other part of me was pitifully weak.

As we moved, like prisoner and gaoler together in some dungeon whose walls were built of both terror and delight, so that who was to say which of us was the more imprisoned, I tried not to look into her eyes. But I could feel them blazing at me so that I was impelled to turn my head. They were smiling boldly, and yet with a tenderness I had never seen in a woman's eyes before, and a yearning which made me catch my breath. And then her mouth closed over mine once more, one hand reached up and dragged my face down to hers. She was murmuring words to me incoherently.

Then she was pulling me down with her on to some bundles of hay which had been stacked in a corner, and the sweet scent of the hay mingled in my nostrils with the scent of her tumbled red hair, the warm perfume of her neck and shoulders.

My brain was spinning in torment, my knees were as water, I was trembling from head to foot, as I felt her hand clinging to my neck as if she might never let go even for the crack of doom itself.

Some portion of my sensibilities clung on the disjointed sequence of images in which Leatherface, still asleep up above in the loft figured; of the Flying Hope speeding through the night on to London, the faces of the self-styled Mr. Fisher flashing before my mind's eye, and of Miss Demarest — and I fancied I could catch a glint of mocking laughter in her expression — and yet all this seemed strangely distant and apart from me, as if it was happening upon some other plane of experience, as if I had become two separate beings; and the one that part of my thoughts held on to was someone else and not myself at all, gasping in this cruelly sweet and tenderly brutal embrace.

Then everything was blotted out from my mind, now all that filled my consciousness was the passion-contorted face before me, white and gleaming and the red, dishevelled hair matted with sweat and the great eyes starry bright as if with fever, blazing up at me out of the darkness.

16

I bent low over the black horse's mane as we sped through the tunnel of trees whose branches formed a lattice-work of shadow and moonlight above me, the horse's hooves beating a rhythmic tattoo on the rough, narrow lane.

Now the tunnel ended and recalling the instructions I had been given, I turned my mount aside to jump a ditch and without slackening speed headed across the undulating stretch of common reaching out before me to a mist-shrouded copse.

That was the next sign-post by which I was to plot the course that the red-haired creature at the inn had mapped out for me, while she had lain beside my trembling frame, smoothing my hair.

I had contrived carefully to note what she said in my memory, despite that every moment of what had recently gone before flooded back to me, overwhelming me with shame and confusion. Then when I had sat upright, trying to reckon what æons must have gone past while we had been locked in our embrace, 'How long can we have been here?' I said, and she had smiled at my agitation.

'Too long and yet not long enough,' she said, and then we helped each other to get to our feet, while she had calmly rearranged her bodice and smoothed her skirts, while I shyly turned away and saw that my own clothes were straightened and put to rights. I put on the black hat and had reached for the leather mask when she put her hand on my arm.

'Wear that now,' she said, 'and you will get no distance at all.' She thrust it down from my face with a click of her tongue. 'Keep it and the pistol out of sight until you're ready to pounce on your prey.'

I nodded, quickly realizing the commonsense in her advice and had slipped the mask into the pocket with the pistol, when there was a movement above us and the sound of a sleepy cursing, as if something had roused the man in the loft out of a vivid dream. I had given a gasp of alarm. Leatherface was waking from the wine-heavy sleep in which he had lain, while almost immediately below him his own sweetheart and I had been enfolded in each other's arms. At any moment he would be descending. If he guessed at what had transpired he would need no rope to take the place of the length I had quietly removed, in order to lower himself, a raising of the trap-door and down he would swing and drop. The red-haired wench had sensed my apprehension. 'He will never know,' she said, her mouth close to my ear. 'But it is time for you to be on your way. Look out to watch that the yard is clear. I will get his horse.'

I hesitated, anxious lest she could not manage the animal without fuss or noise, but as she moved quickly and silently into the shadows where the blur of the black horse showed and the sound of its pawing the floor reached me, I suffered no further doubt that she could carry out her task more efficiently than I. Almost for certain she knew the animal and its ways and it would know her and obey her whispered command. So I went to the stable-door, edging it open to give me a view of the yard in the moonlight.

It appeared empty of anyone, not an ostler stirred, nor any traveller so far as I could perceive as I peered out in the direction of the archway made by the upper storey of the inn, and which opened on to the road. All was quiet and deserted, except for an owl which hooted somewhere nearby and the whining of some scavenging dog, as I looked cautiously round wondering if by chance there was an exit from the courtyard other than that which led into the road. Some way out which appeared more secret would make my chance of departure unmolested more likely, I had thought. The external wall of the stable to my right terminated in a low, rambling mass at right angles to the inn. Here, I had calculated, might be the room where I had encountered the malevolent figure of Old Reuben, with its secret passage leading to the rat-hole in which I had been trapped, I noted that for the whole length of the side of this building no window overlooked the courtyard.

My gaze travelled to a high wall forming the end of the yard and there where it merged into the shadows of the other wing of the rambling inn I thought I could make out the dark rectangle of a door in the wall, suggesting to me at once that it opened on to an alley or some byway. If this was indeed the case this door seemed to offer the best way of quitting the place if I was to leave unwitnessed. I turned back into the stable as the girl led the horse towards me, its hooves deadened by the straw. No further sound or movement came from above. The girl saw my quick upward look and nodded reassuringly. 'Doubtless, he's sleeping again,' she said.

I dragged the stable-door wide as noiselessly as I could. I halted the red-haired doxy and the horse as she urged it forward, and pointed across to the black rectangle in the wall. 'That way? What lies outside?'

She pressed my arm encouragingly. 'You have a good eye,' she said. 'That is the way, it is an alley little used and leads to a lane which is the way you must take. Do you go unbolt the door.' While she waited, quieting the horse with a whisper, I slipped out and keeping close against the wall to the right, I made my way cautiously until I stood opposite the door in the wall which was my objective. I paused breathlessly, my eyes searching all about me for any sign of movement, but the place was so quiet I might have been in a graveyard. I darted boldly out across the cobbles full into the moonlight. Gaining the door swiftly and silently I found the heavy bolt above my head and I drew it back carefully so that it made the slightest grating sound. I pulled at the door and it creaked open.

It was at that moment that a stab of light appeared from somewhere further along the shadowed, straggling building and a figure emerged, moving in the pool of illumination made by the lantern swinging from his hand. In the instant that I saw him I made out the twisted shoulder and sharp, crafty face of the creature who had lured me along the secret passage and slammed the lock on me in my rat-infested prison. Then I had slipped behind the door which I had pulled half-open and waited, my heart thudding in my throat, wondering if I had been discovered. But Old Reuben's evil minion did not appear to have noticed and as the scrape of his scuffling feet drew nearer I decided that so intent was he on his purpose, whatever that was, it was more than likely he would pass me by unconscious of the door behind which I lurked. And then of a sudden I realized what was his purpose indeed, and it brought the hairs bristling upon the back of my neck. For he had turned aside and was crossing the yard, and going straight to the stable.

Whether he was minded to carry out some instruction of Old Reuben's, or was expected by Leatherface, or whether he was merely intent upon locking up for the night made no difference to the dread result of his appearance on the scene. Even if the red-haired doxy had seen him and returned the horse to his stall and hid herself, my position still remained desperate, for supposing the hunched-shouldered man roused Leatherface? What would be my fate, and that of the wench too, at the hands of the highwayman or the proprietor and his cronies of the inn I did not pause to contemplate, my head was over-full of a dozen fears and possibilities.

I knew I had got to do something to stop the creature who had started across the moonlit yard for the stable. But what could I do that would put him out of the way, that would not risk causing a scene and commotion? There seemed to be only one way and as the idea came into my mind I acted. I disarranged my clothes and ruffled my hair, and pushing the door behind which I was hiding open wide so that it creaked loudly, I hung on to it as if trying to support myself. With my head sunk low and my shoulders bent I tried to give the impression that I had just pushed open the door from outside and was weary to the state of collapse. The noise I made at once snapped the man's attention round on me and he stopped in his tracks and stared. Now, if only he would come to me to investigate what was amiss, I stood a chance of encompassing my design. Fortune was kind to me, for at that moment a ragged cloud straggled across the moon and the brightly-lit yard became dimmed and full of shadows, so that my intended victim must come closer if he wanted to see who it was hung there on the gate. In order to lure him even nearer, I muttered hoarsely: 'Help me . . . Help.' I kept my voice low so that it was only just loud enough to carry to him.

Perhaps he thought it was some traveller, sick or overcome with the result of imbibing too freely of liquor; and perhaps he calculated that this seemingly helpless soul might yield up a fat purse merely for the taking. But at any rate, he did not call out, but hurried across to me while I still made a pretence of clinging weakly to the door and muttering for help. He stood off and held up the lantern, thrusting it near my face and I looked up to see the gleam of surprised recognition in his cunning eyes.

'How did you — ?' he began to say, but as he spoke I lurched forward and before he could guess my intention I dealt him a blow with all the strength I could on the side of his head. The lantern fell, clattering to the cobbles and was immediately extinguished, as he staggered back against the wall. Mercilessly I stepped in and hit him with every ounce of my force again. This time fair and square on the point of his jaw, so that I could not resist telling myself that Jack Morgan could not have delivered the punch more skilfully. With a faint groan that died on his thin lips he slid down the wall and crumpled on the ground. I bent, thinking it better not to leave him there, in case he recovered consciousness too quickly for my wish, and took him by the shoulders and dragged him across to the stables where the wench was waiting.

'It was a cool thing you did,' she said, in a whisper quivering with admiration, so that I could not help giving a little breathless laugh of pride at my exploit. She helped dump the figure into a corner, and I took the precaution of knotting a piece of cord I found round his wrists.

The stable had darkened since the moon still hung behind the cloud, and she urged me to the door where the horse stood quiet and ready. 'You should get away,' she said, 'while the moon stays hidden.' She led out the horse and with me at her side, we crossed to the door without further delay. Once in the alley I closed the door after me.

'Into the saddle and then help me up,' she said. What she said took me aback, for I had not considered that she would be accompanying me. She caught my hesitation and said: 'You will need me to guide you out of this maze and set you on the short-cut you must take.' Accordingly I got up into the saddle, and then took her hands and pulled her up behind me. She held on with her arms round my waist, and I urged the horse forward at a walking pace. I had learned to ride almost from the hour I could walk, for my father was an enthusiast, and hunted regularly, and I was accounted a moderately good horseman. The alleyway was rough and narrow, twisting and turning like a snake for some fifty yards or more, and now the moon was temporarily gone, it was as dark as pitch. The wall flanking it on either side echoed and re-echoed to the hoof-beats, but all the way through we met no one, nor was there the sound of any pursuit. Now the alley opened out into a lane, and at a whisper over my shoulder I turned left and with quickening pace proceeded past low hedges and overhanging trees which formed the boundaries of gardens beyond which were situated large houses. Here and there lighted windows shone through the darkness and the trees and from one house came the strains of music and the sound of voices and laughter; as if some late dancing party was in full progress. I felt the wench's fingers playing affectionately about my neck and she hummed softly to the fading music.

For myself, I was in no such spirit. Too anxious I was to get on, lest all I had been through should even now bring me nothing but failure, that I should be too late to waylay the Flying Hope. I estimated that it must have left the inn three-quarters of an hour ago, and whatever short-cut I might take and however fast the animal under me went, it would be impossible to overhaul the coach with such a start. I spurred the black horse into a canter and very soon we emerged on to a road, beyond which stretched a common, a vast expanse it was, looking lonely and desolate with wraiths of mist rising against the night-sky. 'Leave the road,' came the voice once more in my ear, 'and get on to the heath.'

I obeyed and we were speeding towards a small copse, where I could make out a rough track and again obeying the voice over my shoulder I pulled up, looked round and waited. 'This is where we say good-bye.' She spoke softly, and held an arm still about me. 'Keep to the track until you come to a fork at a wood. Take the right fork across another heath, until you see a lane ahead of you overhung with the branches of trees. Along the lane to its end, over the ditch on your right across one more lonely heath. At a copse branch to the left and it must bring you out on the Dover Road. Keep a good speed and you will be there ahead of the Flying Hope, and time enough to hide beneath a cluster of trees at the dip in the road. Then may you wear his mask.'

I glanced ahead at the pathway through the gorse and rough grass that stretched towards the dark line of the horizon. I turned to look into her face, pale in the darkness. Her eyes were bright, her mouth curved over her teeth in a mischievous smile.

'And you?'

'I shall slip back the way I came. Oh, do not fret yourself, I shall not lose my way. I have done that once tonight, but not again.' The bold amusement in her voice brought a hot blush to my face, and the recollection of what had passed between us such a short while ago caused me to stir on my saddle, tongue-tied and unable to meet her gaze.

Her tone and attitude reassured me that she would be safe enough, and I had the impression that she had made this same excursion more than once before, no doubt with Leatherface. I helped her to dismount from behind me and it was at that moment I was filled with an overpowering sense of loss, so that for a moment I could not let her go, and she had to unclasp my hands, still holding on to my left hand as she stood there staring up at me from the shadows. While my brain was clogged with a score of thoughts, and my heart felt choked with an emotion of strange tenderness and longing such as I had never experienced before, yet I could find no words to speak to her. I could only mumble inadequately thanks for her help, and say that I truly hoped she would come to no harm as a result of this night's adventures. And then I murmured something to the effect that she must go her way and I must go mine.

And she all the time staring up at me, her soft mouth parted, her eyes melting and yet oddly mocking at the same time, her red hair caught by capfuls of breeze whipped off the heath, and I with not a glimmer of what thoughts she might be thinking behind her round, pretty face.

Suddenly she bent and her warm mouth was pressed to my hand, passionately and wordlessly, as if she would never let me go. As suddenly she looked up again, watching my face with sharp intakes of breath, her eyes wide and alight with the fire that burned within her.

'Do nothing foolish,' she said hoarsely. 'Think of me sometimes. And good luck go with you.'

Before I could speak she turned abruptly and darted away into the gloom, which now seemed chill and threatening, while I watched her running form heading back the way we had come, until it was lost in the shadows. She had not looked back. I had spurred the black horse and we flung ourselves along the path ahead.

I had kept her directions clearly in my head as I pushed onwards; and now I paused momentarily at the dark copse looming up at me silhouetted against the sky, which was still dulled by the raggle-taggle of clouds which continued to drift across the moon. I concluded that I had been riding for twenty minutes since I had left the red-haired creature though I could not estimate the miles we had covered. Not once had the black horse stumbled or faltered, and now it stood for a moment, the steam rising from the sweating withers, the saliva frothing at the corners of the mouth. The Dover Road, I felt sure, could not be more than half a mile. I listened for the sound of galloping hooves and the rattle of wheels, but there was nothing, except the cry of some night-bird from the black trees nearby, and then the sudden high-pitched squeal of a rabbit, fallen victim to some stoat or fox.

My brow furrowed with the anxiety that, for all I had been reassured, I was too late, and biting my lip, I urged the horse forward again and swinging left past the copse, pushed on even though my hopes were low and my sensibilities warned me that the Flying Hope was by now many miles beyond my reach, speeding unimpeded for London, and that my venture had failed.

17

The track was straight and less rough so that I was able to spur my mount into a steady gallop, my attention at first occupied with guiding the animal underneath me. So I had little time to reflect any more on what had gone before. Only the immediate future counted, my arrival for my rendezvous in time. I pushed on impatiently, the black horse seeming as anxious as I to be moving speedily, shaking his head and whinneying in a mild, somewhat plaintive manner, so that I gave him more rein. I realized that so accustomed was he to travelling fast across country under cover of darkness that he required no guidance from me to keep him steady, and when we ran through a straggle of birch trees it was all I could do to duck and weave out of the way of the overhanging branches.

Up and down the shallow gradients, skirting meadowland and cropped fields, and leaving on one side or the other a dark lonely farmhouse or a woodcutter's cottage whose occupants had long since retired, we met no one, while I could still see nothing resembling a road.

My anxiety was mounting, so that I found myself gritting my teeth and I was beginning to wonder if I should ever reach the Dover Road; that either the young woman from the Fox had erred in her directions or I had misremembered them, when I sighted a clump of trees and an area of thickly-spread shrubs at the top of a steep gradient ahead. The formation of the ground to one side of this suggested that just beyond might be the dip of which the red-haired wench had spoken. It seemed that my conjecture was correct, for the black horse checked his pace before I could do it for him. We began to climb the gradient, and my heart rose with excited anticipation.

We now struck a rough path, with loose stones and boulders in our way, and presently the animal halted, as if waiting for me to dismount. This I did and led the way on foot. Eventually the path ended at where the trees thinned, and a few yards away at the bottom of the gently sloping bank ran the Dover Road.

I glanced in the direction from which I might expect the Flying Hope to appear, and listened for anything that might signal its approach, but neither sound nor sight was there; the only comfort that I could take was that there was no indication either that the coach had passed and was receding in the distance. Buoying myself up with the hope I was yet in time, I surveyed the scene below me. Faint moonlight shimmered from behind the clouds, enabling me to see that it was an ideal position in which to execute my plan. The road dipped abruptly, on its farther side stunted bushes covered low hummocks of ground that swept upwards to a rise topped by trees. This ran either way along as far as the brow of the gradient to my right. On the side I was situated the formation of the ground was similar so that the road here passed through a defile. From where I stood I had the road from Canterbury under observation for a distance of several hundred yards where it came into view round a bend lined with trees. Thus while the road and anything on it was fully exposed, the dip at which I had arrived offered the most generous cover. This was what the wench had meant when she had said that I should be able to hide myself against the approach of the coach.

I took the leather mask from my pocket and proceeded to adjust it over my face, pulling the hat well down over my eyes. I kept the pistol ready in my pocket and I stood still under the trees and waited while the horse quietly nudged me with his muzzle.

The only sound and movement around me was the sighing of the wind and the rustling of the gently swaying branches of the trees. Still the road remained deserted in the gloom, and I was beginning to sag under the oppression of final and complete disillusionment of failure, when suddenly I caught a sound which set every nerve in my body a tingle. From the direction of Canterbury towards which my attention was turned came the faint clip-clop of approaching hooves; and then I thought I could make out the rattle of coach-wheels. Then a movement along the road and in another instant a coach-and-four came into view. There was no question but that it was the Flying Hope.

Trembling with excitement I could do nothing for a moment but stand and watch it approach. I could discern the coachman and the guard silhouetted against the road behind, I could even detect the roll and sway of the coach as it braked against the approaching descent. The rumble of the wheels and the beat of hooves now began to echo against the sides of the dipping road and I thought it was time I moved. Quickly I climbed into the saddle, drawing the pistol from my pocket. I paused for a few more seconds while the horse tossed its head impatiently. I could feel the sweat running down behind the mask and my heart thudded against my ribs, sounding to my quickened imagination like the blows of a blacksmith's hammer.

The horses slowed and I could hear the

coachman's muttered curses as he pulled at the ribbons to steady them. Choosing my moment, I spurred my animal forward and we descended from the trees to come out of hiding a few yards ahead of the coach. I was brandishing the pistol so that its sinister gleam showed clearly. I saw the guard make a furtive attempt to reach for his blunderbuss and I gave such a shout at him in what I hoped was my most convincing imitation of Leatherface's voice.

'Not a move from you, or you will never make another.'

'Leatherface,' the coachman said, and I could see his eyes protruding; with a little growl he added: 'You again.'

I made no answer, but exultation filled me as the guard drew back nervously, the coachman dragged at his horses and the coach came to a stop so that I was alongside the leading pair. 'Now,' I shouted again, most ferociously, 'get down both of you, and no delay.'

The coachman glared at me as if he might burst for a moment. Then, at a wave from my pistol, and grumbling he descended preceded by the guard, and stood watching me warily. My glance was drawn to the window where I recognized Jack Morgan's broad features, contorted with surprise, as he leaned out.

'Leatherface,' he said incredulously, and then for the benefit of those within the coach he added: 'It's him — again. The brazen devil.' I could hear Miss Demarest's voice raised in alarm, and the snapping tones of Lord Deal. No doubt, I thought, the bogus Mr. Fisher would be going through the motions of mouthing his prayers, while Mr. Ellis would be just awaking from a dream of some juicy beefsteak washed down with wine.

'Out of the coach,' I shouted, 'every-one.'

At first I had thought my tone had held a quavery note, and no wonder, since I was so tensed up in every fibre of my being with mingling apprehension at what I was doing and a feeling of nervous triumph at my immediate success. For a certainty I had halted the Flying Hope and there was no doubt that my impersonation of Leatherface had so far been accepted at its face value. It occurred to me that a contributory cause for my initial success was the fact that the moon still lay behind the clouds and that I was being viewed by the victims of my outrageous exploit under the cover of gloom and shadow, whereas before their tormentor had faced them in the full light of the moon. I offered up a hasty prayer that these fortunate conditions which now attended on me would continue long enough for me to complete my task. Jack Morgan had pushed open the door and stepped down to the ground, Lord Deal close on his heels, snarling angrily. 'Must we endure this mummery all over again?' Those slitted watery eyes were fixed on me, smouldering with contempt and hatred.

The false parson came next, slowly descending to the ground and appeared to shake from head to foot as if most deadly affrighted. 'We shall never see London again,' he said, and his voice ended in a wail.

'Obey quickly, and you may continue your journey the sooner,' I said harshly, marvelling at his performance. George Barrington was indeed a consummate play-actor. It was difficult to believe that he was not the nervous man of God he purported to be, and instead the notorious pickpocket secreting on his person the snuff-box. I brandished the pistol in a gesture of impatience. 'And that means you also,' I was addressing myself to Mr. Ellis who now stood hesitantly in the doorway of the coach. I could swear he brushed a crumb from the corner of his plump, coarse face as with an effort he lowered himself to the ground, keeping his eyes on me in a baffled stare all the while.

'Leatherface?' he said. 'But — ?'

I cut short whatever he had in mind to say. 'Stand with the others,' I said. Barrington had already begun to move nervously to join Morgan and Lord Deal, muttering in a trembling voice to Mr. Ellis that he had best do as he was ordered, so that I could not resist saying to him: 'I am glad, Mr. Parson, that you are as eager to please as ever.' I spoke scathingly, and had to make a great effort to control my feelings of loathing for him, lest I lapsed into my normal voice and thus gave myself away.

He ran his tongue over his lips, as if I had given him some encouragement to expect mercy from me. 'You see in me but a poor, humble sinner,' he said, and his cringing manner which I knew he employed to cover his true identity quite sickened me to the stomach.

'Sinner, I dare swear you are,' I said bitingly. 'How poor we shall learn presently.' I took great satisfaction in observing the look of consternation and doubt that suddenly flooded his face, so that now I thought his fear was not stimulated but real. Then my attention was turned to the slim young figure, familiar to me in her cloak, the hood thrown back from the lovely heart-shaped face who stood hesitant, framed in the doorway. Each of them made as if to move towards her, but Lord Deal, stepping out nimbly, reached her before the others. I noted with satisfaction that before he did so, he had glanced in my direction to reassure himself that I would not misinterpret his move, however innocent its intent.

Lord Deal assisted Miss Demarest to alight, and just for a fleeting moment I experienced that strange quiver of exhilaration which her nearness had brought me at our last meeting, the memory of which had been eclipsed by my closer intimacy with the red-haired creature and its more passionate outcome. I heard her thank Lord Deal in her warm, sweet voice as they joined the others. And then concentrating all my attention upon the risky business in hand I saw to it that the coachman and the guard drew near to the passengers, so that all stood where I had them completely under observation. 'And no tricks this time,' I warned Lord Deal and Jack Morgan, jerking the pistol at them, 'or this shall know the reason why.' I had remained in the saddle but now, keeping my eyes and firearm trained upon them I slipped from the horse's back and left the animal to move a few paces away to crop at the grass at the side of the road.

Looking back on it now, I cannot

conceive that I could have proceeded as I did, that I could have put into action what must have seemed to any sane adult a hare-brained schoolboy's prank. Looking back on it, the very idea of it makes me still grow uncomfortably warm about my cravat. But I had no misgivings of that nature as I stood there bold and arrogant, my pistol held most menacingly, there in the middle of the Dover Road, the famous Flying Hope at my mercy. And it must have been my very brashness and my thoughtlessness for the incongruity of the situation that suspended the critical judgment of those whom I held temporarily in the hollow of my hand, for not one of them appeared to doubt that I was that notorious gentleman of the pad, Leatherface himself.

'Step forward, Mr. Parson,' I said crisply, brandishing the pistol. I was anxious to get the business over, the longer I took about it the more did I realize that I would reveal that I was not what I pretended to be.

The black-suited, narrow figure gasped

in terrified surprise. 'You — you — would not shoot me?'

'You would murder a man of God?' I heard Miss Demarest say, in tones of horrified awe.

I shrugged calmly. 'Whether I do or not depends on him.' The disguised George Barrington had hurried forward in response to my order and stood there, bent at the knees and his hands pressed together in a supplicatory attitude. I turned my masked face upon him as if considering whether I should not shoot him down there and then. To Lord Deal I spoke out of the side of my mouth. 'You, Lord Deal, stand next to him.'

I could see Lord Deal stiffen, I could feel his venomous glance upon me, but he too stepped forward obediently. I observed Jack Morgan's ham-like fists clench, and I permitted myself a passing inward smile as I pondered how his iron jaw would sag if he guessed that the hat I was wearing was the one he had handed me as a souvenir, that the pistol in my grip was the very same one I had persuaded him to give me out of the kindness of his heart. As for

Miss Demarest, her hand had flown to her pretty mouth; while Mr. Ellis stood immobile, his eyes that were set too close together kept fixed on me unblinkingly. And not a stir nor a squeak out of the coachman or the guard. They knew which side their bread was buttered.

'What do you expect of me?' Lord Deal stared across the gap between us unflinchingly, his rotting teeth exposed by his drawn-back lips. 'That I empty my pockets?'

'His pockets,' I said, with a nod at the creature beside him, 'interest me more than yours.' And I saw the other start as though I had slapped him unexpectedly across the face, while Lord Deal regarded me in plain astonishment. And coolly, elaborately nonchalant, aping Leather-face, I imagined, as though to the manner born, I let loose my next broadside. 'And,' I said, 'I require of you to empty them.' If I had ever entertained the faintest doubt respecting the truth of Leatherface's accusation which he had conveyed to me at the Fox Inn against the self-styled Mr. Fisher, that doubt must have been dissipated now, for consternation showed upon the latter's face as if the ground had yawned wide open at his feet. A strangled croaking issued from his throat but he failed utterly to get the words out; while for his part Lord Deal's expression was one of incredulity, and he was almost speechless.

'Empty his pockets?' he said finally, and the others murmured amongst themselves obviously nonplussed. As they stared at me silently and with puzzled hostility, I nodded peremptorily to Lord Deal.

'Proceed,' I said, with a razor edge to my tongue.

For a moment I thought he would throw all caution aside and hurl himself at me, so savage was his expression, so consumed with hatred did he appear. 'Do your own dirty work,' he said with acid vehemence.

I kept my head and spoke unwaveringly. 'I shall count three,' I said, and I even contrived to add a lightness to my voice, as if I was quite careless of the consequences.

'Shoot and be damned,' Lord Deal said.

'Not you,' I said, 'but the parson.'

George Barrington's face was working convulsively, while the others recoiled, Miss Demarest uttering a sharp cry, while Lord Deal made a hissing sound between his blackened teeth. 'I'll see you hang for this, if it's the last thing I do.'

I gave another inconsequential shrug, and then I paused dramatically, moving my pistol so that its twin cold gleaming barrels pointed straight at the bogus parson's heart. 'One,' I counted.

'No — no — ' Miss Demarest was wringing her hands in anguish, and it was all I could do not to turn to advise her that the individual upon whose behalf she pleaded was quite unworthy of her intercession, neither was he in the slightest degree of danger. But I could not resist wondering what George Barrington's own feelings must be at this moment; whichever way he turned he faced ruin. If he allowed Lord Deal to accede to my demand, the snuff-box must be discovered upon his person, and he would be exposed for what he was. Alternatively, if he resisted his pockets being searched he would suffer, so it might appear to him, being shot.

'Two,' I said obdurately, as Lord Deal did not move. Jack Morgan made as if to take a step forward, but a slight shift of the pistol deterred him. Still no sign from Lord Deal and a dreadful doubt assailed me, was my bluff going to be called at last? Had I succeeded this far with my design only for the cup of triumphant justification for all that I had carried through to be dashed from my lips. I dare not show that I was wavering. I gripped the pistol-butt more tightly and began to form the number three upon my tongue. Then Miss Demarest threw herself upon her knees before Lord Deal.

'Do as he says. For God's sake do as he says.'

18

Whether it was in response to Miss Demarest's plea, or on account of the apparent implacableness of my attitude, I did not know; at any rate Lord Deal stepped forward reluctantly enough, but he reached the bogus parson's side. For myself I almost gave a great sigh of relief, so thankful was I that my will had prevailed, but I managed to repress it sufficiently, though I was grateful for the leather mask that hid my face which must otherwise have revealed to everyone my true feelings. It flashed through my mind that what prompted the prowler on the pad to go out masked, was not so much that he might be disguised against being identified, but so that his emotions were hidden from his victims who otherwise would surely be encouraged to resist his demands.

'Forgive me, Mr. Parson,' Lord Deal

was saying. 'But unless I obey the villain — '

'Keep off.' The bogus parson spat out the words, his voice rising in a scream that sounded quite out of keeping with his previous attitude, so that Lord Deal stopped short. 'Keep away from me.' And as the other backed away a pace, Jack Morgan, Mr. Ellis and Miss Demarest, who had risen to her feet, were staring at him with blank incredulity.

'Why so affronted?' Mr. Ellis said. 'His lordship likes the situation no better than you.'

'Your only alternative,' Miss Demarest said, with a glance at my menacing pistol, 'is death.' It was plain that, like the rest of them, she was finding it difficult to comprehend the reaction of someone who was suddenly assuming a character totally at variance with that which he had shown before. I watched all this obliquely, my attention being concentrated upon the individual I knew to be George Barrington. He was scowling darkly, in complete contrast with his usual mild and ingratiating demeanour, and I could not help experiencing some exultation at the knowledge of the fearful speculations which the dilemma he was facing must have released in his mind. Lord Deal had dropped his hands and shrugged.

'Do you please yourself, Mr. Parson, of course,' he said.

'It — it is some trap,' the other said as if to explain his attitude, but his tone was thick with frustration and fear, and his eyes shifted from Lord Deal to the others and back again with a hunted look. I thought it was time for me to remind him and everyone else that it was for me to do the talking. I transfixed the figure in parsonical black and moved the pistol slightly to give the impression I was about to squeeze the trigger. 'Raise your hands,' I said, biting off each word, 'that your pockets may be searched without hindrance.'

He eyed me with bitter malevolence, his mouth drawn downwards at the corners, before slowly, reluctantly, he lifted his arms towards Lord Deal. 'I can do nothing but obey,' he said, in a mumbling tone, then with a snarl added out of the corner of his mouth: 'But I'll be revenged.'

'One of your cloth talks of revenge?' I said pleasantly, and then nodded to Lord Deal to proceed. He stepped closer and obviously still most puzzled by the situation, began to dip his hands, if hesitatingly, into the pockets of the creature before him, who stood rigid, as if his bones might crack and he would break in half at any moment.

'There is a prayer-book in this pocket . . . ' Lord Deal next took a handkerchief from the other pocket and paused to let me see there was nothing else there.

'Try inside his coat,' I said. I shifted the pistol again threateningly. Lord Deal's fingers stole inside the other's long coat.

'Some papers . . . And — ' He broke off, an expression of utter astonishment spreading across his thin, enamelled features. There, held betwixt his searching fingers was an object, glinting in the dim light. 'My snuff-box.' While he focussed his watery eyes upon it, and then held it high so that each one could see and identify it, a murmur of wonderment rose from all. I thought my harsh triumphant chuckle was in a good imitation of Leatherface's grim humour. I slanted a look at Lord Deal.

'Safely returned you,' I said.

'His lordship's snuff-box,' Jack Morgan said, his heavy brows knitted together.

'Is not this most strange?' Miss Demarest sounded most bewildered, while Lord Deal's gaze was still firmly rivetted on the object in his hand, his mouth opening and closing like a trout that has just been landed on the bank of a stream. At last, his expression still registering his incredulity, he found his voice.

'How came you by it, Mr. Parson?'

Confronted by a situation from which even his quickwittedness could not extricate him, George Barrington hesitated and then only mumbled unintelligibly, everyone's eyes turned on him, until finally he could do no more than give way to an explosive outburst. 'Rot you, I'll answer no questions.'

The unparsonlike language came startlingly from that mealy mouth which had been uttering little but prayerful phrases, and drew a gasp from everyone, except, I noticed inconsequently, Mr. Ellis, who remained quiescent and withdrawn.

'I — I — that is — I don't understand,' Lord Deal said, fumingly glancing from his snuff-box to the hostile face of the creature from whose pocket he had removed his precious item. 'Why — who are you?'

I thought it was time for another of my imitations of Leatherface's derisive chuckles. 'Permit me to introduce Mr. George Barrington,' I said.

'Barrington,' Lord Deal said, with a gulp that bulged his scrawny adam's apple over his fine cravat. 'The pickpocket?'

'Barrington,' someone else exploded, I think it was the coachman. An exclamation came from Miss Demarest, and her hand had flown to her wide-open mouth characteristically.

'The notorious George Barrington? The pickpocket?'

'In his rôle of a clergyman,' I said, 'and a rôle in which he is not entirely inexperienced.'

'Then it was you on the Dover packet?' Lord Deal was glowering at Barrington now, as the light of understanding began to glint in his watery eyes. 'It was not lost at all.'

Mr. Ellis who, until the moment had remained so still and silent, now suddenly seemed to be galvanized into life. He stepped forward as if the better to study the wicked rogue who stood revealed in their midst. And then he made an observation which made me jerk my gaze to him. 'And I never recognized him,' was what he said.

'Are you then acquainted with him?' Miss Demarest said, taking the words out of my mouth. I confined myself to flicking my eyes to Barrington, tensed anew, his glance darting nervously over the man who had suddenly taken the attention of us all, by his cryptic utterance.

'Who am I to you?' The pickpocket's question rapped out defiantly.

Mr. Ellis regarded him levelly and an air of authority surrounded him which had never been there before. Those close-set eyes were gimlet-sharp, that plump face had grown stern and the jaw, which had been more noticeable for its masticatory movements, had tightened. 'I am bound to confess,' he said, with extraordinary coolness, 'that I also am not what I seem.' He drew himself up with a bearing of some dignity. 'I am an officer from Bow Street Police Office.'

'A Bow Street Runner,' Jack Morgan said, in a hushed voice.

'A Runner — ' George Barrington drew in his breath in a long hiss of despair, throwing a wild stare about him, as the significance of his fellow-passenger's presence upon the scene struck him with all its force.

I had heard, of course, of Sir John Fielding the Blind Beak as he had been dubbed for he was, in fact, stoneblind, who was the magistrate at Bow Street Police Court and who had recruited about him a body of lawenforcement officers in an effort to stamp out the criminality that flourished in London. I never imagined I should encounter a member of this force in such circumstances as those in which I had placed myself. Of all the people in the world I wanted to meet at this critical moment, the last was a Bow Street Runner.

For myself, I had recoiled a pace, and momentarily lowered the pistol. I raised it again automatically, though I hardly realized what I was doing, my brain was reeling before the impact of this entirely unforeseen development. Mr. Ellis, somehow without seeming to move, was of a sudden standing very close to George Barrington and before any one of us realized what was happening there was a metallic glint and a pair of handcuffs appeared from his pocket.

'Look out.' It was Jack Morgan who let out the warning shout, but it came too late. Barrington spun on his heel, ducked as Mr. Ellis tried to close with him and sped off into the shadows. Like the others, I was so staggered by the suddenness and effrontery of the pickpocket's bid to escape that I could only remain where I was, confused and hesitant. Confronted with these mounting and totally unexpected anticlimaxes after the smooth run of luck that had kept me buoyant since I had first held up the Flying Hope, the initiative I had scored at the outset deserted me. Taking advantage of the general confusion which struck us all, Barrington had turned aside from the path he had started to take towards the trees at the side of the road, and bounded for the black horse, which had been quietly cropping at a patch of grass. In another moment he flung himself into the saddle and jerked the reins. Mr. Ellis ran shouting after him, obviously he carried no pistol hidden away, but the fugitive spurred the horse forward, and bending low over its neck, galloped a few paces along the road and then swung up the bank on the farther side, to disappear into the darkness of some trees.

'If only I'd carried a pistol,' Mr. Ellis said, turning back to us, his expression full of mortification.

'And mine being unloaded — ' I said, blurting out the words, in that brief instant completely forgetting the rôle I was supposed to be enacting. Once more everyone's gaze fastened on me, for I had been momentarily forgotten by them in the excitement of the pickpocket's escape. I could only stand there, wishing fervently that I had bitten off my tongue before allowing it to betray me. Helplessly I watched the guard, whose face had lit up as he caught what I said, double past the coach and reach for his blunderbuss that I had ordered him to drop. He ran out on to the road and seemed at first about to fire it after the fled George Barrington. Then, realizing the futility of the action, he swung round upon me, who presented a helpless target.

'If he's got away,' Mr. Ellis said, glancing from the direction that horse and rider had taken and bending his close-set eyes on me, 'here's one who shan't escape.' Lord Deal was already advancing towards me, his thin lips curled and his enamelled face contorted venomously. I stood as if rooted to the spot as I realized to what end my moment of thoughtlessness had brought me. I had trapped myself. If I dared to run for it, then the guard, who was also bearing down on me behind his blunderbuss, would surely fill me with lead. Lord Deal nodded to Jack Morgan. 'Seize him,' he said. 'His pistol is unloaded.'

Jack Morgan moved warily towards me. 'Don't you see — ?' I started to say and did not try to resist when my arms were pinned roughly behind my back. I protested in my normal tone but those huge hands would not relax their grip.

'He was deceiving us all the time,' I heard Miss Demarest say.

'One ruffian, anyway,' Lord Deal said viciously, 'for our Bow Street Runner.'

'Let me go,' my voice rose desperately. 'I'm not Leatherface at all.'

'What does he say?' Mr. Ellis said.

'Tear off his damned mask,' Lord Deal said to Jack Morgan, who obeyed, pulling the leather mask from my face and pushing the hat from my head.

Whatever surprises they had experienced that night, nothing brought such a cry of amazement from their throats, everyone of them, as that which rose now from the circle about me. In the silence that followed, I could see that Miss Demarest looked as much horrified as shocked. I could read in her eyes that she was realizing how I had deceived her so that she had lent herself to my stratagem. Her glance was cast down and she bit into her underlip. As for the others, they seemed quite bereft of words, even Lord Deal was so far taken aback that he could only utter a strangled: 'Rot me.' Jack Morgan's fierce grip relaxed a trifle, but he still held on to me so that I had no hope of slipping free, while Mr. Ellis stood peering at me in a partly curious, partly jubilant attitude, scratching ruminatively at his chin.

'You were left for sick at the inn?' he said. 'So we were informed.'

Miss Demarest looked up, but before she could speak, I plunged in, determined to save her further hurt and embarrassment. 'It is no fault of hers. Miss Demarest was quite innocent of my intention. I had to feign illness and deceive her in order to carry out my plan.' I heard Jack Morgan mutter under his breath, and I could well imagine how he was inwardly reviling me for having fooled him also, and I felt a pang of self-reproachment for the deception I had carried out on him.

'I knew him for a rogue as soon as I set my eyes on him,' Lord Deal said.

'Your plan,' Mr. Ellis said, 'which was to hold up the coach, and rob your erstwhile friends.'

His tone was icy and now the coach and all of them facing me spun round so that I thought I was going to faint. I could not believe that the purpose of my masquerade was not plain to everyone. I could not imagine that what I had done could be misinterpreted. Surely they must see that however rashly and foolishly I had acted, my object had not been one of downright villainy?

'But you don't understand,' I said desperately. 'I masqueraded as Leatherface deliberately. I enacted the rôle for the sole purpose of exposing George Barrington for what he was, to regain the snuff-box for Lord Deal. You all saw how I bluffed him with this empty pistol.'

'Then you'd have bluffed me to hand it on to you,' Lord Deal said, completely unconvinced by my explanation. I threw an anguished look at the others, and read disbelief in every face. I racked my brain for some way of forcing them to realize that every word I spoke was the truth. 'You must believe me,' was all I could say. 'You must. It's true, I swear.'

Mr. Ellis's eyes were cold and hostile. 'If every word you say is true,' he said, slowly, weighing every syllable, 'how did you come by the knowledge that he was the notorious George Barrington, when not even I suspected it?'

'Because I — because — '

I broke off lamely, my throat suddenly dry, as I groped for an answer that I could make. For how in the circumstances in which I now found myself suspect, dare I confess to my meeting with Leatherface at the Fox? How could I begin to explain that none other than he himself had acquainted me with the true character of the parson, who had possessed himself of the snuff-box? Even as I tried to fight my way out of the quicksand of scepticism and distrust which surrounded me on every side, I heard Mr. Ellis's remorseless voice add another to his first penetrating question.

'For that matter,' Mr. Ellis said, 'how did you know that the snuff-box was secreted where it was?'

19

As Mr. Ellis's first and then second question were thrust at me swiftly one after another, so that I felt as if I had been skewered like some helpless animal to a board, I twisted and turned in my mind, seeking a way out of the dreadful dilemma I was in. If I began to give the plain unvarnished facts which had prompted my masquerade I would have got not half-a-dozen words out, before my listeners, with perhaps the exception of Miss Demarest, damned me as no better than Leatherface's accomplice. As being in league with him from the very start. I recalled again that look of Lord Deal's which I had caught over the matter of my stopping Jack Morgan from firing the pistol; and throwing Lord Deal a glance now I felt sure I could see him reflecting upon the incident and putting two and two together. While no doubt the others would be trying to recall something

248

sinister about me, which pointed to my being that which they now suspected. The fact of my travelling alone, for instance. Was it not most unusual for someone of my tender years to be unaccompanied by any parent or guardian? Something significant in that, sure enough.

If only I could have foreseen in my calculations any possibility that the situation would take such an unexpected turn. If only Barrington had not contrived to elude capture but was by now securely handcuffed in Mr. Ellis's custody, I should have been left in the position as I had planned it, to reveal myself when the moment was most ripe and so disarmed any breath of suspicion against me. But recriminations were of little use now, those about me were awaiting my answer to Mr. Ellis.

'Where's your tongue?' he was asking me. 'Answer me how you knew the scoundrel's true identity and the where-abouts of the snuff-box?'

'I could not speak then, for — for the same reason that I — I cannot now.' It was all the fumbling answer I could make, as I tried hard to return his fierce gaze.

'You've got a resourceful rascal here,' Lord Deal said without compassion. 'A desperate young malefactor.'

Mr. Ellis nodded in agreement, and there came the ominous clink of metal as he brought the handcuffs into view again. 'You'd better slip them on,' he said firmly. I pushed back against Jack Morgan who still held me securely, vainly I tried to turn away as Mr. Ellis loomed up at me with the handcuffs. 'It'll only be the worse for you, my lad,' he said. And I seemed to die within me from shame and humiliation as the handcuffs slipped around my wrists and with a dexterous movement he quickly turned the key so that I was pitiable, wretched prisoner. He patted his handiwork and a slow, triumphant smile lit his features. 'That will clip your wings, I fancy.'

And so, with a sense of deepest humiliation, I was escorted to the coach, between Mr. Ellis and Lord Deal, the guard with his blunderbuss plodding close behind. Disillusioned, wretched beyond belief, unable to accept the terrifying predicament into which the unforeseen had forced me, I felt as if I was in a dream, a nightmare from which I must surely awake to find myself safe and sound in my bed at home.

I was now taken, it seemed, for a worse criminal than the one whose duplicity I had revealed; I, who but a few minutes before, had been congratulating myself on the success of my venture, had watched tensed with gratified excitement while George Barrington returned the stolen snuff-box, and was only waiting to throw off Leather face's mask and reveal myself to everyone's astounded gaze, their delighted surprise and praise at my boldness.

Instead, in what desperate straits was I now landed. Denounced as a real highwayman, my denials unheeded, my story unheard, handcuffed like the felon I had pretended to be, while the real culprit had slipped away and was now laughing up his sleeve out of danger.

What could I say or do to save myself from the terrible trap in which I was caught? My mind in a state of black confusion I stumbled up into the coach. Mr. Ellis came close behind me. He instructed Jack Morgan to take his place in the corner so that I was forced to sit between them. Numbly, I noted Lord Deal help Miss Demarest up the step and he quickly followed her and the coachman slammed the door, and called out to his impatient horses. I heard him scramble up on to his seat and a few seconds later came the sound of the guard taking his place. There was a mutter of conversation between them, then a shout from the coachman, the crack of his whip, and the Flying Hope rumbled forward, taking us once more on our journey.

As the coach gathered speed through the night, which was darkened by intermittent scudding clouds, my mind flew ahead to my parents awaiting me in London. Choking back tears of mortification and despair, I pictured them shocked and bewildered at my arrival, handcuffed and guarded by a Bow Street Runner. The sweat broke out on my brow and the palms of my hands, and I bit back a groan of anguish, closing my eyes as if to shut out the sight. Opening them, I was stricken with fresh remorse when I gazed on Miss Demarest. She was silent, leaning back in her corner, her eyelashes dark along her cheeks. Was she asleep or had I so disgraced her she could not bear to look at me? Her cloak was fastened at her neck and its hood concealed her hair and shadowed her forehead.

The sight of her warm generous mouth filled me with a memory of her kiss and our sweet, short interlude together. If she hated me now for taking advantage of her kindness, how much more would she loathe me if she knew of my shameful interlude with the red-haired creature at the Fox? I tried to tell myself, squirming with shame at the memory of it, that I had been forced to sink to lust and wickedness, but I knew Miss Demarest would feel nothing but horrified disgust for the part I had played. Looking at her, my heart contracted with self-reproach at that which, beginning as a wild boyish prank, had led to lies and deception, wantonness and degradation, had after all attained me nothing but humiliating self-pity and self-disgust, which I now endured. I had set out so bravely, overcoming every obstacle and any scruple that would divert me from my purpose and in the moment of achievement had met irreparable disaster.

And her pale beautiful face and closed eyes offered me no thought of solace in my wretchedness, while I knew I should find no pity in the faces of the others. I could read nothing in Jack Morgan's expression; like Miss Demarest he had fallen silent, his eyes closed beneath his heavy brows, as if dozing, his broad face impassive. Lord Deal, in the opposite corner, appeared awake, but after some desultory conversation with Mr. Ellis, his drowsy voice had suggested that he, too, had been struggling to ward off sleep, and he had fallen silent. Now he seemed to have some difficulty in keeping his watery eyes from closing. Mr. Ellis alone appeared to remain alert, his sturdy figure taking up a great deal of the seat beside me with Jack Morgan on the other side of me, so that I was firmly wedged in. Mr.

Ellis fidgeted and then fumbled for the inevitable food-bag which he produced. I saw Lord Deal's lashless eyes flicker as he lazily watched the other bring out a pie from the bag and begin munching it. I noted this out of the corner of my eye, and then Lord Deal said to Mr. Ellis: 'That was bad luck for you, that George Barrington contrived to escape.'

Mr. Ellis nodded, and gulped down a mouthful of pie. 'But for the horse, I do believe I would have caught him.'

'Such blasphemous effrontery, impersonating a parson.'

'Had I been more alert,' said Mr. Ellis, wiping his mouth with the back of his hand, 'I should have suspected him before.'

And while Lord Deal assured the law-officer that no blame attached to him, and that he could not have been expected to penetrate such a wickedly artful disguise, I could not help reflecting, even in my misery and bitterness that Lord Deal and the Bow Street Runner were completely overlooking the credit due to me. For it was I who had been the one to unmask the bogus parson. George Barrington had hoodwinked everyone except Leatherface, and had it not been for my action, however foolhardy and ill-conceived it might seem, neither Mr. Ellis nor anyone else would, I felt sure, have suspected the wolf in sheep's clothing in their midst.

'Doubtless you will warn them at Bow Street,' Lord Deal said through a yawn, 'so that a hue-and-cry may be raised after him?' The other gave a nod of agreement, and then brushed the crumbs from his last mouthful of food from the front of his coat. Lord Deal went on, his voice growing more drowsy: 'Elusive and cunning he may be, he is bound sooner or later to make a false step and then it's the gallows for him.'

'That will be his end,' Mr. Ellis said grimly.

'The inevitable end of all evil-doers,' and Lord Deal had to glance significantly in my direction to emphasize that he was speaking for my benefit and consideration. I remained silent, keeping my eyes downcast. 'Coming to the matter of that other villain,' Lord Deal said, blinking the advance of sleep back from his eye-lids, 'you saw him hanged, you said, at Tyburn, then how explain his reappearance on the Dover Road tonight?'

I lifted my head with sudden interest and waited for Mr. Ellis's reply to this question which had so much intrigued me and which I had longed myself to put to Leatherface. The man from Bow Street hesitated, then he said thoughtfully: 'It must have been that his cronies were waiting ready, and cut him down immediately after the cart had drawn away leaving him to dangle. Then they contrived to revive him.'

'The poxy blackguard must possess a strong neck,' Lord Deal said with a grunt of disapprobation. 'Now you do mention it,' he continued after a pause, 'I recall hearing of a similar case at Tyburn.'

'So that's how it was.' I heard the words come from my tongue involuntarily, as if someone else was speaking, for I spoke my thoughts aloud, having no intention to make myself heard. But this explanation of the mystery of the highwayman's appearance after his public execution so caught my imagination that I automatically spoke up.

Mr. Ellis's eyes raked me with disfavour. 'Were I you,' he said, 'I should not regard it as a reliable means of cheating Justice.'

'I had not meant to speak,' I said lamely, and averted my eyes again as Lord Deal muttered sleepily in obvious agreement with what Mr. Ellis had said. Apart from the clatter of the wheels and the sound of the horses' hooves, a tense silence followed. Then there came some more fidgeting from Mr. Ellis as he delved deeper into his bag and I watched him eventually extract a brandy-flask. Lord Deal's mouth sagged open to disclose those blackened stumps, and his eyes half-closed, his head lolling back, his enamelled face cracked with fatigue and strain. He yawned noisily.

'We have suffered enough to make us more than a trifle weary,' Mr. Ellis said quietly, as if to soothe the other to relax into sleepy oblivion. He proceeded to unscrew the cap from the flask, and there came a sleepy, dry chuckle from the corner.

'Tell me, Mr. Ellis, and do you find it more congenial,' Lord Deal said, 'to adapt your disguise to yourself, or yourself to the disguise?'

The coach rattled and shook from side to side, as the Bow Street Runner concentrated his attention upon pouring brandy from the flask into the cap which he used to drink from. If he intended to make any answer to the question he did not do so, for as he took a mouthful of brandy, Lord Deal yawned again, this time more loudly, smothering his mouth with jewel-bedecked fingers, and then his hand fell down and rested on his thin, bony knees, while his head lolled back. He was fast asleep. I watched him as almost immediately he began to snore faintly. Mr. Ellis took another sip of brandy, smacked his lips, then replenished his make-shift cup. This he gulped off, and wiping his mouth on the back of his hand, he screwed the cap back, to return the flask to his capacious pocket.

He looked round slowly at each silent

figure; Miss Demarest who seemed quite asleep, her hood pushed forward over her face, so that it was in the shadow; Jack Morgan, whose thick shoulder pressed imprisoningly against mine, while his jaw nestled his broad chest as if even in slumber he still kept his guard against an opponent's fist; and Lord Deal himself, now far away in his dreams. Mr. Ellis muttered something to himself, but what it was I could not catch, then casting a sidelong glance at me, which appeared to satisfy him, he also settled back, as if preparing to follow the other's example, while the Flying Hope rushed London-wards.

20

While Mr. Ellis had apparently directed his mumbling observations to no one in particular before falling asleep, as it appeared, I kept my head down and my eyes closed as if I, too, were dozing. I continued to remain perfectly still for some minutes and soon the Bow Street Runner's deep regular breathing convinced me that he was lost deep in sleep. I glanced at him from the corner of my eye. His head drooped, his plump form heaved visibly with every breath he took. No doubt the fatigue exacted from the responsibility of his office, and the pies he had put away into his stomach, topped by the brandy had caused him to fall into unconsciousness deeper than that of the others. I glanced slowly round watching each one of them in turn; not one returned my look. Their eyes were closed, they swayed and shook to the jolting and lurching of the coach; but they slept on soundly and undisturbed.

Their unguarded somnolence could not fail to send my thoughts leaping like a fish freshly hooked, in an effort to jerk itself free; irresistibly my brain became a turmoil of ideas for making my escape. In my confusion and despair I tried to make space for some clear reasoning by which I might get myself out of my awful predicament. That Mr. Ellis and Lord Deal had made up their minds that I was nothing less than a cunning criminal I had no doubt; and I knew that no explanation of mine which I might submit to their consideration would influence them. Short of Leatherface himself riding once again out of the shadows, pistols agleam, to halt the Flying Hope and inform everyone of the true facts, I had no hope of convincing my companions of my innocence. Yet, if I was not to be utterly lost I dare not remain Mr. Ellis's prisoner, to arrive in London and be lodged in gaol. I must break away before that dread moment somehow.

I glanced at my manacled wrists and my heart sank once more. Was it impossible to attempt to jump out of the coach without my hands free? How would I get as far as the door past Jack Morgan or Mr. Ellis, before being hauled back? Yet if only I could get out I was confident of showing my captors a clean pair of heels. The night was still dark enough to hide me, once I could turn aside from the road. Ragged banners of cloud drifted across the moon so that changing light and shadow played over the coach, and the passenger's faces were alternately palely revealed and heavily shadowed. The sudden lurching of the coach brought Mr. Ellis and Jack Morgan alert again. We could hear the muffled shouts of the coachman. 'What the devil — ?' Mr. Ellis said.

Jack Morgan had glanced out of the window. 'Near jolted us through the roof.'

'The coachman grows careless,' Mr. Ellis said.

'It's a wearisome journey,' Morgan said, putting his great hand over his mouth to smother a yawn. Mr. Ellis fidgeted beside me, as if to settle himself once more, when Miss Demarest stirred suddenly, and spoke in strange tones:

''Graves have yawned and yielded up their dead; Fierce, fiery warriors fight upon the clouds — ''

Mr. Ellis jerked up, wide awake once more. 'What — ?' he said, puzzled.

'Talking in her sleep,' Jack Morgan said, sleepily.

''And ghosts did shriek and squeal about the streets.

Oh, Caesar, these things are beyond all use — '' Miss Demarest broke off and woke up with a start.

'You were talking in your sleep,' Mr. Ellis said.

'Do forgive me,' she said. 'I dreamed I was appearing as Calpurnia in *Julius Caesar* . . . ' She paused a little breathlessly. 'To-night's events have excited my mind a trifle.'

'Most understandably, I'm sure,' Mr. Ellis said. 'Do you try to sleep once more.'

Inside the coach once more became wrapped in silence, except for the heavy breathing of Jack Morgan, to be joined by Mr. Ellis; and from the outside sounded the rattle of wheels and hoof-beats.

And then, surely, I told myself, the pace slackened, the coach was beginning to slow up, and I bit my lips in a frenzy of frustration. We were proceeding up what seemed to be a gently-sloping gradient; and a quick glance through the window informed me that on either side of the road lay dark trees, or where they fell away, undergrowth. I looked down at the heavy bands about my wrists. I felt the hot and cold shivers of mounting tension surge through me, impatience and frustration flamed higher, as I told myself over and over again that now, while everyone was asleep, was my only chance for action, my only hope of escape.

I looked up as a shaft of moonlight fell across Miss Demarest's face and I saw that her dark luminous eyes were wide open, staring at me. I did not speak, I could not comprehend what lay behind the look, then suddenly she leaned forward, glancing at the others in a quick, nervous turn of her head. Then I felt her fingers urgently digging into my knee. 'You must get away,' she said, in a whisper.

The revelation of her belief in me filled my being with such exhilaration that for a moment I felt oblivious of the handcuffs, my captors and all the other obstacles that prevented any attempt from resulting in success. Then my sense of realities returned. There was Miss Demarest to think of. Even if she had any idea of helping me, and if I accepted it, what would become of her?

'Thank you,' I said in a whisper. 'Thank you, but if you were caught aiding me — '

I broke off as Lord Deal shifted in the corner and blew noisily through his mouth, muttering something which sounded as if it was to do with his snuff-box. He settled down again and for some moments Miss Demarest and I stared cautiously at him. Then she beckoned me and I leaned towards her to catch her whispered words. 'You behaved foolishly, recklessly. Had you told me frankly of your plan, I could have spoken up boldly.' She shrugged. 'But it is not time now to question that. We must obtain the key to the handcuffs.'

I looked round at Mr. Ellis's sleeping figure and then faced her again. 'How to get it from him?'

'It has slipped half out of his pocket, the other side from you. I can see it gleam.' She smiled at me knowingly. Mr. Ellis stirred at that moment in his sleep. We waited tensely for him to settle down again, and eventually with a faint sigh he lay back and his regular breathing told us he was soundly asleep once more.

'He'd wake for certain,' I whispered, 'if you try to get the key.'

Miss Demarest did not appear to hear me, she studied Mr. Ellis carefully. It occurred to me once more, this time most reassuringly, that his brain might be dulled with the brandy and his stomach heavy with the food he had partaken. The faint smile flickered at the corners of her mouth again. 'You must play your part.' Should he wake, or any of the others, fall to the floor as if in your sleep.'

I had hardly nodded understandingly, before she leaned inch by inch towards

Mr. Ellis. I could not see properly, but I thought she must almost have the key within her grasp, when Jack Morgan shifted slightly, and she sat back quickly and silently.

'Miss Demarest.' It was Jack Morgan who spoke in a low voice. She turned to him startled. 'You need have no fear of waking me.' He glanced significantly at us both. For a moment Miss Demarest seemed stunned into silence and then she gazed at him and although her eyes were shadowed there was a kind of defiant gleam in them.

'You heard all I've been saying?' she said.

He nodded. 'You will raise the alarm?' I said in a whisper.

His broad face creased into a smile. He leaned across to Miss Demarest. 'I agree with you,' he said. He could never know what relaxation of pent-up tension his words brought to me. Here instead of an enemy now I had another able ally. With two comrades, my hopes soared. I refused to consider failure and I was willing to take any risk to prove my cause just. Miss

Demarest had leaned forward to Mr. Ellis once more, and I could not take my eyes off hers, while Jack Morgan glanced either side out of the windows. 'The pace is not fast, but the road rough and jumping into the darkness even at this poor speed might bring disaster.'

'It is a risk I must take,' I said confidently. I was thinking that the slower the coach was travelling when I jumped, the greater chance the guard would have to fetch me down with his blunderbuss. Mr. Ellis, would I knew, instruct the man to fire and kill me, rather than risk losing another prisoner. My object was to encourage Miss Demarest and Jack Morgan to help me to jump for it now while the coach was moving; I felt sure I could manage without mishap at this speed. I glanced quickly out of the windows on either side. The trees offered good cover each side of the road. If I didn't know that part of the world, neither perhaps did Mr. Ellis, and in the dark my eyes would be as good as his.

A spasm of light faintly lit the carriage and I saw Royall Demarest's face, pale and taut, her eyes on me, and in them I read mingled admiration and concern. The moonlight vanished as suddenly as it came and we were once more in shadow and I could see only the vague outlines of my companions, as Miss Demarest, waiting in the darkness, leaned towards us.

'I will try now,' she said in a tense whisper. Even as she spoke another sudden stirring of Lord Deal in his corner held her back and I watched him, hardly daring to breathe, as he moved his head and shoulders into a more restful position. His lips moved in slurred murmur, his words indistinguishable. After grunting two or three times he gave a sniffling wheeze, and then he quietened once more. Was he in his sleep muttering about me? I did not need any proof to know that I could expect no more sympathy or mercy from him than from Mr. Ellis.

Only one great anxiety assailed me, which was that my two friends were risking becoming involved in my troubles and might themselves become dangerously incriminated. 'But you two — ?' I said

But Miss Demarest pressed her fingers against my mouth. 'It matters not what they suspect, once you have gained your liberty.'

Jack Morgan nodded energetically and I protested no more and sat back silent and as still as the swaying coach would allow. The road was certainly in a bad state and the gradient was long. The coach bumped and swayed to such extent that I marvelled that anyone could sleep so soundly as Lord Deal and Mr. Ellis appeared to do. I had braced myself against Jack Morgan's powerful shoulder, and we both stared at Miss Demarest awaiting her move.

Presently, without a word, she began once more cautiously to lean towards Mr. Ellis. Her hands, a pale flutter in the darkness, reached out to the pocket on the further side from me and I had no way of knowing when she found the key-ring, until the faint click of metal reached our ears. Then Jack Morgan's body tensed beside me as there was a movement from Mr. Ellis, and to my horror he raised his head and his eyes were wide open, with such alertness that it was obvious he had not suddenly awakened from a sound sleep. He gripped the groping fingers of Royall Demarest in his.

'You have a warm hand,' he said suavely. Miss Demarest gasped with the shock and withdrew her hand quickly. 'A performance which does not become you.' Mr. Ellis turned to Jack Morgan. 'Neither does such treachery go in keeping with your character.'

'We believe in his innocence,' Miss Demarest said defiantly, as Lord Deal sat up, rubbing his eyes, and looking round vacantly, catching only part of the conversation, and unable to comprehend the situation.

'Your voices woke me,' he said, disagreeably. 'You seem to be at odds with each other.'

'While I was thought to have been asleep,' Mr. Ellis said, 'Miss Demarest, aided and abetted by Mr. Morgan, was plotting to aid this young rascal to escape.'

Lord Deal's mouth opened and closed.

'It cannot be true,' he breathed at length.

'What he says is the truth,' Miss Demarest said quietly, her eyes bright.

Lord Deal had jerked forward to peer at Jack Morgan, who nodded his head slowly. 'I agree with Miss Demarest, that the young gentleman might be misjudged.'

'Young gentleman,' Lord Deal said, his tone rising irately. 'A thorough-paced ruffian — '

Any further words he might have uttered were lost as the nearside coach-wheels bounced over some object in the road, and we were all violently dislodged from our seats. In the confusion I heard the coachman shout and the crack of his whip, and the coach forged relentlessly on. I had been ignored by Mr. Ellis and Lord Deal during their surprised condemnation of the other two. I had hunched there miserably, the handcuffs biting into my wrists. But the wild scramble inside the coach suddenly galvanized me into action. I knew there would never be another opportunity; now that Mr. Ellis was aware that Royall

273

Demarest and Jack Morgan supported my intentions to escape he would keep an even closer eye on me, and Lord Deal also. Despite the handcuffs a voice rang out in my brain with a clarion-call that the Flying Hope's sudden upset was providing me with my only chance. It was now or never.

I fell with the others to the floor of the coach, but while they were trying to regain their feet I was up swiftly and I plunged towards the door. In another moment I had turned the handle and the door flew outwards. For a second I paused, there was a loud shout in my ears, as tensing myself, I leaped out into the night.

21

There was the sound of horses' hooves and the receding clatter of wheels as the Flying Hope sped on, shouts of alarm from inside the coach and the ditch gaped beneath me at the side of the road. I tried to clutch the edge of the ditch to stop myself sliding into it, but the handcuffs were too much of an impediment, and I shot through a cluster of brambles and came to rest in shallow water and mud. But apart from a soreness to my hip and a grazed knee I escaped injury.

A quick glance showed me that the coach was stopping and I had no time to lose. I managed to haul myself up the further side of the ditch by forcing my way through bushes and finally gained the top of the bank. Here a wild hedge barred my path, but by lying flat I was able to wriggle feet-first through the lower part of the hedge and make my way on hands and knees to some bushes. I could hear voices from the direction of the coach, and felt impelled to run for it as fast as possible; but a moment's reflection decided me to remain where I was. The noise I would make, impeded as I was about the wrists, stumbling and tearing through bush and undergrowth, was bound to attract attention. Just to my left I could make out a blur of trees, and I now decided that there might be a safe harbour in which to pause.

I could hear Mr. Ellis's voice and the coachman calling out as I reached the dark, welcome cover. I stood hidden behind a tree-trunk and listened. The coach was not many yards away, but a rise in the ground lay between me and the road. Although the voices sounded near, I felt reasonably safe for the moment. I decided to stay put. I tried to hear what was being said, to pick up any information that might help me to avoid recapture. I heard the coachman speaking: 'I never saw what happened. The wheels caught the branch of a tree blown down in the storm, I shouldn't wonder. But I didn't see no one jump nor nothing, till you called me to stop.'

'The young scoundrel might have injured himself,' Mr. Ellis said hopefully. 'He won't get far anyhow.'

'What chance have you of finding him?' It was Royall Demarest's voice, and I could detect a triumphant mocking note in it. 'Surely you're not going chasing a young boy? And one who's innocent, too.'

'If you'll keep your advice to yourself, it would be better,' Mr. Ellis said, with asperity. 'I haven't forgotten how you and Mr. Morgan aided and abetted the young ruffian.'

'The villain was still handcuffed?' Lord Deal asked querulously.

'That he was. He can't shake them off. And wherever he goes, whoever he asks for help, the handcuffs will reveal him as an escaped criminal.'

'What do you plan to do?' Lord Deal said.

'Go after him, of course. Didn't I say he wouldn't get far with the mark of a felon on him?' A pause and I heard Mr. Ellis call to the guard to hand him a pistol from the arms-chest on the coach. 'That will put the fear of death into him,' he said.

The guard said something to the effect that he would loan him the required firearm, Mr. Ellis reiterated that thus armed he would set about recapturing his escaped prisoner on his own, so that I could not repress a stab of fear at the certainty in his voice.

'And what about us?' the coachman said.

'Yes,' said Lord Deal, 'are we expected to remain here, until you've successfully concluded your task?'

'Surely you can get to the next inn?' said Mr. Ellis to the coachman, a trifle peevishly. 'I will make a search while you rest there against my arrival with the damned boy. I shall require you to convey us to London just the same.'

'But, Mr. Ellis,' I heard Lord Deal say snappishly, 'Surely you're not suggesting we sit about awaiting your return? I for one have had enough of this night's madness, I want to get into my own bed as soon as may be.'

'And I, too,' Miss Demarest said.

'I shall not be long, you can be sure of it,' Mr. Ellis said, in a voice that brooked no disobedience to his commands.

There was the sound of the guard clambering down from his seat and then he brought a pistol to Mr. Ellis. There was a muttering among the others, steps back into the coach and the door was closed. I could hear their voices in the coach but I could not distinguish anything in particular, before there was the sudden stamping of the horses and the jingle of harness. A moment later came the encouraging shout from the coachman and the crack of his whip, then the rumble as the coach moved forward. I heard footsteps, those of Mr. Ellis without a doubt, quickly approaching the spot where I had taken my desperate leap. Suddenly the footsteps died, then after a pause I heard the faint crackle of someone thrusting their way through the bramble and bushes lining the ditch and I guessed Mr. Ellis was forcing a way through for himself.

A short while later I stood flat against the trunk of the tree as I heard the crackle of footsteps along the path. Mr. Ellis passed within twenty yards of me, his footfalls fading and finally died away altogether. I remained where I was for fully another five minutes, but only the faint, rustling sounds of animals and birds in the copse broke the silence.

I set about deciding which would be the best direction to strike out, and finally I set off cautiously at right angles to the road for about a hundred yards, then I turned, and following a parallel course with the Dover Road, going away from Mr. Ellis, until I came out into open fields, just beyond the crest of the hill up which I had proceeded. The moon, faintly curtained by could, shed a diffused light over the landscape, and I could almost pick out the road snaking its way Londonwards. I thought I could see a dark blur which I was almost certain was the coach, well on its way.

I pictured Lord Deal huddled irritably in his corner, snarling at Jack Morgan, who would be silent and withdrawn; and Royall Demarest, and I wondered if she was in turn thinking of that inexperienced clumsy youth with whom she had passed a brief interlude and whom she had done her best to help in his hour of need. I told myself that if I was to take advantage of the aid and encouragement with which Miss Demarest had provided me, and the opportunity I had grasped, then I must rid myself of the wretched handcuffs that hampered me. If only I could come upon some place where I might take the use of a file, it would not be long before I could face the world again. Until then I must skulk in the shadows, hide from everyone's eyes the clinking badge of my shame and humiliation.

I looked across the fields away from the road. Beyond a meadow in front of me was a rough opening in the hedge, made as if it had been trampled down. Perhaps this led on to a farm track fringing the next field? It seemed to me worth investigating and it was not in the direction my pursuer appeared to have taken, so I set off cautiously, keeping low against the skyline, my eyes and ears alert. I moved as quickly as possible, anxious to reach the meadow and the shelter of the hedge before a narrow break in the clouds which I had glimpsed allowed the moon to shine down in its full intensity. Although I tried to convince myself that Mr. Ellis was moving in an altogether different direction from the course I was taking, it was likely that he would stop at intervals, certainly where he was offered a wide view of his surroundings, and search the landscape. Where the moonlight was brighter at a moment when I was moving across the open ground I would make an easy mark for those close-set watchful eyes of his.

I reached my objective apparently without giving my presence away, for no human sound reached me as I paused breathlessly under the hedge. I found it unconscionably wearisome and vexatious making my way with my wrists held in steel, and though I had to thank my fortune that they had not been locked behind my back, as easily might have happened, yet I was handicapped and frustrated enough as I was. If my pursuer had spied me he would have certainly shouted a warning by now and commanded me to stop; he might even have fired the pistol he had taken from the guard, to back up his order. But only the friendly sounds of nature broke the stillness. In the great oak tree that stood in isolation across the meadow an owl hooted, its screech awaking the distant echo of its mate somewhere in the copse I had just left. The scurrying of a rat or field-mouse rustled in the grasses lining the foot of the hedge and I saw the white blob of a rabbit's tail as it dived for its burrow in a hummock near the oak tree. I felt a kinship with all this wild, half-heard, half-seen life, creatures who were also hunted, if not by humans then by others of their kind.

For a few moments longer I stood close in the shelter of the hedge and waited, idly noting the globules of moisture that gleamed and dripped from stem and leaf, reminder of the violent storm that had passed. Then, urged on by the sharp cutting of my wrists, I followed the hedge to the boundary of the meadow where a broken-down farm gate barred a narrow, stony track which divided the meadow from the next field and was screened on either side by the hedgerows. Although I could not see just where it led it seemed reasonable to suppose that it opened on to the Dover Road. Where I stood at the gate, it turned and went deeper into the countryside.

I climbed over the gate, and with a growing sense of hopefulness journeyed along the track, taking myself further from the main road and the starting-point of my escape. I felt sure the track must lead to some isolated farmhouse where I could perhaps find the means of ridding myself of the wretched handcuffs. But as the time passed and the distance I had covered seemed to bring me nowhere nor sight me any place of habitation, my dilemma with all its attendant fear began to flow back to me. I had made perhaps a further half-mile when the stony surface upon which I had been trudging gave way to grass which was soft in places and soggy. Nevertheless, it looked as though it had been used recently by somebody because there was a flattened, firmer path across it. I followed this and eventually came to another hedge which ran before a wide ditch and what would be a meadow beyond. I pushed my way through a thinned-out part of the hedge, slid down the bank and up the other side, to take a view of my surroundings. I hoped to come upon a house or farm-building of some kind, but there was nothing so substantial as that to be seen whichever way I looked. Throwing off my disappointment I turned to skirt the field, keeping near the ditch, so that I could dive into it for cover if I needed.

Then the ditch swung away from me, and straight ahead in a corner made by the ditch and a high hedge that joined it at right angles I saw something which stopped me in my tracks. Two-score yards away underneath the overhanging branches of a tree, almost indistinguishable from the shadows which surrounded it, stood what I took at first to be some sort of coach, then I made it out as a gypsy's caravan. I had seen the gypsies and their brightly-painted houses-on-wheels straggle past my own home many times, bearing the dark-eyed men and women and their children, their thin dogs slinking along between the tall wheels. Just beyond, as I stared at this unexpected sight, I could now distinguish the vague shape of a haystack, as if the caravan was sheltering in its lea, and then a horse moved and I saw that it was cropping at the loose hay.

I stood there staring indecisively, for I could not think whether to turn aside and quietly continue on my way until I found the cottage or farmhouse I needed, when it occurred to me that I might be more fortunate than if I had found the sort of dwelling which I had been seeking. For if this was what it appeared, the home of some Romany, the sort who roamed the land as free as the air, I might well receive more sympathy than I could expect from ordinary beings. Here, I might have help which would rid me of my handcuffs as expeditiously as I had dared to hope. I stepped slowly and cautiously towards the strange habitation, my spirits rising yet tempered with the realization that I must go carefully. I must be on guard lest I find myself in even greater danger than that from which I had escaped. What I had heard of the gypsies and their vaguely sinister practices came to my mind. I recalled the various tales that I had been told of how these strange, swarthy-faced creatures were magicians and soothsayers, that they were acquainted with the acts of sorcery learned from Egypt and the Indies; how they were supposed to kidnap young children and hold them to ransom; of the strange ceremonies and rites in which they indulged, when they drank human blood and vowed death to their foes. Uneasiness mingled in my mind with anticipation, then I made out a square of light in the side of the caravan, and a shadow moved as if someone was stirring within. I went on towards it; and then of a sudden when I was a few yards off came an infernal clatter from beneath the caravan and there leaped forth two snarling, yapping dogs.

They were large animals, or perhaps their size was exaggerated in the dim light, but there was no denying their aggressiveness and I stood still, uncertain as they reached me, their jaws snapping. I called aloud in panic, and saw the top half of the door swing open. A shapeless figure stood there, dark against the illumination inside the caravan, whether it was a man or woman I could not tell, but there was no doubt about the dull gleam along the barrel of the fowling-piece that aimed at me.

22

If the two snapping, bounding dogs surprising me out of the darkness did not appear dangerous enough, then the firearm pointing straight at me made me fear the worst; whatever reception I might have been expecting it was nothing so terrifying as this. I called out again, declaring my friendly intentions, and eventually the figure in the doorway spat out some order unintelligible to my ears and the dogs, growling and baring their fangs, slowly withdrew underneath the caravan, where they squatted, snarling suspiciously. It was a man's voice which had quietened them, and now its owner stepped out on to the top of the short flight of steps which led to the ground, his fowling-piece lying across his arms, silently scrutinizing me as I went hesitantly forward.

In the shadowy light he seemed an enormous figure with thick, matted black hair that joined the untrimmed, curling beard which concealed most of his face, from which his fleshy, bulbous nose stuck out like an ugly promontory. His shaggy brows protruded to such extent that it was impossible to determine his eyes, but I felt they were flickering over me warily, and I sensed them settle on my handcuffed wrists which I held awkwardly before me, like some reluctant supplicant. As far as I could make out his clothes looked as ragged and tawdry as the flea-bitten coats of his dogs, and when I stopped a few paces from the steps the smell that assailed my nostrils brought me close to retching. It was the dirty, liceridden stench of an unwashed body clothed in garments that had not been removed for months on end. This was a typical roaming vagabond, a scavenger; but whether he was as evil as he looked I had yet to find out. But whatever his character I had now committed myself by my very appearance, and since it was in his power to set me free, I must needs throw myself upon his pity.

'Forgive me for disturbing you,' I said

in a pleading voice. 'But I am in desperate straits.'

He said nothing, but I was near enough to see the suspicious glitter beneath his overhanging brows now as he looked down at me, and I realized that my unheralded appearance out of the night would have unsettled any man, whether his life was innocent or sordid with crime. I made up my mind that frankness alone would best repay me.

'I am on the run from an officer of the law,' I said boldly, 'though it is no fault of mine. I am innocent, but he took me without giving me a fair hearing. If I am to prove him wrong I must be rid of these.' I suddenly held up my hands held together by the rings of encircling steel. 'That is why I escaped.'

He stared at them, then put aside his gun and with another sharp order to his dogs crouched between the wheels, when after a brief growling they lapsed into silence, he came slowly down the steps. 'Where was this?' he said, and his voice was thick with some strange accent, so that it was difficult to catch his meaning.

I nodded my head in the direction of the Dover Road. 'I was travelling by the Flying Hope,' I said. 'I jumped from the coach and have so far eluded my captor.'

He tugged at his beard. The stench of him was stronger, but I knew that this was the least hazard that he might contribute to my circumstances. He spoke slowly, and there was a note of scorn in the thick tones. 'I lead my own life away from law and order. I want none of it.' He paused and then turned back up the steps and reached for the fowling-piece again. 'Be gone with ye.'

'Wait,' I pleaded desperately from the foot of the steps. 'Help me to free my wrists. That's all I ask of you. I swear I'll trouble you no more once this iron is off.' The sweat stood out on my brow which he must have observed in the light from his lantern within the caravan. He did not pick up the long-barrelled firearm, but his huge soiled hand returned to his beard, which he pulled at again, reflectively. He looked beyond me whence I had come, and the faint hope rose within me that he was ensuring that I was alone, and I prayed that Mr. Ellis was nowhere in the vicinity, so that our voices, quiet as they were, should not carry to him on the silent night air. But there was only the soft furtive sounds of some wild creatures in the darkness, the sudden rasp as the horse a few yards away tugged at the hay, and in the distance, the lonely screech of a night owl. He moved his head suddenly and looked at me as though he had reached a decision.

'Come in,' he said abruptly.

Murmuring my gratitude, I mounted the steps, and he stood aside for me to enter his abode. Inside was as rancid as was his own foul, unwashed person. There seemed to be no ventilation, the one small window appeared a permanent fixture, and as soon as my strange host closed the half-door again, the fresh air that had drifted in was lost in the warm, nauseating atmosphere. A small fire smouldered in an ash-filled make-shift grate, from which smoke curled up to a chimney-hole in the roof. Over the fire a small cauldron of some dark liquid simmered. There was a jumbled heap of old apparel strewn in one corner and a pair of long hunting knives on top of a shallow cupboard lining one wall. On the opposite side was a narrow space where a filthy-looking blanket covered a tattered straw mattress, and on this lay a hammer and chisels and other odds and ends together with innumerable pieces of wood, some of which were fashioned into clothes-pegs. It appeared as if I had interrupted him in his work. I noticed on the walls were various wooden racks, elaborately carved, which were obviously another example of his handiwork. In a bracket on the wall at the further end a lantern burned fitfully. As I stood there, taking in the small, untidy scene, he indicated me with a grunt to sit down, while he lowered himself on to the floor leaning back. The fowling-piece stood near to his hand.

'Let's see,' he said, and I held out my wrists, while he kept his dark, matted head over the handcuffs. He examined them for what seemed many long minutes, while I wondered anxiously if the problem of loosening them had defeated him. 'It will take time,' he said at last, cautiously. 'And then what will be my reward?'

'I have only a few coins on me,' I said, I had in fact left the rest of my money packed away with my luggage for safety. 'You may have all that.'

His shadowed gaze flicked over me with what seemed to be a faint amusement. But he said nothing, his mouth, almost hidden in the dark hair of his beard, revealed itself in a brief smile. It was on the tip of my tongue to promise him a good payment of gold when I might obtain it from my father; but he did not appear to be the sort who would be impressed by promises of such a nature, so I said no more. He turned aside, and after fumbling among the hammer and chisels for some seconds, he produced a short length of wire.

'I have little time for those bullies,' he said, in his strange, thick accent, 'who dub themselves the law. I live free and hate the chains of authority which enslave a man.'

I murmured some grateful words, not

knowing quite what to say, anxious only that he should free me. Then he began to tinker with the piece of wire in the lock that operated the handcuffs. He worked in a brooding kind of silence. I watched him breathlessly, noticing the glint of a golden ring in the lobe of his ear, half-obscured by the matted beard. I found myself unable to tell him of the events which had led me into my present plight; of anything concerning Leather-face or George Barrington; of the disastrous ending to my scheme, something of which I might have imparted to him, without being too forthcoming with secret information, but merely to help him feel that he was serving the ends of truth and real justice. He gave the impression that he existed in his own strange world, untouched by and uninterested in what went on around him.

Then suddenly the piece of wire he was insinuating in the lock scraped still, there was a click so that the handcuffs opened, and with what joy I let them fall to the floor while I began to chafe where they had gripped my wrists. But my excited happiness was cut short by the sudden growling of the dogs outside. In another moment we heard them move from under the caravan and run barking across the field. In an instant the big figure had crossed to the door, opening the top half noiselessly a few inches, to look out. I was beside him. Someone was out there in the darkness, the dogs' yapping and snarling grew more angry.

'It's him,' I said in desperation. 'Mr. Ellis from Bow Street. He must have seen the lighted window.' He glanced at me, his deep-sunk eyes narrowed, enigmatic beneath the black brows. 'You won't give me away?' I pleaded. 'Where can I hide?'

He looked out again into the night without speaking and I was numb with dread. He had helped me so far, surely he would not desert me now? I glanced round at the clutter, the heap of verminous clothing, the filthylooking bed, here was no place of concealment anywhere. The barking of the dogs came closer and the man reached for his fowling-piece. 'The haystack,' he said suddenly. 'It is old and you can dig yourself into it.'

I needed no second bidding. The door opened wide enough for me to drop quietly to the ground, and I worked my way round to the back of the caravan. As I moved towards the haystack, I heard the bearded man descend the steps; but whether he remained where he was or went forward to meet the newcomer I did not know. I was pulling aside the hay to make a cavity in the stack into which I could hide myself. A pair of startled birds flew from somewhere above my head, and I felt a frightened mouse slip over my hand. Moving swiftly, I dug out a cavity with my hands, and now I wriggled my way in, feet first, and pulling the stalesmelling hay over my head. Just as I finished covering my face, I saw a familiar figure approach out of the darkness.

The hulking shape confronting him had called off the dogs and they moved around the two men, sniffing and growling, suspicious and aggressive towards the stranger. Although there was sufficient light from the caravan by which from my hiding-place I could make out Mr. Ellis and the other, I could not see their faces; but this did not concern me so long as I could hear their conversation. The Bow Street Runner came straight to business.

'I'm looking for an escaped prisoner. Since you are about at this hour, I wonder if you have seen anyone?'

'No one,' I heard the bearded man say at once. 'Not I.'

'Mr. Ellis is my name,' the other went on tenaciously. 'Of the Bow Street Police Office.' He made it sound mighty impressive. 'The young rogue I was taking to London jumped the Flying Hope not two miles from here. He was handcuffed, which will inconvenience his progress.'

'Handcuffed? Then it will serve him little if he show himself here.' And I smiled thankfully towards my benefactor, as his reply reached me where I lay, not daring to move a muscle, scarce breathing.

I thought the big man was about to add something in his thick accents, and I tensed to try and catch the words. But whatever he had in mind remained unsaid, Mr. Ellis had stepped to one side the better to see the pair of dogs which I now noticed had stopped their growling and were moving towards the haystack. They were sniffing the air as they approached the spot where I was hidden. I realized with growing horror that should they persist in their curiosity they must for a certainty bring Mr. Ellis to observe them more closely and speculate upon what it was that was attracting them.

The air seemed to hum with suspense. Silently the men followed the dogs with their eyes as they began leaping up at the hay just below me. They continued to sniff and growl in their throats and their mangy tails threshed with excitement. Mr. Ellis made no move, but I could see that his shadowy figure had become very still and his manner withdrawn and watchful as I had observed in his demeanour before.

'They appear interested in that hay-stack,' he said, at length, his voice growing razor-edged with insinuation. 'What might you have there that should draw their attention?'

23

Mr. Ellis's questions sent a cold stab of fear through me, so that my limbs began to twitch. I tried to check this sudden ague-like attack which rustled the loose hay which engulfed me and that itself filled me with fresh alarm that even this slight disturbance would give my presence away. The two dogs still growled and jumped up at the haystack, but Mr. Ellis did not move, he seemed to be awaiting the reply to his question. The gypsy made no movement towards the restless dogs either. How long it was before he answered the Bow Street man I did not know; the time seemed interminable to me as I lay there, and I closed my eyes tightly, as if by shutting out the sight I could remove the danger of it to me. Then, when he spoke I could hardly believe what he said, or his casual tone.

'What should draw my curs' attention?' he said. 'What would entice your attention or mine to the pastry-cook, or the sweetmeat shop? What but our stomach?' I blinked open my eyes in amazement, for it was almost as if he knew of Mr. Ellis's weakness for his stomach, and for an incredulous moment I wondered if I had informed him of the other's one great interest in life, apart from his duty, which was to gorge himself with food and wine. But it was an irrelevancy which even if I had remembered it, which I hadn't, I should have considered it too unimportant to mention.

'And what does that mean?' Mr. Ellis asked, not a little pompously.

'I shot a fox and threw it on the stack,' I heard the other say, by way of explanation, and I marvelled with gratitude, at his inventiveness. 'It's their meat for tomorrow. But they are greedy.' His voice hardened, he shouted a command and the dogs, growling, with their tails between their legs, slunk back to him. I heard a further mutter from the dark, bearded figure, and the animals retreated to the caravan-steps, where they sat on their haunches. 'If I can be of no further use to you,' the gypsy said shortly, 'so I will bid you good night.'

I could see by Mr. Ellis's attitude that he appeared nonplussed. He was reluctant to go, yet he could think of no reasonable excuse to stay. I heard the jingle of coins from his purse. 'You scratch a poor existence, doubtless,' he said in an insinuatingly cloying voice. 'You would not refuse an honest guinea.'

'Depends with what honesty it's offered.'

'You could keep watch for this young malefactor?' Mr. Ellis paused and again I caught the chink of coins. 'I must continue my search, I'm sure he cannot have got far away. If you should see him hereabouts, you have but to fire your fowling-piece to warn me.'

'I do not want your money,' the gypsy said brusquely, and moved towards his caravan, the Bow Street Runner following after him.

'You want for nothing then?' Mr. Ellis obviously disliked this rebuff, and he must have felt foolish returning the coins to his purse.

'Nothing,' the other said, 'but my own company.' He turned abruptly and climbed to the door of his caravan and there stood silently waiting for Mr. Ellis to depart. On what seemed was some sudden impulse the latter moved to the foot of the steps, as if to obtain a glimpse of the dimly-lit interior. When he spoke he introduced a casual note into his voice in an attempt to cover up his curiosity.

'Good night then,' he said. 'But remember it is your duty to assist a law-enforcement officer whenever you may. Not only is it your duty, you will be suitably rewarded.'

There was no answer, and finally Mr. Ellis swung on his heel and strode away in the direction whence he had come, the gypsy stood watching him out of sight. Then he went into the caravan.

I lay unmoving for several minutes, taut and alert to catch any sound that might signal Mr. Ellis's return, but except for the noise of the horse munching close by and the occasional snarl of the dogs, there was nothing to alarm me. The big, dark man did not re-appear, and I thought I could hear the sounds of him moving about which suggested to me that he was settling down for the night. At any rate he certainly made no sign to me. He might have not been aware of my existence. Did he expect me to remain where I was for the rest of the night, or return to the caravan? Or was he counting on my quietly slipping away into the night? Presently I pulled myself slowly out of the clinging hay and stood leaning against the stack until the life flowed back into my numbed legs.

The night seemed darker, and I saw the last light of the moon extinguished by a massive cloudbank. Then of a sudden lower down towards the horizon a streak of lightning zigzagged its fiery trail across the sky. At the same time as there came a rumble of thunder, the first patter of rain fell around me like myriad ghostly footsteps; the trees and the hedgerows were beginning to vibrate with the breeze. The night was about to launch another stormy onslaught, and I knew what I must do. I must slip away at once, before the storm brought Mr.

Ellis running back for shelter.

With one final glance in the direction of the caravan I moved silently round to the back of the haystack, anxious to avoid alerting the dogs again. Once out of sight, I paused for a moment, listening; but neither the gypsy nor his mangy curs had been disturbed by my movements. I had not expressed my gratitude to the dark, bearded man who had not only freed me from the shamefully impeding handcuffs, but had cunningly hoodwinked the Bow Street detective on my behalf. Now my mind wavered with indecision. Should I thank him with all my heart before taking my leave? At first it seemed that it would be very wrong of me not to. But a wiser counsel prevailed and I set off, reassuring myself with the thought that the gypsy would in fact rather have me go like this than place him in further risk through my presence in the event of Mr. Ellis's early return to the caravan on the excuse of seeking shelter against the coming storm.

I found the weakest part of the hedge along which I had proceeded in the darkness and forced myself through to the other side. Jumping a shallow ditch, I followed the grassy path beside a partly cropped field to a gate at the end. The rain was falling heavily now, the lightning more frequent and the rumblings of thunder nearer overhead. There was no useful shelter that I could see, and even if there was any, it would have been too close to the hiding-place I had just left for me to take advantage of it in safety. I pushed on as quickly as I could along the fringe of another field, keeping as close to the hedge as the narrow ditch would allow.

About half-way along, the field began to slope upwards and beyond the shallow hedge marking its boundary I could make out in the lightning-flashes that the land was uncultivated. When I reached the boundary hedge, pausing for the next lightning stroke to light up the scene I could see why the land ahead was not farmed. It was rough ground on which the grass and bushes grew wildly, and between which the surface was pock-marked with hillocks and trenches, all no doubt infested with rabbit-burrows. The ground rose steeply to a ridge, thinly covered with trees that leaned drunkenly from the wind.

I picked my way cautiously up to the ridge, pausing every now and then between the obstructions during the momentary flashes of light. It was wonderful to experience the freedom from the manacles round my wrists and a sense of exhilaration and hope urged me onwards, as perspiration soaking the clothes next to my skin and the rain drenching my outer garments, I eventually gained the crest. Making the most of the scanty shelter provided by the trunk of a tree, I stood there looking out across the stormy landscape, hoping to pinpoint some shelter wherein I could rest my weary body.

It was during a more prolonged searing zigzag of lightning since reaching the hilltop that I saw the house. It was impossible to tell how far distant it was, but in that and subsequent flashes I saw the light reflected from the windows and the gleam of a rainwashed roof. I watched and waited to plot its position. There was no mistake; it was a large rambling place that might be the manor of some gentry. Once I had the direction implanted firmly in my mind I set off down the hill towards it.

How long I travelled and over what terrain I have but a faint recollection. I know that by the time I reached the gravel track that presumably joined the house to the highway, my sodden clothes were torn, my hands scratched, and the once immaculately polished riding-boots which I had taken from Leatherface were plastered with mud up to the knees. The rain had found its way down my neck and mingled with perspiration so that even as I stumbled and staggered towards the refuge ahead I could not prevent myself shivering. The track curved round between stunted trees and hedges and there suddenly, in a lightning flash, I saw a broken-down gate with the carriage-drive beyond sweeping to the portico of the wide front door.

On reaching the gate, I hesitated filled with some strange apprehension. I could make out that the drive was choked with weeds and the gardens overgrown, the shrubbery was a riot of rampant foliage on either side. The house itself, now that I was close to it, looked deserted, as neglected and dilapidated as the gardens, the tall windows revealed in the lightning-flashes like so many glassy, unseeing eyes. I pushed aside the dejection and exhaustion that had fallen upon me. If it was indeed empty then I should, I told myself, find no one who might refuse me shelter. Thrusting my fears from me, I moved quickly up to the front door. As I stood there in the shelter of the portico, hesitating again, a door banged somewhere within, and for a moment the impulse to take to my heels was almost irresistible, but the driving rain and my flagging spirits, coupled with the certainty that here was no one to turn me away, checked the strange, unreasoning dread that assailed me. I turned the handle and pushed against the front door. I was only half-expecting it to yield and had already made up my mind that I should need to force an entrance through some window. But it opened slowly and groaning to my steady pressure and I stepped inside. A long lightning-flash revealed that I was in a hall with double doors, one of which was swinging to and fro, to my left. This was undoubtedly the banging door that I had heard.

I obtained a brief glimpse of the high ceiling, a wide, bare and broken staircase leading above. To my right two open doorways led into one wing of the house, with here and there the walls all cracked and crumbling. In front of me and beyond the staircase lay another wide doorway apparently leading to the rear of the house and through which a cold draught blew. A fierce draught raged from upstairs, indicative of more broken windows. The silence of the house, in between the rolls of thunder and the anger of the storm, together with the mustiness of decay made it apparent to me that I had come upon a scene that had once been one of beauty and elegance, but how many years it had been slipping into the shambles of a festering derelict I could not tell. I moved towards the double doors on my left. I waited on the threshold for the next flash and saw beyond a room with tall windows fronting the drive. Thick dust carpeted the floor, but the walls and ceiling stood intact. Opposite another door beckoned me across and I opened this to find myself in a long, wide room, which must have run the whole width of the house. High-ceilinged and with tall windows at each end. The musty smell curiously enough seemed less marked, there was less of a feeling of desertion and decay. The rain drove against the windows and the lightning-flashes threw strange, brief shadows across the floor, and in those seconds of brilliance I was able to make out the great, wide ash-strewn fireplace, in the centre of one wall, and some objects of furniture.

Close to the wall I saw a straw palliasse and in the corner a cupboard. I suppose I was too overcome with exhaustion, my brain too fuddled to realize the significance of these signs of recent occupation. I imagined vaguely that this may have been the resting-place of some nomad, some roaming creature. I was only too thankful to have found shelter and a place where I could at long last, after all my wandering, rest my aching limbs. I sat myself on a chair and wrenched off the boots and peeled off the long velvet jacket. I sank down on to the palliasse and in spite of the crashing thunder, the searing flashes of light and the eeriness of my surroundings, I was soon asleep.

Suddenly I was awake again, how long I had slept I had no idea, but I came out of my dreamless oblivion of utter exhaustion with a start. I was conscious of a steady light, then that the storm seemed to have faded somewhat, then of movement above me. My scalp tingling I turned my head and then lay there rigid, unable to credit my senses.

In the light of the lantern which burned nearby, bending over me with that familiar sardonic smile touching the corners of his mouth, stood Leatherface.

24

'My life has been a chequered one,' Leatherface was saying, his eyes veiled with a cloud of smoke which he had puffed from his clay pipe. 'A thing of light and shade, of many vicissitudes suffered in many places. It cannot be said that I started off with all the best advantages of birth and upbringing, though I did not pity myself for that. I have enjoyed the opportunity of taking the straight and narrow path of virtue with its rewards, but instead I chose the wider, wayward road, with its dangers and consequent vagaries of fortune.'

When I had awakened to find him there beside me, my mind still muzzy with sleep, I could not comprehend the why or wherefore of his presence. 'I had no intention of disturbing you,' he had said, 'since I see you are much travel-stained and weary.' His glance had taken in the torn black velvet jacket, and the scratched and mud-caked boots that I had taken from the stable loft at the Fox Inn. 'I can hardly recognize my belongings.'

'I can explain.' I sat bolt upright, my eyes shifting from his face to the rich, panelled walls, then to the fireplace where on the grey ash dead twigs had been placed and were now starting to burn. 'I had thought no more than that some vagabond sheltered here,' I said.

'No one but a stranger would dare set foot here, which has the reputation of being haunted, and so suits my purpose well.' The thunder rumbled in the distance less frequently and the rain did not drive so relentlessly against the windows, while there was the bang of a door and the creaking of loose timbers, stirred by the gusty draughts. I saw him throw another quizzical look at his apparel.

'I only meant to borrow them,' I said. 'But — but my plan went wrong.'

'A fine plan, to rob me of my clothes and my nag, and then steal shelter in here.'

I explained to him quickly what had been the purpose behind the forced loan I had made upon his property, mentioning that Barrington now owned his black horse, and how my great stratagem had gone so dreadfully awry. And as the words tumbled from my lips, the eyes studying mine narrowed, but they did not smoulder with anger, or bitterness; indeed, I fancied I could detect in them a hint of amused admiration, and he said: 'Rot me, for such damned audacity. Go on.' And he had taken from his pocket a blackened clay pipe which he proceeded to fill with a dark, strong-smelling shag from a worn leather pouch.

I plunged on, saying nothing of my shameful interlude with the red-haired girl in the stable beneath him; how success had run with me to the point where Mr. Ellis revealed that he was from the Bow Street Police Office, whereupon those dark, craggy brows were raised a trifle, but he had made no comment, only dragged enigmatically on his pipe. With some bitterness I recounted how despite that Lord Deal had, through my action, retrieved his precious snuff-box, neither he nor Mr. Ellis had believed my good intention, and I was degraded and handcuffed. I told him how I had escaped from the Flying Hope, eluded Mr. Ellis's pursuit, and how I had struggled on through the storm, to finally reach this dark, eerie house.

Exhaling thick clouds of tobacco-smoke, which quickly disintegrated in the draughts, he had watched me closely all the time, and at the end of my account, he said: 'You showed enterprise and courage, out-matched only by your damned folly.' He crossed to the panelled wall near the fire-place and after a moment's operation he slid back one of the panels. Then he had brought out a bundle of clothes which he placed in front of the fire. There was a long velvet jacket like the one I had worn, a pair of polished riding-boots, a hat and a leather mask. The twin barrels of a pistol gleamed in the firelight, and he smiled thinly at my surprise.

'When I discovered my loss I borrowed some garments and a nag to bring me here.' He took the boots I had worn and also the jacket and placed them before the fire, which was now beginning to blaze comfortingly. 'And I hope,' he said, 'that your first venture along the path that leads to Tyburn will be your last.' He glanced round and then regarded his pipe for a moment with a dark scowl. 'Especially now you see,' he said, 'the way we gallants of the toby live.'

His voice had been edged with such a strange bitterness which I had not noticed before, so that I was set wondering, at first idly and then with increasing curiosity, what had driven such as he to take to the pad, an outlaw and an outcast. And so in some odd fashion, how quite it turned that way I cannot recall, he had begun to speak of himself. 'At the moment when I made my small bow upon the stage we call Life,' he was saying now, launching into his story, 'my mother was employed in an establishment in the humble district of St. Giles, which was run by a creature known as Mother Sulphur, later to rise to greater heights when she kept a house of more elegant infamy in Long Acre.'

He went on to relate how for reasons about which he could only conjecture, he had been cast adrift on London's streets when he could have been aged no more than six to become one of the vast pack of vagrant children, deserted and unknown and virtually outlawed by society. By the time he was aged ten he passed among his companions, boys and girls of similar ages and circumstances, as a bold, resolute fellow. As he talked he brought to my mind's eye the streets and alleys of that part of London of which I had heard but never seen. Of the infamous Rookeries of St. Giles, the maze of lanes, cellars and dens, all dark and the air nauseous, where the solitary traveller must be on the alert for the everpresent prowling footpad; and whose wretched crumbling houses, harbouring the lowest beggars and thieves, cut-throats and felons ever gathered together under London's sky, communicated one with another by rotting roof or slimy cellar, a sprawling warren of evil into which it was hopelessly perilous for the minions of the law to penetrate.

I could imagine myself walking beside

him through the streets and courts off Drury Lane or Russell Street, Crown Court or King's Court, all that area of Covent Garden, where gaming-hells and bagnios, drinking-dens and brothels hung about the playhouse like the filth of the streets about the skirts of elegant women of society. Or I stood in the flash-houses and thieves' kitchens, and listened to the slang of the highwaymen and bullies, duellos and footpads, prostitutes and pimps. He became a member of a gang of sneak-thieves; when he was a few days past the age of thirteen he was caught and sent to Clerkenwell, where he was whipped till his back was all wealed and covered with blood. The only result was to corrode his innermost soul and cure him not at all. Within a week he was about his business again at Bartholomew Fair picking pockets.

Now I moved with him through the mobs of people thronging the fair outside St. Bartholomew's Hospital, my ears filled with the squeak of penny trumpets, the banging of drums, the bellowing of stallholders and toy-makers, waxwork-showmen and booth-proprietors; in my nostrils the odours of roast pigs turning on their spits, the heavy fumes of wines and liquors from the taverns and grog-shops; while before my imagination I could see the motley processions of ballad-singers and costermongers, petty chapmen and gingerbread-women, magicians and trinket-sellers, beaux and wide-eyed yokels, elegantly-attired women of the town and servingmaids.

I saw through his eyes all the brilliance of the scene, on every side the stages with brightly coloured backdrapes and painted signs, showing almost every conceivable wonder from wild lions to tame canaries, from massive giants to minute dwarfs, while high above the crowd, perched on slender poles, monkeys gibbered and grimaced at the jeers and laughter of the crowd. Quacks and charlatans yelled and harangued, while here was an Italian dentist who pulled teeth to the accompaniment of the trumpet, drums and trombone, which drowned the shrieks of his victims; here was Dr. Zodiac doing a roaring trade with his sovereign balm which, he claimed, would preserve any purchaser from death for ever; or promised prompt, truthful replies to every question asked him about the future. And everywhere was the swarming crowd, surging here and there, laughing and joking, some drunken and quarrelsome, others continually wide-eyed at the wonders on view.

It was not long before Leatherface was to know the inside of a gaol-cell, this time back again to Clerkenwell New Prison, which had been the scene of his bitterly-remembered flogging. 'They would have committed me straight to Newgate,' he said, 'but that prison being bursting already with villains, there was no room for me.' He contrived to escape; and for the next several years his was a life of arrest and brief imprisonment, of such daring and ingenious escapes, so that as I listened to him while he told me these things, in his dry, rasping voice, my mind grew sombre as I contrasted the tales I was hearing with the story of my own happy childhood, where I took for granted that I had good food in my belly, a warm bed and a roof over my head, and above all the affection of my parents.

Then it was that he decided to extend his activities, and make his bow as a highwayman on Hampstead Heath. And so, as the storm muttered outside, and the rain drove only intermittently against the lonely, crumbling house, I was to hear how he set out on the pad. I leaned forward, my chin upon my hand, and evincing even more avid interest as he began to narrate this chapter of his strange and dangerous career, so that he gave me the benefit of his thin, frosty smile and his dark eyes glittered. While he carefully tapped out the black dottle of tobacco from his clay pipe he said: 'No doubt you fancied you had been the youngest ever to sally forth on the toby. Do not flatter yourself. But then,' noting the passing glum expression that shadowed my face, 'you would do well to remember how I had packed a life-time of apprenticeship to this particular trade into my few years. Consequently, in that respect, I was much more mature than you.'

He ranged the heaths of Hampstead and Hounslow, with underneath him the swiftest cattle that the money he filched from his victims' purses, together with an inborn eye for good horse-flesh, could buy. Bagshot Heath and other roads that led to London knew him, and there the night air rang to his cry: 'Stand and deliver.' And always he rode alone. And while he described to me his adventures as collector of tolls upon the high-toby, he discoursed shrewdly upon his own character and that of the company of the pad. 'Like the rest of my kind, I am a creature of the time and the seasons. I choose the times of action with superstitious care; at certain hours I would sooner refrain though every circumstance seem to favour success. I would rather obey the inner voice of an unreasoning wizardry, than fill my pockets with the gold for which my avariciousness is ever hungry. There is no law of man I fear to break, no, nor of God, neither, yet I shrink from walking under a ladder; and if the date was the 13th and it fell upon a Friday, I would starve that day rather than rob a soul of a penny.'

It seemed to me that in his category of attributes he had omitted courage. I recalled the dryness of my mouth, and the perspiration that had started up all over me when I had ridden on his black horse out of the shadows on the Dover Road a few hours' since. And I had merely been impersonating a highwayman, playing at the part. 'For the real thing,' I said to him, 'you must possess a great fortitude.'

He gave his dry, harsh laugh. 'I know that we are applauded for our courage by the Grub Street hacks and in the chap-books. But that praise is reserved for the occasion when we must make our dying speech at Tyburn.' I gave a shiver, I had not thought to remind him of the penalties that accompanied the pursuit of his profession. 'Until then,' he went on, 'our exploits are vilified as cowardly and brutal, as indeed they may be in the opinion of our victims. As for courage in the face of death we ride in hope. A villain such as I must ever hope, he hopes until despair is inevitable. When the noose is in sight then he walks firmly to the gallows, that none in the crowd may suspect the tremor in the knees.'

A year-and-a-half after having embarked upon his present career, he had left a game of faro in St. James's one night, to gallop by starlight across Blackheath; and meet his first check. He had halted a shay and came off to the tune of a hatful of jingling guineas, when his nag had tripped clearing a hedge and gone lame, so that he was forced to take refuge at the next inn he came to. The inn was unknown to him, and a sense of danger troubled him as soon as he set foot across the threshold, so that he was anxious to be on his way. Over brandy he considered how best to obtain a new horse, when he became drowsy and fell asleep. 'I swear that the poxy innkeeper knew me for what I was and drugged the bottle.' He awoke roughly to find himself staring all befuddled up at his victim of a few hours before, who denounced him to a short, determined-looking individual whom he recognized at once as none other than Townsend, the famous

Bow Street Runner, backed by two more grim-visaged officers.

His wits befuddled, his limbs lethargic, cornered with drawn pistols and with the booty on him, there was nothing for it but to go quietly, and allow himself to be conveyed to Bow Street forthwith. And in my imagination I could see him stood at the bar in the courtroom in the early hours of the morning, before Sir John Fielding, that enormous figure who sat there strangely quiescent and yet alert, the black bandage over his sightless eyes. 'It's said,' Leatherface told me, 'that for all his blindness, he knew any miscreant who'd been up before him previously. He could smell them out, or recognize them by their voice.' The news had spread that a highwayman had been taken and was up before the Blind Beak, and the little court was packed with all manner of spectators come to see the show. Pomaded coxcombs and society-women, street-walkers from Covent Garden Piazza and bullies from the stews, journalists, whose pens scratched noisily, and rakes from the bagnios, all were squeezed together, breathing in the dank, fetid air which no perfume could stifle. There was not much that he could say in answer to the charge against him. The Blind Beak had no alternative than to commit the accused to Tothill Fields Bridewell, there to await his trial at the Old Bailey.

He came to the day when he stood in the dock at the Old Bailey, the court stifling with the press of people, prisoners, guards, turnkeys, witnesses and in the gallery, a packed throng of men-about-town and women of society come to see the sights, snapping snuff-boxes, fluttering fans, giggling, whispering, chattering, even the perfume with which they had liberally drenched themselves failing to overcome the abominable stench. Water streamed down the walls, a damp steam obscured the windows. On one side of the judge, before whom was placed the usual bunch of herbs which were supposed to ward off gaol-fever, sat a duchess and another woman of title, accompanied by the Under-Sheriff and other dignitaries, the cause of this visit had been a wish to gratify their curiosity excited by the presence in the dock of six women convicts. The distinguished spectators remained while the judge passed sentence of death on the prisoners, one of them a young girl, who had been convicted with an older woman beside her, of robbing a bread shop.

Leatherface had elected to defend himself as best he could, he himself was unable to afford a counsel and his friends of the underworld having deserted him in this hour of need, there was no help forthcoming from any other quarter. But the prosecution, backed by indisputable evidence that he was an escaped gaol-bird, had little difficulty in settling his hash. 'I had to thank my lucky stars,' he said, with a reminiscent grunt of thankfulness, 'that the old justice passed a sentence after he had partaken of lunch washed down with a bottle or two of wine which must have mellowed his judgment, otherwise it would have been the trip to Tyburn for me.' As it was he was sentenced to three years' hard labour heaving ballast on the Hulks.

He was duly removed from the Stone

Jug with a batch of other convicts sentenced to the same fate, and conveyed by barge five miles to Woolwich Reach, where several dilapidated old warships were moored off the south bank. These were the notorious Hulks, floatingprisons for criminals ranging from the most hardened felon to young boys. The rotting ship upon which Leatherface found himself was an old East Indiaman, fitted out for its present purpose, as he put it, 'as if to prove the minimum amount of air and breathing-space, food and clothing upon which human life could be supported.' Below decks tiers of wooden bunks, exactly five feet ten inches in which to lie lengthwise, with eighteen inches width, were allowed each occupant. The convicts' clothes were as meagre as their sleeping-space, and their food-supply equally deficient. The Thames supplied their drinking-water, plentifully flavoured with London's sewage.

Guarded by armed overseers the convicts, shackled with iron fetters day and night, were employed raising sand and gravel from the river-bed and dumping it on the shore. After the day's work was done the men were clamped down below in the dark, foul hold, where typhus was rampant, so that they died off like flies. 'Not that there wasn't a never-ending supply of souls to fill up the gaps.' I could not believe how any human being could endure this living death. But he not only endured it, he contrived to survive the horrors of the hell-ship. Moreover, accepting the verminous, revolting surroundings and vile hopelessness of the situation with the realization that escape was impossible, he set about achieving freedom by guile alone. He performed his labours with industry and every appearance of contrite repentance.

His extreme youth was very much in his favour, he was still not yet eighteen, and he came to be regarded sympathetically as a young offender who might be trusted to turn his back upon a life of crime. After he had served two years of his sentence the chief gaoler of his floating prison included his name on a short list of his fellow-prisoners, who were either too aged or ailing to be fit to work, for a remission of sentence. It was not until three months afterwards that the plea achieved the desired result and Leatherface received the royal pardon and release from the Hulks.

Despite all he had gone through, it had not deterred him from returning to his former career. I could not help searching questions springing to my mind at the realization that here was an example where brutal punishment had quite failed to change the wrongdoer's heart for the good. Sensible that he was a marked man if he went back to living by the pad, he decided to shift his ground, and seek fresh fields to exploit his talents. He had picked up the information over the underworld grapevine that London sharpers, adept in the mysteries of their profession had lately swooped across the Irish Sea to descend upon Dublin, there to practise shop-lifting and pocket-picking, swindling and confidence-trickery with lucrative results. It seemed to be just the place, where unknown to the law-officers, he might hope to set up in the only trade he knew with less danger than was attached to his old stamping-ground.

Leatherface took a fancy to Dublin life, he had begun to ape the man of fashion, frequenting playhouses and gambling-places, which not only amused him, but it had occurred to him might prove a source of income. The cutpurses had not yet made their presence felt in these circles, where the gentry were unsuspecting and their pockets unguarded. Leatherface envisaged himself set up as a pickpocket beau, haunting the gaming-houses, and drinking-dens, there to rob the young bucks in their moments of dissipation and debauchery. 'By the winter of that year,' he said, 'I had accumulated over £1,000.'

Then his lucky streak ran out on him. He was nabbed in the act, with his fingers in the pockets of a drunken fop at a playhouse, and he was thrown into the local Black Dog gaol. However the turnkeys were not incorruptible, and Leatherface was quickly able to bribe himself free. But now his reputation in Dublin was as ruined as it had been in London, and his thoughts returned to

England; but he knew that London would have lost none of its dangers for him. And so it was that he hit upon Bath as a likely place for one in his line of business to set up.

25

It was at Bath, as he reminded me, that Leatherface had witnessed Royall Demarest's appearance in *The Tempest*, and his thoughts harked back to his recent meeting with her on the Dover Road. ' ''We are such as dreams are made on,'' he quoted, as she had done in the moonlight beside the Flying Hope and his gaze became faraway and filled with a haunting sadness, ''and our little life is rounded in a sleep.'' He sighed and then throwing off his momentary melancholy, he paraded before my imagination the life he had led in Bath. Of nights the scene of his activities would be the town-hall where the dice rattled, cards glinted under the chandeliers, or to the music of a lively orchestra, gamblers and dancers mingled. Here words sometimes ran high, and hands slapped swordhilts menacingly; here the pickpockets, sharpers and confidence-men from London and the

335

Continent plied their trade. It seemed to him that the road that led from London to Bath might prove more safely worthy of his attention, and accordingly he decided that his best hope for a rich living lay in returning to the pad. 'It was back to my old love,' he said to me, 'and never to leave it again. Except,' with his whimsical smile, 'when sojourning in a prison-cell.'

Shortly before his decision once more to devote his exclusive attention to his erstwhile profession, he had met someone who was to become his close ally and confederate in his every enterprise from now on. 'A sleepingpartner you understand,' he said, 'in every sense of the word.'

The new accomplice was called Fan Holt who was a camp-follower, so to speak, of the raggle-taggle soldiers of fortune who had descended upon Bath. At first I did not realize that he was speaking of the red-haired young woman at the Fox Inn. It was only then as I averted my face so that he should not see it grow hot at the memory of her, that I realized that I had not known her name.

After his will-o'-the-wisp presence had plagued the Bath Road for a year or less, Leatherface began to hanker to return to London's purlieus, and he decided to try his luck once more in his old haunts. Fan Holt accordingly obtained employment for herself at a coaching-inn on the Windsor Road, in order that she might supply him with appropriate intelligence regarding the movements of prospective prey. And so Leatherface's horse, as black as the night itself, galloped the Windsor to London toby, the brace of pistols gleamed in the Brentford moonlight; and the dark eyes glittered imperiously behind the leather mask which he had adopted to further one of the many legends which grew up about him: that he had fought in the wars on the Continent, and had been frightfully wounded in the face by gunshot, or cannon-ball splinter and he must ever wear his leather mask sleeping and waking, so that none could see the horror behind it.

Though there were narrow squeaks, and heart-stopping moments when capture seemed certain, some last-second trick or stroke of luck would enable him to elude every trap and stratagem against him. Nigh on four years he successfully pursued his trade by night, while by day he remained a virtual hermit, rarely venturing forth from the secret inn-room where he might rest, or the cottage or barn where he lay low. Constantly he shifted his ground so that no one, sometimes not even Fan Holt could be sure where he might be located. All this to avoid the risk of being snared through some informer who might be possessed of foreknowledge of his whereabouts.

It was Fan Holt who one day learned through the indiscretion of a tippling guest at the inn where she was employed, that the coach from Windsor would next evening be carrying notes and bills, their value £9,000 from a local bank to the Bull Inn, Holborn, there to be handed over to the banker's London representative. This mouthwatering booty would be contained in a stout iron box, heavily padlocked, the keys in duplicate being held by the bankers at each end. For greater security the iron box had been placed in a canvas bag, fictitiously addressed, to give it the appearance of an ordinary parcel. The next night with Fan beside him, Leatherface sat at the reins of a horse between the shafts of a farm-cart at a selected spot on the lonely Windsor road. Hitched to the back of the cart was his black horse. For this special operation he was not wearing his leather mask, instead he was dressed to look like a farm-labourer, an old wide-brimmed hat effectively shadowing his face; and Fan was got up in a dairymaid's dress, a large shawl about her head and shoulders. The winter sky was starlit with no moon; and presently upon the light breeze that ruffled the branches overhead came the clip-clop of horses' hooves, signalling the approach of the Windsor coach.

With Fan bursting into a drunken song Leatherface drove the cart zigzagging along the road as if returning from an evening at an ale-house. The coach-lamps flickering in the darkness bore down on them, until they were twenty yards away; the coachman began shouting and cursing for him to give way, and Leatherface apparently in his drunkenness persisting in his wild folly, until he slowed his cart across the road under the very muzzles of the coach-horses, effectively barring their path.

While he and Fan kept up their drunken singing and guffawing as if vastly amused by the situation, the guard descended from his place, leaving his armoury behind, with the intention of grabbing the cart-horse's head and leading it out of the coach's way. As he approached Fan took her cue, and half fell, half jumped from the cart and in tipsy fashion began to embrace him, crooning and giggling amorously. When her advances were discouraged, her demeanour changed and she promptly began attacking the object of her seemingly misplaced affection, shouting at him obscenely and beating upon him with her fists; while Leatherface had remained where he was in the cart, laughing and shouting encouragement to the pair as if drunkenly entertained by the performance, but his eyes, gleaming under the shadow of his hat, alert for what he anticipated must be the next move

And sure enough as if he had willed him to act accordingly, the coachman himself must step down from his seat and come between his guard and the vixen who was hampering him with her violent onslaught. The passengers at the windows of the coach added their voices to the din, urging the coachman to proceed with the journey, while he found himself as much involved with the scratching, cursing, kicking wench as his guard. And then when they were both trying to disentangle themselves and beat a hasty retreat they were suddenly staring into the twin muzzles of the two pistols glinting evilly in the light from the coach-lamps. Leatherface grinned reminiscently. 'If I'd been old Nick himself they couldn't have been more taken aback.'

Before the astonished pair could voice their protest or a cry for help, Fan had whipped off her voluminous skirts, and enveloped the heads of both of them so that they were held floundering together, hopelessly blindfolded. Leatherface had ordered the passengers, thunderstruck and paralysed by this sinister turn to the situation, to remain inside the coach under the threat of shooting down whoever was foolish enough to show a face. Handing his pistols to Fan, who meanwhile had bustled the blindfolded coachman and guard into the side of the road, and instructing her loudly to use them on anyone who made a false move, he was smashing off the lock of the boot at the back of the coach and abstracting the canvas bag which held the iron box. In a few moments he had hastened with his load to his cart, and dumped it aboard. Fan rejoined him, returning him his pistols, while he unhitched the black horse and mounted it. At once she drove off the same way they had come into the starlit darkness, leaving Leatherface to cover her retreat. When he judged she was well on the way to their prearranged rendezvous he turned, firing a warning shot over the coachman and the guard, still enveloped in the skirts, and galloped off in the direction Fan had taken.

Everything so far as the hold-up itself

was concerned having gone according to plan, all that remained was to turn that part of the swag, nearly three-quarters of it, that was in the form of bills, into cash. News of the robbery would quickly reach Windsor and London, and Leatherface was aware that he would have to cash the bills which were drawn in Windsor or that neighbourhood, in those places where news of the theft had not yet reached. Speed and plausibility was the essence, and accordingly he and Fan Holt hurried to Oxford where, cashing some of the bills, he was enabled to set himself up with the appearance of a person of wealth and position.

But the Blind Beak at Bow Street had not been altogether idle. He promptly raised the hue-and-cry, and keen pursuit was started at once. Leatherface had reached an inn at Northampton, when he was awakened from a slumber of pleasant dreams by the noise of the arrival of a troop of the military in the inn-yard below. Sensing that something was in the wind which boded him little joy he quietly slipped out with the object of effecting his departure, taking his treasure with him. However, the soldiers were everywhere, and though he reached the stables the chance of leaving unnoticed by shay was obviously hopeless. Taking as much money as he could push into his pockets, he decided to make a dash for it on horseback. His hurried removal attracted the attention of some alert soldiery, however, and they gave chase. There were half-a-dozen of them, better mounted than he, who had been forced to grab the nearest horse he could lay his hands on. All the same he led them a pretty dance until at Banbury, his nag dropped dead from exhaustion beneath him, and the game was up.

And so his journey to Tyburn began. First, the Old Bailey once again, and the black cap perched atop the judge's rusty, sideways wig; and then in my mind's eye I could see the crowds on that fatal morning swelling the route from Newgate Prison, all along High Holborn to Tyburn. I could hear the shouts of the broadsheet-sellers, with their copies of Leatherface's life and crimes compiled of legends and lies by Grub Street hacks, and then the mounting buzz of excitement and anticipation as the hero of the grim procession came into view. I could visualize the mob of bulging-eyed men and women and children all about me, as that lone tall, dark figure in the lumbering cart, leaning negligently against the black coffin which accompanied him, coolly acknowledged the roars of applause, shouts and jeers that greeted him with a show of his shackled wrists. 'I could afford to feel almost as inconsequential as I appeared,' he said to me, 'since I was buoyed up to some extent by the secret hopes of rescue from the very jaws of death itself. A forlorn hope, you may think, but when it is all there is left him, a man may be forgiven if he draws upon it.'

In the fleeting days before his execution-date, even when the last hope that he might be spared faded, Fan Holt, who had escaped the Bow Street Runners, feverishly sought for his rescue on the very gallows. Now I was to hear the truth of his miraculous escape, how he had cheated death itself. Yet despite the hope that lifted up his spirits, when Leatherface beheld the triple tree, and knew that the ultimate moment was near, his mouth went dry as if filled with sand, his knees turned to water, so that he forgot to make a jest to the press milling around his cart. Against the pale sky of that summer morning the wooden triangular structure rose up black and sinister. The cart stopped beneath the cross-bar from which the hangman had already suspended the rope. As he stood there while the noose was slipped over his neck he glanced at the huge grandstand sagging beneath the weight of spectators who filled it, and then his anxious gaze transfixed Fan Holt. His racing heart bounded at the sight of her, and the two hulking fellows on either side. Her red hair flowing in the light breeze gleaming like a banner in the sunlight, seemed to him like a signal that all would yet be well; and she threw him a confident smile from the shouting, swaying mob that enclosed her.

Now was his moment for the customary farewell speech. 'I thought it prudent not to linger over-long, since the sooner I was hanged and cut down the better; I felt quite chilled by the capful of wind, it would have been ironical to have died from pneumonia. So I gave the poxy mob a joke, a quotation or two of doggerel rhyme, and made my adieu with the vow that my ghost should haunt the Dover Road.' The hangman stood back, surveyed his handiwork, the driver of the cart jerked the reins, the horse went smartly forward, and Leatherface was left hanging while a mighty ear-splitting roar rose on all sides. 'Now it was up to Fan and her friends,' he said, 'and their speedy adroitness.'

I had sat there, fingernails dug deep into the perspiring palms of my hands, as I listened to him talking so calmly about it all. It seemed incredible that after what he had endured he was in fact standing there, telling me his story at all. My mind was reeling at the pictures he had conjured up as he came to the climax of his strange and mysterious career. He had taken his pipe from his mouth and I saw his free hand unconsciously finger his throat, while his dark eyes went oddly blank, as if he, himself, was peering within his soul at those last seconds of consciousness while he swung from the gallows. Much as my curiosity urged me to do so, I could not bring myself to ask him the thousand and one questions that rose to my lips. Much as I longed to hear him answer I could not ask him about that moment that must have seemed an æon when he had entered the valley of death, from whence he had yet contrived to turn back and make his safe return.

He himself did not offer to reveal what lay in his thoughts, what agony of apprehension he must have suffered, and physical pain as the rope tightened about his neck. I felt myself irresistibly impelled to glance at him, and wonder if the white cravat at the thick, muscular throat, hid any mark or scar. In the brief silence that hung stretched upon the air he drew reflectively at his pipe. And then he went on to describe what, as he was to learn later, had chanced further. Fan Holt's prearranged plot bore fruit. She and her two companions had surged quickly forward to reach the swinging figure, while two others of her gang appeared, crying out loudly on all sides that this was to save the highwayman from the dissecting-table. The guards combined to hold back those who pressed close out of morbid curiosity to view the condemned's death-struggles.

A knife had flashed in the pale sunlight and Leatherface, inert, his features purpling, was swiftly lifted down, while Fan Holt herself loosened the noose's knot. Even then when they had already accomplished so much and as speedily as they had dared to hope, disaster nearly wrecked the plan. They had proceeded a dozen yards with their precious burden, fighting their way through the crowd, when suddenly a cry went up that they themselves were body-snatchers sent by the surgeons. For a few taut moments, while Fan and her companions shouted down the wild accusation, answering that they were friends anxious to see their hero decently buried, they were held back. Finally, however, Fan's heartrending appeals and tears won them their way to a hearse which had been waiting on the edge of the mob, a surgeon sat within, with hot blankets ready to enwrap the body. All safely inside, the driver whipped up the horses and the black vehicle sped to a house nearby, especially rented to receive the apparently lifeless remains.

Wrapped in a bed of more hot blankets the limp form was blooded copiously, and untiringly massaged to restore the circulation. And so, miraculously as it sounded to my ears, the faint spark of life that still remained despite the strangling noose was gradually warmed to a brighter flame. Presently the almost-stilled heart began to beat more and more strongly, the pulse, which had been so sluggish as to be almost indistinguishable began to respond.

Within one hour after the surgeon had begun to work upon him, Leatherface slowly opened his eyes; his lips drawn back in a ghastly grin, he croaked painfully: 'Water, for Christ's sake, my throat's as sore as hell.'

26

And so he had brought his story up to the present. I was left to wonder how, having suffered so much as he had, even to outstaring death in the face he had still chosen to continue his nefarious career. How was it possible, I asked myself, that he had even not learned the lesson which seemed so apparent to me, which was that anything was better than the precarious existence he had led, the constant balance he must keep on the razor-edge of doom? Any employment however menial, whatever its circumstances, so long as it were honest no matter how poorly paid seemed to me infinitely preferable, however looked at, than the path of crime. But such was the case with him, that he felt impelled to continue as he had before in his old ways, nonchalantly reckless of what next and finally fatal hazard might befall him, so long as he had his black horse between his knees, a brace of his favourite pistols in his pockets, and the prospect, however elusive it may prove, of rich pickings beneath the stars.

He had lit his pipe again, it had grown cold while he reached the climax of his story. As he drew at it his gaze held mine through a puff of tobacco-smoke and I sensed that he guessed what was in my mind, for his eyes narrowed quizzically, he was reading my thoughts. 'I've heard that each one of us is born with the seed of death implanted in ourselves, and since that each breathing moment takes us that much nearer the grave, there are those of us who seek to hurry the process, who are self-destroyers.' He paused to tamp down the tobacco in the clay bowl. 'No doubt such am I,' he said. 'Each time I set out upon the pad I am impelled not by the urge to imperil my victim and rob him of his purse, but because I seek, deep down within my innermost being, to imperil myself, and bring about my own ruin.' He dragged deeply at his pipe, and took a restless turn about the room. 'But these are waters too deep for you to paddle in,' he said. Indeed, what he had been saying had put my thoughts in a haze, I could not follow his reasoning. 'Let it be sufficient,' with a drawling laugh, 'if you have learnt from the lesson that has been taught me. That, however much I may contradict myself, there is nothing more despicable than the desperado; stripped of its false glitter, it is a sorry profession.'

I nodded for I understood his meaning now well enough, and my mind rang with echoes of his words. This much I had learnt as a result of the escapade upon which I had foolishly embarked during the past few hours. That truth and honour, however dull they might appear, are to be cherished far above the antics of rogues and thieves. Moreover I had been taught that even to play at villainy was to risk wretchedness and calumny and lose the love of one's fellow-creatures. "He that toucheth pitch shall be defiled therewith," I heard Leatherface say, and once again it was as if he was reading my thoughts, so that I started with surprise. He gave his harsh laugh. 'So I escaped the noose,' he said, in conclusion, 'even when it was drawn around my neck, with no more harm to me than a dry rasp in my throat.' I remarked the harshness of his tone more closely than I had before, realizing the reason for it.

He had derived much cynical amusement, he said, reading the reports in the newspapers of his execution. Then he thought he might gain no little advantage from the universal belief in his death, his last vow on the gallows that his ghost would haunt the roads where he had plied his trade in the flesh, was quoted extensively. He became inspired with the macabre notion of driving his warning home by appearing in his old guise, leather mask and all, upon the toby. It was not long before he must rest inactive no longer, so that only a week after he had danced on the air at Tyburn, he was back on the pad, impelling folk to believe with superstitious terror that he was his own wraith. Rumour quickly spread that Leatherface's ghost nightly appeared to levy toll from travellers on the roads, as he had threatened the world it would.

Meanwhile, Fan Holt had chanced to

meet an old acquaintance, a fence named Old Reuben, who had established himself like some spider at the centre of a web of intrigue and villainy, at an inn known as the Fox on the Dover Road. The old fence had so dazzled her with accounts of the rich pickings to be had among the steady stream of travellers to and from the Continent, that she persuaded Leatherface to shift his ground once more and he had accordingly lately set out to thrill the neighbourhood of the Fox with proof that his ghost was as troublesome to travellers along the Dover Road, as his living presence had been on that other road where he had not long since successfully preyed. Fan Holt had proceeded to find employment as of old, as a spy at the Fox Inn.

During these revelations of his life both private and professional, I had formed an impression that grew increasingly stronger that Leatherface regarded me as something of his responsibility, that it was up to him to see me as safely out of the entanglement in which I had so foolishly involved myself. I concluded that a bright spark of kindliness towards me burned within him and that he abhorred as much as I any possibility that I should become tainted with the faintest suspicion of anything that smacked of crime or villainy. Perhaps his concern for my welfare and my good name was nothing more than an attempt, if not consciously, to placate the gods, to redeem himself a little for his own sins that he had committed. I could not tell, but convinced as I was that he would do all in his power to clear me of any guilt in the estimation of Lord Deal and Mr. Ellis, I felt that the time was now ripe to convey to him the urgency of overtaking the Flying Hope so that my innocence could be re-established once and for all, before Lord Deal or the Bow Street officer reached London, and my parents would learn of my trumped-up infamy.

The violence of the storm had been slow abating. Now I glimpsed through the windows to the East the first faint glimmer of dawn revealing a cloud-wracked sky torn by an infrequent flash of lightning. Now and again a fitful gust of wind threw a capful of rain against the windows. Instilled with the fervent desire to hurry away to prove my innocence, my impatience impelled me to speak my mind.

'Now that the storm is past and it begins to get light, we can be moving once again.'

He stared at me, his dark eyes preoccupied and his brow furrowed. Then he glanced out of the window as if his thoughts were still somewhere else, caught up with the dark tale he had been relating.

'I'm sure Miss Demarest and Jack Morgan believe that all I did was to make no gain for myself, but only to see the return of the snuff-box. But the other two are positive I'm a criminal. No word or action of mine will change their minds. But you could tell them the truth. You alone can prove me innocent; that I acted in all good faith. If only we can catch the Flying Hope.'

He was regarding me, as if engrossed by my appeal to him. 'Ellis, you say, is somewhere searching for you?'

I nodded. 'Even if he is not with them,' I said, 'Lord Deal will suffice. Once he is won over to me, his word and opinion will influence Mr. Ellis. Besides, isn't it possible that the storm forced him to abandon his search for me and rejoin the rest at the next inn?'

'Nearest would be Faversham.' He seemed to be calculating the lie of the land. 'And we miss them there, we'd catch the coach by Gravesend. Even the two of us on my nag will travel at double the pace; there isn't a short cut between here and London I don't know.' My face brightened with anticipation, and my impatience to be off was apparent, but he seemed in no haste. 'Though why should Lord Deal think so ill of you,' he said scratching his long chin, 'since it was on account of you that he gets back his poxy trinket — ?'

'He had his knife into me from the start,' I said, cutting in on him, so anxious was I to make a move. I recalled my spontaneous and spirited defence of Leatherface on the packet. 'I told you he suspected me over the pistol I believed to be unloaded, that I had aided your flight. Then he could not credit it in his suspicious mind when I persuaded him to find his snuff-box in George Barrington's pocket, that I did not intend filching it from him in turn.'

'We will alter his mind. As for your Bow Street Runner, his business breeds suspicious fancies. While doubtless his pride was wounded, losing Barrington as he did, after you had delivered him so neatly into his hands.'

The stabbing flames from the fire that was beginning to blaze lit up his harshly chiselled features, deepening the lines that ran from his great hooked nose. I could not read what lay behind that jutting, craggy brow, what plan he was conceiving which would accomplish my ends. I was all racked with anxiety to be away; I had completely recovered from the exhaustion that had overcome me as a result of my hazardous escape from the Flying Hope, my fateful game of hide-and-seek in the storm with Mr. Ellis; I was feeling fresh enough for anything, even if the clothes on my back were only half-dry and my belly was wanting for food and drink, still all that could wait until later, when my mind was reassured and I no longer felt like a hunted animal. I had no stomach for eating or drinking; no heart for anything until my utter guiltlessness had been proclaimed. 'I'm eager to be away,' I said.

He stretched his great figure until he looked like some enormous black bat there in the long, high-ceilinged room, with the dawn inching in through the windows. I had begun pulling on his boots, all caked with dried mud, while he threw me a quizzical look, as if noting that I was making mighty free with his property, but I only grinned back at him. I was so elated at the prospect of rehabilitating myself in the eyes of Lord Deal and Mr. Ellis, Jack Morgan, and especially Royall Demarest that thrills of excited anticipation sped through my being and I was unable to prevent myself trembling as I stamped about in the boots that fitted me so ill. I knew for certain that with Leatherface to back me, not even Mr. Ellis could doubt the good intentions behind my actions, wildly foolish though they had been. I already had friendly allies in the persons of Miss Demarest and Jack Morgan, who had voiced their feelings in defence of my integrity and honesty, and now I could not fail, I felt confident, to persuade the others that I had suffered a grave injustice.

My only fear was whether we could overtake the Flying Hope in time. Leatherface would have to proceed warily, too; it would be broad daylight and I could not expect him to risk being seen on a busy highway or at an inn on the road. I glanced at him, and any fears or doubts that had assailed me were pushed into the background. His calm presence reassured me, and not even the sight of his pistol which he produced and began to look over, alarmed me. A sardonic shadow lingered at the corners of his mouth. 'They may come in useful as a means of persuading those who might not otherwise listen, to hear me out.'

Suddenly, he paused, and then without

a word he crossed swiftly to the window and cautiously peered out on the overgrown carriage-way of the house. I did not move. Alarm gripped me as if I was held in a vice. Now, I could hear the faint crunch of gravel from the drive. Leatherface beckoned me to cross to him at the window. I urged my numbed limbs into action and stood beside him, keeping well back so that I might not be observed. I drew in my breath in a whistling gasp of amazement.

Approaching the house, all bedraggled and wretched-looking, was Lord Deal himself, with just behind him Miss Demarest and Jack Morgan.

27

That the Flying Hope should meet disaster yet again, halted once more and sustaining greater damage, on its eventful journey to London and not far distant from the derelict, eerie house where I was sleeping through the wild, howling storm, I could not have envisaged in my most fanciful dreams. That this was what had in fact transpired, and how it came about, I afterwards learned.

Soon after my desperate leap for freedom into the dark, and Mr. Ellis's decision to leave the coach to proceed, while he came in search of me, the coachman had driven at a slower pace. He had feared that the object in the road over which we had bounced with such violence, might have weakened the wheel which had been temporarily repaired at the Fox. So the coach had continued on its way slowly but surely, and without mishap, until the great storm broke. The heavy downpour slowed the cattle almost to walking-pace, but they pushed on, making fair progress, even when the surface of the road changed for the worse. The ditches gave way to shallow banks which hemmed close to the road on either side and down whose slopes the rain flooded loosening the road's surface, and scoring it in places with troughs which filled with water wherein the wheels sank and dragged. But it was not until the Flying Hope rounded a bend, screened on one side by a low, bush-shrouded cliff, that they came upon chaos before the coachman or the guard, blinded by the rain and lightning, could see it.

The torrential rain had dislodged the side of the low jutting cliff where it had almost overhung the road, and a mass of earth and debris had been strewn across the highway. The unexpected barrier suddenly appearing before them, the frightened horses pulled the coach wildly sideways on, so that it was as much as the coachman could do, exerting all his strength and dexterity, to halt the animals before the Flying Hope was toppled over. This disaster was averted, but the coach was swung violently to one side, and the extra strain upon the already damaged wheel was too much for it. Now, it completely splintered and collapsed, tilting the coach down into the mud.

There, half-slewed across the road the coach was forced to remain; even without the harassing of the storm, there was nothing that could readily be employed to overcome the calamity. The coachman, after a cursory examination, confirmed everyone's worst fears. There was no continuing the journey on only three wheels, it would have to wait for the passing of the storm or daylight, when either a fresh coach could be obtained, or a new wheel brought and fitted in place of the shattered one. And so there was nothing for it but that Lord Deal, Miss Demarest, Mr. Morgan and the coachman with the guard must wait inside the coach, against the tempest that roared overhead. There they were forced to remain through those, long, wearisome hours of storm and darkness, to all intents and purposes trapped in the helplessly crippled Flying Hope, its roof presently beginning to leak, thus adding to their wretched, miserable state.

A short while before dawn the thunderous fury, the hissing lightning flashes and the downpour began to abate. By the time the first grey streaks edged the horizon, the thunder had faded to a growl, the lightning was intermittent and the clouds were rolling back, only occasional squalls brought spatters of rain. The coachman and the guard proceeded to examine the damage and consider the position in the faint light. Everything more than confirmed their first opinions. Even if the road ahead had not been blocked by the miniature avalanche of mud and boulders the wheel was smashed beyond repair. There was no prospect of retracing their steps in order to branch off and circumvent the obstruction and so continue their journey. It was impossible to move the coach. There was little likelihood of help from other travellers, for not a soul would be moving yet, everyone would have been sheltering from the raging elements. There remained only one thing to do, which was for the coachman to take one of the horses and proceed forthwith to Faversham, a half-mile distant and there obtain assistance, either in the form of another conveyance or a new wheel, whichever was most expeditiously come by, to enable the passengers to continue their journey. And so, leaving the guard with the others, the coachman surmounted the mass of mud and debris where a way was barely possible, and rode off on his urgent errand.

Soon after his departure when the sky had brightened sufficiently, Jack Morgan clambered to the nearby highest point to return to the coach with the news that he had spied a lone house not far from their position. Chilled and damp, and in the lowest spirits, Lord Deal immediately insisted that they should all repair to the place, at least they would find warmth to dry themselves, rain-soaked and miserable as they were in the leaky topsy-turvy coach. And when the occupants learned of their predicament, he was confident, they would even offer them hot drink and food. So it was decided that the guard should keep watch on the coach, their luggage and the three horses, and keep a look-out for Mr. Ellis, in case he should turn up from his expedition, while the three others made their way along muddy tracks and across flooded meadows to the house. The very house wherein Leatherface and myself were now preparing to leave, and where I now stood, transfixed at the window, watching the drooping trio stumbling up the unkempt carriage-way to the front door. In my astonishment at this unexpected sight I had pushed forward, so that Leatherface had to remedy my careless lack of caution by pulling me back, so that I could see without myself being seen.

'Seems that we're to be spared our trouble,' he said, his voice rasping in my ear. 'Instead of our going to the mountain the mountain is come to Mahomet.'

I had imagined the Flying Hope half-way to Gravesend by now, and I could not fathom the reason for the appearance at this lonely, derelict house of Lord Deal, Royall Demarest and Jack

Morgan all these hours after Mr. Ellis and I had left them to continue on their way. Unaware then of what I knew later, I could only think that somehow they had discovered some hint of my whereabouts and had come for me. I glanced at Leatherface who was now putting on his leather mask, 'They must know I'm here,' I said, in a perplexed whisper.

'What's it matter what they know? They're here, and that's to our favour.' He gave a glance through the window again. 'Look at their appearance,' he said. He gave a drawling laugh. 'They hardly seem like some resolute searching-party. More like stranded travellers in need of shelter.'

Came a sudden, sharp knocking on the front door and I glanced across at the wide door which opened on to the other deserted, dusty room, beyond which lay the hall. The door was open, and I could see the double-doors across the other room. They were closed. All Leatherface and I had to do was wait for our unbidden visitors to make their way into the empty house, as they surely would, and head this way. Now that the daylight had strengthened, I could see our obvious means of retreat should we need to get out quickly. And it was apparent to me why Leatherface had chosen this room of all the others for his quarters. The great windows on the opposite side looked on to a crumbling terrace, and nothing beyond but the overgrown gardens and a large cluster of trees, with glimpses of rising open country, clear as far as the eye could see.

Another bout of loud and longer knocking snapped my attention to the wide-open door and Leatherface and I stood poised silently together waiting. Jack Morgan's voice came to us. 'I do believe the place is deserted, my lord.'

'It looks to me entirely uninhabitable,' we heard Lord Deal say, as irritable as ever, in reply. 'Still, it offers us shelter, where we can make a fire and warm ourselves.' There was a murmur from Miss Demarest, then the sharp-toned voice came again. 'There's little sense in waiting upon nobody. Break open the door.' Now a grunt from Jack Morgan, as if surprised, no doubt when he tried the handle, the door had opened for him. There came its complaining creak as it was pushed back on its rusted hinges. Then suddenly Royall Demarest's tones.

'Should we go in? I feel this place must be haunted and will gain us little comfort. The musty smell, the feeling of decay is most menacing.'

'Rot me,' Lord Deal said, contemptuously. 'Who'd give a damn for ghosts or the like? All I want is warmth and shelter against that fool of a coachman's return.'

We heard him bark a command at Jack Morgan, and then the sound of their footsteps, slow and cautious, reached us. Jack Morgan called out to ask if anyone was at home, his voice echoing hollowly. The footsteps paused as if the trio were looking around them. There ensued a long silence, disturbed finally by footsteps again as Lord Deal's voice sounded, but no less irascible and impatient. 'Been empty for years, I should not wonder. Look at the state of it. Falling in everywhere.'

We heard Jack Morgan make some

observation as if in agreement with the other, then the footsteps drew nearer, they were crossing the hall towards the double-doors which we were watching, and I glanced down at the butt of one of his pistols protruding from the pocket of the tall, black figure beside me, whose attitude was negligent and casual as if he was expecting some friends calling for a dish of tea and genteel gossip.

'I don't like it,' came Miss Demarest's voice, faint and tremulous. 'There's something evil here.'

'Damned superstitious nonsense,' said Lord Deal explosively. 'It's nothing more than an uninhabited ruin, and if we can find somewhere less draughty, we might have a fire going.'

The three pairs of footsteps halted at the double-doors and a handle turned. A door began to creak wide. I felt a touch on my arm, and quickly followed Leatherface, who had stepped out of the newcomer's line of vision. Now the footsteps sounded on the bare floor, approaching us slowly, as if still with a sense of caution, as if the eerie atmosphere of the draughty, crumbling place had not been dissipated by Lord Deal's contemptuous observations.

Steadily the three visitors neared the open door of the room where we waited. Leatherface had moved a pace in front of me; and now I saw, with my blood racing faster, that the pistols had appeared in his hands. I waited, held rigid in a grip of tension for whoever should first come through the door.

It seemed to me that the footsteps would never reach us, they seemed to drag across the floor. Yet it could not have been more than a matter of seconds before they reached the threshold and Jack Morgan halted, to stare at us with a dropping jaw. He could find no words to say as Lord Deal and Miss Demarest joined him and saw us, too. The shocked, incredulous expressions on their faces was a sight I shall never forget. Jack Morgan's jaw continued to sag, without a sound from him. Lord Deal's thin, still rouged lips were clamped into a twisted line, and his watery eyes fixed us unblinkingly, moving from me to Leather-face and back again. Miss Demarest's hand flew to her mouth, and the dark eyes in that wan, but lovely heart-shaped face widened with terror.

'Ghosts,' she said. 'It must be.'

Perhaps we did both present a ghostly appearance, motionless and unsmiling, as we stood there in the greyness of that neglected, dusty room, thrown into curious relief against the dawn light that edged its way through the rain-splashed, begrimed windows. But whatever super-natural spell we may have cast, it was of brief duration. Lord Deal snapped the silence with his waspish snarl.

'The place is haunted right enough,' he said. And then, spitting out the words, as he took in the pistols glinting at him. 'But not by any ghost, but by the damned Leatherface.'

28

'You are right,' Leatherface said. 'Masked, as you see, against being recognized should I see any of you yet again. Though that I'm damned, as you say, time must tell.'

Lord Deal chocked apoplectically, then recovered himself sufficiently to say in his sharp, waspish voice: 'My hope is even more fervent that next time I see you, it will be at Tyburn.' He shifted his vicious contorted expression upon me. 'And you too, who are in league with this damned villain.'

I could not help a shiver at the malevolence in his gaze, and turned appealingly to the towering figure beside me. Miss Demarest who had been staring at me, nonplussed, now said: 'Where are we, what is this house?'

'A den of thieves,' Lord Deal said, 'that's for certain.'

'Out of the frying-pan into the fire,'

Jack Morgan muttered.

'It was one of my hiding-places,' Leatherface was saying. 'Until it was discovered, and that most recently.' He threw a glance at me.

'I came upon it by accident in the storm,' I said.

Lord Deal gave a loud snort of disbelief. I caught Jack Morgan's stony look, as if even he, who had been the least suspicious of the company in the Flying Hope towards me, could not quite stomach that my presence there together with the very man who had held up the coach was purely chance. Leatherface turned to me with a twitch of amusement at the corners of his mouth beneath his mask. 'You are indeed a victim of fell coincidence,' he said.

'I have only myself to blame for that,' I said wretchedly.

' "The fault, is not in our stars," ' Miss Demarest said, not without a rising hint of sympathy in her tone. ' "But in ourselves." '

'Neatly quoted,' Leatherface said, 'even though it happens that it does not altogether fit the case.' He turned to Lord Deal, who had made a surreptitious movement to bring him closer to Jack Morgan as if he would inspire the other to make a further attempt to launch himself against that rakish, black figure. But if this desperate manœuvre had in fact been in Lord Deal's mind he must have been dissuaded by the wicked glint of those twin-barrelled pistols, as Leatherface, his casually-spoken words belied by the purposefulness of his demeanour, said to him: 'One of your company appears to be missing.'

'Mr. Ellis?' Royall Demarest said, and then she looked at me, and her gaze fell for a moment on my wrists, now happily unmanacled. 'Still out searching for you, no doubt.'

I wondered what had happened to the man from Bow Street. If he had, perhaps, made his way back to the gypsy's caravan, to shelter from the storm. If so, it further occurred to me, would he have noticed the handcuffs which had been removed from me, and which might have been left carelessly amongst the rest of the jumble that had strewn the gypsy's abode? Or perhaps Mr. Ellis had been able to find somewhere else where he could shelter until the storm had passed. I glanced through the windows at the sky from which the pink of that early dawn was slowly beginning to give place to a steely-blue. I could make out the branches of a great oak tree which were outflung as if weighed down still by the pressure of the storm which had heaped the torrential rain upon it. The storm seemed to have blown itself out, birds were beginning to sing in the hedgerows and bushes all around the house.

'Pity he is not present to hear what I have to say,' I heard Leatherface saying.

'No doubt your meeting,' Lord Deal said, caustically, 'is, for the present, merely postponed.'

'A dubious pleasure,' Leatherface said, 'which I would willingly omit, in ordinary circumstances. This, however, is different. He also should hear that which will exonerate this youth whom you and he have blindly misjudged, so wrongfully accused.'

Lord Deal gave another of his disbelieving snorts, and for a moment my heart sank once more, as I gauged how difficult it was going to be to convince the irascible, suspicion-filled old man of the truth concerning me. Then I caught the expressions on the faces of Miss Demarest and Jack Morgan which showed that they at any rate were disposed to listen with unbiassed judgment. Royall Demarest turned impatiently upon Lord Deal. 'What motive can he have,' she said, with a flash of her dark eyes, 'in this case for speaking less than the truth?'

Leatherface gave her a thin, frosty smile. 'What I have to say,' he said dryly, 'draws most of the blame upon me, while the rest George Barrington must answer for.'

'Another poxy rogue who'll swing for it,' Lord Deal said. And he snapped his blackened tooth-stumps together, and reached into his pocket with an air of finality. From the corner of my eye I saw the pistols jerk in his direction, and my heart was in my mouth as I wondered what next might happen. Then Lord Deal produced his snuff-box, that precious snuff-box which glinted and sparkled in the pale light that slanted into the long room, the golden snuff-box which had been the cause for much of the disaster and misery of the past several hours. Lord Deal snapped open the lid and with his bejewelled, claw-like fingers, took a pinch of snuff, returning the cherished object to his pocket before dabbing his nose with his lace handkerchief.

All this time the leather mask had been bent unmoving upon him, and then that grating voice was heard to say quietly: 'Rot me, but you have a rare impertinence, prompted either by courage or senile forgetfulness.'

Lord Deal's rat-trap of a mouth opened. 'What do you mean?'

'That snuff-box, of whose weight I failed to lighten you earlier in our acquaintance, what's to prevent me lifting it now?'

The watery eyes flickered to the pistol-barrels menacing him, and I heard Miss Demarest give a little gasp. I turned to the brooding figure beside me, but he answered me before I could say anything. 'No fear; he may keep his damned trinkets whose safe return he owes entirely to you.' I relaxed, muttering thankfully, as he turned back to Lord Deal. 'Which is why,' he said, 'I find incomprehensible your bitterness against him, since what loss or harm have you suffered at his hands?'

'On the contrary,' I heard myself speaking up spiritedly, 'if it hadn't been for me you might never have seen your snuff-box again.'

Leatherface made a slight movement of his hand towards me, as if advising me that I should hold my tongue and leave everything safely to him. 'Let me tell you,' he said to Lord Deal, his jaw jutting forward in emphasis, 'that if it wasn't for this resolute, if ill-advised young cockerel, I should pluck that snuff-box and every valuable from your pestilential carcass, and if you resisted, blow your brains out with no more compunction than I would shoot a dog.' A tense silence hung on the dusty, neglected room, broken only by the crackle of wood burning in the fireplace, and the shrill song of the birds beyond the windows. There was no doubt in the minds of those facing us that Leatherface meant every syllable he had uttered. And I could sense in their expressions that their mood was undergoing a subtle but definite change. Even Lord Deal, I felt sure, was viewing me with a less speculatively hostile eye.

'The only one,' Leatherface was continuing in that tone of quiet conviction, 'to be the loser on account of this business is myself. Items: a brace of favourite pistols, a hat and — ah — other attire, and one black horse lost to George Barrington.' With swift incisiveness he went on to acquaint them faithfully of the past night's happenings, wherein I had been involved. And where he could not fill in the picture I put in what interjections I thought were required. What had occurred at the Fox Inn, for instance, though I made no reference to Old Reuben, thinking it indiscreet to do so, considering Leatherface's situation there; nor, needless to say, did I mention my brief, if well-remembered acquaintance with the young woman I now knew was named Fan Holt.

With no show of brazenness, Leather-face did not spare himself so far as his own complicity in the matter was concerned; but speaking frankly and with evident sincerity he made it plain that I was no villainous accomplice or party to the theft of the snuff-box. At the same time he damned George Barrington for the evil fashion in which he had deluded me into aiding him in all innocence, and purely out of good intentions become his unwitting confederate. When he reached the end of it all nor did he fail in blaming me for my wild, hare-brained venture and hazardous prank, so that I could not help hanging my head under his scathing censure.

But that he had succeeded in clearing my name and re-establishing me in the others' good opinions, even including Lord Deal, was plain enough. 'I will take it upon myself,' Lord Deal said, with remarkable good grace, I thought, consid-ering his hitherto viciously implacable attitude towards me, 'to acquaint Mr. Ellis of the indisputed facts as I now believe them to be. I am sure he will concur with all of us in accepting what we have heard as the unvarnished truth.'

Spontaneously I crossed to him as he extended his hand to me in a token of friendship. As I did so, Leatherface moved behind me and now stood in the doorway. I thought I detected a wariness in his attitude, as if he was forewarned of some imminent danger as he spoke. 'Much as it pains me to quit such charming company,' he was saying, 'not to mention forgoing the pleasure of relieving you of all your valuables, I must bid you adieu.'

And he turned on his heel and was gone, but I broke free of Miss Demarest's hand clasping my arm, to rush after him. His footsteps echoed somewhere in the direction of the back of the house, and I followed speedily. I hurried through the large, derelict kitchen and through a door which swung on one rusty hinge open to the stable-yard, and was in time to see him already mounted on a black horse, the animal he had ridden over from the Fox Inn. He turned as I cried out to him, and I saw that he no longer wore his leather mask. There was a vibrant urgency in every line of his tall, broad-shouldered figure. He paused momentarily while I hurried across to him, muttering incoherently words of gratitude for what he had done which had lifted the load of wretchedness and black suspicion entirely from me.

Those saturnine features with that great hooked nose and long chin were bent upon me as I stood there. The dark piercing eyes beneath the craggy brows regarded me unsmilingly; and I thought I caught in them an expression of infinite sadness, as he spoke to me gratingly. 'Get home,' he said, 'and be thankful to Christ that you have a home and loving hearts to go to.'

Without another word he swung away and galloped out to the drive. I darted after him and stood at the corner of the house, as instead of proceeding along the weed-filled gravel for the road, he reined his horse aside and leaping a hedge headed across the fields which lay covered in the early-morning mist. I watched the tall, black figure swallowed up in the grey wraiths, and then for a moment he reappeared again and stood on the brow of a hill, starkly silhouetted against the pale horizon, lit now by a golden promise of the sun. Then I fancied he gave a glance back, at any rate I will swear that he raised a hand in farewell, and was gone.

I stood there, staring out across the mist, hoping to sight him again. But I never did, he had vanished as if he might never have been.

Presently I began to make my way back to the house, my heart a turmoil of emotions; one moment I felt swamped with a feeling of forlornness at an innermost knowledge that I had seen the last of one whom I had come to know so intimately in such a brief time; next moment I felt uplifted and exhilarated, knowing that after all I had suffered, I could hold my head high again, that I was freely acquitted of any part in the desperate evil in which I had been entangled, and was held in the best estimation by those to whom I was returning.

I went back into the house the way I had come. I crossed the hall and reached the room where I had left the others, and now I realized the reason for Leather-face's hasty adieu, and marvelled at his intuition which had forewarned him to go while the going was good. For there, in a state of semi-collapse and supported by Jack Morgan before the fire, which Miss Demarest was tending with more wood, was Mr. Ellis. I do not know which of the two of us was most surprised as at the sound of my approach, he turned with the others, and saw me stood in the doorway.

Soaked to the skin as he was, completely exhausted and lacklustre-eyed, yet he made as if to advance upon me purposefully, but Lord Deal's claw-like fingers on his arm quietly restrained him. 'All right, Mr. Ellis, he is not to blame.'

29

All this, as I said when I began, was long ago, that I have been telling you, though much of it remains imprinted so indelibly upon my memory that some parts of that strange tempestuous night on the Dover Road might have happened only yesterday. In my mind's eye I can see the man who was known to the world as Leatherface as if he had only just ridden away through the mists of the dawn that followed the long night; while Fan Holt's face rises up before me as if it was but an hour since our encounter at the Fox Inn. Royall Demarest, she also is as clear in my imagination as if I was still sitting opposite her in the coach that duly arrived from Faversham, to take us as far as the inn there, where we breakfasted and dried the damp out of our clothes, before we set forth once more for London, which we reached at last, without any further misadventures.

My story, then, must draw to a close, there is no more to add. Poor Mr. Ellis, who had wandered around, buffetted by the storm, had eventually found himself at dawn on the Dover Road. Trudging onwards, having given up the search for me, seeking only shelter, warmth and breakfast, he had come upon the Flying Hope, abandoned except for the guard who had directed him to the derelict house where we were. He was much taken aback at my appearance on the scene, but when the truth about me was given him by Lord Deal and the others, he finally ceased eyeing me sourly. In the end he agreed, if a little ungraciously, that I had been misjudged. He even apologized for the ill-treatment I had suffered, and that for his part he had no more to say, so far as I was concerned, and proceeded to fulminate over the fact that Leatherface had been in that very spot only a short while since, only to vanish like a will-o'-the-wisp. I never saw Mr. Ellis again; neither did I ever encounter any of the other passengers of the Flying Hope, after we had said good-bye to one another on arrival at the Red Lion, Charing Cross, in London.

I still recall the sickening pang I experienced as I saw Miss Demarest greeted most demonstratively by a tall, startlingly handsome man as she stepped from the coach. But whatever my youthfully jealous thoughts that attacked me, they were all forgotten at the sight of my father, somewhat stern of demeanour and my mother, anxious-eyed, and their faces lighting up as they saw me. I was to hear something of Royall Demarest's subsequent triumphs at Drury Lane, how she became a famous leading lady, and how several years later she had married, though whether to the tall, handsome man, I do not know, and retired from the stage. Tales too, I heard of Jack Morgan's career which reached me from time to time, his appearances in the prize-ring up and down the country, in Ireland and on the Continent, and how Lord Deal won and lost vast sums according to the fortunes of his protégé.

I heard too, that the notorious George

Barrington was finally taken and transported for life to Botany Bay; while, from time to time, tales reached me of the exploits of the Bow Street Runners, and the achievements of the Blind Beak in his never-ending battle against the criminals of London. But of course, although I was a nine days' wonder on my return home with my parents to Rochester, my friends and relatives agog to hear of my adventures that night, and my school-mates plying me with questions for many weeks afterwards, at length other interests took my attention. Many of the impressions of what had happened, the images that I had held in my imagination, began to fade. There were my studies at school to occupy me, my future to be planned and to be fulfilled; there were the varied strokes of Fate that fell, as is only natural in this life, upon my family and as the years advanced upon myself, which are no part of the present tale.

To-day, however, these many years later, finds me still in the house that once belonged to my parents, and where from my window I can see the road running past into Rochester. And sometimes at night as I sit alone watching the road, white in the moonlight, my thoughts turn again around that tall, swaggering figure, his back as wide as a door, wearing the shining leather mask that gave him his name. I hear his rasping voice once more, and that wry, short laugh of his.

I wonder vainly, as I have done so many times, what his last thoughts must have been as he stood for the second time on the gallows at Tyburn; for, some eighteen months after he had waved me adieu across the dawn mist and disappeared from my sight for ever, he was taken by Townsend and his Runners. In my mind's eye I seem to see him, the roaring mob on every side, but there had been no devoted and resolute Fan Holt with her waiting hearse, though what had happened to her meanwhile, I never heard. Perhaps the guards and soldiers formed too strong a ring about the gallows, or his friends failed him at the last; no one this time was there swiftly to cut down that figure as it swung from the tree.

Only sometimes as I stare at the road to

Rochester in the lonely moonlit hours, I experience the strange fancy that I see a wraith astride a black horse ride past, and catch a glimpse of that sardonic grin cast in my direction from beneath the leather mask.

Leatherface in Real Life

John Neville, nicknamed Leatherface, existed in real life to the extent that he is an amalgam of several notorious highwaymen operating between 1751–1778, during which years this novel is placed. He is made up, then, of Sixteen String Jack Rann, who worked the Hounslow Road, and was a great frequenter of Ranelagh Gardens; Charles Fleming, whose undisputed territory, while he lived, was the roads north of London, until he was caught near Harrow; and others whose exploits are recorded in the never-ending, musty, crime-blotched pages of the Newgate Calendar; such as Jack Sheppard, youthful thief and rogue whom no prison of his day could hold, and 'Gentleman' Harry Simms, expelled from Eton for robbing his schoolfellows, and whose elegant, fleeting form became known to most roads from Bagshot to Bath.

As for some others who appear in Leatherface's story, such as the Bow Street Runner, Townsend; Sir John Fielding, the Blind Beak; and George Barrington the pickpocket, they were real people whom readers may have encountered in two previous novels of eighteenth-century London's underworld; while Fan Holt, like her hero, is also an amalgam, partly the auburn-haired Ellen Roach, Jack Rann's doxy; and Jane Webb, ingenious and resourceful pickpocket who was known as Diving Jenny, and it is said was the origin of Jenny Diver of *The Beggar's Opera* fame.

As for the youthful narrator himself, while juvenile delinquency, due to the terrifying conditions among which the poor were born and bred, was one of eighteenth-century London's greatest problems, teenagers of better circumstances, then as they do now, emulated their social inferiors on occasion. To have ventured on the youthful escapade which has been described would not have been unusual for a more dare-devil scion of many a respectable family; in fact the criminal records of the latter end of the eighteenth century contain many instances of youths of good birth who having once tasted the gaudy excitement behind a mask and a brace of pistols, would not be deterred by warnings or the salutary sight of Fruit hanging from the Tree, but continued their reckless way, until they themselves danced one morning on the Tyburn air.

We do hope that you have enjoyed reading this large print book.

Did you know that all of our titles are available for purchase?

We publish a wide range of high quality large print books including:
Romances, Mysteries, Classics
General Fiction
Non Fiction and Westerns

Special interest titles available in large print are:
The Little Oxford Dictionary
Music Book, Song Book
Hymn Book, Service Book

Also available from us courtesy of Oxford University Press:
Young Readers' Dictionary
(large print edition)
Young Readers' Thesaurus
(large print edition)

For further information or a free brochure, please contact us at:
Ulverscroft Large Print Books Ltd.,
The Green, Bradgate Road, Anstey,
Leicester, LE7 7FU, England.
Tel: (00 44) **0116 236 4325**
Fax: (00 44) **0116 234 0205**

DR. MORELLE AND THE DOLL

Ernest Dudley

In a wild, bleak corner of the Kent Coast, a derelict harbour rots beneath the tides. There the Doll, a film-struck waif, and her lover, ex-film star Tod Hafferty, play their tragic, fated real-life roles. And sudden death strikes more than once — involving a local policeman ... Then, as Dr. Morelle finds himself enmeshed in a net of sex and murder, Miss Frayle's anticipated quiet week-end results in her being involved in the climactic twist, which unmasks the real killer.